Guide

Vicksburg
Campaign

The U.S. Army War College Guides to
Civil War Battles

Antietam

Edited by Jay Luvaas and Harold W. Nelson

Chancellorsville & Fredericksburg

Edited by Jay Luvaas and Harold W. Nelson

Chickamauga

Edited by Matt Spruill

Gettysburg

Edited by Jay Luvaas and Harold W. Nelson

Shiloh

Edited by Jay Luvaas, Stephen Bowman,
and Leonard Fullenkamp

Vicksburg Campaign

Edited by Leonard Fullenkamp, Stephen Bowman,
and Jay Luvaas

Guide to the

Vicksburg Campaign

Edited by

Leonard Fullenkamp,

Stephen Bowman,

and Jay Luvaas

University Press of Kansas

Published by the University Press of Kansas (Lawrence, Kansas 66049), which was
organized by the Kansas Board of Regents and is operated and funded by Emporia
State University, Fort Hays State University, Kansas State University, Pittsburg State
University, the University of Kansas, and Wichita State University

Library of Congress Cataloging-in-Publication Data

Guide to the Vicksburg Campaign / edited by Leonard Fullenkamp,
    Stephen Bowman, and Jay Luvaas.
        p.   cm. — (U.S. Army War College guides to Civil War battles)
    Includes bibliographical references and index.
    ISBN 0-7006-0922-9 (alk. paper). — ISBN 0-7006-0923-7 (pbk. :
alk. paper)
    1. Vicksburg (Miss.)—History—Siege, 1863.   2. Vicksburg National
Military Park (Miss.)—Guidebooks.   3. Historic sites—Mississippi—
Vicksburg Region—Guidebooks.   I. Fullenkamp, Leonard.
II. Bowman, Stephen.   III. Luvaas, Jay.   IV. Series.
E475.27.G77   1998
973.7'344—dc21   98-8423

British Library Cataloguing in Publication Data is available.

Printed in the United States of America

10   9   8   7   6   5   4   3   2

CONTENTS

MAPS AND ILLUSTRATIONS

Maps

Illustrations

PREFACE

The authors wish to acknowledge a debt of gratitude to the many people without whose support, encouragement, and assistance the preparation of this book would not have been possible. Maj. Gen. Richard Chilcoat, then commandant of the U.S. Army War College, Carlisle Barracks, Pennsylvania, and his successor, Maj. Gen. Robert Scales, unfailingly and enthusiastically provided the resources and command support so essential for this project to go forward. Equally supportive was Dr. Gary Guertner, chairman of the Department of National Security and Strategy, who similarly encouraged our efforts and afforded us time to prepare the manuscript for publication while continuing our normal faculty duties.

The U.S. Army Military History Institute, also at Carlisle Barracks, and its director, Col. Tom Vossler, in countless ways contributed to this effort. The Institute's staff, including Louise Arnold Friend, Michael J. Winey, and Randy W. Hackenburg, rendered invaluable assistance, advising us in our research and aiding us in the selection of photographs and lithographs to accompany the text. A special debt of thanks is due to the technical experts in the Army War College photo lab who brought to life the many faded photographs found throughout the book. James E. Kistler patiently accommodated countless changes and editing as he drew the maps that accompany the text. The final renderings of the maps are the product of our interpretations and Jim's artistic skills.

Unit designations and tactical information on the maps were derived from multiple sources, including the *Atlas to Accompany the Official Records of the Union and Confederate Armies*, reports and accounts from the various participants as contained in the *War of the Rebellion: Official Records of the Union and Confederate Armies*, numerous secondary sources, and, ultimately, our own interpretation of events. Almost without fail all maps were checked against those found in *The Vicksburg Campaign* by Edwin C. Bearss. His three-volume study of the Vicksburg campaign was an invaluable aid to our research efforts. We are equally grateful to Col. Robert Doughty, head of the Department of History, U.S. Military Academy, West Point, New York, for permission to use the superb maps contained in *The West Point Atlas of American Wars*, drawn by Edward Krasnoborski and George Giddings, as a basis for interpreting the battles and depicting the terrain.

Vicksburg Park historian Terrence J. Winschel was extremely helpful to us during many phases of work on the book. During our trips to the battlefields and Vicksburg, he shared his ideas and offered suggestions on what to see and where to go. He graciously read the manuscript and provided many useful comments and recommendations. A prolific author and expert on the Vicksburg campaign, he has prepared battlefield guides to a number of the battle sites. We are grateful to him for his insights and his work on drawings and maps that aided our interpretation of the many engagements in the campaign.

A group of special friends who know and share the unique joy of walking old battlefields and discovering new insights, the self-styled "Army of the Cussewago," walked the ground with us on two occasions and provided sound advice and wise counsel. We are indebted to them for their steadfast support and encouragement.

Finally, a special thanks to our secretary, Chris Hockensmith, for all she did, typing, editing, proofing, catching countless mistakes, and asking good questions the answers to which greatly enhanced clarity and improved the book immeasurably.

HOW TO USE THIS BOOK

A noted English historian declared some eighty years ago that "the skilled game of identifying positions on a battlefield innocent of guides, where one must make out everything for oneself—best of all if no one has ever done it properly before—is almost the greatest of outdoor intellectual pleasures."

This guide is designed to help you enjoy such an experience with the Vicksburg campaign. Part I begins with the strategic setting for the campaign and culminates with the Confederate surrender in July 1863. It can be read, as with any history of the campaign, during leisure hours at home. For those with the time and the inclination to explore the campaign in all its complexity, to see for themselves where and how the battles and maneuvers were fought, and to gauge how well their mental pictures of events matched the ground, there are guided tours in Parts II and III.

Driving tours or excursions to peripheral sites such as Fort Pemberton, Chickasaw Bayou, Grant's Canal, and Deer Creek and battlefields at Port Gibson, Raymond, Champion Hill, and Big Black River bridge can be found in Part II of the guide. For each stop the reader will find a brief context to set the stage for events that occurred there and references to Part I, where more detailed accounts may be found. Part III is a guided tour of the siege lines at the Vicksburg National Military Park.

This book is not intended to serve as a *history* of the battle—for that you should consult the more standard works on the Civil War or narrative histories of this campaign. Those who visit battlefields with us report that the most productive study begins *after* they have stopped at key points, viewed the terrain, and shared the recollections of participants—the approach you will experience by using this guide.

INTRODUCTION

Notwithstanding the passage of time and the increasing complexity of modern warfare, Ulysses S. Grant's Vicksburg campaign endures as an example of successful campaign planning. Spanning more than six months and thousands of square miles, the campaign eventually culminated with the capture of its strategic objective, the city of Vicksburg, and with it control of the Mississippi River. In later years, when recounting his recollections of events, Grant tended to convey the impression that the campaign unfolded pretty much according to plans he had developed when first setting about to capture the city. If that is so, one wonders why anyone would construct such an obtuse and complex plan.

Grant's campaign to wrest control of the Mississippi River from the Confederates was not the first great campaign of the war. Others before him had formulated campaign plans remarkable for their sophistication and complexity. In 1862, Maj. Gen. George B. McClellan designed a plan to capture Richmond with a line of operations extending from the Atlantic coast up the James Peninsula to the gates of Richmond. Although confounded in his attempt by his own deficient generalship and the brilliance and audacity of his opponent, Confederate general Robert E. Lee, McClellan's Peninsula campaign plan was nonetheless remarkable for its vision and complexity. In short, although McClellan's plan was basically sound, the primary cause of failure was his generalship. Daring plans demand leaders who can accept and manage risk. McClellan could do neither. At the decisive moment he lost his nerve and withdrew his forces when Lee did not capitulate, instead launching a series of sharp counterattacks that compelled McClellan to abandon his effort.

When Grant's plan to capture Vicksburg did not unfold as initially planned, he did not abort the campaign, but with dogged determination and persistence triumphed. Although by doctrine one did not change a line of operations without serious provocation, during the Vicksburg campaign Grant changed his line of operations at least three times, not counting the failed attempts to open lines through the rivers and bayous surrounding the city. He carefully weighed the gravity of his decisions when changing lines, balancing risks with his instinctive feel for opportunities to be had from the changes. Throughout the

1

campaign Grant displayed remarkable intuition. He seemed to have a sense of how effective his operations were in relation to his opponent and adjusted his actions accordingly.

Initially, Grant planned a very traditional and secure overland line of operations from La Grange, Tennessee, to the southwest following the railroad, which was to be used as a line of communications, in the direction of Vicksburg. He launched his campaign in December 1862, seeking to draw the Confederate defenders away from the city in order to permit a force under the command of Maj. Gen. William T. Sherman to take the Vicksburg defenses from the rear. When Confederate cavalry attacked Grant's base of operations at Holly Springs, Mississippi, he was forced to abandon this line and withdraw back to Tennessee. Sherman, who with his army was already en route by river to the city, only learned of Grant's change of plans after he was bloodily repulsed in his efforts to take the high ground north of Vicksburg. Thus the stage was set for the campaign as it eventually evolved.

Over the next six months, between January and July 1863, Grant and his naval counterpart, Acting Rear Adm. David D. Porter, developed a series of imaginative initiatives to capture the river city. An earlier joint army and navy expedition against Vicksburg's defenses had failed the previous summer but in the undertaking had illustrated the essential nature of cooperation between the services. Although joint operations involving the army and the navy were essential, no joint structure existed at the time that compelled either service to submit to the command of the other. Instead, army and navy forces were enjoined to cooperate with one another.

Making matters worse, relations between the army and navy were particularly sensitive at the time in view of the recent creation of the Mississippi Squadron. Until late 1862 the ironclad gunboats on the Mississippi had been largely built, owned, and operated by the army. Following a bruising bureaucratic struggle, which Lincoln himself arbitrated, between Secretary of War Henry Stanton and Secretary of the Navy Gideon Wells, the navy assumed command of the squadron. Fortunately, Grant and Porter took an immediate liking to one another and over the course of the campaign forged a professional relationship of mutual trust and respect that was conveyed to their respective services. Without the effective cooperation and joint service operations of the army and navy, it is unlikely the campaign would have succeeded.

Grant's Vicksburg campaign illustrates operational art. The operational level of war connects battles, or the tactical level, with strategic end states. Operational art principally encompasses the fundamentals

INTRODUCTION [3]

that link the two. In very simple terms, campaigns may be defined as a series of distributed operations or events that are conducted to secure strategic ends. Grant's strategic objective was control of the Mississippi River, which gave the Union the strategic initiative in the West.

Vicksburg was important because it was a junction of railroad and river traffic. Valuable commodities from Confederate states and territories west of the Mississippi crossed the river at Vicksburg and continued east and south on the rail lines that terminated in the city. Guarding Vicksburg was a vast network of secondary rivers and bayous, not to mention the mighty Mississippi River, which obstructed the northern and western approaches to the city. Confederate armies, one under Lt. Gen. John C. Pemberton and another under Gen. Joseph E. Johnston, protected the eastern and southern approaches. Unlike the Union, the Confederates had few naval forces in the vicinity of Vicksburg, suggesting a vulnerability to be exploited if ways to do so could be found.

During the campaign, Grant and Porter sought a variety of ways to leverage the combined strengths of their forces. Work on a canal intended to bypass the city's defenses, begun opposite Vicksburg in the summer of 1862, was resumed in March 1863. This attempt to bypass the Confederate stronghold was eventually abandoned as impractical, as were other even more elaborate schemes involving rechanneling rivers and bayous. Certainly the most remarkable of these peripheral operations was the Steele's Bayou expedition. Seeking to attack and seize the high ground north of the city known as Walnut Hills, Porter devised a plan whereby ironclads would proceed up Steele's Bayou and into a series of adjoining bayous and creeks, some hardly wider than the beam of his boats, with the intention of making their way into the Yazoo River north of the city and above the defenses on the Walnut Hills. From there soldiers accompanying the boats, assisted by the fire from their heavy guns, would assault and capture the defensive works. Although bold and imaginative, the endeavor proved both foolhardy and nearly disastrous when Confederate forces came very close to trapping the boats in the tree-choked bayous. Only an eleventh-hour rescue effort led by Sherman himself averted disaster.

Eventually Grant and Porter settled on a course of action that called for bypassing the city's defenses and opening a line of operations from south and east of the city. Grant's generalship becomes a critical factor in this phase of the campaign as does the generalship of his opponents. In the early months of the campaign, the Confederate high command was fairly confident of its ability to defend the city.

Lt. Gen. John C. Pemberton was personally chosen by Confederate president Jefferson Davis for the task. Later, seeking to strengthen the Confederate military situation in Tennessee and Mississippi, Gen. Joseph E. Johnston was assigned to command a geographical area that encompassed Vicksburg but did not specifically include Pemberton or his forces.

As Grant's forces maneuvered east of the river and began to close in on the city, confusion arose within the Confederate chain of command. Johnston, failing for whatever reason to comprehend the duties of his command, did not exercise effective direction of all the forces within his theater of operations, a shortcoming that contributed directly to the loss of Vicksburg. Correspondence between Johnston and Pemberton reflects this confusion. Much of it seems to have been written with one eye on the future, as though both were seeking to lay the blame on the other for any disaster that might befall their efforts.

Grant is blessed in this campaign with subordinates of incomparable talent. Whereas the Union army in the east was burdened with political generals, many of mediocre talents, Grant's army was remarkable for men such as Sherman, James McPherson, and Edward Ord. The exception was John A. McClernand. A War Democrat politician turned soldier and a supposed friend of Lincoln, McClernand was incompetent, or at best inadequate, as a general in the eyes of Grant, Sherman, and Porter. Indeed, it was McClernand's seniority to Sherman that caused Grant to assume personal command of the Vicksburg campaign. Were it not for his fear that McClernand would do harm to the army, Grant would probably have remained in Tennessee and left the details of the campaign to his talented subordinate, Sherman.

Grant eventually removed McClernand from command, although not until quite late in the campaign and then only after receiving assurances from Washington that he had permission to do so. Readers can sift through the events leading up to and including the details surrounding Grant's decision to relieve McClernand of his command and decide for themselves if it was warranted. The episode is informative not simply for what it says about Grant's command style but also for what it implies about his evolving relationship with Lincoln and Henry Halleck, his general in chief. Initially tentative in his dealings with the high command in Washington, by summer 1863 Grant had begun to evince a sense of confidence not seen earlier. In effect, he was transformed by the campaign: as he struggled with its challenges and complexities, his confidence in himself and his judgment grew. The extent to which he learned from these experiences becomes evident the following spring when, in May 1864, he undertook a campaign of comparable complexity and importance in the eastern theater against Robert E. Lee.

Readers will note that this book draws almost exclusively on two primary sources. Reports and correspondence from the *War of the Rebellion: Official Records of the Union and Confederate Armies* and from the *Official Records of the Union and Confederate Navies in the War of the Rebellion* have been woven together to form the narrative of the campaign. Where necessary to provide context or clarity, selections from memoirs of key participants, principally Grant, are included. Other secondary sources have been used sparingly. Historians draw from many sources and distill from their research an interpretation of events. As this guide is not intended to be a detailed history of the Vicksburg campaign, no effort to distill events or provide an interpretation has been made. Rather, it is for the reader, unencumbered by the analysis of others, to arrive at his own interpretations and insights. Editor's notes are used sparingly and only when necessary to clarify the historical material.

Readers also will note what seems to be excessive attention given to minor subjects. Engineering operations, as an example, are covered extensively. Vicksburg was a traditional siege in every sense of the term. One would imagine that with such a large number of Union and Confederate officers having been educated as engineers at the U.S. Military Academy at West Point, knowledge of siege operations was commonplace in Grant's army. Indeed, the opposite was the case. As with most military tasks, siege work was a science with its own arcane language. Reports on these operations are laced with technical terms and phrases, generally in French, reflecting their origin. Notes, where appropriate, have been provided for ease of understanding. Engineering operations are important not only as they apply to the ultimate capture of Vicksburg and its formidable defenses, but also for what they portend for the great campaign against Richmond the following summer.

Those who may assume that this volume will be of interest only to the military professional should be assured that it contains something of interest to everyone. Beyond the details of campaign planning, joint operations, military strategy, and generalship are to be found countless insights into the ephemeral aspects of war, such as courage, initiative, and the ordeal of combat. For those with the time and inclination to walk the ground, there are directions to that end. Those who choose to read the accounts of events and see them only in their mind's eye will likewise be rewarded for their efforts. The many maps, diagrams, and illustrations included in the guide will prove useful to both. For a variety of reasons the situation maps represent a blend of the historical and modern topographical features. Modern roads are included when necessary to assist the visitor in moving around the battlefields. Similarly, tree lines and vegetation are different today than at the time of the battle.

Anyone familiar with Civil War correspondence knows that spelling was not a particularly strong suit for many. Thus readers will note many variations in the spelling of locations, rivers, settlements, and so forth. Haynes' Bluff is variously cited as Haines or Haynes's Bluff, and Chickasaw Bayou and Chickasaw Bluffs refer to the same general location. Champion Hill was located on property belonging to a family by that name, which explains why the possessive form is often associated with reports on the battle. Grant at different times spells Yalobusha as Yalabusha and Talahatchie as Talahatachee when it is obvious he is referring to the same rivers. Similarly, although other proper names are given in several variations, the reader will have no difficulty sorting things out. Where clarity is essential, "sic" is used sparingly, or the proper spelling is given in brackets.

There is one final consideration for those who spend time with this book. The Vicksburg campaign provides insights into the education and development of a general who was to play a pivotal role in the outcome of the Civil War. Generals in that war did not learn their profession in schools like today's Army Command and General Staff College or the Army War College. Such schools did not appear until the turn of the century. As cadets at the U.S. Military Academy at West Point, Grant and his contemporaries were taught the fundamentals of tactics and engineering, not the skills of generalship. Moreover, little in their prewar careers, the Mexican War notwithstanding, prepared them for the work they would be called upon to perform in the Civil War. Campaign planning is vastly more complex than simple tactics, and mastery of *Hardee's Tactics* or the manual of drill in no way ensured that one could command forces over vast distances. Knowledge of logistics, the art of supplying forces in war, was essential, yet there was no school or college to teach the subject. Grant ultimately proved himself to be a master logistics planner. Sherman did likewise. For both, the Vicksburg campaign was an experience to be mined for lessons on many subjects, but perhaps none so important as logistics.

Those who believe that too great an emphasis has been placed on the role of a single general in the planning and execution of this campaign should remember that the staff system for planning and directing operations in no way compares with today's system. During the Civil War the commanding general of the army on campaign performed many of the staff functions personally, and although Grant had a very capable chief of staff, quartermaster, engineer, medical officer, and so forth, ultimately the ideas and the orders were his and his alone. Writing in his memoirs after the war about Grant's role in the campaign, Sherman was unstinting in his praise: "The campaign of Vicksburg, in its conception and execution, belonged exclusively to General Grant, not only in the great whole, but in the thousands of details. I still retain many of his letters and notes, all in his own handwriting, prescribing the routes of march for divisions and detachments, specifying even the amount of food and tools to be carried along . . . no commanding general of an army ever gave more of his personal attention to details, or wrote so many of his own orders, reports, and letters, as General Grant."[1]

Grant was the primary architect for the Vicksburg campaign. Stereotypes of him as a rather dull and colorless man of little imagination who simply bludgeoned his opponents into submission must be thrust aside by any who seriously study this campaign. In the Vicksburg campaign Grant displayed the generalship, intelligence, and broad talents he truly possessed.

NOTE

1. William T. Sherman, *Memoirs of General William T. Sherman, by Himself* (New York: Appleton, 1875), 1:362.

PART I
THE VICKSBURG CAMPAIGN

Vicksburg as seen from the Mississippi River during the Civil War. (U.S. Army Military History Institute)

THE STRATEGIC SITUATION

By the winter of 1862, Vicksburg had become perhaps the most important city in the conflict between North and South. Geography was the main reason. Vicksburg dominated the Mississippi River, controlling passage up and down the river and thus all commerce from the upper Mississippi to the Gulf of Mexico. Union control of the Mississippi would cut the Confederacy in two and deny the footstuffs, matériel, and manpower coming from Arkansas, Louisiana, and Texas. In addition, the Southern Railroad of Mississippi (Alabama and Vicksburg), sometimes called the Vicksburg and Jackson Railroad, further enhanced the strategic significance of the city. Thus Vicksburg was a political, economic, and military prize of great value—for both sides. President Abraham Lincoln, who had worked a flatboat down the Mississippi as a young man, understood this fact well.

The military situation for the Union further enhanced the key role of Vicksburg. In May 1862, Flag Officer David Glasgow Farragut had steamed his fleet up the Mississippi from New Orleans to try to capture Vicksburg by naval bombardment. He had a small (1,400 men) army detachment with him to occupy the city after its surrender. Upon reaching the city, Farragut found its defenses impregnable to the naval forces with him. The ships' guns could not be sufficiently elevated to fire on the Vicksburg batteries high on the bluffs overlooking the river. The defenses were also too strongly defended for the weak infantry force accompanying him. Farragut moved back to New Orleans.

Other actions in the various theaters confirmed the importance of Vicksburg. In September 1862, the Confederate invasion of the North had been turned back at Antietam, but the battle was at best a draw. Major General Ambrose Burnside's Union Army of the Potomac had been bloodily repulsed in December 1862 at Fredericksburg and in January 1863 Federal Maj. Gen. William S. Rosecrans ended Confederate Gen. Braxton Bragg's attempt to invade Kentucky at Murfreesboro (Stones River) but did not pursue Bragg's defeated force, thus gaining tactical victory but failing to gain strategic advantage.

Theater of operations for the Vicksburg campaign.

War weariness was overtaking the North. The elections of 1862 had seen the Republican majority in Congress reduced. Economic stagnation in the Northwest (i.e., Illinois, Iowa, Wisconsin, Minnesota, and so forth) because of insufficient outlets for crops and products added to the pressure to start negotiations with the Confederacy. The Union needed a victory.

Capturing Vicksburg would be no easy task, however. It sat on bluffs more than 200 feet above the river. The land north of the city was a maze of shallow lakes, meandering streams, dense swamps, and sluggish rivers, covered by trees and bushes, all of which were prone to flooding by the mighty Mississippi, especially in winter and spring. An army attacking from the north had to negotiate all these significant obstacles before ever dealing with Confederate Lt. Gen. John C. Pemberton's defending army. By moving east of Vicksburg, the attacking Union force could avoid the difficulties of the horrendous terrain north of the city, but it would find itself in the heart of the deep South, with a hostile population and a tenuous line of communications vulnerable to attack or raids. Any movement from the west had to include crossing the Mississippi River before attacking the city, thus again facing a serious logistics problem. Grant considered all of these problems as he pondered the course of action he would take to capture Vicksburg.

1. FORTRESS VICKSBURG

Summary of Principal Events:
April 24, 1862–January 3, 1863

April
24–28   Evacuation of New Orleans by Maj. Gen.
               Mansfield *Lovell**, CSA, and surrender of the
               city to Commo. David G. Farragut, USN, and
               Maj. Gen. Benjamin Butler, USA.
               Arrival in Vicksburg of Confederate forces
               from New Orleans and strengthening of river
               batteries at Vicksburg.
May
12   Capture of Baton Rouge, Louisiana, and
               Natchez, Mississippi, by U.S. Navy.
18   Arrival of vanguard of U.S. fleet at Vicksburg
               and first hostile shots fired by U.S. Navy against
               the city's defenses.
June
6   Federal gunboats under Commo. Charles Davis,
               USN, defeat Confederate gunboats under the
               command of Capt. James E. *Montgomery*, CSN,
               in the Battle of Memphis, Tennessee, resulting
               in the surrender of the city to Federal forces.
10   Maj. Gens. Ulysses S. Grant, Don C. Buell, and
               John Pope ordered to resume command of
               their separate army corps.
15   Expedition to Holly Springs and skirmish at
               Tallahatchie Bridge, Mississippi.
28   Brig. Gen. Thomas Williams, USA, begins
               work on a canal designed to enable gunboats

*Editors' note: The convention used in this book is that all Confederate surnames
are italicized, while Union names are in standard type.

to bypass Vicksburg's defenses. Commo. David G. Farragut, USN, steams his gunboats upriver past Vicksburg's defenses.

July

1   Arrival of gunboats of Western Flotilla (USN) from Memphis.

2   Confederate Districts of the Mississippi and of the Gulf constituted under the commands of Maj. Gen. Earl *Van Dorn* and Brig. Gen. John H. *Forney.*

11   Maj. Gen. Henry W. Halleck, USA, assigned to command as general in chief of all the land forces of the United States.

15   CSS *Arkansas* engages U.S. fleets.

16   The District of West Tennessee, Major General Grant commanding, extended to embrace the Army of the Mississippi.

17   Grant assumes command of all troops in the armies of the Tennessee and the Mississippi, and in the Districts of Cairo and of the Mississippi.

23   Work on Williams's canal abandoned.

24   Farragut and Williams withdraw downriver.

28   Davis's Western Flotilla withdraws upriver.

August

5   Confederate forces are repulsed in their attempt to retake Baton Rouge, Louisiana. CSS *Arkansas* scuttled to prevent capture by Federal forces.

30   Operations along the Mississippi Central Railroad.

September

5   Brig. Gen. Daniel *Ruggles,* CSA, assigned to command of the District of the Mississippi.

24   District of West Tennessee reorganized. Maj. Gens. William T. Sherman, Edward O. Ord, and William S. Rosecrans, and Brig. Gen. Issac Quinby, USA, assigned to divisions.

October

12   Maj. Gen. Earl *Van Dorn,* CSA, assumes command of the troops in the state of Mississippi.

14	Lt. Gen. John C. *Pemberton,* CSA, assumes command of the Department of Mississippi and East Louisiana, including forces intending to operate in southwestern Tennessee.
16	Department of the Tennessee constituted under the command of Maj. Gen. Ulysses S. Grant.
31–January 10	Operations on the Mississippi Central Railroad from Bolivar, Tennessee, to Coffeeville, Mississippi.

November

| 24 | Gen. Joseph E. *Johnston,* CSA, assigned to a command embracing western North Carolina, Tennessee, northern Georgia, Alabama, Mississippi, and eastern Louisiana. |

December

12	Expedition up the Yazoo River, Mississippi. USS *Cairo* sunk by torpedo.
13–19	Raid on the Mobile and Ohio Railroad from Corinth to Tupelo, Mississippi.
18	The U.S. Fifteenth, Sixteenth, and Seventeenth Army Corps constituted under the commands of Maj. Gens. William T. Sherman, Stephen A. Hurlbut, and James B. McPherson. Maj. Gen. John A. McClernand, USA, assigned to command the Thirteenth Army Corps.
20–January 3	Operations against Vicksburg result in Federal defeat at Chickasaw Bayou.

Narrative of Maj. Samuel H. Lockett, CSA, Chief Engineer of the Vicksburg Defenses

The occupation of Vicksburg was the immediate result of the fall of New Orleans on the 25th of April, 1862. The first military operations were the laying out and construction of some batteries for heavy guns, by Captain (afterward Colonel) D. B. *Harris* of the Confederate States Engineers, the work being mostly done by a force of hired negroes. These batteries were located chiefly below the city; their positions were well chosen; they had fine command of the river against a fleet coming from below.

On the 12th of May, 1862, Brigadier-General Martin Luther Smith arrived and took command, under orders from Major-General Mansfield *Lovell,* the Department commander. From that day to the end General *Smith* was never absent from his post, was always equal to every emergency, and never once, while in control, failed to do the right thing at the right time.

On the 20th of June, 1862, I was ordered from the Army of Tennessee, then under General *Bragg,* to report to General *Smith* as his Chief Engineer. I was with him in that capacity until the 1st of November, when I was made, by General *Pemberton,* Chief Engineer of the Department of Mississippi and East Louisiana, of which General *Pemberton* had just taken command. This change extended my field of operations from Holly Springs to Port Hudson, but I never relinquished immediate charge of the defenses of Vicksburg. Hence I may safely claim to have been identified with the defense almost from the beginning to the end of operations.

The series of irregular hills, bluffs, and narrow, tortuous ridges, apparently without system or order, that constitute the strong defensive position of Vicksburg, raised some two hundred feet above the level of the river, owe their character, with all their strangely complex arrangement and configuration, to the natural erosive action of water on the fine, homogeneous, calcareous silt peculiar to the lias [loess] or bluff formation.

At the time of my arrival no enemy was near, but the work of preparation was going on vigorously. The garrison was engaged in strengthening the batteries already constructed, in making bombproof magazines, and in mounting new guns recently arrived. Several new batteries were laid out by myself on the most commanding points above the city; these were afterward known as the "Upper Batteries." The work of making an accurate map of Vicksburg and vicinity was also begun.

But we had not many days for these preliminaries. On the 26th of June the advance of [Rear Adm. David G.] Farragut's fleet arrived in sight. The next morning found it in position for bombarding. A flotilla of mortar-boats was moored close to the farther shore of the river just beyond the range of our lower batteries. A second flotilla had crept along the bank next to us with their masts so covered with the boughs of trees that we did not discover them until they were quite near. They were completely protected from our guns by the bank.

At a signal-gun from one of the iron-clads the guns were opened. I measured one of the holes made by the mortar-shells in hard, compact clay, and found it seventeen feet deep. It was a difficult matter to make bomb-proofs against such destructive engines. A few shots were fired from our batteries in answer to the challenge of the mortar-boats, but these shots were harmless, and soon were discontinued. The Federal bombardment was likewise nearly harmless. . . . Vertical fire is never very destructive of life. . . .

June 28th was a memorable day. At early dawn the mortar-fleet renewed its heavy bombardment. At the same time the vessels and gun-boats moved up toward the city and opened fire with all their heavy ordnance. Under cover of this tremendous shelling the *Brooklyn* and *Hartford* and several of the iron-clads boldly pushed up stream, and went past our batteries under full headway, pouring into the city broadside after broadside with astonishing rapidity. The Confederate batteries responded with equal energy.

The results of this first encounter with the hitherto redoubtable fleet was highly gratifying. . . . True, the fleet got past the batteries; but the *Brooklyn* and *Octorora* were temporarily disabled. All the vessels suffered more or less, and many Federal sailors were killed and wounded, as we learned from people who lived across the river. On the Confederate side no gun was disabled, no battery injured, and only thirteen were killed or wounded. Our batteries mounted 29 guns, of which 2 were 10–inch Columbiads, the rest being old style 42 and 32 pounders. The *Brooklyn* alone carried 24 11-inch Dahlgren guns. We expected a land attack at the same time, and were prepared for it by the presence of as many as ten thousand troops, under *Breckinridge, Bowen,* and *Preston* who . . . were in near-supporting distance. They were not called upon, however, and no troops were under fire except the brigade of General M. L. *Smith.*

After this, for two weeks, things moved along at Vicksburg with something akin to monotony. The mortar-fleets kept up a steady bombardment, but even the citizens of the town became so accustomed to it that they went about their daily occupations . . . [and] would only betake themselves to their shelters when the fire seemed to be concentrated in their particular neighborhoods. Finally the upper fleet, under Flag-Officer C. H. Davis, came down the river, joined the vessels that had run our batteries, put a flotilla of mortar-boats in position, and took part in the grand but nearly harmless sport of pitching big shells into

Vicksburg. During this period General Thomas Williams commenced the famous canal across the narrow neck of land in front of Vicksburg [in May 1862, as part of Adm. David Farragut's offensive launched from New Orleans]. But the water fell faster than the ditch was dug, the river refused to make a cut-off, and this effort also proved a failure.

On the 15th of July the monotony of the situation was greatly relieved by one of the most stirring episodes of the war. The little Confederate ram, *Arkansas,* . . . came out of Yazoo River, where she had been built in imitation of the famous *Merrimac,* and ran the gauntlet of the whole upper fleet. . . . For several days . . . the regulation bombardment was kept up. Suddenly, however, on the 25th of July, the lower fleet, big ships, gunboats, and mortar-boats, weighed anchor and dropped down the river to a distance of several miles below their former position. On the 27th both lower and upper fleets took leave of us. . . .

Working parties were at once put upon the river-batteries to repair damages and increase their strength wherever recent experience had shown it to be necessary. It was also determined to construct a line of defense in rear of Vicksburg, to prepare against an army operating upon land. As chief engineer, it became my duty to plan, locate, and lay out that line of defense. A month was spent in reconnoitering, surveying, and studying the complicated and irregular site to be fortified.

No greater topographical puzzle was ever presented to an engineer. The difficulty of the situation was greatly enhanced by the fact that a large part of the hills and hollows had never been cleared of their virgin forest of magnificent magnolia-trees and dense undergrowth of cane. At first it seemed impossible to find anything like a general line of commanding ground surrounding the city; but careful study gradually worked out the problem.

The most prominent points I purposed [*sic*] to occupy with a system of redoubts, redans, lunettes, and small field-works, connecting them by rifle-pits so as to give a continuous line of defense.[1] The work of construction was begun about the 1st of September with a force of negro laborers hired or impressed from the plantations of the adjacent counties. Haynes's Bluff on the Yazoo River and Warrenton, about six miles below Vicksburg, were fortified as flank protections to the main position.

On the 14th of October, 1862, Lieutenant-General John C. *Pemberton* took command of the Department of Mississippi and East

Lt. Gen. John C. *Pemberton,* CSA, Commander, Department of Mississippi
and East Louisiana. (U.S. Army Military History Institute)

Louisiana, establishing his headquarters at Jackson. About the same time General [Ulysses S.] Grant was placed in supreme command of the Federal forces in north Mississippi. Then followed a succession of movements against Vicksburg, having for their object the turning of that point. They were all uniformly unsuccessful, and were so remote from the city, with one exception, that the garrison of Vicksburg was not involved in the operations which defeated them.[2]

PEMBERTON TAKES COMMAND

George W. Randolph, Secretary of War, CSA, to Maj. Gen. John C. Pemberton, CSA, September 30, 1862

You will proceed to Jackson and relieve General *Van Dorn* from the command of the district assigned to him by General *Bragg*, for the purpose of permitting him to command the forces ordered to advance into West Tennessee. You will turn your attention immediately to the defense of the States of Mississippi and Louisiana east of the Mississippi River, and consider the successful defense of those States as the first and chief object of your command.

You will also organize the troops in your department and prepare them for the field, and give such assistance to the officers charged with the enrollment of conscripts as they may require. The commandants of the camps of conscripts are charged with the duty of enrolling and assigning them. They act under general orders and report directly to this Department; but it will be in your power to assist them in the discharge of their duties.

If a favorable opportunity offer [*sic*] for an attack on New Orleans you will avail yourself of it, and act in concert with Maj. Gen. Richard *Taylor*, who commands the District of Louisiana west of the Mississippi. You will communicate with him as speedily as possible and concert with him a joint plan of operations for the defense of the river and the capture of New Orleans.

Your military department will comprise the State of Mississippi and so much of Louisiana as lies east of the Mississippi River. Until further orders you will report directly to this Department.[3]

NOTES

1. These engineering terms describe specific types of field fortifications: *redoubt*—multisided or circular enclosed earthworks. Large

redoubts are referred to as forts; *redan*—two-sided angular earthwork, pointed toward the enemy; *lunette*—a fortification with two projecting faces (like a redan) and two parallel flanks extending from the faces. Henry Lee Scott, *Military Dictionary: Comprising Technical Definitions; Information on Raising and Keeping Troops; Actual Service, Including Makeshift and Improved Matériel; and Law, Government, Regulations, and Administration Relating to Land Forces* (New York: D. Van Nostrand, 1861), pp. 394, 497–99.

    2. Samuel H. Lockett, "The Defense of Vicksburg," in *Battles and Leaders of the Civil War,* 4 vols., ed. Robert U. Johnson and Clarence C. Buel (New York: Century, 1887–88), 3:482–84.

    3. U.S. War Department, *War of the Rebellion: Official Records of the Union and Confederate Armies,* 128 vols., ed. Robert N. Scott et al. (Washington, D.C.: Government Printing Office, 1891–1901), XVII, pt. 2, pp. 716–17; hereafter cited as *O.R.*

2. GRANT TAKES COMMAND

Summary of Principal Events:
October 3, 1862–January 3, 1863

October

3–12   Battle of Corinth, Mississippi, and pursuit of Confederate forces.

14   Lt. Gen. John C. *Pemberton,* CSA, assumes command of all troops in the State of Mississippi and eastern Louisiana, including the forces intended to operate in southwestern Tennessee.

16   Department of the Tennessee constituted under the command of Maj. Gen. Ulysses S. Grant, USA. Grant also assumes command of the Thirteenth Army Corps.

31–January 10   Union operations on the Mississippi Central Railroad from Bolivar, Tennessee, to Coffeeville, Mississippi.

November

24   Gen. Joseph E. *Johnston,* CSA, assigned to a command embracing western North Carolina, Tennessee, northern Georgia, Alabama, Mississippi, and eastern Louisiana.

December

12   Expedition up the Yazoo River, Mississippi.

13–19   Raid on the Mobile and Ohio Railroad from Corinth to Tupelo, Mississippi.

15   Brig. Gen. Nathan B. *Forrest*'s expedition into west Tennessee.

18   The Fifteenth, Sixteenth, and Seventeenth Army Corps constituted under the commands of Maj. Gens. William T. Sherman, Stephen A. Hurlbut, and James B. McPherson, USA. Maj.

Gen. John A. McClernand, USA, assigned to
command the Thirteenth Army Corps.
20–January 3   Operations against Vicksburg, Mississippi.

Narrative of Maj. Gen. Ulysses S. Grant, USA

The battle of Corinth [Mississippi, October 3–4, 1862], . . . a
decided victory, though not so complete as I had hoped for, . . .
relieved me from any further anxiety for the safety of the territory
within my jurisdiction, and soon after receiving reinforcements I
suggested to the general-in-chief [Maj. Gen. Henry W. Halleck] a
forward movement against Vicksburg.

On the 23rd of October I learned of *Pemberton*'s being in command at Holly Springs and much reinforced by conscripts and
troops from Alabama and Texas. On the 25th . . . I was placed in
command of the Department of the Tennessee. Reinforcements
continued to come from the north and by the 2d of November I
was prepared to take the initiative. This was a great relief after the
two and a half months of continued defence [*sic*] over a large district of country, and where nearly every citizen was an enemy ready
to give information of our every move.

Vicksburg was important to the enemy because it occupied the
first high ground coming close to the river below Memphis. From
there a railroad runs east, connecting with other roads leading to
all points of the Southern States. A railroad also starts from the
opposite side of the river, extending west as far as Shreveport,
Louisiana. Vicksburg was the only channel . . . connecting the parts
of the Confederacy divided by the Mississippi. So long as it was
held by the enemy, the free navigation of the river was prevented.
Hence its importance. Points on the river between Vicksburg and
Port Hudson were held as dependencies; but their fall was sure to
follow the capture of the former place. . . .

At this time my command was holding the Mobile and Ohio railroad from about twenty-five miles south of Corinth, north to Columbus, Kentucky; the Mississippi Central from Bolivar north to its
junction with the Mobile and Ohio; the Memphis and Charleston
from Corinth east to Bear Creek, and the Mississippi River from
Cairo to Memphis. My entire command was no more than was necessary to hold these lines, and hardly that if kept on the defensive.
By moving against the enemy and into his unsubdued . . . territory,

Maj. Gen. Ulysses S. Grant, USA, Commander, Army of the Tennessee. Grant was forty years old in the fall of 1862 at the beginning of the Vicksburg campaign. (U.S. Army Military History Institute)

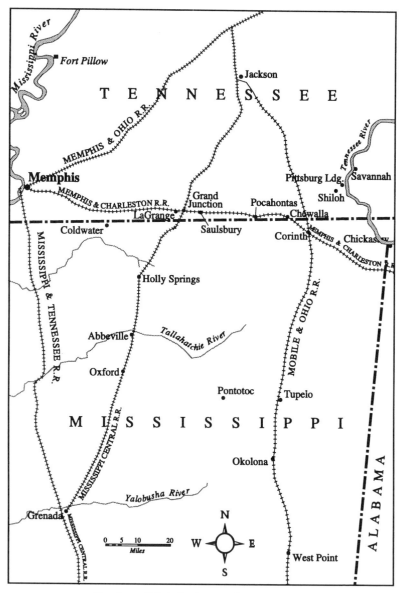

Northern Mississippi area of operations.

driving their army before us, these lines would nearly hold themselves; thus affording a large force for field operations. My moving force at that time was about 30,000 men, and I estimated the enemy confronting me, under *Pemberton,* at about the same number. General [James B.] McPherson commanded my left wing and General C. S. Hamilton the centre [*sic*], while [William T.] Sherman was at Memphis with the right wing.

Pemberton was fortified at the Tallahatchie [*sic*], but occupied Holly Springs and Grand Junction on the Mississippi Central railroad. On the 8th we occupied Grand Junction and La Grange, throwing a considerable force seven or eight miles south, along the line of the railroad. The [rail]road from Bolivar forward was repaired and put in running order as the troops advanced.

Up to this time it had been regarded as an axiom in war that large bodies of troops must operate from a base of supplies which they always covered and guarded in all forward movements. There was delay therefore in repairing the road back, and in gathering and forwarding supplies to the front. . . . Holly Springs I selected for my depot of supplies and munitions of war, all of which at that time came by rail from Columbus, Kentucky, except the few stores collected about La Grange and Grand Junction. This was a long line (increasing in length as we moved south) to maintain in an enemy's country.

On the 12th I received a dispatch from General [Henry W.] Halleck saying that I had command of all the troops sent to my department and authorizing me to fight the enemy where I pleased. The next day my cavalry was in Holly Springs and the enemy fell back south of the Tallahatchie.

On the 15th of November, while I was still at Holly Springs, I sent word to Sherman to meet me at Columbus. . . . At that meeting, besides talking over my general plans I gave him his orders to join me with two divisions and to march them down the Mississippi Central railroad if he could. Sherman, who was always prompt, was up by the 29th to Cottage Hill, ten miles north of Oxford. He brought three divisions, leaving a garrison of only four regiments of infantry, a couple of pieces of artillery, and a small detachment of cavalry. Further reinforcements he knew were on their way from the north to Memphis.

About this time General Halleck ordered troops from Helena, Arkansas—territory west of the Mississippi was not under my command then—to cut the [rail]road in *Pemberton*'s rear. The expedition

. . . was successful so far as reaching the railroad was concerned, but the damage done was very slight and was soon repaired.

The Tallahatchie, which confronted me, was very high, the railroad bridge destroyed and *Pemberton* strongly fortified on the south side. A crossing would have been impossible in the presence of an enemy. I sent the cavalry higher up the stream and they secured a crossing. This caused the enemy to evacuate their position. . . . The enemy was followed as far south as Oxford by the main body of troops, and some seventeen miles farther by McPherson's command. Here the pursuit was halted to repair the railroad from the Tallahatchie northward, in order to bring up supplies. The piles on which the railroad bridge rested had been left standing. The work of constructing a roadway for the troops was but a short matter, and, later, rails were laid for cars.

During the delay at Oxford in repairing railroads I learned that an expedition down the Mississippi now was inevitable and, desiring to have a competent commander in charge, I ordered Sherman on the 8th of December back to Memphis to take charge. . . .*

Neither my orders to General Sherman, nor the correspondence between us or between General Halleck and myself, contemplated at that time my going further south than the Yalabusha [River]. *Pemberton's* force in my front was the main part of the Garrison of Vicksburg, as the force with me was the defence [*sic*] of the territory held by us in West Tennessee and Kentucky. *I hoped to hold Pemberton in my front while Sherman should get in his rear and into Vicksburg. The further north the enemy could be held, the better* [emphasis added].

It was understood, however, between General Sherman and myself that our movements were to be cooperative; if *Pemberton* could not be held away from Vicksburg I was to follow him; but at that time it was not expected to abandon the railroad north of the Yalabusha. With that point as a secondary base of supplies, the possibility of moving down the Yazoo until communications could be opened with the Mississippi was contemplated.

It was my intention, and so understood by Sherman and his command, that if the enemy should fall back I would follow him even to the gates of Vicksburg. I intended in such an event to hold

---

*See Part I, Chapter 4, and Part II, Phase 1, Stop 1, Chickasaw Bayou, for additional information on Grant, Sherman, and McClernand.

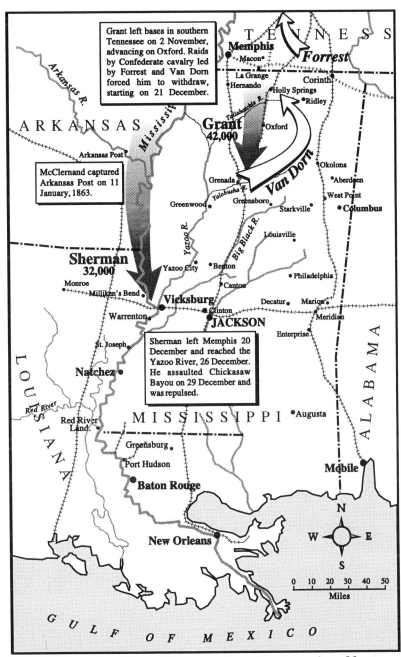

Grant's initial drive on Vicksburg, November–December 1862.

the road to Grenada on the Yalabusha and cut loose from there, expecting to establish a new base of supplies on the Yazoo, or at Vicksburg itself, with Grenada to fall back upon in case of failure.... At the time ... it had not been demonstrated that an army could operate in an enemy's territory depending upon the country for supplies. A halt was called at Oxford with the advance seventeen miles south of there, to bring up the [rail]road to the latter point and to bring supplies of food, forage and munitions to the front....

On the 20th [Maj. Gen. Earl] *Van Dorn* appeared at Holly Springs, my secondary base of supplies, captured the garrison of 1,500 men ... and destroyed all our munitions of war, food and forage.... At the same time [Brig. Gen. Nathan Bedford] *Forrest* got on our line of railroad between Jackson, Tennessee, and Columbus, Kentucky, doing much damage to it. This cut me off from all communication with the north for more than a week, and it was more than two weeks before rations or forage could be issued from stores obtained in the regular way.

This demonstrated the impossibility of maintaining so long a line of road over which to draw supplies for an army moving in an enemy's country. I determined, therefore, to abandon my campaign into the interior with Columbus as a base, and returned to La Grange and Grand Junction, destroying the road to my front and repairing the road to Memphis, making the Mississippi River the line over which to draw supplies. *Pemberton* was falling back at the same time....

After sending the cavalry to drive *Van Dorn* away, my next order was to dispatch all the wagons we had, under proper escort, to collect and bring in all supplies of forage and food from a region of fifteen miles east and west of the road from our front back to Grand Junction, leaving two months' supplies for the families of those whose stores were taken. I was amazed at the quantity of supplies the country afforded. It showed that we could have subsisted off the country for two months instead of two weeks without going beyond the limits designated. This taught me a lesson which was taken advantage of later in the campaign when our army lived twenty days with the issue of only five days' rations by the commissary. Our loss of supplies was great at Holly Springs, but it was more than compensated for by those taken from the country and by the lesson taught.[1]

GRANT'S CONCEPT

Grant to Maj. Gen. Henry W. Halleck, December 8, 1862, 10 P.M.

General Sherman will command the expedition down the Mississippi. He will have a force of about 40,000 men. Will land above Vicksburg, up the Yazoo, if practicable, and cut the Mississippi Central Railroad and the railroad running east from Vicksburg where they cross Black River.

I will co-operate from here, my movements depending on those of the enemy. With the large cavalry force now at my command I will be able to have them show themselves at different points on the Talahatchie [sic] and Yalabusha [sic], and where an opportunity occurs to make a real attack. After cutting the two railroads General Sherman's movements to secure the ends desired will necessarily be left to his judgment. I will occupy the railroad to Coffeeville.[2]

HOLLY SPRINGS: THE CONFEDERATES STRIKE FIRST

Maj. Gen. Earl Van Dorn to Pemberton, December 20, 1862

I surprised the enemy at this place [Holly Springs] at daylight this morning; burned up all the quartermaster's stores, cotton, etc.—an immense amount; burned up many trains; took a great many arms and about 1,500 prisoners. I presume the value of stores would amount to $1,500,000. . . .[3]

Grant to Halleck, December 21, 1862, 8 P.M.

The rebel cavalry commanded by *Van Dorn* made a dash into Holly Springs yesterday at daylight, capturing the troops, stores, etc. Their movement from the Yalabusha [sic] was very rapid. I heard of their crossing and ordered force to Pontotoc to intercept them, but they traveled as fast as the scouts who brought the news.

Next their departure from Pontotoc, going north, was reported. All my available cavalry was ordered in pursuit and are still out. As the rebels outnumber them three to one I do not expect much.

When communication was broken with the north I had troops concentrate to resist an attack on Jackson [Tennessee]. Do not know the result. If enemy are falling back north of the Tallahatchie I may find it necessary to send forces to Corinth. I would like to send two divisions more to Memphis and join the river expedition with them. This would make it necessary to fall back to Bolivar. The enemy are falling back from Grenada.[4]

Grant to Col. J. C. Kelton, December 25, 1862 (Washington, D.C.)

I am now occupying the line of the Tallahatchie, with the road strongly guarded to the rear, waiting for communication to be opened, to know what move next to make. It is perfectly impracticable to go farther south by this route, depending on the road for supplies, and the country does not afford them. Our immense train has so far been fed entirely off the country, and as far as practicable the troops have been also. For 15 miles east and west of the railroad, from Coffeeville to La Grange, nearly everything for the subsistence of man or beast has been appropriated for the use of our army, and on leaving our advanced position I had the principal mills destroyed.[5]

JOHNSTON IS SENT WEST

Special Orders, Adjutant and Inspector General's Office No. 275, Richmond, Virginia, November 24, 1862

III. General J. E. *Johnston,* CSA, is hereby assigned to the following geographical command, to wit: Commencing with the Blue Ridge range of mountains running through the western part of North Carolina, and following the line of said mountains through the northern part of Georgia to the railroad south from Chattanooga; thence by that road to West Point, and down the west or right bank of the Chattahoochee River to the boundary of Alabama and Florida; following that boundary west to the Choctawhatchee River, and down that river to Choctawhatchee . . . to the Gulf of Mexico.

All that portion of the country west of said line to the Mississippi River is included in the above command. General Johnston will . . . establish his headquarters at Chattanooga, or such other

Gen. Joseph E. *Johnston,* CSA, Commander, Confederate forces in the western theater. *Johnston,* fifty-six, was still recovering from wounds received at Seven Pines in May 1862, when he assumed command of the Department of the West. (U.S. Army Military History Institute)

place as in his judgement will best secure facilities for ready communication with the troops within the limits of his command, and
will repair in person to any part of said command whenever his
presence may for the time be necessary or desireable.[6]

J. E. Johnston to the President, January 2, 1863

General *Pemberton* continues to command at Vicksburg; he has
asked for all the troops here [Jackson, Mississippi], after being re-
enforced by *Maury's* division, in addition to those brigades agreed
upon between us. The line of 12 miles to Snyder's Mill probably
requires them all; I fear difficulty of subsisting them, however. A
report just handed in by the inspecting officers shows that the supply of provision is much smaller than General *Pemberton* supposed.
The place may be reduced I fear in consequence of this; or should
it be invested we shall not have a sufficient force to break the investment.

Grant is still on the Tallahatchie, so that the remainder of
Loring's and *Price's* troops cannot be withdrawn from Grenada.
From his halting I suppose he is repairing the railroad. The force
at Grenada (about 11,000 effective) is too weak to do more than
delay the passage of the river by the enemy. My hope of keeping
him back is in *Van Dorn,* under whom I propose to unite all the
available cavalry when *Forrest* and *Roddey* can be found.

Should Grant join Sherman at Vicksburg it would be very em-
barrassing; for as he could reach the place from Memphis as soon
as we could learn whether he was embarking or moving along the
railroad to Grenada it could be invested by the combined armies.
We could not break the investment with 11,000 men, but it would
be necessary to try.

The necessity of holding the Yazoo as well as Vicksburg em-
ploys a large force too widely distributed to be in condition for the
offensive.

We have no news from Arkansas, which proves I think that we
are to get no help from that side of the Mississippi. The Legisla-
ture has done nothing yet.

We require about 20,000 men, the number you have asked
for from Arkansas, to make headway against both Grant and
Sherman. Will the great victory at Fredericksburg [December 13,
1862] enable General *Lee* to spare a part of his force?

Should the enemy's forces be respectably handled, the task you have set me will be above my ability.[7]

Pemberton to Johnston, January 24, 1863

Enemy in full force again opposite the city, with indications of attempting to force his way below. This necessarily separates my command. Must have large force at Warrenton. Cannot place troops at Meridian without weakening this place. Book captured from Yankee colonel, killed yesterday, says Vicksburg must be taken. If necessary, will send his whole force; also states canal cut across.[8]

Pemberton to Johnston, February 6, 1863

Unless the enemy designs landing below Vicksburg and a protracted investment, perhaps first capturing Port Hudson, I can see no purpose in his arrangements. . . .[9]

NOTES

1. Ulysses S. Grant, *Personal Memoirs,* 2 vols. (New York: Charles L. Webster, 1885), 1:419–35 passim.
2. *O.R.,* XVII, pt. 1, p. 474.
3. *O.R.,* XVII, pt. 1, p. 503.
4. *O.R.,* XVII, pt. 1, p. 477.
5. *O.R.,* XVII, pt. 1, p. 478.
6. *O.R.,* XVII, pt. 2, pp. 757–58.
7. *O.R.,* XVII, pt. 2, p. 823.
8. *O.R.,* XXIV, pt. 3, pp. 599–600.
9. *O.R.,* XXIV, pt. 3, p. 618.

3. "A PERFECT CONCERT OF ACTION"

Summary of Principal Events:
November 24, 1862–January 12, 1863

November

24   Gen. Joseph E. *Johnston*, CSA, assigned to a command embracing western North Carolina, Tennessee, northern Georgia, Alabama, Mississippi, and eastern Louisiana.

December

4   General *Johnston* assumes the command to which he was assigned November 24.

7   The Confederate Department of Mississippi and East Louisiana reorganized; Maj.-Gens. Earl *Van Dorn* and Sterling *Price* commanding First and Second Corps.

9   Major General *Van Dorn* temporarily in command of the Army of the Mississippi.

12   Expedition up the Yazoo River, Mississippi.

13–19   Raid on the Mobile and Ohio Railroad from Corinth to Tupelo, Mississippi.

27   Sherman's force attacks Snyder's Bluff.

27–28   Skirmishes at Chickasaw Bayou.

29   Assault on Chickasaw Bluffs.

January

2–3   Sherman's forces reembark and proceed to Milliken's Bend, Louisiana.

4–17   Expedition against and capture of Arkansas Post, or Fort Hindman, Arkansas.

11   Maj. Gen. James B. McPherson, USA, assumes command of the Seventeenth Army Corps.

12   Maj. Gen. William T. Sherman, USA, assumes command of the Fifteenth Army Corps.

Grant to Maj. Gen. William T. Sherman, December 8, 1862

You will proceed with as little delay as possible to Memphis, Tenn., taking with you one division of your present command. On your arrival at Memphis you will assume command of all the troops there, and that portion of General [Samuel R.] Curtis' forces at present east of the Mississippi River, and organize them into brigades and divisions in your own army.

As soon as possible move with them down the river to the vicinity of Vicksburg, and with the co-operation of the gunboat fleet under command of Flag-Officer [David D.] Porter proceed to the reduction of that place, in such manner as circumstances as your own judgment may dictate. The amount of rations, forage, land transportation, etc., necessary to take will be left entirely with yourself.

The quartermaster at Saint Louis will be instructed to send you transportation for 30,000 men. Should you still find yourself deficient, your quartermaster will be authorized to make up the deficiency from such transports as may come into the port of Memphis.

On arriving in Memphis put yourself in communication with Admiral [Andrew H.] Foote and arrange with him for his co-operation. Inform me at the earliest practicable day of the time when you will embark and such plans as may then be matured. I will hold the forces here in readiness to co-operate with you in such manner as the movements of the enemy may make necessary.

Leave the District of Memphis in the command of an efficient officer, and with a garrison of four regiments of infantry, the siege guns, and whatever cavalry may be there.[1]

Narrative of Adm. David D. Porter, USN

I assumed command of the Mississippi Squadron at Cairo, Illinois, in October, 1862. There were the sturdy ironclads that had fought their way from Fort Henry to Donelson, to Island No. 10, and White River, and destroyed the enemy's navy at Memphis. . . . As soon as I arrived, the ironclads were put in the hands of five hundred loyal mechanics, and in a week were ready for any service. The rest of the vessels under my command were not very formidable, consisting of some side-wheel river steamboats and three or four "tin-clads," and this was the force with which the navy was expected to batter down Vicksburg![2]

Soon after my arrival at Cairo I sent a messenger to General Grant informing him that I had taken command of the naval forces, and should be happy to co-operate with him in any enterprise he might think proper to undertake. I also informed him that General [John A.] McClernand had orders to raise troops at Springfield, Illinois, prior to undertaking the capture of Vicksburg. I thought it my duty to tell him this, as it was not information given me in confidence.

Several weeks later Captain McAllister, quartermaster at Cairo, gave a supper party to me and the officers on the station on board the quartermaster's steamer, a large, comfortable river boat.

Supper had been served when I saw Captain McAllister usher in a travel-worn person dressed in citizen's clothes. McAllister was a very tall man, and his companion was dwarfed by his superior size. McAllister introduced the gentleman to me as General Grant, and placed us at a table by ourselves and left us to talk matters over.

Grant, though evidently tired and hungry, commenced business at once. "Admiral," he inquired, "what is all this you have been writing to me?"

I gave the general an account of my interviews with the President and with General McClernand, and he inquired, "When can you move with your gun-boats, and what force have you?"

"I can move tomorrow with all the old gun-boats and five or six other vessels; also the *Tyler, Conestoga,* and *Lexington.*"

"Well, then," said Grant, "I will leave you now and write at once to Sherman to have thirty thousand infantry and artillery embarked in transports ready to start for Vicksburg the moment you get to Memphis. I will return to Holly Springs tonight, and will start with a large force for Grenada as soon as I can get off.

"General Joe *Johnston* is near Vicksburg with forty thousand men, besides the garrison of the place under General *Pemberton.* When *Johnston* hears I am marching on Grenada, he will come from Vicksburg to meet me and check my advance. I will hold him at Grenada while you and Sherman push on down the Mississippi and make a landing somewhere on the Yazoo. The garrison at Vicksburg will be small, and Sherman will have no difficulty in getting inside the works. When that is done I will force *Johnston* out of Grenada, and, as he falls back on Vicksburg, will follow him up with a superior force. When he finds Vicksburg is occupied, he will retreat via Jackson."

I thought this plan an admirable one. Grant and myself never indulged in long talks together; it was only necessary for him to tell me what he desired, and I carried out his wishes to the best of my ability. . . . Here in twenty minutes Grant unfolded his plan of campaign, involving the transportation of over one hundred thousand men.

Three days after, with all the naval forces, I started down the Mississippi, and at Memphis found General Sherman embarking his troops on a long line of river steamers. . . . This was the first time I had ever met General Sherman, and my impressions of him were very favorable. I thought myself lucky to have two such generals as Grant and Sherman to co-operate with. . . .

No one, at that time, had any idea of the magnitude of the defenses that had been erected in every quarter to keep a foe out of Vicksburg. . . . Sherman at every point encountered obstacles of which he had never dreamed.[3]

Sherman to Porter, November 16, 1862

My opinion is that a perfect concert of action should exist between all the forces of the United States operating down the [Mississippi] valley, and I apprehend some difficulty may arise from the fact that you control on the river, [Maj. Gen. Samuel R.] Curtis on the west bank, and Grant on the east bank. Were either one of you in absolute command, all, of course would act in concert. Our enemies are now also disconcerted by divided counsels; *Van Dorn* and [Maj. Gen. Mansfield] *Lovell* are superior in lineal rank to *Pemberton,* and yet the latter is in command of the Department of Mississippi and Louisiana.

I think the forces now under Grant are able to handle anything in Mississippi; and our men are now confident and pretty well drilled. We can advance southward, striking Grenada and interposing between Vicksburg and Jackson, but your fleet should be abreast or ahead of the army. You invite these suggestions, and I think General [Henry W.] Halleck [general in chief] would order a concert of action any time you are prepared.

The possession of the river, with an army capable of disembarking and striking inland, would have a mighty influence.

I know that the people, though full of southern ardor, are getting tired of the devastations of war. Our new troops came with

Maj. Gen. Frederick Steele, USA, Commander, First Division, Fifteenth
Army Corps (Sherman). (U.S. Army Military History Institute)

ideas of making vigorous war, which means universal destruction, and it requires hard handling to repress excesses.

I take freely of corn, horses, wood, and lumber, brick—everything for the Government, but allow no individual plunder.

I was very anxious to see you before departing for the interior, but now expect soon to be off, acting under Grant, but hope we may meet below. I have admirable maps of Memphis and country round about, of which I could give you copies; but as your operations are by water, these would be of little service.[4]

Sherman to Col. John A. Rawlins, Assistant Adjutant General on Grant's Staff, December 19, 1862

I estimate we have enough boats to carry our command. We are now embarking and will be all aboard tomorrow. I will go ahead to Helena tomorrow and conclude the arrangements for the garrison at Friar's Point and cavalry force operating to the Tallahatchie. Enough boats have gone forward to carry Steele's command, so that I calculate to leave Helena December 21st, Gaines' Landing 22d, and be at Vicksburg 24th. No final return from Helena, but estimated total 32,000 men.

Admiral Porter is here and goes to Helena tomorrow. He expects all to meet at Milliken's Bend, 25 miles above Vicksburg, on the 24th. Shall at once break railroad west of Vicksburg and then enter the Yazoo. You may calculate on our being at Vicksburg by Christmas. River has risen some feet, and all is now good navigation. Gunboats are at mouth of Yazoo now, and there will be no difficulty in effecting a landing up Yazoo within 12 miles of Vicksburg.

General Gorman proposes to move all his forces from Helena to Napoleon, at mouth of Arkansas. I will see him tomorrow. He says he could then, if called, bring all his men to Vicksburg or act up the Arkansas. Colonel Howe and four companies of regular cavalry have arrived with pistols and sabers. I leave him with the garrison hitherto detailed for Memphis. I take Thielemann's cavalry, 70 men; at Helena will make up the necessary cavalry force.

At Vicksburg we will act so as to accomplish the original purpose, and will calculate to send you rations up the Yazoo. Yazoo City is the best point and can be reached after the reduction of the battery at Haines' [sic] Bluff.[5]

Maj. Gen. William T. Sherman, USA, Commander, Fifteenth Army Corps during the Vicksburg campaign. (U.S. Army Military History Institute)

Sherman to Col. John A. Rawlins, Assistant Adjutant General on Grant's Staff, December 21, 1862

I arrived here [Helena, Arkansas] last evening, and immediately saw Generals Gorman, Steele, and Blair. Their share of transports had previously been sent and were here loaded so as to receive their troops.

Already, 9 A.M., two of my Memphis divisions . . . have passed down to the first rendezvous, Friar's Point, and I expect A. J. Smith every hour. Steele's division will be afloat today and drop down to Friar's Point, so that by tomorrow morning my whole command will be embarked and underway. I will reach Gaines' Landing tomorrow, the 22d, and Milliken's Bend 23d, and be at mouth of Yazoo Christmas. . . .

General Morgan L. Smith reported to me this A.M. in passing that some men, 25 in number, had come into Memphis after I left, reporting that Holly Springs had been captured by the enemy and that they were the sole survivors. I hardly know what faith to put in such a report, but suppose whatever may be the case you will attend to it. . . . Admiral Porter is here and most of his gunboats are below.[6]

CHICKASAW BAYOU

For directions to this site, see Part II, Phase 1, Stop 1.

Sherman to Col. John A. Rawlins, Assistant Adjutant General on Grant's Staff, January 3, 1863

I have heretofore reported my progress and the organization of the forces placed under my command up to the date of their embarkation at Memphis, on December 20, 1862. This was two days later than fixed by your instructions, but was as soon as transports could possibly reach us from Cairo and Saint Louis.

On the 20th I proceeded to Helena and there met General [Willis A.] Gorman, commanding officer, and arranged with him for the establishment at Friar's Point of a regiment of infantry and a section of artillery, and a cavalry force of 2,000 men, under General [Cadwalader C.] Washburn, to operate from Friar's Point over to the Tallahatchie, and if possible to communicate with General Grant. I also met General Frederick Steele, who was assigned

to command the forces detailed to join me at that place. All of these
were embarked on the 21st, and by my orders were rendezvoused
at Friar's Point. My whole force there being assembled, we proceeded in order, led by Admiral Porter in his flag boat *Black Hawk*,
to Gaines' Landing, and next day to Milliken's Bend.

From that point I dispatched [Stephen G.] Burbridge's brigade, of the First Division (A. J. Smith's) to destroy a large section
of the Vicksburg and Shreveport Railroad, near the Tensas River.
This duty was admirably performed, the roadway destroyed for
many miles, and several long pieces of bridge and trestle work
burned. General Burbridge found a great deal of cotton, corn, and
cloth, the property of the Confederate Government, which he
burned. Cotton, the property of private individuals, was left un-
disturbed. . . .

On December 15, without waiting for the return of Burbridge,
I left General A. J. Smith, with the remainder of his division, to
follow as soon as that detachment came in. With the other three
divisions I proceeded opposite the mouth of the Yazoo, landing
on the west bank of the Mississippi, whence I dispatched General
Morgan L. Smith, with one of his brigades, to destroy another
section of the same road at a point nearer Vicksburg. This work
of destruction was also accomplished fully, so that the Vicksburg
and Shreveport Railroad, by which vast amounts of supplies reach
Vicksburg, is, and must remain for months, useless to our enemy.

On December 25, according to my promise made to General
Grant, I had my force at the mouth of the Yazoo. The whole naval
squadron of the Mississippi, iron-clads and wooden boats, were
also there, Admiral D. D. Porter in command. Conferring with
him, and with all positive information gained from every available source, we determined that the best point of debarkation was
at a point on the Yazoo, 12 miles up, on an island formed by the
Yazoo and Mississippi Rivers and a system of bayous or old channels.

On the 26th all the fleet proceeded in order up the Yazoo,
gunboats leading and distributed along the column of transports
to cover them against sharpshooters from the jungle and cane-
brake that cover the low banks of the Yazoo. . . . As soon as we
reached the point of debarkation, De Courcy's, Stuart's, and Blair's
brigades were sent forward in the direction of Vicksburg about 3
miles, and on the 27th the whole army was distributed and moved
out in four columns: Steele's above the mouth of Chickasaw Bayou;
Morgan's, with Blair's brigade of Steele's division, below the same

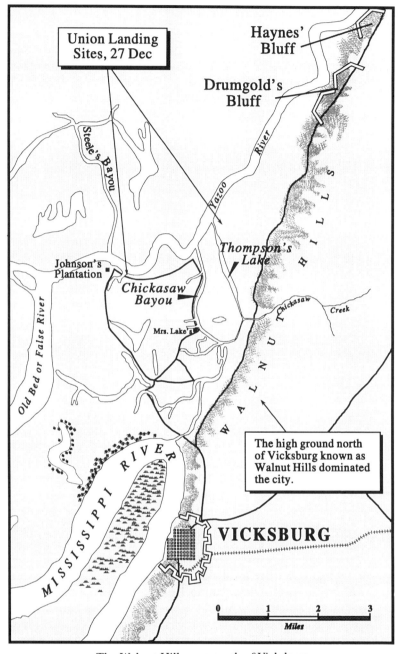

Union Landing
Sites, 27 Dec

Haynes'
Bluff

Drumgold's
Bluff

Steele's Bayou

Yazoo River

Thompson's
Lake

Johnson's
Plantation

Chickasaw
Bayou

WALNUT HILLS

Chickasaw Creek

Mrs. Lake's

Old Bed or False River

The high ground north
of Vicksburg known as
Walnut Hills dominated
the city.

MISSISSIPPI RIVER

VICKSBURG

0   1   2   3
Miles

The Walnut Hills area north of Vicksburg.

bayou; Morgan L. Smith's on the main road from Johnson's plantation to Vicksburg, with orders to bear to his left, so as to strike the bayou about a mile south of where Morgan was ordered to cross it, and A. J. Smith's division keeping on the main road.

All the heads of columns met the enemy's pickets and drove them toward Vicksburg. During the night of the 27th the ground was reconnoitered as well as possible, and it was found to be as difficult as it could possibly be from nature and [military] art. Immediately in our front was a bayou passable only at two points—on a narrow levee and on a sand bar which was perfectly commanded by the enemy's sharpshooters that line the levee or parapet on the opposite bank. Behind this was an irregular strip of bench or table land, on which was constructed a series of rifle-pits and batteries, and behind that a high, abrupt range of hills, whose scarred sides were marked all the way up with rifle-trenches and the crowns of the principal hills presented heavy batteries.

The county road leading from Vicksburg to Yazoo City was along the foot of these hills, and answered an admirable purpose to the enemy as a covered way along which he moved his artillery and infantry promptly to meet us at any point at which we attempted to cross this difficult bayou. Nevertheless, that bayou with its levee parapet, backed by the lines of rifle-pits, batteries, and frowning hill, had to be passed before we could reach *terra firma* and meet our enemy on anything like fair terms.

Steele in his progress followed substantially an old levee back from the Yazoo to the foot of the hills north of Thompson's Lake, but found that in order to reach the hard land he would have to cross a long corduroy causeway with a battery enfilading it, others cross-firing it, with a similar line of rifle-pits and trenches before described. He skirmished with the enemy on the morning of the 28th, while the other columns were similarly engaged; but on a close and critical examination of the swamp and causeway in his front, with the batteries and rifle-pits well manned, he came to the conclusion that it was impossible for him to reach the county road without a fearful sacrifice.

As soon as he reported this to me officially, and that he could not cross over from his position to the one occupied by our center, I ordered him to retrace his steps and cross back in steamboats to the southwest side of Chickasaw Bayou, and to support General Morgan's division, which he accomplished during the night of the

28th, arriving in time to support him and take part in the assault of the 29th.

General Morgan's division was evidently on the best of all existing roads from the Yazoo River to the firm land. He had attached to his train the pontoons with which to make a bridge in addition to the ford or crossing which I knew was in his front— the same by which the enemy's pickets had retreated. The pontoon bridge was placed during the night across a bayou supposed to be the main bayou, but which turned out to be an inferior one, and it was therefore useless; but the natural crossing remained, and I ordered him to cross over with his division and carry the line of works to the summit of the hill by a determined assault.

During the early part of the . . . 28th a heavy fog enveloped the whole country, but General Morgan advanced De Courcy's brigade and engaged the enemy; heavy firing of artillery and infantry were sustained, and his column moved on until he encountered the real bayou; this again checked his progress, and was not passed until the next day.

At the point where Morgan L. Smith's division reached the bayou was a narrow sand-spit, with *abatis* thrown down by the enemy on our side, with the same deep, boggy bayou, with its levee parapet and system of cross-batteries and rifle-pits on the other side. To pass it in his front by the flank would have been utter destruction, for the head of the column would have been swept away as fast as it presented itself above the steep bank. General Smith, while reconnoitering it early on . . . the 28th, was, during the heavy fog, shot in the hip by a chance rifle-bullet, which disabled him, and lost to me one of my best and most daring leaders. . . . General D. [David] Stuart succeeded to his place and to the execution of his orders.

General Stuart studied the nature of the ground . . . and saw all its difficulties, but made the best possible disposition to pass over his division . . . whenever he heard General Morgan engaged on his left.

To his right General A. J. Smith had placed Burbridge's brigade . . . next to Stuart, with orders to make rafts and cross over a portion of his men; to dispose his artillery so as to fire at the enemy across the bayou and produce the effect of a diversion. His other brigade [Landram's] occupied a key position on the main road, with pickets and supports pushed well forward into the tangled *abatis* within three-fourths of a mile of the enemy's forts and in plain view of the city of Vicksburg.

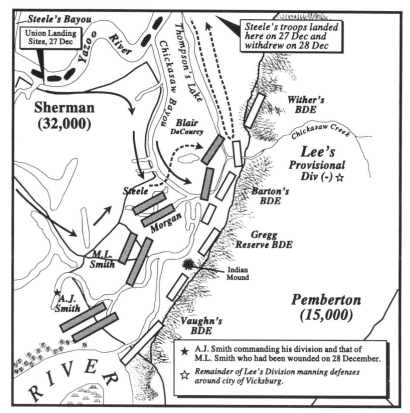

Sherman's forces attacking across Chickasaw Bayou, December 29, 1862.

Our boats still lay at our place of debarkation, covered by the
gunboats and by four regiments of infantry—one of each division.
Such was the disposition of our forces during the night of the 28th.

The enemy's right was a series of batteries or forts 7 miles
above us on the Yazoo, at the first bluff, near Snyder's house, called
Drumgould's Bluff; his left, the fortified city of Vicksburg, and his
line connecting these was near 14 miles in extent, and was a natural fortification strengthened by a year's labor of thousands of
negroes, directed by educated and skilled officers.

My plan was by a prompt and concentrated movement to
break the center near Chickasaw Creek, at the head of a bayou
of the same name, and once in position to turn to the right

(Vicksburg) or left (Drumgould's Bluff). According to information then obtained I supposed their organized forces to amount to about 15,000, which could be re-enforced at the rate of about 4,000 a day, provided General Grant did not occupy all the attention of *Pemberton's* forces at Grenada, or Rosecrans those of *Bragg* in Tennessee.

Not one word could I hear from General Grant, who was supposed to be pushing south, or of General [Nathaniel] P. Banks, supposed to be ascending the Mississippi [to Port Hudson]. Time being everything to us, I determined to assault the hills in front of Morgan on the morning of the 29th—Morgan's division to carry the position to the summit of the hill; Steele's division to support him and hold the county road. I had placed General A. J. Smith in command of his own division and that of M. L. Smith, with orders to cross on the sand-spit, undermine the steep bank of the bayou on the farther side, and carry at all events the levee parapet and first line of rifle-pits, to prevent a concentration on Morgan.

It was near 12 m. [noon] when Morgan was ready, by which time Blair's and Thayer's brigades, of Steele's division, were up to him and took part in the assault; and Hovey's brigade was close at hand. All the troops were massed as close as possible, and all our supports were well in hand.

The assault was made and a lodgment effected on the hard table-land near the county road, and the head of the assaulting columns reached different points of the enemy's works, but there met so withering a fire from the rifle-pits and cross-fire of grape and canister from the batteries that the column faltered, and finally fell back to the point of starting, leaving many dead, wounded, and prisoners in the hands of the enemy. . . .

General Morgan's first report to me was that the troops were not discouraged at all, though the losses in Blair's and De Courcy's brigades were heavy, and he would renew the assault in half an hour; but the assault was not again attempted.

I urged General A. J. Smith to push his attack, though it had to be made across a narrow sand bar and up a narrow path, in the nature of a breach, as a diversion in favor of Morgan, or [a] real attack, according to its success.

During Morgan's progress he passed over the Sixth Missouri under circumstances that called for all the individual courage for which that admirable regiment is . . . famous. Its crossing was covered by the Thirteenth U.S. Regulars, deployed as skirmishers up to the near bank of the bayou, covered as well as possible by fallen trees, and firing at any of the enemy's sharpshooters that showed a mark above the levee. Before this crossing all the ground opposite was completely swept by our artillery. . . .

The Sixth Missouri crossed over rapidly by companies, and lay under the bank of the bayou, with the enemy's sharpshooters over their heads within a few feet—so near that these sharpshooters held out their muskets and fired down vertically upon our men. The orders were to undermine this bank and make a road up it, but it was impossible; and after the repulse of Morgan's assault I ordered General A. J. Smith to retire this regiment under cover of darkness. Their loss was heavy. . . .

While this was going on Burbridge was skirmishing across the bayou at his front, and Landram pushed his advance, through the close *abatis* or entanglement of fallen timber, close up to Vicksburg.

When the night of the 29th closed in we stood upon our original ground and had suffered a repulse. The effort was necessary to a successful accomplishment of my orders, and the combinations were the best possible under the circumstances. I assume all the responsibility and attach fault to no one, and am generally satisfied with the high spirit manifested by all.

During this night it rained very hard, and our men were exposed to it in the miry, swampy ground, sheltered only by their blankets and rubber shawls. . . . I visited Admiral Porter on his flagboat and advised him of the exact condition of affairs, and on the following day, after a personal examination of the various positions, I was forced to the conclusion that we could not break the enemy's center without being too crippled to act with any vigor afterward.

New combinations therefore became necessary. I proposed to Admiral Porter if he would cover a landing at some high point close to the Drumgould batteries I would hold the present ground and send 10,000 choice troops and assault the batteries there . . . which, if successful, would give us the substantial possession of the Yazoo River and place us in connection with General Grant. Admiral Porter promptly and heartily agreed; and on a full conference, after close questioning some negroes as to the nature of the ground about the mouth of the Skillet Goliah, we came to the conclusion that no road or firm ground could be found south of that bayou.

Example of abatis during the Civil War. (U.S. Army Military History Institute)

It was therefore agreed that the 10,000 should be embarked immediately after dark during the night of December 31, and under cover of all the gunboats proceed before day slowly and silently up to the batteries above and engage them, the gunboats to silence the batteries, the troops then to disembark, storm the batteries, and hold them. While this was going on I was to attack the enemy here and hold him in check, preventing re-enforcements going up to the bluff, and in case of success to move all my forces to that point. Steele's division and the First Brigade of my Second Division were designated and embarked; the gunboats were all in position and up to midnight everything appeared favorable.

I left the admiral about 12 o'clock at night and the assault was to take place about 4 A.M. I went to my camp and had all the officers at their posts ready to act on the first sound of cannonading in the direction of Drumgould's Bluff; but about daylight I received a note from General Steele stating that the admiral had found the fog so dense on the river that the boats could not move, and that the expedition must be deferred to another night; but before the night of January 1, 1863, I received a note from Admiral Porter that "inasmuch as the moon does not set tonight until 5.25 the landing must be a daylight affair, which, in my opinion, is too hazardous to try."

Of course I was sadly disappointed, as it was the only remaining chance of our securing a lodgment on the ridge between the Yazoo and Black Rivers from which to operate against Vicksburg, and the railroad east, as also to secure the navigation of the Yazoo River; but I am forced to admit the admiral's judgment was well founded and that even in case of success the assault on the batteries of Drumgould's Bluff would have been attended with a fearful sacrifice of life.

One-third of my command had already embarked for the expedition; the rest were bivouacked in low, swampy, timbered ground, which a single night's rain would have made a quagmire, if not a lake. Marks of overflow stained the trees 10 and 12 feet above their roots, and further attempts against the center were deemed by all the . . . commanders as impracticable, I saw no good reason for remaining in so unenviable a place. . . . All the necessary orders were made and all the men and materials were re-embarked on the original transports by sunrise of January 2.

During all this time the enemy displayed in our front, whenever we presented ourselves, large masses of infantry and cavalry; artillery crowned the summits of the hills, appeared in the batteries on their faces, and field-guns presented themselves everywhere along the county road. We could hear their [rail] cars coming and departing all the time, and large re-enforcements were doubtless arriving, and as the rumor of General Grant having fallen behind the Tallahatchie became confirmed by my receiving no intelligence from him, I was forced to the conclusion that it was not only prudent but proper that I should move my command to some other point.

Two suggested themselves—the Louisiana shore opposite the mouth of the Yazoo, and Milliken's Bend. The latter had many advantages, large extent of cleared land, some houses for storage, better roads back, a better chance for corn and forage, with all the

Confederate defenses at Chickasaw Bayou. (U.S. Army Military History Institute)

same advantages for operating against the enemy inland on the river below Vicksburg or at any point above where he might attempt to interrupt the navigation of the Mississippi. My mind had settled down on this when, all my troops being on board their transports ready to move, on the morning of January 2, I learned from Admiral Porter that General McClernand had arrived at the mouth of the Yazoo. Fearing that any premature move on my part might compromise his plans . . . I determined to remain where we were until I consulted him, which I did in person, and with his approval I then proceeded . . . to land my command at Milliken's Bend and dispatch back to the north the fleet of transports which had carried them.[7]

THE CONFEDERATE DEFENSE

Report of Lt. Gen. John C. Pemberton, CSA,
Commanding Department of Mississippi and
East Louisiana, December 12, 1862–January 2, 1863

On December 21, [1862], while at Grenada awaiting the approach of the enemy in that direction, information was received that his large fleet of gunboats and transports was moving down the Mississippi River for the supposed purpose of attacking Vicksburg. Brig. Gen. [J. C.] *Vaughn's* brigade of East Tennesseeans was at once ordered to that point.

On the 24th definite and reliable information reached me that the enemy's gunboats had arrived at the mouth of the Yazoo River, 6 miles above Vicksburg, and that his transports were not far in their rear. Thereupon Brig. Gen. [John] *Gregg* with his brigade was immediately sent forward.

On the 25th [I] left Grenada and reached Vicksburg at 12 m. [noon] on the 26th. While on the route the Fortieth Alabama Regiment . . . was ordered from Columbus to Vicksburg. On my arrival I found the enemy's gunboats were engaged in shelling the banks of the Yazoo River up to the vicinity of the first bluffs at Snyder's Mill, and under their cover he was disembarking his troops from his transports.

Snyder's Mill is situated 13 miles north of Vicksburg, on a bluff which overlooks the Yazoo River. At this point a strong battery had been planted and the river blockaded by a raft. Swamps, lakes and bayous running parallel with the river intervene between the bank and the hills, and leave but four practicable approaches to the high ground from Snyder's Mill to the Mississippi River, but all outside of the fortifications erected for the defense of Vicksburg: one in Blake's field, running along his levee nearly at right angles with the river; the next about a mile below, along the Chickasaw bayou; the third passing through a dry part of the lake opposite to an Indian mound, and the fourth by a road leading from Johnson's [house] by the race track. Before my arrival Major-General [M. L.] *Smith* had arranged his guns and disposed of his troops so as to guard these several approaches, under the immediate command of Brig. Gen. [S. D.] *Lee.*

On this day skirmishing began soon after the disembarkation of the enemy's troops, which resulted in driving his advanced parties from Mrs. Lake's plantation into the swamps bordering the river.

On the 27th, at an early hour, demonstrations in force were made at the Indian mound, Chickasaw Bayou, Blake's Levee, and Snyder's Mill, thus showing on the part of the enemy accurate knowledge of all the approaches.

About 2 o'clock three of the enemy's gunboats moved up to attack our battery at Snyder's Mill, and continued a heavy firing for three hours, when they returned down the river. Our guns were handled with spirit and precision, and the officers and men deserve the highest praise for their gallant conduct during the engagement.

About the time of the attack at Snyder's Mill another was made along the Chickasaw Bayou with great violence and in heavy force. This was gallantly and successfully met by the Seventeenth Louisiana Regiment, two companies of the Forty-sixth Mississippi Regiment, and a section of Capt. [J. L.] *Wofford*'s battery, all under command of Col. [W. T.] *Withers,* First Mississippi Artillery.

During the evening and night of this day Brigadier-Generals *Vaughn* and *Gregg,* with their brigades, arrived from Grenada, and also Brig. Gen. [S. M.] *Barton* and his brigade, of Maj. Gen. [C. L.] *Stevenson*'s division. Before daylight they were moved to the front and Brigadier-General *Vaughn* assigned to the command of the left, at the race course; Brigadier-General *Barton* to the center, fronting on the Indian mound, and Brigadier-General *Lee* to the right, reaching to Snyder's Mill. Brigadier-General *Gregg* at first was held in reserve with his troops, but was subsequently placed in position between Generals *Vaughn* and *Barton.*

On the 28th, at 4:30 A.M., the enemy opened fire with his sharpshooters and six pieces of artillery, on the rifle-pits in front of the Indian mound and the section of artillery upon it. The Thirty-first Louisiana Regiment . . . occupied the trenches, and during the day was re-enforced by five companies of the Fortieth Georgia. . . . The enemy's fire was kept up with great vigor and without intermission throughout the day. In the evening it was so severe that our men were unable to stand to their guns on the mound when two sections of Maj. [M. S.] *Ward*'s artillery were ordered up to aid in preventing the enemy from planting a battery in close range, which was successfully effected.

On the previous night the command of Colonel *Withers* was removed from Chickasaw Bayou to Blake's Levee, and the Twenty-eighth [Twenty-ninth] Louisiana Regiment . . . of *Lee's* brigade, was sent to occupy *Withers'* position of the previous day.

About daylight the enemy, with six pieces of artillery, supported by at least a brigade of infantry, opened a heavy fire upon this gallant regiment, which held him in check until 12 m., when it retired in good order. The enemy, elated with his success, followed rapidly, but his progress was soon checked by a well-timed volley from the Twenty-sixth Louisiana . . . which occupied the rifle pits hurriedly thrown up opposite the dry part of the lake.

On the same morning another strong column advanced upon the position held by the Seventeenth Louisiana Regiment, Forty-sixth Mississippi . . . and [Capt. Robert] *Bowman's* battery, all under command of Colonel *Withers,* on Blake's Levee, which was resisted in gallant style and the enemy finally driven back with heavy loss. . . .

On the conclusion of this day's fighting it seemed highly probable that on the next the enemy would make the attempt to carry our position by assault. The dispositions were made accordingly. The works were repaired and strengthened, some additional trenches dug, and just before daylight it was deemed advisable, owing to its isolated position, to withdraw the Twenty-sixth Louisiana Regiment.

On the 29th, about 9 o'clock, the enemy was discovered in his attempt to throw a pontoon bridge across the lake. In this he was foiled by a few well-directed shots from a section each of *Wofford's* and *Ward's* batteries. . . .

About 10 o'clock a furious cannonade was opened on General *Lee's* lines. This ceased about 11 o'clock, when a whole brigade—about 6,000 strong, understood to have been Brig. Gen. [F. P.] Blair's . . . emerged from the woods in good order and moved gallantly forward under a heavy fire of our artillery. They advanced to within 150 yards of the pits when they broke and retreated, but soon rallied, and dividing their forces sent a portion to their right, which was gallantly driven back by the Twenty-eighth Louisiana and Forty-second Georgia Regiments with heavy loss.

Their attack in front was repulsed with still greater disasters. By a handsome movement on the enemy's flank the Twenty-sixth and part of the Seventeenth Louisiana threw the enemy into inextricable confusion, and were so fortunate as to capture 4 stands of regimental colors, 21 commissioned officers, 311 non-commissioned officers and privates, and 500 stand of arms. The Third, Thirtieth, and

View of Chickasaw Bayou. (U.S. Army Military History Institute)

Eightieth Tennessee Regiments occupied the rifle-pits and behaved with distinguished coolness and courage.

During the assault upon the right the enemy in force was
endeavoring to carry our center, commanded by General *Barton,*
by storm. Five resolute efforts were made to carry our breastworks
and were as often repulsed with heavy loss. Three times he succeeded in mounting the parapet and once made a lodgment and

attempted to mine. . . . At this point the enemy did not give up his attack until night-fall.

On the left, commanded by Brigadier-General *Vaughn*, the heavy *abatis* prevented the approach of the enemy except with sharpshooters, who advanced continuously, but were met firmly by his East Tennesseeans.

Our sharpshooters were everywhere, by their coolness, vigilance, and accuracy of aim, rendered the most valuable service and contributed greatly to the general result.

On the morning of the 29th Major-General *Stevenson* arrived at Vicksburg, and by reason of seniority was assigned to the command of the troops in front of the enemy.

On the 30th, although the enemy still occupied his position in front of our lines, the firing was confined to the sharpshooters on either side. Maj. Gen. [D. H.] *Maury* arrived during this day from Grenada with a portion of his division and was assigned to the command of the right wing, reaching from the signal station to Snyder's Mill.

On the 31st the enemy sent in [a] flag of truce, asking permission to bury his dead and care for his wounded, which was granted.

On January 1 it became evident that some new movement was on hand, and on the 2d it was ascertained that the enemy was re-embarking. General *Lee* was sent with five regiments to harass him in this operation. The noble Second Texas, whose fortune it was to be in advance of the assaulting column, charged and routed the enemy, formed on the bank of the river, and continued (although under the incessant fire of twelve gunboats) their attack on the crowded transports until they passed beyond range. . . .

During these several engagements our entire loss was 63 killed, 134 wounded, and 10 missing.[8]

Report of Maj. Gen. Martin L. Smith, CSA, Commanding Forces in Front of Vicksburg, of Operations December 25–30, 1862

The broken ridge of hills touching the Mississippi at Vicksburg extends into the interior in nearly a direct line and has a direction at about right angles with the general course of the river. The Yazoo in its course touches the base of these hills at a point 12 miles in the interior known as Snyder's Mill; thence, diverging from

Brig. Gen. Stephen D. *Lee*, CSA, Commander, Provisional Division at Chickasaw Bayou. (U.S. Army Military History Institute)

them, empties into the Mississippi some 6 miles above the city. There is thus between the hills and the Yazoo a triangular-shaped area of bottom land, densely wooded, with the exception of one or two plantations on it, and intersected with bayous and low, swampy ground. Skirting the hills from Snyder's Mill down to near the Mississippi is first a swamp and then an old bed of the Yazoo, containing considerable water, and only to be crossed without bridging at three points, where torrents from the hills have borne along sufficient matter to fill up a bed. From the termination of this old bed to the Mississippi a belt of timber is felled, forming a heavy *abatis*. There was thus a continuous obstacle 12 miles long, formed of *abatis* and water, skirting the base of the hills and but a short distance from them, terminated at one end by our fixed batteries and fortified position at the mill; at the other end by the heavy batteries and field-works above Vicksburg. Through this obstacle there are but three natural passages. . . .

The fortifications proper encircling this city are disconnected and entirely independent of the line described and the one selected on which to meet the enemy. The inquiry naturally arises, Why meet the enemy outside of our fortifications and on a line so extended? The reasons determining were as follows: The Yazoo drains a section of country of great wealth and fertility, has its source in the heart of the State, is navigable at an ordinary stage of water to the Mississippi Central, and has accumulated in its waters a large amount of property in steamboats. All this wealth of products and boats it was important to protect, but still more important to prevent the enemy from getting control of the river, which, once possessed, would give him a base for operations most dangerous to our success. So long as the works at Snyder's Mill were held the whole Yazoo Valley was defended. It was believed those works could be held provided the enemy was forced to make a direct assault upon them from the river and not permitted to disengage himself from the bottom described, break through our line, and, establishing himself in the open country between the mill and Vicksburg, be able to take those works in rear.

Another object was also accomplished: The enemy, without gaining the hills, could make no attempt to cut the line of the Vicksburg and Jackson Railroad.

The base of the hills being determined upon as the proper line, preparations were made in advance to guard the three natural approaches to it by throwing up earthworks, felling timber, etc. It was further strengthened during the progress of the attack as the enemy's plans developed themselves.

Certain information regarding the proximity of the enemy's fleet was first received on the morning of December 23, and by 10 o'clock that night seventy-four transports were known to be in the vicinity of the mouth of the Yazoo, together with some twelve gunboats that had previously arrived. This number was increased during the succeeding two or three days to about one hundred and twenty.

At daylight on the . . . 25th the troops of the command were ordered in the trenches, which they did not leave again until the attack was abandoned, except to re-enforce different portions of the line as circumstances required.

The 25th and part of the 26th were occupied by the enemy in debarking and making demonstrations of attack at Snyder's Mill, where one of their most formidable iron-clads was very severely handled and driven out of range by the open batteries. . . . The gunboats did not afterward venture another attack, their iron armor being rather readily penetrated.

About noon on the 26th it began to be apparent that the main attack would be against the center of our line, in the endeavors to gain the high ground by the crossing-points mentioned. The available infantry under Brigadier-General *Lee* was accordingly placed at these exposed points, with directions to hold the enemy in the bottom to the last and give time for re-enforcements to arrive. This was handsomely done, and they were completely held in check during the remainder of the day at the two points where their columns appeared.

The arrival of the three brigades, under Brigadier-Generals *Barton, Gregg,* and *Vaughn* during the afternoon and night of the 26th added greatly to our strength and confidence. These troops were moved promptly forward and by daylight were in position, thus enabling the exposed points to be held in force and the whole front to be watched by skirmishers.

The line was now immediately commanded as follows; General *Lee* was on the right, General *Barton* in the center, General *Vaughn* on the left, General *Gregg,* with brigade, being held in reserve, although subsequently placed in position between Generals *Barton* and *Vaughn.* The order was for each brigade to draw re-enforcements from the one immediately on its left, the left itself to be re-enforced by fresh arrivals from the interior or from the reserve.

The 27th was apparently occupied by the enemy in getting their batteries in position and preparing extensive rifle-pits.

Early on the morning of the 28th the enemy opened with a heavy fire of both artillery and musketry along the entire line, which increased with intensity as the day advanced and only ceased with night.

The night of the 28th was spent by both parties in placing new batteries in position, strengthening the works and preparing for the morrow.

At daylight on the 29th the attack commenced with renewed fury and soon the appearance of a largely increased force in front indicated an intention to assault, which was attempted almost simultaneously along the whole line. In front of General *Lee* the attack was the most formidable, as, owing to the ground, they could deploy on a greater front, thus taking advantage of their superiority of numbers. The assaulting force—estimated at 6,000—moved from their concealed position in the woods, advanced rapidly on an open space of say 400 yards, and made a determined attack upon his intrenched position. Taken in flank by the artillery and met in front by a withering sheet of musketry fire, the enemy struggled up to within a short distance of our line, when he wavered, stopped, and soon fled in irretrievable panic and confusion, strewing the ground with his dead and wounded, leaving in our position 4 regimental colors, over 300 prisoners, and 500 stands of arms.

In front of General *Barton* the assault, although not made in such numbers, was persisted in with a tenacity indicating a determined purpose to succeed. Five different times did they attempt to storm his most advanced work, each time repulsed with loss, and from daylight until sunset the troops were under as severe a fire of musketry and artillery as it was practicable for an enemy almost enveloping them to pour into the work.

The formidable *abatis* in front of General *Vaughn*, together with the batteries in position in the line to his rear, seemed to have disheartened the enemy there from the first, rendering his attack uncertain, feeble, and easily repulsed. His skirmishers, as they advanced in the fallen timber, were boldly met by our sharpshooters and their progress arrested. A few well-directed shots from some 12 and 24 pounders drove them back into the woods and their masses disappeared.

On the 30th the enemy's fire sensibly slackened, and permission to bury their dead and care for their wounded being granted on the 31st, it was not afterward renewed to any great extent. . . .

The manner in which the troops . . . bore themselves during the six days and nights of continuous service in the field and trenches cannot be too much admired. Under General *Lee* they met the enemy in superior numbers and hurled him back with heavy loss. Under General *Barton* they endured unflinchingly a fire from which veteran troops might well have shrunk and gave a bloody reception to his repeated assaults. Those under Generals *Gregg* and *Vaughn* showed perfect steadiness throughout. . . .

To the intelligent activity of my chief quartermaster and commissary much praise is due. Cooked rations were furnished the troops during the whole operations, and transportation provided promptly . . . to the extent that resources, both public and private, admitted of.[9]

SAFEGUARDING THE LINE OF COMMUNICATIONS— ARKANSAS POST

Narrative of Maj. Gen. William T. Sherman, USA

On the 4th of January, 1863, our fleet of transports was collected at Millikin's Bend, about ten miles above the mouth of the Yazoo, Admiral Porter remaining with his gunboats at the Yazoo. General John A. McClernand was in chief command. General George W. Morgan commanded the First Corps and I the Second Corps of the Army of the Mississippi.

I had learned that a small steamboat, the *Blue Wing* . . . towing coal-barges and loaded with ammunition, had left Memphis for the Yazoo, about the 20th of December, had been captured by a rebel boat which had come out of the Arkansas River, and had been carried up that river to Fort Hindman. We had reports from this fort, usually called the "Post of Arkansas," about forty miles above the mouth, that it was held by about five thousand rebels, was an inclosed work, commanding the passage of the river, but supposed to be easy of capture from the rear.

At that time I don't think General McClernand had any definite views or plans of action. If so, he did not impart them to me. He spoke in general terms of opening the navigation of the Mississippi, "cutting his way to the sea," etc., etc., but the *modus operandi* was not so clear.

Knowing full well that we could not carry on operations against Vicksburg as long as the rebels held the Post of Arkansas, whence to attack our boats coming and going without convoy, I visited him on his boat, the *Tigress*, took with me a boy who had been on the

Rear Adm. David D. Porter, USN, Commander, Union naval forces for the Vicksburg campaign. (U.S. Army Military History Institute)

Blue Wing, and had escaped, and asked leave to go up the Arkansas to clear out the Post. He made various objections, but consented to go with me to see Admiral Porter about it. We got up steam in the *Forest Queen* during the night of January 4th, stopped at the *Tigress,* took General McClernand on board, and proceeded down the river by night to the admiral's boat, the *Black Hawk,* lying in the mouth of the Yazoo.

It must have been near midnight, and Admiral Porter was in *deshabille.* We were seated in his cabin and I explained my views about Arkansas Post and asked his cooperation. He said that he was short of coal, and could not use wood in his iron-clad boats. Of these I asked for two, to be commanded by Captain Shirk or Phelps, or some officer of my acquaintance. . . . Porter's manner to McClernand was so curt that I invited him out into a forward-cabin where he had his charts, and asked him what he meant by it. He said that "he did not like him"; that in Washington, before coming West, he had been introduced to him by President Lincoln, and he had taken a strong prejudice against him. I begged him, for the sake of harmony, to waive that, which he promised to do.

Returning to the cabin, the conversation was resumed, and, on our offering to tow his gunboats up the river to save coal, and on renewing the request for Shirk to command the detachment, Porter said, "Suppose I go along myself?" I answered, if he would do so, it would insure the success of the enterprise. At that time I supposed General McClernand would send me on this business, but he concluded to go himself and to take his whole force. Orders were at once issued for the troops not to disembark at Milliken's Bend, but to remain . . . on board the transports. . . .

The whole army, embarked on steamboats convoyed by the gunboats, of which three were iron-clads, proceeded up the Mississippi River to the mouth of White River, which we reached January 8th. On the next day we continued up White River to the "Cut-off"; through this to the Arkansas, and up the Arkansas to Notrib's farm, just below Fort Hindman. Early the next morning we disembarked.[10]

Report of Maj. Gen. W. T. Sherman, USA, Commanding Fifteenth Army Corps, January 13, 1863

It was about dark when the advance of the fleet reached the place of debarkation, about 3 miles below the point of attack, and darkness set in, so that it was impracticable to place the boats at suitable points for landing. During the night it rained hard, but cleared away at 4 A.M., when I proceeded to arrange the boats of my corps and begin the work of disembarkation. This was not advanced far enough to put the troops in motion till 11 A.M., when General Steele's column entered the woods back of Notrib's farm, which soon became a deep, ugly swamp, but wading through it for about 2 miles in an easterly direction the head of the column reached a field and cabin on hard ground.

There, upon questioning closely the occupants of the cabin and some prisoners who gave themselves up, we ascertained that in crossing the swamp we were on the south side of a bayou which in a northeasterly direction extended to Bayou La Cruz, a tributary of the White River, and that to reach the Little Prairie, behind the Arkansas Post, we would have to march a circuit of 7 miles, although in an air-line the distance did not exceed 2.

Satisfied that this route would not fulfill the conditions of General McClernand's plan of attack, I sent my chief of staff, Major Hammond, back to him to explain the state of facts and the conclusion to which I had arrived.

Having also learned that the enemy had abandoned his first line of rifle-pits on the river bank, about a mile above our landing, I had previously ordered General Stuart to march his division directly by that route, following the bank of the river. General McClernand soon overtook us and, confirming my conclusion, ordered me to countermarch Steele's division and hasten to lead Stuart's. Sending orders immediately to General Steele, who was some distance in advance, to make a feint on that road with his cavalry and one regiment of infantry and with the balance of his division retrace his steps, I rode back and over-took Stuart's column, which had reached within half a mile of the Post. I hastily made an examination of the ground and directed Captain Pitzman, of the Topographical Engineers, to make a reconnaissance to the right, while I gave orders to dispense of the troops coming from the rear. Night closed in before these preparations were complete and the troops, already in position, bivouacked without fires through that bitter cold night.

The moon rose about 1 A.M., when I rode forward and examined the position of the enemy as well as possible and gave General Stuart some general instructions about throwing up an *epaulement* to a battery of field guns. General Steele's division was at the time passing to his position on the right, so that when day broke, Steele was on the extreme right and Stuart next to him; Morgan's corps was on the left, resting on the river. We could hear the enemy all night busy at work chopping and felling trees, and became convinced he was resolved on a determined resistance. His position was: his right in a strong earth fort, with four bastion fronts, inclosing a space of about 100 yards square, and a line of hastily-constructed rifle-pits or parapet extending across the neck of level ground to a bayou west and north of this fort; the length of this line was about three-quarters of a mile. In the fort were mounted three heavy iron guns, two in embrasure and one *en barbette,* with four small rifled 3-inch guns and four smooth bore 6-pounders, distributed at the salients and flanks. Along the rifle-pits were also six other field pieces—12-pounder howitzers and 3-inch rifled guns.[11]

Late in the evening of the 10th Admiral Porter's fleet made a furious attack upon the fort, continuing the cannonading till after it was dark; but although I had pushed one brigade of Stuart's division, commanded by Col. Giles A. Smith, close up to the enemy's line, our forces were not then in position to make an assault.

Early the next morning, however, I moved all my corps into an easy position for assault, looking south across ground encumbered by fallen trees and covered with low bushes. The enemy could be seen moving back and forth along his lines, occasionally noticing our presence by some ill-directed shots, which did us little harm and accustomed our men to the sound of rifled cannon.

By 10 A.M. I reported to General McClernand in person that I was all ready for the assault, and only waited the simultaneous movement of the gunboats. They were to silence the fort and save us from the enfilading fire of its artillery along the only possible line of attack. About 12:30 I received notice from General McClernand that the gunboats were in motion.

The four 20-pounder rifled guns . . . were then in position to my left in the thick woods and brush and their men had been cutting the trees away to open a field of fire, but as Burbridge's brigade of Morgan's corps occupied ground to their front, these guns could not be used during the engagement. . . .

My orders were that as soon as the gunboats opened their fire all our batteries in position should commence firing, and continue until I ordered "Cease firing," when after three minutes' cessation

Lithograph of the attack on Arkansas Post (Fort Hindman) by troops under the command of Major General McClernand and boats under the command of Rear Admiral Porter. (Frank Leslie's *Illustrated History of the Civil War*)

the infantry columns of Steele and Stuart were to assault the enemy's line of rifle-pits and defenses.

The gunboats opened [fire] about 1 P.M., and our field batteries at once commenced firing, directing their shots at the enemy's guns, his line of defenses, and more especially enfilading the road which led directly into the fort, and . . . separated General Morgan's line of attack from mine. I could not see the gunboats, and had to judge of their progress by the sound of their fire. This was at first slow and steady, but rapidly approached the fort and enveloped it with a complete hail-storm of shot and shell. Our field batteries continued their fire rapidly for about fifteen minutes; the enemy not replying, I ordered the firing to cease and the infantry columns to advance to the assault. The line of skirmishers had been withdrawn and the infantry sprang forward with a cheer. About 100 yards of clear space was to our immediate front, and then a belt of ground about 300 yards wide separated us from the enemy's parapet. This belt of ground was slightly cut up by gullies and depressions and covered with standing trees and brush, with a good deal of fallen timber and tree tops. Into this the attacking columns dashed rapidly, and there encountered the fire of the enemy's artillery and infantry, well directed from their perfect cover, which checked the speed of our advance, which afterward became more cautious and prudent.

By 3 P.M. our lines were within 100 yards of the enemy's trenches, outflanking him on our right and completely enveloping his position. The gunboats could be seen close up to the fort, and I saw the admiral's flag directly under it. All artillery fire from the fort had ceased, and only occasionally could be seen few of the enemy's infantry firing from its parapets; but the strongest resistance continued in our immediate front, where the enemy's infantry was massed, comparatively safe from the gunboats, whose fire was properly directed well to the front lest it should reach our men, whose colors they could plainly distinguish. A brisk fire of musketry was kept up along our whole front, with an occasional discharge of artillery through the intervals of the infantry lines until about 4 P.M., when reports reached me at the same instant that the white flag had been shown all along the enemy's lines. I myself saw a large, conspicuous white flag displayed at the point where the main road intersected the parapet, and sent forward my aide, Captain Dayton, to communicate with the commander.

Sending orders as fast as possible along the line to the right to cease firing, I followed Captain Dayton and found the place surrendered. . . . I immediately sent orders to General Steele to push one of his brigades along the bayou to his extreme right, to prevent escape in that direction, and dispatched every mounted man near me . . . in the same direction, to secure all squads of men who . . . might attempt to escape. I soon however became convinced that the surrender was perfect and in good faith, and that we had gained the enemy's position, with his fort, guns, men, and all the *materiel* of war. . . .

The 12th instant was mostly consumed in collecting captured property . . . and enrolling and embarking the prisoners. . . . Major Sanger reports . . . that he has put on board the steamboats designated for the purpose 4,791 prisoners. . . . Among the captured property I was rejoiced to find the ammunition shipped for me from Memphis for Vicksburg, which had been captured by the enemy on the *Blue Wing.*[12]

Narrative of Maj. Gen. William T. Sherman, USA (*continued*)

The next day the prisoners were all collected on their boats, lists were made out, and orders given for their transportation to St. Louis, in charge of my aide, Major Sanger. We then proceeded to dismantle and level the forts, destroy or remove the stores, and we found in the magazine the very ammunition which had been sent for us in the *Blue Wing*, which was secured and afterward used in our twenty-pound Parrot guns.

On the 13th we reembarked; the whole expedition returned out of the river by the direct route down the Arkansas during a heavy snow-storm, and rendezvoused in the Mississippi, at Napoleon, at the mouth of the Arkansas. Here General McClernand told me he had received a letter from General Grant at Memphis, who disapproved of our movement up the Arkansas; but that communication was made before he learned of our complete success. When informed of this, and of the promptness with which it had been executed, he could not but approve. We were then ordered back to Milliken's Bend, to await General Grant's arrival in person. We reached Milliken's Bend January 21st.[13]

NOTES

1. *O.R.*, XVII, pt. 1, p. 601.
2. A "tin-clad" is a lightly armored steamship, more vulnerable than the more heavily armored "iron-clad."
3. David D. Porter, *Incidents and Anecdotes of the Civil War* (New York: D. Appleton, 1885), pp. 124–28 passim.
4. *O.R.*, XXIII, pt. 1, pp. 487–88.
5. *O.R.*, XVII, pt. 1, pp. 603–4.
6. *O.R.*, XVII, pt. 1, p. 604.
7. *O.R.*, XVII, pt. 1, pp. 605–10.
8. *O.R.*, XVII, pt. 1, pp. 665–68.
9. *O.R.*, XVII, pt. 1, pp. 671–74.
10. William T. Sherman, *Memoirs of General William T. Sherman, by Himself*, 2 vols. (New York: Appleton, 1875), 1:324–25.
11. These terms are defined in Henry Lee Scott, *Military Dictionary: Comprising Technical Definitions; Information on Raising and Keeping Troops; Actual Service, Including Make-shift and Improvised Matériel; and Law, Government, Regulations, and Administration Relating to Land Forces* (New York: D. Van Nostrand, 1862). An *epaulement* is an elevation thrown up to cover troops from the fire of an enemy, usually composed of gabions (cylindrical barrels open at both ends) filled with earth (pp. 258, 320). An *embrasure* is a hole cut through the wall of an earthwork (p. 255). *En barbette* refers to artillery pieces elevated by raising the earth behind the parapet or placing them on a high carriage, allowing them to be fired over the top of the parapet. In this position the guns have a wide range, instead of being limited by firing through the embrasure (p. 79).
12. *O.R.*, XVII, pt. 1, pp. 754–57.
13. Sherman, *Memoirs*, 1:330–31.

4. OPERATIONS WEST OF THE RIVER

Summary of Principal Events:
December 20, 1862–February 26, 1863

January
30   Maj. Gen. Ulysses S. Grant, USA, assumes immediate command of the expedition against Vicksburg.

February
2–3   Passage of the Vicksburg and Warrenton batteries.
14–26   Expedition to Greenville, Mississippi, and Deer Creek.
16   Maj. Gen. Stephen A. Hurlbut, USA, assumes command of the Sixteenth Army Corps. Skirmish at Yazoo Pass, Mississippi.

Narrative of Maj. Gen. Ulysses S. Grant, USA (*continued*)

Sherman's attack [at Chickasaw Bluff] was very unfortunate, but I had no opportunity of communicating with him after the destruction of the road and telegraph to my rear on the 20th. He did not know but what I was in the rear of the enemy and depending on him to open a new base of supplies for the troops with me. I had, before he started from Memphis, directed him to take with him a few small steamers suitable for the navigation of the Yazoo, not knowing but that I might want them to supply me after cutting loose from my base at Grenada.

On the 23d I removed my headquarters back to Holly Springs . . . [and] on the 10th of January, the work on the [rail]road from Holly Springs to Grand Junction and thence to Memphis being completed, I moved my headquarters to the latter place. . . .

When Sherman started on his expedition down the river he had 20,000 men, taken from Memphis, and was reinforced by 12,000 more at Helena, Arkansas. The troops on the west bank of the river had previously been assigned to my command. McClernand having received the orders for his assignment, reached the mouth of the Yazoo on the 2d of January, and immediately assumed command of all the troops with Sherman, being a part of his own corps, the 13th, and all of Sherman's, the 15th.

Sherman and Admiral Porter with the fleet had withdrawn from the Yazoo. After consultation they decided that neither the army nor navy could render service to the cause where they were, and learning that I had withdrawn from the interior of Mississippi, they determined to return to the Arkansas River and attack Arkansas Post, about fifty miles up that stream and garrisoned by about five or six thousand men. Sherman had learned of the existence of this force through a man who had been captured by the enemy . . . [and] had made his escape. McClernand approved this move reluctantly. . . . After three days' bombardment by the navy an assault was made by the troops and marines, resulting in the capture of the place, and in taking 5,000 prisoners and 17 guns.

I was at first disposed to disapprove of this move as an unnecessary side movement having no especial bearing upon the work before us; but when the result was understood I regarded it as very important. Five thousand Confederate troops left in the rear might have caused us much trouble and loss of property while navigating the Mississippi.

Immediately after the reduction of Arkansas Post and the capture of the garrison, McClernand returned with his entire force to Napoleon, at the mouth of the Arkansas River. From here I received messages from both Sherman and Admiral Porter, urging me to come and take command in person, and expressing their distrust of McClernand's ability and fitness for so important and intricate an expedition.

On the 17th I visited McClernand and his command at Napoleon. It was here made evident to me that both the army and navy were so distrustful of McClernand's fitness to command that . . . it would have been criminal to send troops under these circumstances into such danger. By this time I had received authority to relieve McClernand, or to assign any person else to the command of the river expedition, or to assume command in person. I felt great embarrassment about McClernand. He was the senior major-general after myself within the department. It would not do, with his rank and ambition, to assign a junior over him. Nothing was left, therefore, but to assume the command myself. I would have been glad to put Sherman in command, to give him an opportunity to accomplish what he had failed in ... December, ... but there seemed no other way out of the difficulty. ... Sherman's failure needs no apology. ...

On the 20th I ordered General McClernand with the entire command to Young's Point and Milliken's Bend, while I returned to Memphis to make all the necessary preparation for leaving the territory behind me secure. [Maj. Gen. S. A.] Hurlbut with the 16th corps was left in command. The Memphis and Charleston railroad was held, while the Mississippi Central was given up. Columbus was the only point between Cairo and Memphis, on the river, left with a garrison. All the troops and guns from the posts on the abandoned railroad and river were sent to the front.

On the 29th of January I arrived at Young's Point and assumed command the following day. ... The real work of the campaign and siege of Vicksburg now began. The problem was to secure a footing upon dry ground on the east side of the river from which the troops could operate against Vicksburg. The Mississippi River, from Cairo south, runs through a rich alluvial valley of many miles in width, bound on the east by land running from eighty up to two or more hundred feet above the river. On the west side the highest land, except in a few places, is but little above the highest water. Through this valley the river meanders in the most tortuous way, varying in direction to all points of the compass. At places it runs to the very foot of the bluffs. After leaving Memphis, there are no such highlands coming to the water's edge on the east shore until Vicksburg is reached.

The intervening land is cut up by bayous filled from the river in high water—many of them navigable for steamers. All of them would be, except for overhanging trees, narrowness and tortuous course, making it impossible to turn the bends with vessels of any considerable length. Marching across this country in the face of an enemy was impossible; navigating it proved equally impracticable. The strategical way according to the rule, therefore, would have been to go back to Memphis; establish that as a base of supplies; fortify it so that the storehouses could be held by a small garrison, and move from there along the line of railroad, repairing as we advanced, to the Yallabusha [sic], or to Jackson, Mississippi.

At this time the North had become very much discouraged. Many strong Union men believed that the war must prove a failure. The elections of 1862 had gone against the party which was

Milliken's Bend, Young's Point, and the area west of the Mississippi
River. (*Atlas to Accompany the Official Records of the Union and
Confederate Armies*)

for the prosecution of the war to save the Union if it took the last man and the last dollar. Voluntary enlistments had ceased throughout the greater part of the north, and the draft had been resorted to fill up our ranks.

It was my judgment at the time that to make a backward movement . . . from Vicksburg to Memphis would be interpreted . . . as a defeat, and that the draft would be resisted, desertions ensue and the power to capture and punish deserters lost. There was nothing left to be done but to *go forward to a decisive victory* [emphasis in the original]. This was in my mind from the moment I took command in person at Young's Point.

The winter of 1862–63 was a noted one for continuous high water in the Mississippi and for heavy rains along the lower river. To get dry land . . . to encamp the troops upon took many miles of river front. We had to occupy the levees and the ground immediately behind. This was so limited that one corps, the 17th, under General McPherson, was at Lake Providence, seventy miles above Vicksburg.

GRANT'S CANAL

For directions to this site, see Part II, Phase 1, Stop 2.

Narrative of Maj. Gen. Ulysses S. Grant, USA (continued)

It was in January the troops took their position opposite Vicksburg. The water was very high and the rains were incessant. There seemed no possibility of a land movement before the end of March or later, and it would not do to lie idle at this time. The effect would be demoralizing to the troops and injurious to their health. Friends in the North would have grown more and more discouraged, and enemies in the same section more and more insolent in their gibes and denunciation of the cause and those engaged in it. . . .

Vicksburg . . . is on the first high land coming to the river's edge below . . . Memphis. . . . The bluff, or high land, follows the left bank of the Yazoo for some distance and continues in a southerly direction to the Mississippi River, thence it runs along the Mississippi to Warrenton, six miles below. The Yazoo River leaves the high land a short distance below Haines' Bluff and empties into the Mississippi nine miles above Vicksburg. Vicksburg is built on this high land where the Mississippi washes the base of the hill.

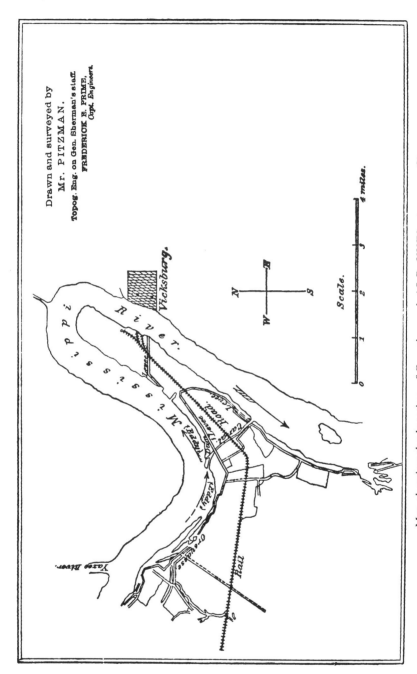

Map showing the location of Grant's canal. (*O.R.*, XXIV, pt. 1, p. 118)

Haines' Bluff, eleven miles from Vicksburg, on the Yazoo River, was strongly fortified. The whole distance from there to Vicksburg and thence to Warrenton was also intrenched, with batteries at suitable distances and rifle-pits connecting them.

From Young's Point the Mississippi turns in a north-easterly direction to a point just above the city, when it again turns and runs south-westerly, leaving vessels, which might attempt to run the blockade, exposed to the fire of batteries six miles below the city before they were in range of the upper batteries. *Since then the river has made a cut-off, leaving what was the peninsula in front of the city, an island* [emphasis added]. North of the Yazoo was all a marsh, heavily timbered, cut up with bayous, and much overflowed. A front attack was therefore impossible, and was never contemplated; certainly not by me.

The problem then became, how to secure a landing on high ground east of the Mississippi without an apparent retreat. Then commenced a series of experiments to consume time, and to divert the attention of the enemy, of my troops and of the public generally. I, myself, never felt great confidence that any of the experiments resorted to would prove successful. Nevertheless I was always prepared to take advantage of them in case they did.

In 1862 General Thomas Williams had come up from New Orleans and cut a ditch ten or twelve feet wide and about as deep, straight across from Young's Point to the river below. The distance across was a little over a mile. It was Williams' expectation that when the river rose it would cut a navigable channel through; but the canal started in an eddy from both ends, and, of course, it only filled up with water on the rise without doing any execution in the way of cutting. Mr. Lincoln had navigated the Mississippi in his younger days and understood well its tendency to change its channel, in places, from time to time. He set much store accordingly by this canal. General McClernand had been, therefore, directed before I went to Young's Point to push the work of widening and deepening this canal. After my arrival the work was diligently pushed with about 4,000 men—as many as could be used to advantage—until interrupted by a sudden rise in the river that broke a dam at the upper end, which had been put there to keep the water out until the excavation was completed. This was on the 8th of March.

Even if the canal had proven a success, so far as to be navigable for steamer, it could not have been of much advantage to us. It runs in a direction almost perpendicular to the line of bluffs on the opposite side . . . of the river. As soon as the enemy discovered what we were doing he established a battery commanding the canal throughout its length. This battery soon drove out our dredges, two in number, which were doing the work of thousands of men. Had the canal been completed it might have proven of some use in running transports through, under the cover of night, to use below, but they would yet have to run batteries, though for a much shorter distance.

While this work was progressing we were busy in other directions, trying to find an available landing on high ground on the east bank of the river, or to make water-ways to get below the city, avoiding the batteries.

On the 30th of January, the day after my arrival at the front, I ordered General McPherson, stationed with his corps at Lake Providence, to cut the levee at that point. If successful in opening a channel for navigation by this route, it would carry us to the Mississippi River through the mouth of the Red River, just above Port Hudson and four hundred miles below Vicksburg by the river.

Lake Providence is a part of the old bed of the Mississippi. . . . It is six miles long and has its outlet through Bayou Baxter, Bayou Macon, and the Tensas, Washita and Red Rivers. The last three are navigable streams at all seasons. Bayous Baxter and Macon are narrow and tortuous, and the banks are covered with dense forests overhanging the channel. They were also filled with fallen timber, the accumulation of years. The land along the Mississippi River, from Memphis down, is in all instances highest next to the river, except where the river washes the bluff, which form the boundary of the valley through which it winds. Bayou Baxter, as it reaches lower land, begins to spread out and disappears entirely in a cypress swamp before it reaches the Macon. There was about two feet of water in this swamp at the time. To get through it, even with vessels of the lightest draft, it was necessary to clear off a belt of heavy timber wide enough to make a passage way. As the trees would have to be cut close to the bottom—under water—it was an undertaking of great magnitude.

On the 4th of February I visited General McPherson. . . . The work had not progressed so far as to admit the water from the river into the lake, but the troops had succeeded in drawing a small steamer, of probably not over thirty tons' capacity, from the river into the lake. With this we were able to explore the lake and bayou as far as cleared. I saw then that there was scarcely a chance of this ever becoming a practicable route for moving troops through an enemy's country. The distance from Lake Providence to the point where vessels going by that route would enter the Mississippi again, is about four hundred and seventy miles by the main river. The distance would probably be greater by the tortuous bayous through which this new route would carry us. The enemy held Port Hudson, below where the Red River debouches, and all the Mississippi above to Vicksburg. The Red River, Washita and Tensas were . . . all navigable streams, on which the enemy could throw small bodies of men to obstruct our passage and pick off our troops with their sharpshooters. I let the work go on believing employment was better than idleness for the men.

Then, too, it served as a cover for other efforts which gave a better prospect of success. This work was abandoned after the canal proved a failure.[1]

NOTES

1. Ulysses S. Grant, *Personal Memoirs*, 2 vols. (New York: Charles L. Webster, 1885), 1:438–49.

5. OPERATIONS ALONG YAZOO PASS AND FORT PEMBERTON

Summary of Principal Events:
February 10–April 8, 1863

February

10–14	Operations on the Red, Atchafalaya, and Black Rivers, Louisiana.
13	Passage of the Vicksburg batteries by the *Indianola.*
19	Skirmish near Coldwater River, Mississippi.
	Skirmish near Yazoo Pass, Mississippi.
24	Capture of the *Indianola.*
24–April 8	Yazoo Pass Expedition (by Moon Lake, Yazoo Pass, and the Coldwater and Tallahatchee Rivers), including engagements (March 11, 13, and 16, April 2 and 4) at Fort Pemberton, near Greenwood, Mississippi.

March

| 14–27 | Steele's Bayou Expedition (to Rolling Fork, Mississippi, by Muddy, Steele's, and Black Bayou and Deer Creek), with skirmishes on Deer Creek (21st and 22d) and on Black Bayou (24th and 25th). |

Narrative of Maj. Gen. Ulysses S. Grant, USA (continued)

Lieutenant-Colonel Wilson of my staff was sent to Helena, Arkansas, to examine and open a way through Moon Lake and the Yazoo Pass if possible. Formerly there was a route by way of an inlet from the Mississippi River into Moon Lake, a mile east of the river, thence east through Yazoo Pass to Coldwater, along the latter to the Tallahatchie, which joins the Yallabusha [*sic*] about two hundred and fifty miles below Moon lake and forms the Yazoo River. These were formerly navigated by steamers trading with the rich plantations along their banks, but the State of Mississippi had built a strong levee across the inlet some years before, leaving the only entrance for vessels into this rich region the one by way of the mouth of the Yazoo several hundreds of miles below.

On the 2d of February this dam, or levee, was cut. The river being high the rush of water through the cut was so great that in a very short time the entire obstruction was washed away. The bayous were soon filled and much of the country was overflowed.

This pass leaves the Mississippi River but a few miles below Helena. On the 24th General [L. F.] Ross, with his brigade of about 4,500 men on transports, moved into this new water-way. The rebels had obstructed the navigation of Yazoo Pass and the Coldwater by felling trees into them. Much of the timber in this region being of greater specific gravity than water, and being of great size, their removal was a matter of great labor; but it was finally accomplished and on the 11th of March Ross found himself, accompanied by two gunboats . . . confronting a fortification at Greenwood, where the Tallahatchie and Yalabusha unite and the Yazoo begins. The bends of the rivers are such at this point as to almost form an island, scarcely above water at that stage of the river. The island was fortified and manned. It was named Fort Pemberton.[1]

For directions to Fort Pemberton, see Part II, Phase 2, Optional Sites.

FORT PEMBERTON

Porter to Lt. Comdr. Watson Smith, Commanding First Division Light-Draft Vessels, Mississippi Squadron, February 6, 1863

You will proceed with the *Rattler* and *Romeo* to Delta, near Helena, where you will find the *Forest Rose* engaged in trying to enter the Yazoo Pass. You will order the *Signal*, now at White River, to accompany you; and if the *Cricket* comes down while you are at Delta, detain her also or the *Linden*. . . . You will obtain coal enough from Helena to enable you to carry on operations for some time. Your vessels had better all go to Helena and coal and start from there with as much coal in two . . . barges as will answer.

The USS *Cairo*. (U.S. Army Military History Institute)

Do not enter the Yazoo Cut until the current is quite slack; and some small transport will have to go ahead, and the soldiers will cut away the trees and branches, so as not to endanger the smokestacks of the steamers.

Proceed carefully, and only in the daytime; 600 or 800 soldiers will be detached to accompany you, and you will take 100 on board of each light-draft. See that the army sends a very small steamer, with stores from Helena.

Get all the pilots you can who are acquainted with the different branches of the rivers. You may find them at Helena.

You will keep perfect order among the troops while on board your vessels or under your orders. Subject them to strict military rules, and see that every order . . . is promptly obeyed.

When you get to the Tallahatchie, proceed with all dispatch to ascend it as far as the railroad crossing, and completely destroy the railroad bridge at that point, after which you will, if possible, cut the telegraph wires and proceed down the river to the mouth of the Yalabusha.

You will fill up with coal and leave the coal barges at that place . . . and dash on to Grenada; destroy completely the railroad bridge, and retire at once down the river without any further damage, excepting to destroy means of transportation . . . and . . . all small boats.

When you get to the Yalabusha, you will proceed with all your force down the Yazoo River and endeavor to get into Sunflower River, where, it is said, all the large steamers are stowed away. These you will not have time to capture; therefore you will destroy them, keeping an account . . . of the value of the property that falls into your hands.

Obtain all the information you can in relation to ironclads, and destroy them if you can while they are on the stocks.

If this duty is performed . . . we will strike a terrible blow at the enemy, who do not anticipate an attack from such a quarter. But you must guard against surprise, and if overwhelmed run your vessels on the bank and set fire to them.

Be careful of your coal, and lay in wood where you can find it. By going along only in the daytime, under low steam, you can cruise some time. But after doing the damage . . . mentioned in my orders, ascend the river again to the Yazoo Cut-off, and report to me by a dispatch boat. . . . Do not engage batteries with the light vessels. The *Chillicothe* will do the fighting.[2]

Report of Brig. Gen. Leonard F. Ross, USA, Commanding Division, Thirteenth Army Corps

I embarked my command on steamers *Volunteer, Lebannon* No. 2, *Cheeseman, Diana, L. Logan, Saint Louis, Mariner, Moderator, Ida May, Emma, Citizen,* and *John Bell,* and made every preparation required "to be used with the Yazoo Expedition," proceeded at once to Yazoo pass, and joined the fleet of gunboats lying at Moon Lake. I entered the Pass on the 25th of February; was detained by high winds and the difficulty in moving coal-barges, but succeeded in entering the Coldwater on the evening of March 1, having been five days in going the distance of 16 miles.

The steamer *Emma,* being reported totally disabled, was ordered back to Helena, and the *Key West* taken in her stead. We arrived in the Tallahatchee on the evening of the 6th of March. Here we determined on leaving the coal-barges behind, and pushing forward with all possible dispatch. As we moved . . . through a well-cultivated country, cotton fires were seen on all sides.

On the evening of the 10th, we came upon the wreck of the steamer *Parallel* and barge, loaded with cotton, and in flames. The enemy being unable to get them away, had set them on fire. The boats were reported to contain over 3,000 bales, and I think we saw over that number on fire at the different plantations passed by us.

On the morning of the 11th, arrived in front of Fort Greenwood [Fort Pemberton], a strong fortification about 3 miles from the village of Greenwood. . . . I sent Colonel Slack, of the Forty-seventh, and Colonel Bringhurst, of the Forty-sixth Indiana . . . out on a reconnaissance by land. We soon met the outposts of the enemy, when a brisk skirmish followed, in which 2 of our men were wounded. . . . We drove them back into their fortifications, which . . . are very difficult of access, being entirely surrounded by water. . . .

On the 12th, a reconnaissance was made by a small party. . . . The *Chillicothe* was making some repairs, and two 30-pounder Parrot guns and one 68-pounder howitzer were placed in battery.

On the 13th, our land battery fired a few rounds; the gunboats were not yet ready to renew the attack. . . .

On the 16th, it was arranged to make another effort to take the fort. The gunboats were to engage at close quarters, and the land battery to open at the same time, and, if successful in silencing the batteries of the enemy, the infantry were to move down in light-draught gunboats and assault the fort. The . . . *Chillicothe* was disabled within fifteen minutes after she became engaged, and withdrew; the *De Kalb* followed, and the movement was a failure. The *Chillicothe* was so severely damaged, and the supply of ammunition was so short, that it was considered unsafe to renew the attack.

We remained in front of the fort until the morning of the 20th, occupying the time constantly reconnoitering the country thoroughly by strong parties . . . but every attempt to find any feasible point of attack for infantry failed. The rebels' works were so surrounded by swamps, bayous, and overflowed country as to be inaccessible for land forces. The iron-clads were nearly out of ammunition, and the *Chillicothe* so damaged as to be disabled. We had heard nothing from re-enforcements that were expected; our dispatch boats had been so long delayed as to excite our apprehensions for their safety, and we had information of rebel movements to establish a blockade at the mouth of the Coldwater by sending infantry and artillery by railroad to Panola, and thence down the Tallahatchee. Under these circumstances . . . it was thought advisable to fall back.[3]

Lt. Col. James H. Wilson to Grant, April 9, 1863

On the 23d day of February, 1863, the Yazoo Pass was opened for navigation. On the 24th, the expedition left Moon Lake, and on the 10th . . . of March arrived . . . near Fort Pemberton. The distance traversed was about 225 miles. The difficulties of navigation . . . were great, and some of the transports were old and unseaworthy, yet all of these things are insufficient to account for all of the delay. . . . To the timidity, over cautiousness, and lack of interest displayed by Lieut. Commander Watson Smith, commanding the gunboats, and the delays growing out of them, is attributable to the failure of the entire expedition. [He] was frequently urged by General Ross, myself, and Captains Walker and Foster, of the Navy, to move with more rapidity, or, at least, allow the iron-clads and rams to proceed with all practicable dispatch to the mouth of the Tallahatchee. . . . Had these suggestions been followed, the entire expedition could have reached Fort Pemberton from three to five days sooner . . . and the ironclads . . . could have arrived there by the 2d of March. . . .

In the attack upon Fort Pemberton Lieutenant Commander Smith again failed to exhibit the decision and intelligence necessary under such circumstances. . . . After the *Chillicothe* and *De Kalb* had silenced the fort, he failed to push the latter close enough to it to ascertain the cause of its not replying to her fire. . . . It was ascertained a few days afterward . . . that had the *De Kalb* been advanced she would have met with no further resistance, because the rebel ammunition was exhausted.[4]

DEFENSE OF FORT PEMBERTON

Report of Maj. Gen. William W. Loring, CSA

I left Jackson, Miss., on the morning of February 17 . . . with the view to finding some suitable place on the Yazoo or Tallahatchee whereat to erect works and place obstructions to the passage down of the enemy. An examination of the two rivers from Yazoo City to 100 miles above here satisfied me that this position was the only one offering the slightest advantage for defensive works, and having previously ordered Major *Meriwether,* of the engineers, to this place, determined to avail myself of its strong points. Accordingly, a line of works composed of cotton bales and earth was thrown up, extending from the Yazoo to the Tallahatchee, and a raft constructed by the able and united labors of Maj. Thomas *Weldon* and Mr. John *McFarland,* and with great skill placed in the Tallahatchee on our right. These necessary arrangements were prosecuted with the utmost diligence day and night; and notwithstanding every exertion to perfect our defenses, the enemy made his descent of the river and found us but poorly prepared to receive him.

On March 11, the enemy made his appearance before us with nine gunboats and twenty-four transports, a land force of 7,000 infantry and artillery. The raft in an unfinished state was hastily swung across the Tallahatchee, and the Confederate States steamer *Star of the West* sunk behind it. My inspector-general, Capt. John D. *Myrick,* was placed in command of the batteries, and we awaited the assault.

At 10 A.M. the formidable iron-clad *Chillicothe* steamed around the bend of the river in our front, as though it was intended to rush upon the raft and destroy it. A well-directed shell from our 32-pounder fell upon her turret, and she sensibly diminished her

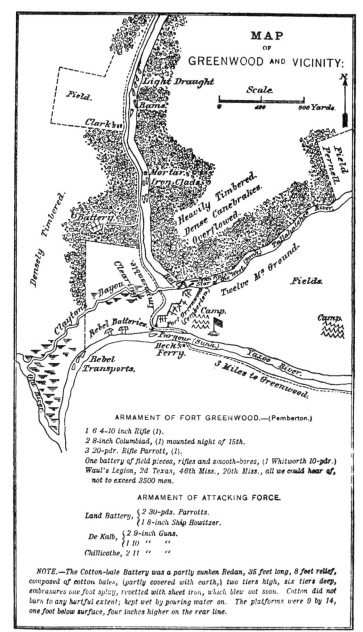

ARMAMENT OF FORT GREENWOOD.—(Pemberton.)

1 6 4-10 inch Rifle (1).
2 8-inch Columbiad, (1) mounted night of 15th.
3 20-pdr. Rifle Parrott, (1).
One battery of field pieces, rifles and smooth-bores, (1 Whitworth 10-pdr.)
Waul's Legion, 2d Texas, 46th Miss., 20th Miss., all we could hear of,
    not to exceed 3500 men.

ARMAMENT OF ATTACKING FORCE.

Land Battery, { 2 30-pds. Parrotts.
              { 1 8-inch Ship Howitzer.

De Kalb, { 2 9-inch Guns.
         { 1 10 " "

Chillicothe, 2 11 " "

NOTE.—The Cotton-bale Battery was a partly sunken Redan, 35 feet long, 8 feet relief,
composed of cotton bales, (partly covered with earth,) two tiers high, six tiers deep,
embrasures one foot splay, revetted with sheet iron, which blew out soon. Cotton did not
burn to any hurtful extent; kept wet by pouring water on. The platforms were 9 by 14,
one foot below surface, four inches higher on the rear line.

Sketch map of Fort Pemberton. (*O.R.*, XXIV, pt. 1, p. 389)

speed. This was followed by a solid shot from an 18-pounder rifle, which also struck, and the *Chillicothe* backed up stream until her hull was hidden around the bend, save her bow and that portion of her which contained the 11-inch guns. She then opened fire, and cannonading was kept up for an hour, when the gunboat withdrew, having been struck several times by three of our guns.

At 4 o'clock in the afternoon the fight was resumed by another gunboat, which we supposed to be the iron-clad *De Kalb*. After two hours hard fighting, the boat withdrew. During the day, Colonel [T. N.] *Waul*, commanding the post, sent out a detachment of his Legion as skirmishers, who engaged a large body of the enemy's infantry and cavalry and drove them back to their transports.

Thursday, the 12th, the enemy was engaged in erecting a battery upon a point in front, thickly wooded, which we could not prevent in consequence of the scarcity of ammunition.

On Friday morning, at 10 o'clock, the enemy again opened upon our works from two gunboats abreast, their land batteries, and a 13-inch mortar. We promptly responded with every gun we had in position, and the fight raged furiously the entire day, night putting an end to it.

It was in this day's engagement that an 11-inch shell from the *Chillicothe* passed through the parapet, displaced a cotton bale, and ignited a tub of cartridges in the magazine of the Whitworth gun. The fire was communicated by the fuse. Fortunately the shell itself did not explode. . . . In this day's engagement we experienced our only loss. A shell exploded over one of our guns, wounding three of the gunners, one of whom died in a few hours. Our troops labored the entire night in repairing damages to the parapet and strengthening the works.

Monday, as we afterward discovered, was fixed by the enemy for a grand assault with their entire force upon our works. Accordingly, the gunboat *Chillicothe* (the other iron-clad having been disabled in Friday's engagement) got into position, bow on, at 1,200 yards range, and with their land batteries and sharpshooters the day's work began. In about twenty minutes after the engagement commenced, a shot from one of our heavy guns penetrated the *Chillicothe* and so badly injured her that the proposed assault was abandoned and she withdrew, leaving the land batteries and sharpshooters to keep up the fight until sunset. . . . Total of casualties: 21.

A significant silence characterized their movements the three following days, although we could see them plainly at their batteries. On Friday, before day, they abandoned their breastworks and commenced a rapid retreat up the river.

Thus was conducted the battle of the Tallahatchee.... This expedition was the prominent one of a great plan for the attack of Vicksburg in rear. It was to move rapidly down the Yazoo River to the mouth of the Sunflower; there await another expedition down that river; the two united were to meet a third up the Yazoo; the three to force the raft at Snyder's Bluff; united, to turn Vicksburg. After many months of secret preparations, they were certain of success. With but little time to fortify, they were determinedly met and forced to an ignominious retreat, leaving behind them evidences that their loss was great in men and material— a check which will undoubtedly prevent a further invasion of the State of Mississippi by the way of Tallahatchee and Yazoo Rivers.[5]

Narrative of Maj. Gen. Ulysses S. Grant, USA (continued)

Fort Pemberton was so little above the water that it was thought that a rise of two feet would drive the enemy out. In hope of enlisting the elements on our side, which had been so much against us up to this time, a second cut was made in the Mississippi levee, this time directly opposite Helena, or six miles above the former cut. It did not accomplish the desired result, and Ross, with his fleet, started back. On the 22nd he met Quinby with a brigade at Yazoo Pass. Quinby was the senior of Ross, and assumed command. He was not satisfied with returning to his former position without seeing for himself whether anything could be accomplished. Accordingly Fort Pemberton was revisited by our troops; but an inspection was sufficient this time without an attack. Quinby, with his command, returned with but little delay.

In the meantime I was much exercised for the safety of Ross, not knowing that Quinby had been able to join him. Reinforcements were of no use in a country covered with water, as they would have to remain on board of their transports. Relief had to come from another quarter. So I determined to get into the Yazoo below Fort Pemberton.

DEER CREEK

For directions to this site, see Part II, Phase 2, Optional Sites.

Narrative of Maj. Gen. Ulysses S. Grant, USA (continued)

Steele's Bayou empties into the Yazoo River between Haines' Bluff and its mouth. It is narrow, very tortuous, and fringed with a very heavy growth of timber, but it is deep. It approaches to within one mile of the Mississippi at Eagle Bend, thirty miles above Young's Point. Steele's Bayou connects with Black Bayou, Black Bayou with Deer Creek, Deer Creek with Rolling Fork, Rolling Fork with the Big Sunflower River, and the Big Sunflower with the Yazoo River about ten miles above Haines' Bluff in a right line but probably twenty or twenty-five miles by the winding of the river. All of these waterways are of about the same nature so far as navigation is concerned, until the Sunflower is reached; this affords free navigation.

Admiral Porter explored this waterway as far as Deer Creek on the 14th of March, and reported it navigable. On the next day he started with five gunboats and four mortar-boats. I went with him for some distance. The heavy, overhanging timber retarded progress very much, as did also the short turns in so narrow a stream. The gunboats, however, ploughed their way through without other damage than to their appearance. The transports did not fare so well although they followed behind. The road was somewhat cleared for them by the gunboats.

In the evening I returned to headquarters to hurry up reinforcements.[6]

Report of Acting Rear Adm. David D. Porter, USN, March 26, 1863

Since my last communication with the Department I have been absent on an expedition into the enemy's country, or that part which he professes to hold.

I have for some time past been under the impression that by cutting our way through the woods (which are all under water) that I could find an entrance into the Yazoo River, and thus get into the rear of Vicksburg without loss of life or vessels.

In consequence of this idea, and from information obtained from a negro, I made a reconnoissance with Lieutenant Commanding Murphy.

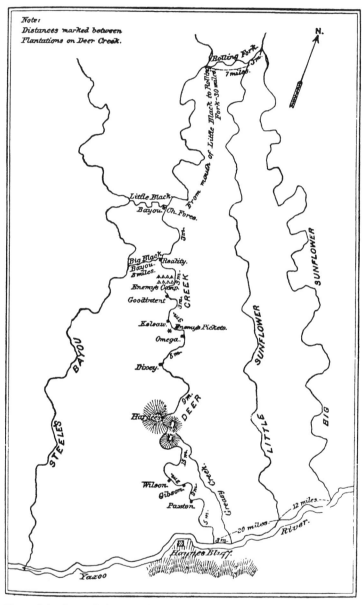

Map of the intended route through Deer Creek. Porter's boats are stopped just as they are about to enter the Rolling Fork. (*O.R.,* XXIV, pt. 1, p. 463)

We started up Steele's Bayou, which at low stages of water is nothing but a ditch, following it for about 30 miles. This part of the route was perfectly practicable; the creek though very narrow, having 5 fathoms of water in it. Black Bayou seemed to oppose our further progress, but on a closer examination we found that by removing the trees we could heave the vessels around the bends, which were very short and left us not a foot to spare.

All we could hear of the route in advance was very favorable. Having obtained as pilot a man well acquainted with the country, I determined to start immediately, having made arrangements with General Grant by which the army could cooperate with us.

On the 14th [of March] I started with the *Louisville,* Lieutenant Commanding Owen; *Cincinnati,* Lieutenant Commanding Bache; *Carondelet,* Lieutenant Commanding Murphy; *Mound City,* Lieutenant Commanding Wilson; *Pittsburg,* Lieutenant Commanding Hoel; 4 mortars and 4 tugs.

The expedition went along finely until it reached Black Bayou, a place about 4 miles long leading into Deer Creek. Here the crews of the vessels had to go to work to clear the way, pulling up trees by the roots or pushing them over with the ironclads, and cutting away the branches above. It was terrible work, but in twenty-four hours we succeeded in getting through these 4 miles and found ourselves in Deer Creek, where we were told there would be no more difficulties.

General Sherman had arrived with a small portion of his command, and as he had only 12 miles to march to Rolling Fork (where we would meet with no further difficulties), while I had to go 21 miles by water, I determined to push on. I found the channel much narrower than I expected, filled with small willows, through which we could scarce make our way, and the branches much overhanging. Still we made at first about a mile an hour, being assured by the pilot that we would find it better as we advanced—it certainly could not get worse.

We had succeeded in getting well into the heart of the country before we were discovered. No one would believe that anything in the shape of a vessel could get through Black Bayou, or anywhere on the route. Still, however, as we molested no one, the inhabitants looked on in wonder and astonishment, and the negroes flocked in hundreds down to the banks of the creek to see the novel sight. Soon we were discovered by the Government agent, who immediately began to apply the torch to the cotton—public and private. All along, as far as the eye could see, there was nothing but cotton fires burning up, and many dwellings consuming with it. The only persons who saved their cotton were those who would not obey the order to burn. They felt confident [that] we were not going to molest private property, and their confidence saved them their cotton, which is still in their possession.

It was melancholy to see such fanatical destruction; but as we abstained from anything of the kind ourselves it placed the two parties in strong contrast before the people of the country, and there were many remarks made not at all complimentary to the Confederate Government.

Finding that our presence was discovered, I pushed on the vessels as fast as the obstacles would permit, not making more than half a mile an hour. We were passing through a beautiful country filled with livestock of all kinds, and containing large granaries of corn belonging to the Confederate Government. The people were more than surprised at the presence of such an expedition, having supposed themselves far removed from the horrors of war, and there was a good deal of change of opinion on the part of some who never supposed they would be under the protection of the American flag once more.

After very great labor we arrived within 7 miles of the Rolling Fork, where everything would be plain sailing before us. We were here informed that some Confederate agents and some of the citizens were forcing the negroes to cut down trees in our path. I immediately pushed on the tug *Thistle,* which had a boat howitzer on her, and she succeeded in reaching the first tree before it was cut down. She proceeded on under charge of Lieutenant Commanding Murphy, while I followed on the *Carondelet,* the leading ship. The enemy succeeded at last in getting a large tree down, which stopped the progress of the tug, and then the negroes, with muskets at their breasts, were made to ply their axes until the creek was supposed to be sealed against our further advance.

The labor of clearing out these obstructions was very great, but there is nothing that can not be overcome by perseverance. The character of the American sailors for endurance was particularly manifested on this occasion, as they worked night and day, without eating or sleeping, until the labor was accomplished.

I hoped by this time to have seen something of our Army coming on, but they had their difficulties to contend with as well as ourselves, and did not reach us in time. The transportation could not be procured at a moment's notice, and we had gone on faster than they expected.

When within 3 miles of Rolling Fork we discovered smoke in the direction of Yazoo River, and I was informed that the enemy were already landing troops to dispute our passage. I did not mind the troops so much as the timber they would cut in Rolling Fork.

I immediately sent on Lieutenant Commanding Murphy with two boat howitzers and 300 men to hold Rolling Fork until we could cover it with our guns, which he did, occupying also an Indian mound some 60 feet high, which commanded the whole country.

After working all night and clearing out the obstructions, which were terrible, we succeeded in getting within 800 yards of the end of this troublesome creek. We had only two or three large trees to remove, and one apparently short and easy lane of willows to work through. The men being much worn-out, we rested at sunset.

In the morning we commenced with renewed vigor to work ahead through the willows, but our progress was very slow. The lithe trees defied our utmost efforts to get by them, and we had to go to work and pull them up separately, or cut them off under water, which was a most tedious job. In the meantime the enemy had collected and landed about 800 men and 7 pieces of artillery (from 20 to 30 pounders), which were firing on our fieldpieces from time to time, the latter not having range enough to reach them.

I was also informed that the enemy were cutting down trees in our rear to prevent communication by water, and also prevent our escape. This looked unpleasant. I knew that 5,000 men had embarked at Haynes' Bluff for this place immediately they heard that we were attempting to go through that way, and as our troops had not come up I considered it unwise to risk the least thing; at all events, never to let my communication be closed behind me. I was somewhat strengthened in my determination to advance no farther until reinforced by land forces when the enemy at sunset opened on us a cross fire with six or seven rifled guns, planted somewhere off in the woods where we could see nothing but the smoke. It did not take long to dislodge them, though a large part of the crew being on shore at the time, we could not fire over them . . . until they got on board.

I saw at once the difficulties we had to encounter, with a constant fire on our working parties and no prospect at present of the troops getting along. I had received a letter from General Sherman, informing me of the difficulties in getting forward his men, he doing his utmost, I knew, to expedite matters.

The news of the falling trees in our rear was brought infrequently by negroes who were pressed into the service for cutting them, and I hesitated no longer what to do. We dropped down again, unshipped our rudders, and let the vessels rebound from tree to tree.

As we left the enemy took possession of the Indian mound, and in the morning opened fire on the *Carondelet,* Lieutenant Murphy, and *Cincinnati,* Lieutenant Bache. These two ships soon silenced the batteries, and we were no longer annoyed.

The sharpshooters hung about us, firing from behind trees and rifle pits, but with due precaution we had very few hurt; only 5 wounded by rifle balls, and they were hurt by being imprudent.

On the 21st we fell in with Colonel Smith, commanding Eighth Missouri and other parts of regiments. We were quite pleased to see him, as I never knew before how much the comfort and safety of ironclads, situated as we were, depended on the soldiers. I had already sent out behind a force of 300 men to stop the felling of trees in our rear, which Colonel Smith now took charge of. The enemy had already felled over forty heavy trees, which Lieutenant Commander Owen, in the *Louisville,* working night and day, cleared away almost fast enough to permit us to meet with no delay.

Colonel Smith's force was not enough to justify my making another effort to get through. He had no artillery and would frequently have to leave the vessels in following the road.

On the 22d we came to a bend in the river where the enemy supposed they had blockaded us completely, having cut a number of trees all together and so intertwined that it seemed impossible to move them. The *Louisville* was at work at them pulling them up, when we discovered about 3,000 rebels attempting to pass the edge of the woods to our rear, while the negroes reported artillery coming up on our quarter.

We were all ready for them, and when the artillery opened on us we opened such a fire on them that they scarcely waited to hitch up their horses. At the same time the rebel soldiers fell in with Colonel Smith's troops, and after a short skirmish fled before the fire of our soldiers. After this we were troubled no more, and dropped down quietly until we fell in with General Sherman, who, hearing the firing, was hurrying up to our support.

I do not know when I felt more pleased to see that gallant officer, for without the assistance of the troops we could not, without great loss, have performed the arduous work of clearing out the obstructions. We might now have retraced our steps, but we were all worn-out. The officers and men had for six days and nights been constantly at work, or sleeping at the guns. We had lost our coal barge, and the provision vessel could not get through, being too high for such purposes. Taking everything into consideration, I thought it best to undertake nothing further without being better prepared, and we finally, on the 24th, arrived at Hill's plantation, the place we started from on the 16th.

Altogether this has been a most novel expedition. Never did those people expect to see ironclads floating where the keel of a flat boat never passed. . . . We destroyed a large amount of Confederate corn and captured a large number of mules, horses, and cattle. The rebels themselves burnt over 20,000 bales of cotton, and we burned all that we found marked "C.S.A.", having taken on our decks and on the mortar boats enough to pay for the building of a good gunboat.

The soldiers enjoyed the excursion amazingly, the fine country through which we traveled being quite different from the swamp where they have spent the winter. Had we succeeded entirely it would have been a severe blow to this part of the country, but it was not to be, and we must console ourselves and the moral effect of penetrating into a country deemed inaccessible. There will be no more planting in these regions for a long time to come. The able-bodied negroes left with our army, carrying with them all the stores laid up by their masters—for whom they showed little affection—for harder times.

I regret to say that we lost one officer . . . who was struck by a rifle shot and died of his wounds. Only two were severely wounded. The boats of some of the vessels were badly damaged—which was about the only serious injury—in crashing through the trees.

We performed a distance of 70 miles each way, making 140 miles of the most severe labor officers and men ever went through. We found our new mortar boats, though badly built, well adapted for this kind of business and very useful in clearing the woods of sharpshooters.

[*Additional and confidential*]

I look upon it as a great misfortune that this expedition did not get through, for it would have been a most perfect surprise; would have thrown into our hands every vessel in the Yazoo and every granary from which the rebels could draw a supply.

The great difficulty seems to have been for want of more promptness in moving the troops, or rather, I should say, want of means for the moving of troops; for there was never yet any two men who would labor harder than Generals Grant and Sherman to forward an expedition for the overthrow of Vicksburg.

At one time I felt most uncomfortable, finding the enemy increasing in strength in front of me, cutting down trees behind me, and, in front, a chance of blocking up the feeders of the canal and letting the water out and not a soldier of ours in sight or (by the answers I received to my communication) any prospect of any coming in time to prevent a landing of the enemy. I never knew how helpless a thing an iron clad could be when unsupported by troops. Our guns were 3 feet below the level, the woods stood just far enough back to enable the sharpshooters to pick off our men without our being able to bother them except with the mortars, which kept them off.

When the army did come up it was without provisions, and we had to subsist them, partly. They left their artillery at Hill's Landing to protect that place, and I felt uneasy about them whenever they would get away from the guns of the ironclad. Under the circumstances, I could not afford to risk a single vessel, and therefore abandoned the expedition. I knew the difficulties to be overcome ahead after we were once discovered. . . . The army officers worked like horses to enable them to accomplish what was desired, but they were behind time and that ended the matter. No other general could have done better or as well as Sherman, but he had not the means for this peculiar kind of transportation.

With the end of this expedition ends all my hopes of getting into Vicksburg in this direction. Had we been successful, we could have made a sure thing of it, provided the army had been pushed on in sufficient numbers. . . . All we can do here now is to harass the enemy by keeping his troops moving to and fro. They will never again be caught by surprise, for after this attempt they will guard every ditch leading into the Yazoo. . . .

There is but one thing now to be done, and that is to start an army of 150,000 men from Memphis, via Grenada, and let them go supplied with everything required to take Vicksburg. . . . Had General Grant not turned back when on the way to Grenada he would have been in Vicksburg before this.[7]

Narrative of Maj. Gen. William T. Sherman, USA (continued)

Admiral Porter was then working up Deer Creek with his iron-clads, but he had left me a tug, which enabled me to reconnoitre the country, which was all under water except the narrow strip along Deer Creek. During the 19th I heard the heavy navy-guns, booming more frequently than seemed consistent with mere guerrilla operations; and that night I got a message from Porter, written on tissue-paper, brought me through the swamp by a negro, who had it concealed in a piece of tobacco.

The admiral stated that he had met a force of infantry and artillery which gave him great trouble by killing the men who had to expose themselves outside the iron armor to shove off the bows of the boats, which had so little headway that they would not steer. He begged me to come to his rescue as quickly as possible.

[Col.] Giles A. Smith had only about eight hundred men with him, but I ordered him to start up Deer Creek at once, crossing to the east side by an old bridge at Hill's plantation, which we had repaired for the purpose; to work his way up to the gunboat-fleet, and to report to the admiral that I would come up with every man I could raise as soon as possible. I was almost alone at Hill's, but took a canoe, paddled down Black Bayou to the gunboat *Price,* and there, luckily, found the *Silver Wave* with a load of men just arrived from Gwin's plantation. Taking some of the parties who were at work along the bayou into an empty coal-barge, we tugged it up by a navy-tug, followed by the *Silver Wave,* crashing through the trees, carrying away pilot-houses, smoke-stacks, and every thing above-deck; but the captain . . . was a brave fellow, and realized the necessity. The night was absolutely black, and we could only make two and a half of the four miles. We then disembarked, and marched through the canebrake, carrying lighted candles in our hands, till we got into the open cotton-fields at Hill's plantation, where we lay down for a few hours' rest. These men were a part

of Giles A. Smith's brigade . . . the senior officer present being
Lieutenant-Colonel Rice, Fifty-fourth Ohio, an excellent young
officer. We had no horses.

On Sunday morning, March 21st, as soon as daylight appeared, we started, following the same route which Giles A. Smith
had taken the day before; the battalion of the Thirteenth United
States Regulars, Major Chase, in the lead. We could hear Porter's
guns, and knew that moments were precious. Being on foot myself, no man could complain, and we generally went at the double-
quick, with occasional rests. The road lay along Deer Creek,
passing several plantations; and occasionally, at the bends, it
crossed the swamp, where the water came above my hips. The
smaller drummer-boys had to carry their drums on their heads,
and most of the men slung their cartridge-boxes around their
necks. The soldiers generally were glad to have their general
and field officers afoot, but we gave them a fair specimen of
marching, accomplishing about twenty-one miles by noon. Of
course, our speed was accelerated by the sounds of the navy-guns,
which became more and more distinct, though we could see
nothing.

At a plantation near some Indian mounds we met a detachment of the Eighth Missouri, that had been up to the fleet, and
had been sent down as a picket to prevent any obstructions below.
This picket reported that Admiral Porter had found Deer Creek
badly obstructed, had turned back, that there was a rebel force
beyond the fleet, with some six-pounders, and nothing between
us and the fleet. So I sat down on the door-sill of the cabin to rest,
but had not been seated ten minutes when, in the wood just ahead,
not three hundred yards off, I heard quick and rapid firing of
musketry. Jumping up, I ran up the road, and found Lieutenant-
Colonel Rice, who said the head of his column had struck a small
force of rebels with a working gang of negroes, provided with axes,
who on the first fire had broken and run back into the swamp. I
ordered Rice to deploy his brigade, his left on the road, and extending as far into the swamp as the ground would permit, and
then to sweep forward until he uncovered the gunboats. The
movement was rapid and well executed, and we soon came to some
large cotton-fields and could see our gunboats in Deer Creek,
occasionally firing a heavy eight-inch gun across the cotton-field
into the swamp behind.

About that time Major Kirby, of the Eighth Missouri, galloped down the road on a horse he had picked up the night before. He explained the situation of affairs, and offered me his horse. I got on *bareback*, and rode up the levee, the sailors coming out of their iron-clads and cheering most vociferously as I rode by, and as our men swept forward across the cotton-field in full view.

I soon found Admiral Porter, who was on the deck of one of his iron-clads, with a shield made of the section of a smoke-stack, and I doubt if he was ever more glad to meet a friend than he was to see me. He explained that he had almost reached the Rolling Fork, when the woods became full of sharp-shooters, who, taking advantage of trees, stumps, and the levee, would shoot down every man that poked his nose outside the protection of their armor; so that he could not handle his clumsy boats in the narrow channel. The rebels had evidently dispatched a force from Haines's [*sic*] Bluff up the Sunflower to the Rolling Fork, had anticipated the movement of Admiral Porter's fleet, and had completely obstructed the channel of the upper part of Deer Creek by felling trees into it, so that further progress in that direction was simply impossible.

It also happened that, at the instant of my arrival, a party of about four hundred rebels, armed and supplied with axes, had passed around the fleet and had got below it, intending in like manner to block up the channel by the felling of trees, so as to cut off retreat. This was the force we had struck so opportunely at the time before described. I inquired of Admiral Porter what he proposed to do, and he said he wanted to get out of that scrape as quickly as possible. He was actually working back when I met him, and, as we then had a sufficient force to cover his movement completely, he continued to back down Deer Creek. . . . There being no longer any sharp-shooters to bother the sailors, they made good progress; still it took three full days for the fleet to back out of Deer Creek into Black Bayou, at Hill's plantation, whence Admiral Porter proceeded to his post at the mouth of the Yazoo, leaving Captain Owen in command of the fleet.

I reported the facts to General Grant, who was sadly disappointed at the failure of the fleet to get through to the Yazoo above Haines's Bluff, and ordered us all to resume our camps at Young's Point. We accordingly steamed down, and regained our camps on the 27th.[8]

CONFEDERATE OPPOSITION

Report of Maj. Gen. Carter L. Stevenson, CSA,
Commanding Second District, Department of Mississippi
and East Louisiana, Vicksburg, March 29, 1863

On the evening of the 20th [March] I received information
that the enemy were endeavoring to turn my right by an expedition, which, entering Steele's, passed into Black Bayou and Deer
Creek, and was at the time that the intelligence reached me within
20 miles of Rolling Fork, through which they expected to make
their way into the Sunflower River and thence into the Yazoo.

The expedition consisted of five iron-clad boats, three armed
stern-wheel boats, four transports, three tugs, and nine barges, all
heavily laden with troops. The importance attached to it by the
enemy may be estimated by the fact that the boats were commanded
by Acting Rear-Admiral Porter and the troops by General Sherman.

Some time before, I had sent off sharpshooters, under the
command of Major [H. W.] *Bridges,* with orders to report to Colonel *Ferguson,* and co-operate with him in protecting the country
drained by Deer Creek and the Sunflower from the raids of the
enemy. This command reported to him on the 16th instant.

As soon as possible after the receipt of the intelligence, I directed Major-General *Maury,* commanding the right wing, to send
Brigadier-General *Featherston*'s brigade to Rolling Fork, to check
their farther advance, and immediately afterward to dispatch a
force, under Brigadier-General [Stephen D.] *Lee,* with orders to
make their way up Deer Creek, fortify and obstruct it at the high
ground at Hardee's, and cut off, if possible, the retreat of the
enemy.

The attack made upon them by our forces in front was successful. They were repulsed in confusion, with a loss of some camp
and garrison equipage and several fine barges on the first day, and,
being closely followed up subsequently, were steadily driven back,
and, at last, completely foiled, relinquished their attempt, and,
returning, resumed their former position in front of the city on
the evening of the 27th. . . .

The damage done their boats was so great that it could easily
be discovered from the lookout station at this point.

I regret that not even the energy of General *Lee,* who gener-
ously volunteered for the occasion, could overcome the difficul-

ties in his way in time to intercept the retreat. Had it been possible, he would have done it.[9]

Report of Maj. Gen. Dabney H. Maury, CSA, Commanding Division

I have the honor to report that the expedition under General
Sherman and Admiral Porter, which endeavored to penetrate, by
way of Steele's Bayou, Black Bayou, Deer Creek, Rolling Fork, and
Sunflower River, into Yazoo River, has been defeated and driven
back. Colonel *Ferguson* now occupies Black Bayou, and has established communication with General *Lee* at Lower Deer Creek.

As soon as I was informed of this movement of the enemy, I
ordered General *Featherston* to proceed with a portion of his brigade to re-enforce Colonel *Ferguson,* and to assume command of
his force. I also gladly availed myself of General *Lee's* offer to conduct a force from Haynes' Bluff up Lower Deer Creek, and ordered
him to attack, if possible, the enemy on Black Bayou. These measures have resulted in the complete defeat of the enemy.

I cannot too highly commend Colonel *Ferguson's* energy and
daring. To his prompt soldiership we are indebted for the arrest
of the progress of the expedition until such re-enforcements came
to him as have enabled us to defeat it. He has been in the advance
all the time, continually pressing the enemy back. His only fear
has been lest the enemy should escape.[10]

Report of Brig. Gen. Winfield Scott Featherston, CSA

About 3 A.M., March 19, I was ordered to move my brigade to
Snyder's Bluff as rapidly as possible; to take two regiments from
that point and one section of artillery, and proceed up Sunflower
River and Rolling Fork to the junction of Rolling Fork and Deer
Creek, to which point the enemy was said to be directing his movements. The order was promptly obeyed, and on Friday (20th),
about 3 P.M., we arrived at the mouth of Rolling Fork, and disembarked the troops, who had to march through water three quarters of a mile before reaching land. Colonel *Ferguson* had preceded
me from near Greenville, Miss., with his command, consisting of
a battalion of infantry, six pieces of artillery, and a squadron of
cavalry some 40 or 50 in number. Colonel *Ferguson* had previously
engaged the enemy and driven back his advance guard from Dr.

Chaney's house, immediately in the fork of Rolling Fork and Deer Creek.

My artillery and infantry were moved rapidly from the boat landing, a distance of some 6 or 7 miles, to the head of Rolling Fork, and arrived there from 4:30 to 5 P.M. I immediately assumed command of all the forces, and placed them in position for an immediate attack. The battalion of infantry was placed on the right, extending up to Deer Creek. The Twenty-second and Twenty-third Mississippi Regiments were placed on the left in the nearest strip of woods to the enemy, and extending down Deer Creek below the enemy's line of boats; the artillery on the more elevated position in the center. The enemy's boats (five in number), commanded by Admiral Porter, were lying a few hundred yards below the junction of Rolling Fork and Deer Creek, surrounded by an open field from one-half to a mile wide, and near a large, elevated mound, upon which he had planted a land battery of not more than two guns.

The infantry were ordered to throw out companies of skirmishers in advance, with instructions to fire at every man who made his appearance on the boats. This disposition of the troops having been made, a brisk fire was opened by our artillery and continued until dark. This fire was responded to by the enemy's gunboats as well as their land battery until night. There was no hope of boarding the boats at this time by the infantry, as they were in the middle of the stream, and could not be reached without passing through water from 10 to 20 feet deep.

The troops remained in position during the night, with instructions that if the boats landed on the east side of Deer Creek to board whenever an opportunity offered. During the night their land battery moved from the Mound to the boats, and the boats commenced moving down stream.

Next morning the attack was renewed. Skirmishers were thrown forward to the nearest points of woods on both sides of the creek, and a constant fire kept up during the day. The artillery was not used on the second day, for the reason that the supply of ammunition was nearly exhausted by the firing on Friday. The country from the head of Rolling Fork down Deer Creek to Black Bayou is nearly a continuous chain of plantations, cleared on both sides, and but few points of woods running to the bank of the stream to serve as a covert and protection for sharpshooters. Owing to the high stage of water in Deer Creek, their guns could be sufficiently depressed on the boats to use grape and canister.

On Saturday evening, the Fortieth Alabama . . . arrived and was placed, with the Twenty-second and Thirty-third Mississippi Regiments, under the command of Col. D. W. *Hurst,* Thirty-third Mississippi Regiment, who had prior to that time had the immediate command of the Twenty-second and Thirty-third Mississippi Regiments, W. Colonel *Ferguson* retaining . . . the immediate command of his own force. The enemy continued to retire down the creek.

On Sunday morning the attack was continued at Moore's plantation, some 6 or 7 miles below the head of Rolling Fork. Two regiments were thrown below in advance of the boats (Twenty-second and Thirty-third Mississippi) in a point of woods running up to the creek, where it was thought they could be successfully assailed. The Fortieth Alabama and artillery [were] ordered to open a brisk fire on them until it had exhausted its supply of ammunition. This order was promptly obeyed, and the fire of our guns most cordially responded to by the guns of the enemy's boats. The two regiments thrown below were met by Sherman's division coming up, when a sharp skirmish ensued.

While this . . . was going on . . . two regiments of the enemy advanced from the boats immediately to the front, evidently with a view of cutting off the Twenty-second and Thirty-third Mississippi, then in advance. These two regiments were ordered back to a strong position then held by the Fortieth Alabama and artillery. This was done in good order through the skirt of woods on the enemy's left.

The enemy advancing some half a mile through the field, and finding our forces united, fell back to the boats. I am satisfied, from reliable information received from citizens as well as a captured dispatch from General Sherman to Admiral Porter, that the enemy's force could not now have consisted of less than eight or nine regiments.

On Monday [23d], our troops were not moved, for the reason that our artillery was out of ammunition and hourly expecting a supply by our boats, and the men were without rations, and had been scantily and irregularly supplied up to that time, owing to the fact that we arrived without rations and without transportation, and it required time to collect both.

On Tuesday morning the march was again resumed, but the artillery was carried but little distance until the roads were found impassable, and it was left.

On Wednesday [25th], the enemy was overtaken on Watson's farm, about 3 miles above Black Bayou. They were posted in a dense cane-brake and woods, from which they retired before our skirmishers, the boats having preceded them. The woods were occupied by our troops that night.

On Thursday morning our troops again advanced through Fore's plantation, when a skirmish ensued between their rear guard and our sharpshooters.

On Friday morning, when preparing to advance through the last skirt of woods on the east side of Deer Creek, before reaching Black Bayou, I learned from cavalry scouts sent in advance that the enemy's boats had gone down Black Bayou and his land forces retired.

On Monday evening, the Thirty-first Mississippi . . . arrived. . . . On Friday night, after the first engagement, the cavalry was sent several miles below to fell trees into the stream to prevent the escape of the boats, but were driven from their work at an early hour by a body of the enemy's infantry without having accomplished much. The cavalry that night did capture a negro, a bearer of a dispatch from General Sherman to Admiral Porter. . . .

The capture of the gunboats could only have been accomplished by the presence of a land force strong enough to have moved a part of it boldly to the rear of the boats, and taken a position where the succoring land force of the enemy might have been held firmly in check, while the remaining part might have felled trees and otherwise obstructed the stream in rear of the boats, annoying them with sharpshooters and compelled their surrender from absolute stress and calamity of situation after their ammunition, and perhaps provisions, should have been exhausted. The entire force under my command up to Monday did not exceed 1,300 men.

The visionary absurdity of the over-sanguine expectations of capturing gunboats entertained by some military men becomes apparent when it is considered that from 12 to 15 feet depth of water, with a width of from 6 to 10 feet, is always interposed between the assailants and the object assailed, and the boats wellnigh incapable of entrance when boarded, and each arranged with reference to the protection of the other. This entire expedition was full of hardships to the troops, who endured them with patience and fortitude, and were always cool and spirited in the presence of the enemy. . . .

Our loss in the slight combats . . . was small, not exceeding 2 killed and 6 or 8 wounded. . . . The success of the expedition consists in turning and driving back the enemy, who in a very short time would have been through Rolling Fork into Sunflower River, and had the uncontested control of the Yazoo Waters.[11]

NOTES

1. Ulysses S. Grant, *Personal Memoirs,* 2 vols. (New York: Charles L. Webster, 1885), 1:449–51.

2. U.S. Navy Department, *Official Records of the Union and Confederate Navies in the War of the Rebellion,* 31 vols., ed. Richard Bush et al. (Washington, D.C.: Government Printing Office, 1894–1927), 24:244; hereafter cited as *O.R.N.*

3. *O.R.,* XXIV, pt. 1, pp. 397–98.

4. *O.R.,* XXIV, pt. 1, pp. 386–90.

5. *O.R.,* XXIV, pt. 1, pp. 415–17.

6. Grant, *Memoirs,* 1:451–53.

7. *O.R.N.,* series I, vol. 24, pp. 474–78.

8. William T. Sherman, *Memoirs of General William T. Sherman, by Himself,* 2 vols. (New York: Appleton, 1875), 1:336–39.

9. *O.R.,* XXIV, pt. 1, p. 455.

10. *O.R.,* XXIV, pt. 1, p. 456.

11. *O.R.,* XXIV, pt. 1, pp. 458–61.

6. RUNNING THE BATTERIES

Summary of Principal Events:
March 19–May 1, 1863

March

19	Passage of the Grand Gulf batteries by the *Hartford* and *Monongahela*.
23	Attack on the Warrenton batteries by the *Hartford* and *Monongahela*.
25	Passage of the Vicksburg batteries by the *Switzerland* and destruction of the *Lancaster*.
31	Engagement at Grand Gulf, Mississippi.
31–April 30	Operations from Milliken's Bend to New Carthage, Louisiana.

April

2–14	Expedition to Greenville, Black Bayou, and Deer Creek, Mississippi, with skirmishes on April 7, 8, and 10.
16	Passage of the Vicksburg batteries by gunboats and transports.
17–May 2	Grierson's raid from La Grange, Tennessee, to Baton Rouge, Louisiana.
22	Passage of the Vicksburg and Warrenton batteries by transports.
29	Bombardment of Grand Gulf, Mississippi, and passage of the batteries.
29–May 1	Demonstration against Haynes's and Drumgould's Bluffs, or engagement at Snyder's Mill.

May

1	Battle of Port Gibson, or Thompson's Hill.

For directions to this site, see Part II, Phase 2, Stop 1, Running the Batteries.

Narrative of Maj. Gen. Ulysses S. Grant, USA (continued)

The original canal scheme[1] was also abandoned on the 27th of March. The effort to make a waterway through Lake Providence and the connecting bayous was abandoned as wholly impracticable about the same time.

At Milliken's Bend, and also at Young's Point, bayous or channels start, which, connecting with other bayous passing Richmond, Louisiana, enter the Mississippi at Carthage twenty-five or thirty miles above Grand Gulf. The Mississippi levee cuts the supply of water off from these bayous or channels, but all the rainfall behind the levee, at these points, is carried through these same channels to the river below. In case of a *crevasse* in this vicinity, the water escaping would find its outlet through the same channels. The dredges and laborers from the canal having been driven out by overflow and the enemy's batteries, I determined to open these other channels, if possible. If successful the effort would afford a route, away from the enemy's batteries, for our transports. There was a good road back of the levees, along these bayous, to carry the troops, artillery and wagon trains over whenever the water receded a little, and after a few days of dry weather. Accordingly, with the abandonment of all the other plans for reaching a base . . . this new one was undertaken.

As early as the 4th of February I had written to Halleck about this route, stating that I thought it much more practicable than the . . . Lake Providence route. The upper end of these bayous being cut off from a water supply, further than the rainfall back of the levees, was grown up with dense timber for a distance of several miles from their source. It was necessary, therefore, to clear this out before letting in the water from the river. This work was continued until the waters of the river began to recede and the road to Richmond, Louisiana, emerged from the water. One small steamer and some barges were got through this channel, but no further use could be made of it because of the fall in the river. Beyond this it was no more successful than the other experiments with which the winter was whiled away.

All these failures would have been very discouraging if I had expected much from the efforts; but I had not. From the first the most I hoped to accomplish was the passage of transports, to be used below Vicksburg, without exposure to the long line of batteries defending that city.

This long, dreary, and, for heavy and continuous rains and high water, unprecedented winter was one of great hardship to all engaged about Vicksburg. The river was higher in its natural banks from December, 1862, to the following April. The war had suspended peaceful pursuits in the south, further than the production of army supplies, and in consequence the levees were neglected and broken in many places and the whole country was covered with water. Troops could scarcely find dry ground on which to pitch their tents. Malarial fevers broke out among the men. Measles and small-pox also attacked them. The hospital arrangements and medical attendance were so perfect, however, that the loss of life was much less than might have been expected. . . . Because I would not divulge my ultimate plans to visitors, they pronounced me idle, incompetent and unfit to command men in an emergency, and clamored for my removal. . . . With all the pressure brought to bear upon them, both President Lincoln and General Halleck stood by me to the end of the campaign. I had never met Mr. Lincoln, but his support was constant.

At last the waters began to recede; the roads crossing the peninsula behind the levees of the bayous were emerging from the waters; the troops were all concentrated from distant points at Milliken's Bend preparatory to a final move. . . .

I had in contemplation the whole winter the movement by land to a point below Vicksburg from which to operate, subject only to the possible but not expected success of some one of the expedients resorted to for the purpose of giving us a different base. I did not therefore communicate this plan, even to an officer of my staff, until it was necessary to make preparations for the start. My recollection is that Admiral Porter was the first one to whom I mentioned it. The cooperation of the navy was absolutely essential to the success (even to the contemplation) of such an enterprise.

I had no more authority to command Porter than he had to command me. It was necessary to have part of his fleet below Vicksburg if the troops went there. Steamers to use as ferries were also essential. The navy was the only escort and protection for these steamers, all of which in getting below had to run about fourteen miles of batteries. Porter fell in with the plan at once, and suggested that he had better superintend the preparation of the steamers selected to run the batteries, as sailors would probably understand the work better than soldiers.

Porter's gunboats approaching Vicksburg on the night of April 16, 1863. (*Harper's Pictorial History of the Civil War*)

I was glad to accept his proposition, not only because I admitted his argument, but because it would enable me to keep from the enemy a little longer our designs. Porter's fleet was on the east side of the river above the mouth of the Yazoo, entirely concealed from the enemy by the dense forests that intervened. Even spies could not get near him, on account of the undergrowth and overflowed lands. . . .

Admiral Porter proceeded with the preparation of the steamers for their hazardous passage of the enemy's batteries. The great essential was to protect the boilers from the enemy's shot, and to conceal the fires under the boilers from view. This he accomplished by loading the steamers, between the guards and boilers on the boiler deck up to the deck above, with bales of hay and cotton, and the deck in front of the boilers in the same way, adding sacks of grain. The hay and grain would be wanted below, and could not be transported in sufficient quantity by the muddy roads over which we expected to march.

Before this I had been collecting, from St. Louis and Chicago, yawls and barges to be used as ferries when we got below. By the 16th of April Porter was ready to start on his perilous trip.[2]

SHERMAN'S ALTERNATIVE PLAN

Gen. William T. Sherman to Col. John A. Rawlins,
Adjutant General, Grant's Staff, April 8, 1863

I would most respectfully suggest, for reasons which I will not name, that General Grant call on his corps commanders for their opinions, concise and positive, on the best general plan of campaign. Unless this be done, there are men who, in any result falling below the popular standard, claim that their advice was unheeded, and that fatal consequences resulted therefrom. My own opinions are:

1. That the Army of the Tennessee is far in advance of the other grand armies.

2. That a corps from Missouri should forthwith be moved from St. Louis to the vicinity of Little Rock, Arkansas, supplies collected while the river is full, and land communication with Memphis opened via Des Ark on the White, and Madison on the St. Francis rivers.

3. That as much of Yazoo pass, Coldwater, and Tallahatachie rivers as can be gained and fortified be held, and the main army

be transported thither by land and water; that the road back to Memphis be secured and reopened; and as soon as the waters subside, Grenada be attacked, and the swamp road across to Helena be patrolled by cavalry.

4. That the line of the Yalabusha be the base from which to operate against the points where the Mississippi Central crosses Big Black above Canton, and lastly where the Vicksburg and Jackson railroad crosses the same river.

The capture of Vicksburg would result.

5. That a force be left in this vicinity, not to exceed ten thousand men, with only enough steamboats to float and transport them to any direct point. This force to be held always near enough to act with the gunboats, when the main army is known to be near Vicksburg, Haines's bluff, or Yazoo City.

6. I do doubt the capacity of Willow bayou (which I estimate to be fifty miles long and very tortuous) for a military channel, capable of supporting an army large enough to operate against Jackson, Mississippi, or Black river bridge; and such a channel will be very valuable to a force coming from the west, which we must expect.

7. The chief reason for operating *solely* by water was the season of the year and high water in Tallahatchie and Yalabusha. The spring is now here, and soon these streams will be no serious obstacle, save the ambuscades of the forest, and whatever works the enemy may have erected at or near Grenada. North Mississippi is too valuable to allow them to hold and make crops.

I make these suggestions, with the request that General Grant simply read them, and give them, as I know he will, a share of his thoughts. I would prefer he should not answer them, but merely give them as much or as little weight as they deserve.

Whatever plan of action he may adopt will receive from me the same zealous cooperation and energetic support, as though conceived by myself.[3]

Narrative of Maj. Gen. Ulysses S. Grant, USA (*continued*)

When General Sherman first learned of the move I proposed to make, he called to see me about it. I recollect that I had transferred my headquarters from a boat in the river to a house a short distance back from the levee. I was seated on the piazza engaged in conversation with my staff when Sherman came up. After a few moments' conversation, he said that he would like to see me alone.

We passed into the house together and shut the door after us. Sherman then expressed his alarm at the move I had ordered, saying that I was putting myself in a position voluntarily which an enemy would be glad to manoeuvre a year—or a long time—to get me in. I was going into the enemy's country, with a large river behind me and the enemy holding points strongly fortified above and below. He said that it was an axiom in war that when any great body of troops moved against an enemy they should do so from a base of supplies, which they would guard as they would the apple of the eye, etc.

He pointed out all the difficulties that might be encountered in the campaign proposed, and stated in turn that what would be the true campaign to make. This was, in substance, to go back until high ground could be reached on the east bank of the river; fortify there and establish a depot of supplies, and move from there, being always prepared to fall back upon it in case of disaster.

To this I replied, the country is already disheartened over the lack of success on the part of our armies; the last election went against the vigorous prosecution of the war, voluntary enlistments had ceased throughout most of the North and conscription was already resorted to, and if we went back so far as Memphis it would discourage the people so much that bases of supplies would be of no use: neither men to hold them nor supplies to put in them would be furnished. The problem for us was to move forward to a decisive victory, or our cause was lost. No progress was being made in any other field, and we had to go on.

Sherman wrote to my adjutant general, Colonel J. A. Rawlins, embodying his views of the campaign that should be made, and asking him to advise me to at least get the views of my generals upon the subject. Colonel Rawlins showed me the letter, but I did not see any reason for changing my plans. The letter was not answered, and the subject was not subsequently mentioned between Sherman and myself to the end of the war, that I remember of. I did not regard the letter as official, and consequently did not preserve it. General Sherman furnished a copy himself to General Badeau, who printed it in his history of my campaigns.

I did not regard either the conversation between us or the letter to my adjutant-general as protests, but simply friendly advice which the relations between us fully justified. Sherman gave

the same energy to make the campaign a success that he would or
could have done if it had been ordered by himself.[4]

RUNNING THE VICKSBURG BATTERIES

General Order of Acting Rear Adm. David D. Porter, USN, Preparatory to Running the Batteries, April 10, 1863

You will prepare your vessel for passing the batteries at Vicksburg, taking every precaution possible to protect the hull and
machinery against any accidental shot.

When the vessels do move, it will be at night and in the following order: *Benton, Lafayette, Price, Louisville, Mound City, Pittsburg,
Carondelet;* other vessels that may arrive hereafter, and army transports, passing as fast as they can. Every vessel will take in tow a coal
barge, to be carried on the starboard side. No lights will be shown
in any part of the ships. All ports will be covered up until such time
as the vessels open fire, which they will do when their broadsides
bear upon the town, or when it can safely be done without inter-
fering with the pilot or endangering the other vessels. Before starting, the hour of departure will be given, and every vessel will have
her fires well ignited, so that they will show as little smoke as possible.

On approaching the batteries, every vessel will exhaust in the
wheel, so as to make but little noise.

If any vessel should receive such damage as to cause her to be
in a sinking condition, the best plan will be to land her on the island below the canal. The vessels must not crowd each other, nor
fire their bow guns when abreast of the town or batteries; 50 yards
is the closest they should be to each other. After rounding the point
below, and being clear of the shoal water, hug the shore enough
(on the side opposite Vicksburg) to get into the shade of the trees
and hide the hulls of the vessels. The crew must work the guns
without light on the decks, and all the guns must be set for about
900 yards, which will reach light fieldpieces and infantry. Fire shell
and sometimes grape. Don't fire after passing the town and main
batteries; the lower batteries are not worth noticing.

When arrived below Warrenton, the flagship *Benton* will burn
a Coston signal, when each vessel will hoist a red light, that I may
know who is missing.

The sterns of the vessels must be protected securely against
raking shot.

Porter's boats passing Vicksburg. (U.S. Army Military History Institute)

The coal barges must be so arranged that they can be easily cut adrift.

No vessel must run directly astern of the other, so that in case of the headmost vessel stopping the sternmost one won't run into her.

In case any vessel should ground under the enemy's batteries at Vicksburg, with no prospect of getting off, she must be set fire to, thoroughly and completely destroyed.

Avoid running on the sunken levees opposite Vicksburg.[5]

Porter to Hon. Gideon Welles, Secretary of the Navy, April 17, 1863

I have the honor to inform you that I passed the batteries at Vicksburg on the night of the 16th of April, with a large force for operations below. Three army transports were prepared to resist shot and accompanied the squadron.

I led in the *Benton*, and having drifted down on the batteries, got up with the first one without being discovered.

At 11:16 P.M. the batteries opened on us, we immediately responded with a rapid fire; the vessels of the squadron all in line followed our example.

The enemy lighted up the river on both sides, and we were fair targets for them, still we received but little damage.

The squadron was under fire for two hours and thirty minutes. No one was killed and only 8 wounded; the greatest number on board this ship, which, being ahead, received a concentrated fire.

An army transport, the *Henry Clay*, was sunk by a heavy shot. The *Forest Queen* (transport) became temporarily disabled and was turned into safe quarters by the *Tuscumbia*.

The fire from the forts was heavy and rapid, but was replied to with such spirit that the aim of the enemy was not so good as usual.

The conduct of all the commanders met my entire approbation.

All the vessels were ready for service half an hour after passing the batteries.[6]

Narrative of Maj. Gen. Ulysses S. Grant, USA (continued)

The enemy were evidently expecting our fleet for they were ready to light up the river by means of bonfires on the east side and by firing houses on the point of land opposite the city on the

Secretary of the Navy Gideon Welles, whose wholehearted cooperation with the Union army helped ensure success in the Vicksburg campaign. (U.S. Army Military History Institute)

Louisiana side. The sight was magnificent, but terrible. I witnessed it from the deck of a river transport, run out into the middle of the river and as low down as it was prudent to go. My mind was much relieved when I learned that no one on the transports had been killed and but few, if any, wounded. During the running of the batteries men were stationed in the holds of the transports to partially stop with cotton shot-holes that might be made in the hulls. All damage was afterwards soon repaired under the direction of Admiral Porter.

The experiment of passing batteries had been tried before this, however, during the war. Admiral Farragut had run the batteries at Port Hudson with the flagship *Hartford* and one iron-clad and visited me from below Vicksburg. The 13th of February Admiral Porter had sent the gunboat *Indianola,* Lieutenant-Commander

George Brown commanding, below. She met Colonel Ellet of the Marine brigade below Natchez on a captured steamer. Two of the Colonel's fleet had previously run the batteries, producing the greatest consternation among the people along the Mississippi from Vicksburg to the Red River.[7]

THE VIEW FROM VICKSBURG

Narrative of Maj. Samuel H. Lockett, CSA, Chief Engineer of the Vicksburg Defenses (continued)

On the night of the 16th of April, 1863, a large part of the upper fleet . . . ran the batteries at Vicksburg. Gun-boats had frequently passed the batteries during the operations of the preceding ten months, but up to that time no one had dreamed that the ordinary river steamboats could do so. They were protected by cotton-bales and by large barges loaded with coal and forage, lashed alongside. One of the transports was fired by our shells, and burned to the water's edge in front of the city. Two other boats were partly disabled, and several of the barges were sunk. Yet eight boats succeeded in getting past both Vicksburg and Warrenton in more or less serviceable condition.

The movement of the boats was soon discovered by the Confederate pickets, who nightly patrolled the river in small boats. They immediately crossed the river and fired several houses in the village of DeSoto, so as to illuminate the river. To appreciate the boldness of this action one must try to put himself in the place of these pickets, who ran great risks of being captured in landing on the opposite shore, which was occupied by the Federal forces. In addition, as soon as their work was accomplished, they were exposed to the enemy's sharpshooters, on the now brightly lighted river, and were in the direct line of fire of the batteries of their friends. Yet they neither failed nor faltered.

Two nights later four more boats, towing barges of large capacity, passed down the river and joined the others at New Carthage, a village in Louisiana about half-way between Vicksburg and Grand Gulf. Here there was a fleet of formidable gun-boats, and transports and barges enough to ferry a large force across the river. This gave a serious and threatening aspect to the movement.

At the same time a force under General Sherman was again menacing Haynes' Bluff; Grierson's raid was playing havoc with railroads and depots of supplies in the interior of Mississippi; rumors of movements of Federal troops in north Mississippi were rife; and Port Hudson in Louisiana was threatened.

General *Pemberton,* just previous to this time, had sent some troops from his department to General [Braxton] *Bragg,* at Tullahoma, and had others *en route* to the same destination. As soon as he became convinced that Vicksburg was seriously threatened by General Grant's last move, he strongly pleaded for the return of his troops, and made rapid dispositions of those still left, to meet the various forces operating against him. Lack of reliable information, however, made his efforts unavailing. Before he could determine which was the real attack, and which were mere diversions, General Grant had perfected his arrangements, attacked and temporarily silenced the batteries of Grand Gulf, and passed that point with his fleet.

This was on the 29th of April. On the next day he crossed the river at Bruinsburg and obtained a lodgment on the eastern shore.[8]

Pemberton to Gen. Joseph E. Johnston, April 17, 1863 (Tullahoma, Tennessee)

There is no doubt a considerable part of Grant's army did go up the river as high as Memphis, and, perhaps, into the Cumberland, but there seems now to be no doubt that re-enforcements are being sent down again.

The arrival of Adjt. and Insp. Gen. Lorenzo Thomas, U.S. Army, who is now at Vicksburg, has, I think, made a great change in enemy's plan of campaign. Under the circumstances, I think that not only should no more troops be sent from here, but that those who have just gone should be at once returned. A large force of Grant's army has established itself at New Carthage, below Warrenton, on west bank; another is at Richmond, La. Five boats (I suppose gunboats, though not yet positively informed), as I telegraphed you this morning, passed the Vicksburg batteries last night. I am momentarily expecting a report as to their character and condition.

These five, together with the three gunboats and small steamer under Farragut, give nine vessels available for crossing troops or operating from above against Port Hudson. I am also somewhat apprehensive that the Charleston expedition failing there, may join Banks against Port Hudson. The raft at Snyder's Mill, a great and important assistant in the flank defense of Vicksburg, has entirely given way, in consequence of the increased current and enormous pressure of drift. This compels additional guns at Snyder's, and they must come from Vicksburg. . . .

My special purpose in this communication is to endeavor to recover the troops I put *en route* for the Army of Middle Tennessee, believing when I started them that I might temporarily reenforce it without immediate and pressing danger to my position here. I have no precise information as to the defenses of Corinth. I learn, however, that they have been greatly strengthened since our army abandoned them.[9]

NOTES

1. See Part II, Phase 1, Stop 2, Grant's Canal, for a discussion of this topic.

2. Ulysses S. Grant, *Personal Memoirs*, 2 vols. (New York: Charles L. Webster, 1885), 1:456–63 passim.

3. Adam Badeau, *Military History of Ulysses S. Grant, from April 1861 to April 1865*, 3 vols. (New York: D. Appleton, 1868–81), 1:618–20.

4. Grant, *Memoirs*, 1:542–43.

5. *O.R.N.*, series I, vol. 24, pp. 554–55.

6. *O.R.N.*, series I, vol. 24, pp. 552–53.

7. Grant, *Memoirs*, 1:463–64.

8. Samuel H. Lockett, "The Defense of Vicksburg," in *Battles and Leaders of the Civil War*, 4 vols., ed. Robert U. Johnson and Clarence C. Buel (New York: Century, 1884), 3:485–86.

9. *O.R.*, XXIV, pt. 3, pp. 752–53.

7. GRIERSON'S RAID

Summary of Principal Events:
April 16–May 3, 1863

April

16 Porter's gunboats and transports run the batteries at Vicksburg.

17–May 2 Grierson's expedition from La Grange, Tennessee to Baton Rouge, Louisiana.

18–24 Diversionary expedition from Memphis to Cold-water, Mississippi.

22 Passage of the Vicksburg and Warrenton batteries by transports.

25–29 Expedition to Hard Times Landing, Louisiana, and skirmishes at Phelps's and Clark's Bayous (26th) and at Choctaw Bayou, or Lake Bruin (28th).

29 Bombardment of Grand Gulf, Mississippi, and passage of the batteries. Demonstration against Haynes's and Drumgould's Bluffs, or engagement at Snyder's Mill, Mississippi.

May

1 Battle of Port Gibson, Mississippi.

2 Skirmish on the South Fork of Bayou Pierre, Mississippi.

3 Skirmishes on the North Fork of Bayou Pierre, at Willow Springs, Ingraham's Heights, Jones's Cross Roads, Forty Hills, and Hankinson's Ferry, Big Black River, Mississippi.

Grant to Maj. Gen. Stephen A. Hurlbut, USA, Commanding Sixteenth Army Corps, March 9, 1863

I send Colonel Dickey, commanding cavalry division, to report to you. I have explained to Colonel Dickey, verbally, that I want the available cavalry put in as good condition as possible in the next few weeks for heavy service.

My plan is to have the cavalry from your command co-operate with the cavalry [*sic*] it is in contemplation to start from some point on the Yazoo. . . . The object will be to have your cavalry move southward from La Grange in as large a force as possible, destroying the bridge over the Tallahatchee; thence move east of south, so as to head [*sic*] Black River or strike it where it can be crossed; the larger portion of the cavalry to move from about Yalabusha River eastward, as if to threaten the Mobile [rail]road, but in reality to cover a move of a select portion of the cavalry, which will go south and attempt to cut the railroad east of Jackson. [Brig. Gen. Cadwalader C.] Washburn will move eastward, and cut the Mississippi Central road where it crosses the Big Black.

It is hoped by these moves of large forces of cavalry to cover the smaller party sufficiently to ensure their success in reaching the [rail]road east of Jackson, and to do what they are sent for, and return to the main body. No vehicles should be taken along, except ambulances, and they should have an extra pair of horses each. The troops should be instructed to keep well together, and let marauding alone for once, and thereby better secure success.

I regret that the expedition you had fitted out was not permitted to go. The weather, however, has been so intolerably bad ever since that it might have failed.

I look upon Grierson as being much better qualified to command this expedition than either [Albert L.] Lee or [John K.] Mizner. I do not dictate, however, who shall be sent. The date when the expedition should start will depend on movements here. You will be informed of the exact time for them to start.[1]

Maj. Gen. Stephen A. Hurlbut to Lt. Col. John A. Rawlins, Assistant Adjutant General, Grant's Staff, April 17, 1863

Grierson's cavalry expedition started at daylight from La Grange. I do not expect to hear from him for fifteen or twenty days, unless from Southern papers.

General Smith started today with three regiments and a battery for Panola, by Holly Springs, going down on railroad, thence by land on north side of Tallahatchee to Panola.

Three regiments and a battery of Lauman's, with 200 cavalry, move tomorrow morning direct on Coldwater and Panola.

Maj. Gen. Stephen A. Hurlbut, USA, Commander, Sixteenth
Army Corps, during the Vicksburg campaign. (U.S. Army
Military History Institute)

These various movements along our length of line will, I hope, so distract their attention that Grierson's party will get a fair start and be well down to their destination before they can be resisted by adequate force. God speed him, for he has started gallantly on a long and perilous ride. I shall anxiously await intelligence of the result.[2]

Report of Maj. Gen. Stephen A. Hurlbut, Sixteenth Army Corps, Memphis, Tennessee, May 5, 1863

I consider it proper to report directly to the General in Chief [Halleck] the transactions in this army corps during the latter part of April, because the recent change of headquarters Department of the Tennessee isolates me from my immediate commander [Grant].

As the spring opened, I was daily more and more impressed with the feasibility of a plan, long entertained, of pushing a flying column of cavalry through the length of Mississippi, cutting the Southern Railroad. By consent and approval of General Grant, I prepared a system of movements along my entire line from Memphis to Corinth for the purpose of covering this cavalry dash. At the same time General Rosecrans proposed to me to cover a movement of 1,800 cavalry from Tuscumbia down into Alabama and Georgia. This did not interfere with my plan, but simply required extra force to be developed from Corinth. Delays incident to combined movements, especially from separate commands, kept his expeditionary column back for six days.

I commenced the movement from Corinth on the 15th. . . . On the 17th, Col. B. H. Grierson, Sixth Illinois Cavalry, with his own regiment, the Seventh Illinois, and Second Iowa, moved from La Grange by way of Pontotoc, with orders, after passing Pontotoc, to proceed straight down, throwing one regiment to the left toward Okolona, and to push for and destroy the Chunkey River Bridge and any others they could reach, and either return, or proceed to Baton Rouge, as might be found advisable.

On the same day . . . a column of infantry 1,400 strong, and one battery, moved by railroad from La Grange to Coldwater, with orders to push rapidly between Coldwater and the Tallahatchee, and take *Chalmers* in flank and rear while attacked in front by three regiments, a battery, and 200 cavalry from Memphis, which left here on the 18th. I considered that the effect of these movements

Col. Benjamin H. Grierson, USA, Commander, Union Cavalry forces, during a raid between La Grange, Tennessee, and Baton Rouge, Louisiana. (U.S. Army Military History Institute)

would be to puzzle the enemy and withdraw his force from the central line, which has proven to be correct.

Chalmers was attacked at Coldwater; the stream found to be unfordable, but was held there until Smith's column from his rear approached from La Grange, when he broke into squads and disappeared. After holding the ground for three days, gathering 400 horses and mules and large supplies of bacon and forage, this force returned with small loss.

Grierson, on the 19th, detached the Second Iowa below Pontotoc, which fought its way gallantly back to La Grange and came home well mounted. The main cavalry column (Sixth and Seventh Illinois) proceeded, without loss or engagement, to Newton, on the Southern Mississippi Railroad, and there destroyed bridges, etc. They then swept around to Hazlehurst, on the New Orleans and Jackson road, and destroyed heavy trestle. . . . I have no doubt they are before this at Baton Rouge, or have joined General Grant at or below Grand Gulf.

I desire especially to call the attention of the General-in-Chief to this gallant exploit of Colonel Grierson, one, I think, unequaled in the war.[3]

Report of Col. Benjamin H. Grierson, USA, Sixth Illinois Cavalry, Commanding Expedition

In accordance with instructions, received . . . at La Grange, Tenn, I left that place at daylight on . . . April 17, with the effective force of . . . 1,700. . . . We moved southward without material interruption, crossing the Tallahatchee River on the afternoon of the 18th at three different points. One battalion of the Seventh Illinois . . . crossing at New Albany, found the bridge partially torn up, and an attempt was made to fire it. As they approached the bridge they were fired upon, but drove the enemy from their position, repaired the bridge, and crossed. The balance of the Seventh Illinois and the whole of the Sixth crossed at a ford 2 miles above, and the Second Iowa crossed about 4 miles farther up. After crossing, the Sixth and Seventh Illinois moved south on the Pontotoc road, and encamped for the night on the plantation of Mr. Sloan. The Second Iowa also moved south from their point of crossing, and encamped about 4 miles south of the river. The rain fell in torrents all night.

The expedition eastward communicated with Colonel [Edward] Hatch, who was still moving south parallel to us. The one to New Albany came upon 200 rebels near the town, and engaged them, killing and wounding several. The one northwest found that Major *Chalmers'* command, hearing of our close proximity, had suddenly left in the night, going west.

After the return of these expeditions, I moved with the whole force to Pontotoc. Colonel Hatch joined us about noon, reporting having skirmished with about 200 rebels the afternoon before and that morning, killing, wounding, and capturing a number.

We reached Pontotoc about 5 P.M. The advance dashed into the town, came upon some guerrillas, killed 1, and wounded and captured several more. Here we also captured a large mill, about 400 bushels of salt, and camp equipage, books, papers, etc., of Captain *Weatherall's* command, all of which were destroyed. After slight delay, we moved out, and encamped for the night on the plantation of Mr. Daggett, 5 miles south of Pontotoc, on the road toward Houston.

At 3 o'clock the next morning, April 20, I detached 175 of the least effective portion of the command, with one gun of the battery and all the prisoners, led horses, and captured property, under command of Major Love, of the Second Iowa, to proceed back to La Grange, marching in column of fours, before daylight, through Pontotoc, and thus leaving the impression that the whole command had returned. Major Love had orders also to send off a single scout to cut the telegraph wires south of Oxford.

At 5 A.M. I proceeded southward with the main force on the Houston road, passing around Houston about 4 P.M., and halting at dark on the plantation of Benjamin Kilgore, 11½ miles southeast of the latter place on the road toward Starkville.

The following morning at 6 o'clock I resumed the march southward, and about 8 o'clock came to the road leading southeast to Columbus, Miss. Here I detached Colonel Hatch, with the Second Iowa Cavalry and one gun of the battery, with orders to proceed to the Mobile and Ohio Railroad in the vicinity of West Point, and destroy the road and wires; thence move south, destroying the railroad and all public property as far south, if possible, as Macon; thence across the railroad, making a circuit northward; if practicable, take Columbus and destroy all Government works in that place, and again strike the railroad south of Okolona, and, destroying it, return to La Grange by the most practicable route.

Of this expedition, and the one previously sent back, I have since heard nothing, except vague and uncertain rumors through secession sources.

These detachments were intended as diversions, and even should the commanders not have been able to carry out their instructions, yet, by attracting the attention of the enemy in other directions, they assisted us much in the accomplishment of the main object of the expedition.

After having started Colonel Hatch on his way, with the remaining portion of the command, . . . about 950 strong, I continued

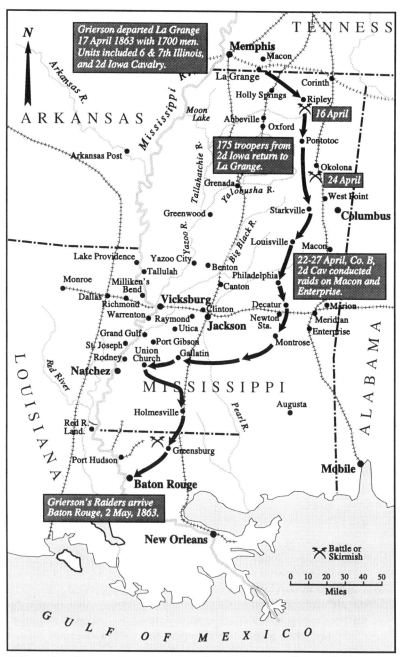

N

TENNESS

Memphis
Macon
La Grange
Corinth
Holly Springs
Ripley
Abbeville
Oxford
Pontotoc
16 April

ARKANSAS

Moon Lake

175 troopers from 2d Iowa return to La Grange.

Okolona
24 April
West Point
Columbus

Arkansas Post

Grenada

Greenwood

Starkville

Louisville
Macon

22-27 April, Co. B, 2d Cav conducted raids on Macon and Enterprise.

Lake Providence
Yazoo City
Benton
Tallulah
Philadelphia
Monroe
Milliken's Bend
Canton
Dallas
Richmond
Vicksburg
Clinton
Decatur
Marion
Warrenton
Raymond
Jackson
Newton Sta.
Meridian
Grand Gulf
Utica
Enterprise
St. Joseph
Port Gibson
Montrose
Rodney
Union Church
Gallatin
Natchez

MISSISSIPPI

Augusta

Holmesville

Pearl R.

Red R. Land.

Greensburg

Port Hudson

Baton Rouge

Mobile

Grierson's Raiders arrive Baton Rouge, 2 May, 1863.

New Orleans

Battle or Skirmish

0 10 20 30 40 50
Miles

GULF OF MEXICO

LOUISIANA

ALABAMA

Arkansas R.

Mississippi R.

Tallahatchie R.

Yalobusha R.

Yazoo R.

Big Black R.

Red River

Grierson's raid was a deception operation designed to distract *Pemberton* as Grant moved his army south of Vicksburg.

on my journey southward, still keeping the Starkville road. Arriving at Starkville about 4 P.M., we captured a mail and a quantity of Government property, which we destroyed. From this point we took the direct road to Louisville. We moved out on this road about 4 miles, through a dismal swamp nearly belly-deep in mud, and sometimes swimming our horses to cross streams, when we encamped for the night in the midst of a violent rain. From this point I detached a battalion of the Seventh Illinois Cavalry . . . to proceed about 4 miles, and destroy a large tannery and shoe manufactory in the service of the rebels. They returned safety, having accomplished the work most effectually. They destroyed a large number of boots and shoes and a large quantity of leather and machinery . . . and captured a rebel quartermaster from Port Hudson, who was there laying in a supply for his command.

We now immediately resumed the march toward Louisville, distant 28 miles, mostly through a dense swamp, the Noxubee River bottom. This was for miles belly-deep in water, so that no road was discernible. The inhabitants . . . generally did not know of our coming, and would not believe us to be anything but Confederates.

We arrived at Louisville soon after dark. I sent a battalion of the Sixth Illinois . . . in advance to picket the town and remain until the column had passed, when they were relieved by a battalion of the Seventh Illinois, under Major Graham, who was ordered to remain until we should have been gone an hour, to prevent persons leaving with information of the course we were taking, to drive out stragglers, preserve order, and quiet the fears of the people. They had heard of our coming a short time before we arrived, and many had left, taking only what they could hurriedly move. The column moved quietly through the town without halting, and not a thing was disturbed. Those who remained at home acknowledged that they . . . had expected to be robbed, outraged, and have their houses burned. On the contrary, they were protected in their persons and property.

After leaving the town, we struck another swamp, in which, crossing it . . . in the dark, we lost several animals drowned, and the men narrowly escaped the same fate. Marching until midnight, we halted until daylight at the plantation of Mr. Estes, about 10 miles south of Louisville.

The next morning, April 23, . . . we took the road for Philadelphia, crossing Pearl River on a bridge about 6 miles north of the town. This bridge we were fearful would be destroyed by the citizens to prevent our crossing, and upon arriving at Philadelphia we found that they had met and organized for that purpose; but hearing of our near approach, their hearts failed and they fled to the woods. We moved through Philadelphia . . . without interruption, and halted to feed about 5 miles southeast, on the Enterprise road.

Here we rested until 10 o'clock at night, when I sent two battalions of the Seventh Illinois Cavalry, under Lieutenant-Colonel Blackburn, to proceed immediately to Decatur, thence to the railroad at Newton Station. With the main force I followed about an hour later. The advance passed through Decatur about daylight, and struck the railroad at 6 A.M. I arrived about an hour afterward with the column. Lieutenant-Colonel Blackburn dashed into the town, took possession of the railroad and telegraph, and succeeded in capturing two trains in less than half an hour after his arrival. One of these, 25 cars was loaded with ties and machinery, and the other 13 cars were loaded with commissary stores and ammunition, among the latter several thousand loaded shells. These, together with a large quantity of commissary and quartermaster's stores and about five hundred stand of arms stored in the town, were destroyed. Seventy-five prisoners captured at this point were paroled. The locomotives were exploded and otherwise rendered completely unserviceable. Here the track was torn up and a bridge half a mile west of the station destroyed. I detached a battalion of the Sixth Illinois Cavalry, under Major Starr, to proceed eastward and destroy such bridges, etc., as he might find over Chunkey River. Having damaged as much as possible the railroad and telegraph, and destroyed all Government property in the vicinity of Newton, I moved about 4 miles south of the road and fed men and horses. The forced marches which I was compelled to make, in order to reach this point successfully, necessarily very much fatigued and exhausted my command, and rest and food were absolutely necessary for its safety.

From captured mails and information obtained by my scouts, I knew that large forces had been sent out to intercept our return, and having instructions from Major-General Hurlbut . . . to move in any direction from this point which, in my judgment would be best for the safety of my command and the success of the expedition, I at once decided to move south, in order to secure the necessary rest and food for men and horses, and then return to La Grange through Alabama, or make for Baton Rouge, as I might hereafter deem best. Major Starr in the mean time rejoined us, having destroyed most effectually three bridges and several hundred feet of trestle-work, and the telegraph from 8 to 10 miles east of Newton Station.

After resting about three hours, we moved south to Garlandville. At this point we found the citizens, many of them venerable with age, armed with shot-guns and organized to resist our approach. As the advance entered the town, these citizens fired upon them and wounded one of our men. We charged upon them and captured several. After disarming them, we showed them the folly of their actions and released them. Without an exception they acknowledged their mistake, and declared that they had been grossly deceived as to our real character. . . .

After slight delay at Garlandville, we moved southwest about 10 miles and camped at night on the plantation of Mr. Bender, 2 miles west of Montrose. Our men and horses having become gradually exhausted, I determined on making a very easy march the next day, looking more to the recruiting of my weary little command than to the accomplishment of any important object; consequently I marched at 8 o'clock the next morning, taking a west, and varying slightly to a northwest course. We marched about 5 miles, and halted to feed on the plantation of Elias Nichols.

After resting until about 2 P.M., during which time I sent detachments north to threaten the line of railroad at Lake Station and other points, we moved southwest toward Raleigh, making about 12 miles during the afternoon, and halting at dark on the plantation of Dr. Mackadora.

From this point I sent a single scout, disguised as a citizen, to proceed northward to the line of the Southern Railroad, cut the telegraph, and, if possible, fire a bridge or trestle-work. He started on his journey about midnight, and when within 7 miles of the railroad he came upon a regiment of Southern cavalry from Brandon, Miss., in search of us. He succeeded in misdirecting them . . . and having seen them well on the wrong road, he immediately retraced his steps to camp with the news. When he first met them they were on the direct road to our camp, and . . . would have come up with us before daylight.

From information received through my scouts and other sources, I found that Jackson and the stations east as far as Lake Station had been re-enforced by infantry and artillery; and hearing that a fight was momentarily expected at Grand Gulf, I decided to make a rapid march, cross Pearl River and strike the New Orleans, Jackson and Great Northern Railroad at Hazlehurst, and, after destroying as much of the road as possible, endeavor to get upon the flank of the enemy and cooperate with our forces, should they be successful in the attack upon Grand Gulf and Port Gibson [see Chapter 8].

Having obtained during the day plenty of forage and provisions, and having had one good night's rest, . . . at 6 o'clock on the morning of the 26th, we crossed Leaf River, burning the bridge behind us to prevent any enemy who might be in pursuit from following; thence through Raleigh, capturing the sheriff of that county, with about $3,000 in Government funds; thence to Westville, reaching this place soon after dark. Passing on about 2 miles, we halted to feed, in the midst of a heavy rain. . . . After feeding, Colonel Prince, of the Seventh Illinois Cavalry, with two battalions, was sent immediately forward to Pearl River to secure the ferry and landing. He arrived in time to capture a courier who had come to bring intelligence of the approach of the Yankees and orders for the destruction of the ferry. With the main column, I followed in about two hours. We ferried and swam our horses, and succeeded in crossing the whole command by 2 P.M.

As soon as Colonel Prince had crossed . . . he was ordered to proceed immediately to the New Orleans, Jackson and Great Northern Railroad, striking it at Hazlehurst. Here he found a number of cars containing about 500 loaded shells and a large quantity of commissary and quartermaster's stores, intended for Grand Gulf and Port Gibson. These were destroyed, and as much of the railroad and telegraph as possible. Here, again, we found the citizens armed to resist us, but they fled precipitately upon our approach.

From this point we took a northwest course to Gallatin, 4 miles; thence southwest 3½ miles to the plantation of Mr. Thompson, where we halted until the next morning.

Directly after leaving Gallatin we captured a 64-pounder gun, a heavy wagon load of ammunition, and machinery for mounting the gun, on the road to Port Gibson. The gun was spiked and the carriages and ammunition destroyed. During the afternoon it rained in torrents, and the men were completely drenched.

At 6 o'clock the next morning, April 28, we moved westward. After proceeding a short distance, I detached a battalion of the Seventh Illinois Cavalry, under Captain Trafton, to proceed back to the railroad at Bahala and destroy the road, telegraph, and all Government property he might find. With the rest of the command, I moved southwest toward Union Church. We halted to feed at 2 P.M. on the plantation of Mr. Snyder, about 2 miles northeast of the church. While feeding, our pickets were fired upon by a considerable force. I immediately moved out upon them . . . and drove them through the town, wounding and capturing a number. It proved to be a part of *Wirt Adams'* (Mississippi) cavalry. After driving them off, we held the town and bivouacked for the night. After accomplishing the object of his expedition, Captain Trafton returned to us about 3 o'clock in the morning of the 29th, having come upon the rear of the main body of *Adams'* command. The enemy having a battery of artillery, it was his intention to attack us in front and rear at Union Church about daylight . . . but the appearance of Captain Trafton with a force in his rear changed his purpose, and, turning to the right, he took the direct road to Port Gibson. From this point I made a strong demonstration toward Fayette, with a view of creating the impression that we were going toward Port Gibson or Natchez, while I quietly took the opposite direction, taking the road leading southeast to Brookhaven, on the railroad.

Before arriving at this place, we ascertained that about 500 citizens and conscripts were organized to resist us. We charged into the town, when they fled, making but little resistance. We captured over 200 prisoners, a large and beautiful camp of instruction, comprising several hundred tents and a large quantity of quartermaster's and commissary stores, arms, ammunition, etc. After paroling the prisoners and destroying the railroad, telegraph, and all Government property, about dark we moved southward and encamped at Mr. Gill's plantation, about 8 miles south of Brookhaven.

On the following morning we moved directly south along the railroad, destroying all bridges and trestle-work to Bogue Chitto Station, where we burned the depot and fifteen freight cars and captured a very large secession flag. From thence we still moved along the railroad, destroying every bridge, water-tank, etc., as we passed, to Summit, which place we reached soon after noon. Here we destroyed twenty-five freight cars and a large quantity of Government sugar. We found much Union sentiment in this town, and were kindly welcomed and fed by many of the citizens.

Hearing nothing more of our forces at Grand Gulf, I concluded to make for Baton Rouge to recruit my command, after which I could return to La Grange, through Southern Mississippi and Western Alabama; or, crossing the Mississippi River, move through Louisiana and Arkansas. Accordingly, after resting about two hours, we started southwest on the Liberty road, marched about 15 miles, and halted until daylight on the plantation of Dr. Spurlark.

The next morning we left the road and threatened Magnolia and Osyka, where large forces were concentrated to meet us; but, instead of attacking those points, took a course due south, marching through woods, lanes, and by-roads, and striking the road leading from Clinton to Osyka. Scarcely had we touched this road when we came upon the Ninth Tennessee Cavalry [Battalion], posted in a strong defile, guarding the bridges over Tickfaw River. We captured their pickets, and, attacking them, drove them before us, killing, wounding and capturing a number. Our loss in this engagement was 1 man killed and Lieut. Col. William D. Blackburn and 4 men wounded.

I cannot speak too highly of the bravery of the men upon this occasion, and particularly of Lieutenant-Colonel Blackburn, who, at the head of his men, charged upon the bridge, dashed over, and, by undaunted courage, dislodged the enemy from his strong position. After disposing of the dead and wounded, we immediately moved south on the Greensburg road, recrossing the Tickfaw River at Edwards' Bridge. At this point we met [W. H.] Garland's rebel cavalry, and, with one battalion of the Sixth Illinois and two guns of the battery, engaged and drove them off without halting the column.

The enemy were now on our track in earnest. We were in the vicinity of their stronghold, and from couriers and dispatches which we captured it was evident they were sending forces in all directions to intercept us. The Amite River, a wide and rapid stream, was to be crossed and there was but one bridge . . . and this was in exceedingly close proximity to Port Hudson. This I determined upon securing before I halted. We crossed it at midnight, about two hours in advance of a heavy column of infantry and artillery which had been sent there to intercept us. I moved on to Sandy Creek, where Hughes' cavalry [battalion] under Lieutenant-Colonel [C. C.] Wilbourn, were encamped, and where there was another main road leading to Port Hudson.

We reached this point at first dawn of day [and] completely surprised and captured the camp with a number of prisoners.

Having destroyed the camp, consisting of about one hundred and fifty tents, a large quantity of ammunition, guns, public and private stores, books, papers, and public documents, I immediately took the road to Baton Rouge. Arriving at the Comite River we utterly surprised *Stuart's* cavalry [Miles Legion], who were picketing at this point, capturing 40 of them with their horses, arms, and entire camp. Fording the river, we halted to feed within 4 miles of the town. Major-General [Christopher C.] Augur, in command at Baton Rouge, having now, for the first, heard of our approach, sent two companies of cavalry . . . to meet us. We marched into the town about 3 P.M., and we were most heartily welcomed by the United States forces at this point. . . .

During the expedition we killed and wounded about 100 of the enemy, captured and paroled over 500 prisoners, many of them officers, destroyed between 50 and 60 miles of railroad and telegraph, captured and destroyed over 3,000 stand of arms and other army stores and Government property to an immense amount; we also captured 1,000 horses and mules. Our loss during the entire journey was 3 killed, 7 wounded, 5 left on the route sick; the sergeant-major and surgeon of the Seventh Illinois left with Lieutenant-Colonel Blackburn, and 9 men missing, supposed to have straggled. We marched over 600 miles in less than sixteen days. The last twenty-eight hours we marched 76 miles, had four engagements with the enemy, and forded the Comite River, which was deep enough to swim many of the horses. During this time the men and horses were without food or rest.

Much of the country through which we passed was almost entirely destitute of forage and provisions, and it was but seldom that we obtained over one meal per day. Many of the inhabitants must undoubtedly suffer for want of the necessaries of life, which have reached most fabulous prices.

Two thousand cavalry and mounted infantry were sent from the vicinity of Greenwood and Grenada northeast to intercept us; 1,300 cavalry and several regiments of infantry with artillery were sent from Mobile to Macon, Meridian, and other points on the Mobile and Ohio [rail]road; a force was sent from Canton northeast to prevent our crossing Pearl River, and another force of infantry and cavalry was sent from Brookhaven to Monticello, thinking we would cross Pearl River at that point instead of Georgetown. Expeditions were also sent from Vicksburg, Port Gibson, and Port Hudson to intercept us. Many detachments were sent out from my command at various places to mislead the enemy, all of which rejoined us in safety. Colton's pocket map of Mississippi, which, though small, is very correct, was all I had to guide me; but by the capture of their couriers, dispatches, and mails, and the invaluable aid of my scouts, we were always able by rapid marches to evade the enemy when they were too strong and whip them when not too large.[4]

Narrative of Maj. Gen. Ulysses S. Grant (continued)

It was at Port Gibson I first heard through a Southern paper of the complete success of Colonel Grierson. . . . He had started from La Grange April 17th with three regiments of about 1,700 men. On the 21st he had detached Colonel Hatch with one regiment to destroy the railroad between Columbus and Macon and then return to La Grange. Hatch had a sharp fight with the enemy at Columbus and retreated along the railroad, destroying it at Okalona and Tupelo, and arriving in La Grange April 26. Grierson continued his movement with about 1,000 men, breaking the Vicksburg and Meridian railroad and the New Orleans and Jackson railroad, arriving at Baton Rouge May 2d.

This raid was of great importance, for Grierson had attracted the attention of the enemy from the main movement against Vicksburg.[5]

NOTES

1. *O.R.,* XXIV, pt. 3, p. 95.
2. *O.R.,* XXIV, pt. 3, p. 202.
3. *O.R.,* XXIV, pt. 1, pp. 520–21.
4. *O.R.,* XXIV, pt. 1, pp. 522–29.
5. Ulysses S. Grant, *Personal Memoirs,* 2 vols. (New York: Charles L. Webster, 1885), 1:488–89.

8. OPERATIONS BELOW VICKSBURG

Summary of Principal Events:
March 11–May 2, 1863

March

14–27   Steele's Bayou expedition (to Rolling Fork, Mississippi, by Muddy, Steele's, and Black Bayous, and Deer Creek).

19   Passage of the Grand Gulf batteries by the *Hartford* and *Monongahela.*

25   Passage of the Vicksburg batteries by the *Switzerland,* and destruction of the *Lancaster.*

31   Engagement at Grand Gulf, Mississippi.

31–April 17   Operations from Milliken's Bend to New Carthage, Louisiana.

April

2–14   Expedition to Greenville, Black Bayou, and Deer Creek, Mississippi, with skirmishes on April 7, 8, and 10.

16   Passage of the Vicksburg batteries by gunboats and transports.

17–May 2   Grierson's raid.

22   Passage of the Vicksburg and Warrenton batteries by transports.

25–29   Expedition to Hard Times Landing, Louisiana, and skirmishes at Phelps's and Clark's Bayous and at Choctaw Bayou (Lake Bruin).

29   Bombardment of Grand Gulf, Mississippi, and passage of the batteries.

30–May 1   Two corps from Grant's army cross the Mississippi at Bruinsburg.

May

1   Demonstration against Haynes's and Drumgould's
             Bluffs (Snyder's Mill), Mississippi. Battle of Port
             Gibson (Thompson's Hill), Mississippi.

"THE OTHER SIDE OF THE HILL": MARCH 11–MAY 1

*Report of Lt. Gen. John C. Pemberton, CSA, Commanding
Department of the Mississippi and Eastern Louisiana*

The enemy, after long-continued and strenuous efforts to
reach the right flank of Vicksburg by forcing a passage through
the Upper Yazoo River, finally relinquished his design, and on the
night of April 4 and 5 re-embarked his troops, and before daylight
was in rapid retreat. About the same time a heavy force of the
enemy, which had been collected at Baton Rouge [Banks] was
mostly withdrawn and transferred to Western Louisiana, leaving
but one division to occupy that place. After consultation by telegraph with Major-General [F.] *Gardner,* commanding Port Hudson
and the Third Military District, deeming the garrison at Port Hudson
more than sufficient under existing circumstances, and to save
supplies at a point so difficult to provide, the navigation of the
Mississippi River being then obstructed to us, and the mouth of
Red River, from whence large quantities of subsistence stores were
drawn, being blockaded by one of the enemy's gunboats, I ordered
[A.] *Rust's* brigade, and two regiments under Brigadier-General
[A.] *Buford,* to proceed immediately to Jackson, Miss., with the then
view of employing them against raids of the enemy in Northern
Mississippi, my great deficiency in cavalry leaving that portion of
the department almost without protection.

About March 11, fearing that the enemy might succeed in
opening a canal practicable for the passage of transports across
the peninsula opposite Vicksburg, I [had] deemed it necessary to
occupy Grand Gulf, near the mouth of the Big Black, and as a
secondary obstacle to the navigation of the Mississippi River. General [J. S.] *Bowen* was also directed to look well to the approaches
by the Bayou Pierre. He subsequently informed me that he had
prepared for the defense on both sides of the bayou.

On the 22d, five heavy guns were mounted and ready for service.
Two of these were removed from the batteries at Vicksburg, and

three, intended for gunboats being built in the Trans-Mississippi Department, were detained by my order, it being impracticable to obtain them elsewhere. At the same time the enemy commenced his movement to reach Vicksburg by the Hushpuckanaw and Deer Creek. Another expedition was also attempted through Steele's Bayou via Rolling Fork and the Sunflower, the object of both being to enter the Yazoo River above Haynes' Bluff. In these designs he was completely baffled. Many of our smaller boats, which were alone fitted for the navigation of these streams, and which were employed in the transportation of supplies for Vicksburg, were necessarily diverted from this purpose to transport troops to meet and repel these expeditions. The same interruption in the transportation of supplies was also of constant occurrence during the protracted expedition via the Yazoo Pass.

On April 7, I received a telegram from the President, inquiring as to the practicability of sending re-enforcements to General *Bragg* in Middle Tennessee, and directing me to send them if existing circumstances in the department would admit of it. On the same day I informed the President by telegram that, in my judgment, it was not safe to diminish the forces in this department at that time.

On April 9, I telegraphed General S. *Cooper,* Adjutant and Inspector General, as follows:

> I am confident that few re-enforcements, if any, have been sent to Rosecrans from Grant; no troops whatever are reported to have gone above the mouth of the Yazoo Pass. I endeavor to keep General [Joseph E.] *Johnston* advised of any movement which may affect his army. The enemy is constantly in motion in all directions. He appears now to be particularly engaged with Deer Creek by land from Greenville. I have forces there to meet him. It is reported, but not yet confirmed, that a movement under McClernand in large force, by land, is in progress west of the river and southward. I doubt it. My operations west of the Mississippi must greatly depend on the movement of the enemy's gunboats. I have several regiments now near New Carthage. I will inform you promptly of anything important, and if I ascertain that part of Grant's army is re-enforcing Rosecrans, will dispatch troops to General *Johnston* as rapidly as possible.

On April 11, I again telegraphed General *Cooper* . . . and General J. E. *Johnston,* at Tullahoma, as follows:

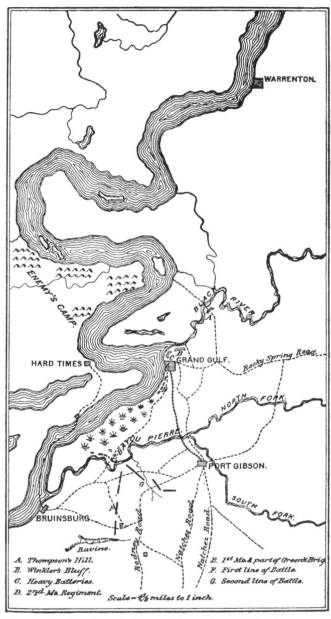

Sketch showing the relative positions of Grand Gulf, Bruinsburg, and Port Gibson. (*O.R.*, XXIV, pt. 1, p. 665)

A scout from Austin reports that forty transports, loaded down, but without troops, passed up the Mississippi River on the 3d and 4th instant.

Brigadier-General *Chalmers* reports that:

Ellet's Marine Brigade passed up the Mississippi on the 7th. The same evening three gunboats and nineteen transports loaded with troops passed up, the last ten boats from Tallahatchee, 20 miles up Coldwater, on Wednesday, going up. *I think that most of Grant's forces are being withdrawn to Memphis* [emphasis added].

On the same day I again telegraphed General *Johnston*. . . .

The following report just received: Scout *Kemp* reports: Near Byhalia, on the 10th, the enemy is strengthening his guard on the Memphis and Charleston Railroad. Twelve thousand troops passed Memphis going up the river on the 7th. The same day fifty pieces of artillery were landed at Memphis and taken to the Memphis and Charleston depot. Part of Grant's army reported to be going to Corinth and down the Mobile and Ohio Railroad; the balance to re-enforce Rosecrans.

Lawson reports near Memphis, 10th:

Marine Brigade gone up the Cumberland River; also fourteen transports and two gunboats passed up the river. On the night of the 7th, a corps of engineers reached Memphis from below.

Acting on these and other corroborating reports, I said to General *Johnston,* in closing my dispatch, "I am collecting troops here, and can send you 4,000 at once, if absolutely necessary"; and accordingly the brigades of Generals *Tilghman, Rust,* and *Buford* were, on April 13, placed under orders to move with dispatch to Tullahoma, while General *Vaughn*'s brigade of East Tennesseeans was ordered to be held in readiness to move at short notice. Maj. L. *Mims,* chief quartermaster, was instructed to furnish the necessary transportation as speedily as possible, and the following dispatch, dated April 12, was transmitted to General Johnston:

I will forward troops to you as fast as transportation can be furnished—about 8,000 men. Am satisfied Rosecrans will be re-enforced from Grant's army. Shall I order troops to Tullahoma?

On April 15, statements made by persons just out of Memphis, of which I was notified by telegraph, indicated that the retrograde movement from Vicksburg was probably a ruse, and that an early attack might be expected on that place; and on the 16th I telegraphed General *Johnston* . . . :

I can send you only two brigades. The latest information induces the belief that no large part of Grant's army will be removed.

On the same day General *Stevenson* was directed to delay the movement of [J. O.] *Vaughn's* brigade, and on the 17th Major *Mims,* chief quartermaster, was instructed that no more troops would be forwarded in the direction of Tullahoma until further orders. General *Tilghman's* brigade was held in position between Jackson and the Big Black Bridge, and on the same day the following telegram was dispatched to General *Cooper,* Adjutant and Inspector General:

General *Stevenson* reports that eight boats attempted to pass Vicksburg last night; five succeeded in passing, one was burned and sunk, and two disabled. General *Chalmers* reports sixty-four steamers left Memphis on the 15th instant, loaded with troops and negroes, apparently with intention of making an assault on Vicksburg. The enemy has nine boats between Vicksburg and Port Hudson. I cannot send any more troops, and think that those on the way to General *Johnston* should come back.

General *Bowen,* at Grand Gulf, was immediately advised of the passage of the boats . . . and instructed to withdraw his troops from the Louisiana shore at the first favorable opportunity. He was also immediately re-enforced by the Sixth Mississippi Regiment, the First Confederate Battalion and a field battery.

On the same day the following telegram was dispatched to General Johnston:

The troops sent you were taken from Port Hudson—a brigade, under Brigadier General *Buford,* aggregate present 4,065. The enemy has nine boats between Vicksburg and Port Hudson. He has landed forces at New Carthage from Grant's army, and can re-enforce them to any extent. He can use his nine boats to cross his troops to this side. The arrival of General Lorenzo Thomas [Adjutant General, USA] has changed the enemy's plans, or his movement up the river was a ruse. I ought to have back *Buford's* brigade; certainly no more troops should leave this department. A dispatch from Brigadier-General *Chalmers* yesterday says sixty-four boats left Memphis since Thursday, loaded with soldiers and negroes, ostensibly to assault Vicksburg.

The raft in the Yazoo at Snyder's Mill has given away, and is entirely destroyed. I am, therefore, compelled to strengthen the batteries there at the expense of Vicksburg.

General *Stevenson* reports that eight boats passed the Bend last night. One was burned and two apparently disabled; the other five escaped uninjured.

Indications of an attack on Vicksburg are so strong that I am not warranted in sending any more troops from this department.

From information received after this dispatch was sent, I learned that eight of the enemy's most formidable gunboats, besides his transports and barges, succeeded in passing safely on the 16th.

I found it a very difficult matter to obtain the necessary hawsers and chains for the raft in the Yazoo, but it was speedily replaced under the active and energetic supervision of Mr. Thomas *Weldon.*

My request for the return of the troops forwarded to Middle Tennessee to re-enforce General *Bragg* was immediately complied with. A portion of them, however, had reached Chattanooga; the remainder were halted by telegraph at various points on the route, and the whole were restored to this department as soon as was practicable.

The enemy's vessels of war occupying the river between Vicksburg and Grand Gulf, it was impossible for me to operate effectually in the Trans-Mississippi Department to prevent the advance of the enemy to the west bank of the river.

On April 17, therefore, I addressed the following telegraphic communication to Capt. E. *Powell,* assistant quartermaster at Natchez:

> Forward the following to Lieutenant-General *Smith* or Major-General *Taylor,* viz: For the want of the necessary trans-

portation, I cannot operate effectually on the west bank of the river; the enemy is now in force at New Carthage and Richmond. I beg your attention to this.

Captain Powell notified me at once that this dispatch had been forwarded by courier.

On the 18th, I addressed a second communication through the same medium. . . .

The enemy are cutting a passage from near Young's Point to Bayou Vidal, to reach the Mississippi River near New Carthage. Without co-operation it is impossible to oppose him. Inform me what action you intend to take.

To these communications . . . I received no reply until after the capitulation of Vicksburg. . . .

On the 19th, reports of raids in Northern Mississippi from several points in Tennessee reached me. All the available cavalry north of the Southern Railroad was at once placed at the disposal of Brigadier-Generals *Ruggles* and *Chalmers,* commanding, respectively, the First and Fifth Military Districts, which embraced all the northern portion of the State of Mississippi, and both were notified of the expected raids. Two companies of cavalry of *Waul's* Legion alone were ordered to report to Brigadier-General *Barton* at Warrenton.

One of these marauding expeditions, under Colonel [Brig. Gen.] Grierson, which crossed the Tallahatchee River at New Albany, succeeded in passing directly through the State, and eventually joined General Banks' forces at Baton Rouge, La. So great was the consternation created by this raid that it was impossible to obtain any reliable information of the enemy's movements, rumor placing him in various places at the same time.

On the 20th, I addressed the following telegram to General *Johnston:*

Can you not make a heavy demonstration with cavalry on the Tallahatchee toward Abbeville, if only for 50 miles? The enemy are endeavoring to compel a division of my troops to Northern Mississippi.

The same day the following communication was addressed to General *Johnston,* in response to one from him, asking if I could not send re-enforcements to the assistance of Colonel [P. D.] *Roddey:*

I have not sufficient force to give an efficient assistance to Colonel *Roddey* [at Tuscumbia]. The enemy are advancing from Memphis via Herndon, from Grand Junction and LaGrange via Holly Springs and Salem, and from Corinth via New Albany. . . . I have but a feeble cavalry force, but I shall certainly give you all the aid I can. I have literally no cavalry from Grand Gulf to Yazoo City, while the enemy is threatening to pass the river between Vicksburg and Grand Gulf, having now twelve vessels below the former place. A gunboat and one transport passed Austin on the 18th, having in tow fifteen flat-boats, or pontoons, with twenty-five skiffs on them. Another transport passed Austin on the 19th, towing sixteen flats, or pontoons.

Brigadier-General *Ruggles* was directed to send all his available cavalry . . . at once toward Corinth, as a diversion in favor of Colonel *Roddey;* General *Johnston* having informed me that a superior force of the enemy from Corinth was in front of *Roddey* at Tuscumbia, and desiring me, if possible, to send aid to the latter. Having no available cavalry to meet the raid of Grierson, which was ravaging the northern portion of the State, I endeavored to employ a portion of *Buford's* brigade (infantry), then returning to the department, and directed the commanding officer of the first regiment, on his arrival at Meridian, to remain until further orders, to protect the most important points on the Mobile and Ohio Railroad, and thereby succeeded in saving the valuable property, machinery, etc., at Enterprise, upon which town the enemy advanced and demanded its surrender, but Major-General *Loring* having reached there with a sufficient force of infantry in time, their object was frustrated. The enemy had previously succeeded in destroying several miles of the track of the Southern Railroad west of Chunkey River, which for more than a week greatly delayed the transportation of troops and entirely prevented that of supplies (except by wagons) from our depots on the Mobile and Ohio Railroad.

To meet these raids as far as possible, Major-General *Loring* was placed in command of all the troops then on the Mobile and Ohio Railroad. He was directed not to leave the line of the road for any great distance, to keep in telegraphic communication with me, and constantly to advise me of his position, and that, operations upon that line being minor in importance to those upon the

Mississippi River, his troops must be so disposed as to enable him to move them in that direction at a moment's notice. The same day the following communication was addressed to General *Johnston* at Tullahoma:

> Heavy raids are making from Tennessee deep into this State. One is reported now at Starkville, 30 miles west of Columbus. Cavalry is indispensable to meet these expeditions. The little that I have is on the field there, but totally inadequate. Could you not make a demonstration with a cavalry force on their rear?

Another expedition having been reported moving across the county in a southwesterly direction from Pontotoc, Brigadier-General *Featherston,* then commanding Fort Pemberton, on the Yazoo was ordered to move without delay toward Duck Hill or Winona, and General *Tilghman,* then at Canton, was directed to hold trains in readiness to move to Winona at a moment's notice. This became more necessary, as a heavy column of infantry as well as cavalry was reported moving from Memphis with the supposed view of taking possession of Grenada. The same day the following communication was telegraphed to General *Cooper,* Adjutant and Inspector General:

> I have so little cavalry that I am compelled to divert a portion of my infantry to meet raids in Northern Mississippi. If any troops can possibly be spared from other departments, I think they should be sent here.

Every effort was made . . . to provide cavalry to arrest Grierson's raid; also to accumulate a force for operations in the direction of Warrenton and Grand Gulf, thinking it quite as probable that Grierson would return by the route on which he was advancing as that he would continue his progress southward.

On the 24th, Brigadier-General *Chalmers,* at Panola, was directed to move, with all his cavalry and light artillery, via Oxford, to Okolona, to intercept the force of the enemy then at Newton Station, on the Southern Railroad. Captain [Samuel] *Henderson,* commanding special scouts at Grenada, was also instructed to send couriers to Generals *Loring, Buford,* and *Ruggles,* notifying those officers by telegrams from the nearest telegraph office, and advising each station on the road, that the enemy had reached Newton, on the Southern [rail]road. A force was also ordered to proceed from Jackson to Forrest, or Lake Station, or to such other points as circumstances might render necessary. Major-General *Gardner,* at Port Hudson, was notified that the enemy had reached the Southern Railroad—that it was probable he would endeavor to form a junction with Banks at Baton Rouge—and was instructed to send all his disposable cavalry to intercept him. Brigadier-General *Featherston,* with his brigade, then at or *en route* for Winona, was ordered to move to Grenada, if there was any approach of the enemy (as was reported) from the north on that place, unless he was also threatened by an advance from the east.

As it was possible that Grierson's forces might return by Jackson, such arrangements as my means allowed were made to defend the capital of the State. Brigadier-General *Tilghman,* then at Canton, was authorized to mount one of his regiments at that place, by the impressment of horses or otherwise, and immediate steps were taken to mount the Twentieth Mississippi and a detachment of the Fourteenth Mississippi, both of these regiments being at the time on duty in Jackson. Similar authority was given to General *Loring,* then on the Mobile and Ohio Railroad, to mount what force he could on that line. In the impressment of horses and their necessary equipments, Maj. L. *Mims,* chief quartermaster, was materially aided by His Excellency the Governor of Mississippi, who was also earnestly advised to mount by the same process a portion of the State troops in Northern Mississippi. All the cavalry I could thus collect south of the Southern Railroad was placed under the orders of Col. R. V. *Richardson* until he should fall in with Col. Wirt *Adams,* who was then directed to assume command and direct the movements of the whole.

On the 28th, it was ascertained that Grierson was continuing his movement south of Hazlehurst, and not toward Grand Gulf or the Big Black Bridge. Colonel [Wirt] *Adams* was directed to follow him up and ambuscade him, if possible. These instructions were carried out as far as practicable, and resulted in a smart skirmish near Union Church. Colonel *Adams'* force, however, was too weak to effect anything important. Grierson, after suffering considerable loss by an ambuscade farther south, which was well planned and executed by a cavalry force from Major-General *Gardner's* command, eventually succeeded in joining General Banks at Baton Rouge.

I have been thus circumstantial in reciting the incidents connected with this celebrated raid that I might clearly demonstrate the great deficiency—I may almost say absence—of cavalry in my department, and the absolute impossibility of protecting my communications, depots, and even my most vital positions, without it; and, further, to show that consequent upon this want of cavalry I was compelled to employ infantry, and thus weaken my force in that arm at other important points.

I wrote to General *Johnston* on March 25, urgently requesting that the division of cavalry under Major-General *Van Dorn*, which had been sent to the Army of Tennessee for special and temporary purposes, might be returned to me. . . . Col. B. S. *Ewell*, assistant adjutant-general, replied to my request:

> In the present aspect of affairs, General *Van Dorn's* cavalry is much more needed in this department than in that of Mississippi and Eastern Louisiana, and cannot be sent back as long as this state of things exists. You have now in your department five brigades of the troops you most require, viz. infantry, belonging to the Army of Tennessee. This is more than a compensation for the absence of General Van Dorn's cavalry command.

I will terminate this subject with the following telegram . . . to General *Johnston* at Tullahoma on April 27:

> However necessary cavalry may be to the army in Tennessee, it is indispensable for me to maintain my communications. The enemy are today at Hazlehurst, on the New Orleans and Jackson Railroad. I cannot defend every station on the roads with infantry. I am compelled to bring cavalry here from Northern Mississippi, and thus the whole of that section of the State is left open; further, these raids endanger my vital positions.

When it seemed probable that the enemy would succeed in opening a navigable canal across the peninsula opposite Vicksburg, and thus to a great extent avoid the batteries established there, I directed that Grand Gulf should be occupied, and as many heavy guns placed in position as could be without too much weakening the defenses of Vicksburg. Believing that the urgency of the case demanded it, I assumed the responsibility of detaining three heavy guns *en route* for the Trans-Mississippi Department, and withdrew two others from the batteries at Vicksburg. Insufficient as I knew this battery to be, it was the heaviest I could place there.

Fort Pemberton, on the Tallahatchee, then occupied our attention. The enemy in large force, by land and water, was exerting all his energies against that position, with the view of turning the right flank of Vicksburg, and every available gun was required for its defense. This necessity continued to exist until the fall of the rivers rendered an approach by water impracticable.

Grand Gulf was not selected as a position for land defense, but for the protection of the mouth of the Big Black and also as a precautionary measure against the passage of transports, should the canal . . . prove a success, which then seemed highly probable. The necessary works were, however, constructed, under the direction of Brigadier-General *Bowen*, to defend the batteries against an assault from the river front and against a direct attack from or across Big Black. When, however, the enemy succeeded in passing sufficient transports to cross his troops from the west bank of the river below Grand Gulf, there being a practicable route by which to move his land forces from above Vicksburg to a point nearly opposite Bruinsburg, the position of Grand Gulf itself lost much of is value; but so great were his facilities of transportation and so rapid his movements that it was impracticable to withdraw the heavy guns.

The only means of subsisting an army south of Big Black are from Vicksburg or Jackson, the former requiring a transportation by dirt road of 40 and the latter of 45 miles, in addition to that by rail. Without cavalry I could not have protected my own communications, much less have cut those of the enemy. To have marched an army across Big Black of sufficient strength to warrant a reasonable hope of successfully encountering his very superior forces would have stripped Vicksburg and its essential flank defenses of their garrisons, and the city itself might have fallen an easy prey into the eager hands of the enemy.

The enemy having succeeded . . . in passing the batteries at Vicksburg with a number of his gunboats and transports, and the report of a heavy movement to the southward on the Louisiana shore being fully confirmed, I immediately made the necessary dispositions for more perfectly guarding all points between Vicksburg and Grand Gulf, and re-enforced Brigadier-General *Bowen* with *Green's* brigade, the Sixth Mississippi Regiment, the First Confederate Battalion, and a battery of field artillery. Other troops were collected on the line of the railroad between Jackson and the Big Black Bridge, and measures were taken to get the troops that were being returned from Middle Tennessee into such positions that they could be readily moved at a moment's notice. Major-General *Stevenson* was directed to place 5,000 men in easy supporting distance of Warrenton, in addition to the brigade already there. Major *Lockett,* my chief engineer, was sent to Grand Gulf.

On the 22d I addressed a communication to Lieut. Gen. E. Kirby *Smith,* acknowledging the receipt of one from him of the 15th asking my co-operation on the west side of the Mississippi, and stating my inability to do so because of the enemy's gunboats in the river and from want of transportation, and again asking his co-operation in front of Grand Gulf and New Carthage.

The following telegram was addressed to Major-General *Stevenson* on the 23d:

> I consider it essential that communications, at least for infantry, should be made by the shortest practicable route to Grand Gulf. The indications now are that the attack will not be made on your front or right, and all troops not absolutely necessary to hold the works at Vicksburg should be held as a movable force for either Warrenton or Grand Gulf.

On the 28th, Brigadier-General *Bowen* telegraphed that "transports and barges loaded down with troops are landing at Hard Times, on the west bank." I immediately replied . . .

> Have you force enough to hold your position? If not, give me the smallest additional number with which you can. My small cavalry force necessitates the use of infantry to protect important points.

Major-General *Loring,* then at Meridian, was ordered to send two of his regiments across the break on the Southern Railroad, near Chunkey River, and Colonels *Ferrell* and *Reynolds,* who were west of the break, were ordered to proceed immediately to Jackson. Major-General *Buckner,* commanding at Mobile, was notified that I should look to him to assist me in protecting the Mobile and Ohio Railroad, as I required all the troops I could spare to strengthen General *Bowen.* Major-General *Gardner,* at Port Hudson, was also ordered to move *Gregg's* brigade rapidly to Jackson. Brigadier-General *Tilghman,* then on the Mississippi Central Railroad, was directed to move promptly, with all of his troops (save bridge guards) to Jackson. Major *Clark,* commanding at Brookhaven, was instructed to send couriers to all cavalry commanders near him, ordering them to move toward Grand Gulf, with directions not to encounter the main body of the enemy, but to harass him in the rear and flank. Similar instructions were forwarded to Osyka and Hazlehurst. To General *Johnston*, at Tullahoma, the following telegram was sent.

> The enemy is at Hard Times, La., in large force, with barges and transports, indicating an attack on Grand Gulf, with a view to Vicksburg. I must look to the Army of Tennessee to protect the approaches through Northern Mississippi.

The following also to Major-General *Stevenson* at Vicksburg:

> Hold 5,000 men in readiness to move to Grand Gulf, and on the requisition of Brigadier-General *Bowen* move them. With your batteries and rifle-pits manned, the city front is impregnable.

To General *Bowen* . . . the following was sent:

> I have directed General *Stevenson* to have 5,000 men ready to move on your requisition, but do not make requisition unless absolutely necessary for the safety of your position. I am also making arrangements for sending you 2,000 or 3,000 men from this direction in case of necessity. You cannot communicate with me too frequently.

I believe that I fully estimated the importance of preventing an advance upon Jackson, if it could be done without sacrificing Vicksburg; but if the latter was lost, the former was comparatively of little value. Vicksburg might still be held with Jackson in possession of the enemy, but it was the hope of being able to hold the position on Bayou Pierre, upon which the safety of Jackson depends, that made me most anxious to re-enforce General *Bowen*, or, failing in that, at least to have a sufficient force at hand to secure his retreat across the Big Black.

On April 30, I received the first information of the landing of the enemy on the east bank of the Mississippi River. General *Bowen* reported by telegraph that 3,000 Federal troops were at Bethel Church, 10 miles from Port Gibson, at 3 o'clock on the evening of the 29th, and that they were still landing at Bruinsburg. Brigadier-General *Tracy*, of *Stevenson's* division, had reached Grand Gulf with his brigade on the 30th. Lieutenant-Colonel [William N.]

Lithograph of the Union naval attack on Grand Gulf. (Frank Leslie's *The American Soldier in the Civil War*)

Brown, of the Twentieth Mississippi, with 50 mounted men of his regiment, left Jackson for the same place on the 29th, and Maj. J. D. *Bradford,* a good artillery officer, was sent to replace the lamented Colonel [William] *Wade* as chief of artillery.

Between 12 M. and 2 P.M. on the 30th, Brigadier-General *Baldwin,* with his brigade, of *Smith's* division, had crossed the Big Black at Hankinson's Ferry.

At 9 A.M. May 1, General *Bowen* informed me by telegraph, his army being then in position 3 miles south of Port Gibson, that General *Baldwin* was entering the latter place. On the same day General *Bowen* telegraphed me that prisoners taken reported McClernand in command . . . and that the enemy's force was estimated at 20,000 men. . . . At 3 P.M. the same day General *Bowen* advised me that he still held his position but that he was hard pressed.[1]

Maj. Gen. Carter L. Stevenson, CSA, to Pemberton, April 28, 1863

The men will be ready to move promptly to cross the Mississippi. Both gunboats and transports must pass the batteries at Grand Gulf. Our army, large enough to defend itself on this side, would consume much time in crossing [the Mississippi to delay Union forces there].

As it is not known what force has been withdrawn from this front, it is not improbable that the force opposite Grand Gulf is there to lay waste the country on that side, and a feint to withdraw troops from a main attack here [Vicksburg]. I venture to express the hope that the troops will not be removed far until further developments below render it certain that they [Union forces] will cross in force.[2]

Johnston to Pemberton, May 1, 1863

If Grant's army lands on this side of the river, the safety of Mississippi depends on beating it. For that object you should unite your whole force.[3]

ASSAULT ON GRAND GULF

For directions to this site, see Part II, Phase 3.

Report of Maj. Gen. Ulysses S. Grant, USA, Headquarters, Department of the Tennessee, Commanding

The Thirteenth Army Corps being all through to the Mississippi, and the Seventeenth Army Corps well on the way, so much of the Thirteenth as could be got on board of the transports and barges were put aboard, and moved to the front of Grand Gulf on April 29. The plan here was that the Navy should silence the guns of the enemy, and the troops landed under the cover of the gunboats, and carry the place by storm.[4]

Grant to Maj. Gen. John A. McClernand, Commanding Thirteenth Army Corps, April 27, 1863

Commence immediately the embarkation of your corps, or so much of it as there is transportation for. Have put aboard the artillery and every article authorized in orders limiting baggage, except the men and hold them in readiness, with their places assigned, to be moved at a moment's warning.

All the troops you may have, except those ordered to remain behind, send to a point nearly opposite Grand Gulf, where you see, by special orders of this date, General McPherson is ordered to send one division.

The plan of the attack will be for the navy to attack and silence all the batteries commanding the river. Your corps will be on the river, ready to run to and debark on the nearest eligible land below the promontory first brought to view passing down the river. Once on shore, have each commander instructed beforehand to form his men the best the ground will admit of, and take possession of the most commanding points, but avoid separating your command so that it cannot support itself. The first object is to get a foothold where our troops can maintain themselves until such time as preparations can be made and troops collected for a forward movement.

Admiral Porter has proposed to place his boats in the position indicated to you a few days ago, and to bring over with them such troops as may be below the city after the guns of the enemy are silenced.

It may be that the enemy will occupy positions back from the city, out of range of the gunboats, as to make it desirable to run past Grand Gulf and land at Rodney. In case this should prove the plan, a signal will be arranged, and you duly informed when the transports are to start with this view. Or it may be expedient for the boats to run past, but not the men. In this case, then, the transports would have to be brought back to where the men could land, and move by forced marches to below Grand Gulf, re-embark rapidly, and proceed to the latter place. There will be required, then, three signals to indicate that the transports can run down and debark the troops at Grand Gulf—one that the transports can run by without the troops, and the last that transports can run by with the troops on board.

Should the men have to march, all baggage and artillery will be left to run the blockade.

If not already directed, require your men to keep three days' rations in their haversacks, not to be touched until a movement commences.[5]

Report of Acting Rear Adm. David D. Porter, USN

I had the honor of sending you a telegraph announcing that we had fought the batteries at Grand Gulf for five hours and thirty-five minutes with partial success. Grand Gulf has been very strongly fortified since Admiral Farragut went down, to prevent his coming up [the river] again, and four batteries (some of very heavy guns) are placed at the distance of a quarter of a mile apart, on high points, and completely command the river.

I ordered the *Louisville, Carondelet, Mound City,* and *Pittsburg* to lead the way and attack the lower batteries, while the *Tuscumbia, Benton,* and *Lafayette* attacked the upper ones, the *Lafayette* lying in an eddy and fighting stern down stream. The vessels below silenced the lower batteries, and then closed up on the upper one, which had been hotly engaged by the *Benton* and *Tuscumbia,* both ships suffering severely in killed and wounded. The *Pittsburg* came up just at the moment when a large shell passed through the *Benton's* pilot house, wounding the pilot . . . and disabling the wheel. This made the vessel unmanageable for a short time, and she drifted down to the lower batteries, which she opened upon while repairing damages.

The *Pittsburg* . . . for a short time bore the brunt of the fire, and lost 8 killed and 16 wounded.

The *Tuscumbia* was cut up a great deal (and proved herself a poor ship in a hot engagement). As the fire of the upper battery slackened (I presume from want of ammunition), I passed up a short distance above the fort to communicate with General Grant, to see whether he thought proper to send the troops to the transports by the battery, under what was rather a feeble return to our fire.

He concluded to land the troops and march them across by a road 2 miles long, coming out below the batteries. As there was a prospect of spending a good deal of ammunition on the upper battery, without being able to occupy it if it was silenced, the vessels moved up-stream again by signal, without being much fired at or receiving any damage, while the enemy had a raking fire on them. I then sent down Captain Walke in the *Lafayette* to prevent them from repairing damages, which they were doing with great diligence. He opened on them, to which they responded a few times, and finally left the fort, when he fired at intervals of five minutes until dark.

At 6 o'clock P.M. I again got underway (with the transports following us) and attacked the batteries again, the transports all passing safely down under cover of our fire. We are now in a position to make a landing where the general pleases. I should have preferred this latter course in the first instance; it would have saved many lives and many hard knocks. The *Benton* received 47 shots in her hull alone, not counting the damage done above her rail;

but she was just as good for a fight when she got through as when she commenced.

All the vessels did well, though it was the most difficult portion of the river in which to manage an ironclad; strong currents (running 6 knots) and strong eddies turning them round and round, making them fair targets; and the *Benton's* heavy plates did not stand the heavy shot, which, in many instances, bored her through.

The *Tuscumbia* showed great weakness as a fighting ship, though her commander did his best to keep her in a position where she did excellent service. The current turned her round and round, exposing her at every turn. It was a hard fight and a long one on both sides. The enemy fought his upper battery with a desperation I have never yet witnessed, for though we engaged him at a distance of 50 yards, we never fairly succeeded in stopping his fire but for a short time. It was remarkable that we did not disable his guns, but though we knocked the parapets pretty much to pieces, the guns were apparently uninjured.[6]

Report of Maj. Gen. Ulysses S. Grant, USA (continued)

This [failure to take Grand Gulf by storm] determined me again to run the enemy's batteries, turn his position by effecting a landing at Rodney, or at Bruinsburg, between Grand Gulf and Rodney. Accordingly, orders were immediately given for the troops to debark at Hard Times, La., and march across to the point immediately below Grand Gulf.

At dark the gunboats again engaged the batteries, and all the transports run by, receiving but two or three shots in the passage, and these without injury. I had some time previously ordered a reconnaissance to a point opposite Bruinsburg, to ascertain, if possible, from persons in the neighborhood the character of the road leading to the highlands back of Bruinsburg. During the night I learned from a negro man that there was a good road from Bruinsburg to Port Gibson, which determined me to land there.[7]

Grant to Sherman, April 29, 1863

We have had terrific cannonading all day, without silencing the enemy's guns. Finding the position too strong, late in the day I decided to again run the blockade, which has been successfully done.

I shall be able to effect a landing tomorrow, either at the lower end of Grand Gulf or below Bayou Pierre, with all of McClernand's corps and Logan's division. Have also a second division of McPherson's command that can be landed next day.

Move up to Perkins' plantation with two divisions of your corps as rapidly as possible. Leave the other division for the present to occupy from Young's Point to Richmond, and to hasten up supplies and ordnance stores. Under the directions sent a few days ago, . . . rations ought to get along to supply the army. The cavalry can collect beef-cattle and grain for some little time.[8]

SHERMAN'S DIVERSION

Sherman to Grant, May 1, 1863
On Board Flagship Black Hawk, Below Haynes's Bluff

Am this moment in receipt of yours from below Grand Gulf. Have sent orders for Steele's and Tuttle's divisions to move to Perkins', and shall follow tomorrow. We will be there as soon as possible.

Tuttle will move by the new road, and Steele by Richmond.

Yesterday the new *Choctaw*, followed by all the other gunboats and our transports, approached the [Haines's] Bluff. We kept up a heavy fire, which was returned by the enemy. The *Choctaw* was struck fifty-three times, but her injuries are not in any vital part. Strange to say, no one was hurt. The *De Kalb* also was uninjured. The *Tyler* caught one shot on her water-line, which is repaired. I disembarked the command at Blake's negro quarters, and made disposition as for attack, which was kept up till after dark, drawing heavy fire.

Today I have felt all the paths and levees back, the ground, except the levees, being all under water still; and at 3 P.M. we will open another cannonade to prolong the diversion, and keep it up till after dark, when we shall drop down to Chickasaw, and so on back to camp.

Tomorrow I will move Blair's division up to Milliken's Bend, just below your headquarters, and with Steele's and Tuttle's divisions will obey your order and reach Perkins'. I hear the enemy has crossed over to Biggs' plantation in yawls, doubtless to see what we are about. They will not find out much. The road to Richmond cannot be reached from Biggs' on account of the overflow.

All our regimental wagons must be on the road, which will leave me without wagons, but I will get to Perkins' somehow. Steele will write you all of interest from Milliken's.

All well with us here, and I do not apprehend any serious loss in the cannonade proposed for this P.M. I want to prolong the diversion as much as possible in your favor.[9]

ESTABLISHING THE BEACHHEAD

Report of Maj. Gen. Ulysses S. Grant, USA (continued)

The work of ferrying the troops to Bruinsburg was commenced at daylight . . . the gunboats as well as transports being used for the purpose.

As soon as the Thirteenth Army Corps was landed, and could draw three days' rations to put in haversacks (no wagons were allowed to cross until the troops were all over), they were started on the road to Port Gibson. I deemed it a matter of vast importance that the highlands should be reached without resistance. The Seventeenth Corps followed as rapidly as it could be put across the river.

About 2 o'clock, May 1, the advance of the enemy was met 8 miles from Bruinsburg, on the road to Port Gibson. He was forced to fall back, but, as it was dark, he was not pursued far until daylight.[10]

NOTES

1. *O.R.*, XXIV, pt. 1, pp. 249–58.
2. *O.R.*, XXIV, pt. 1, pp. 574–75.
3. *O.R.*, XXIV, pt. 3, p. 808.
4. *O.R.*, XXIV, pt. 1, p. 48.
5. *O.R.*, XXIV, pt. 3, pp. 237–38.
6. *O.R.N.*, series I, vol. 24, pp. 610–11.
7. *O.R.*, XXIV, pt. 1, p. 48.
8. *O.R.*, XXIV, pt. 3, p. 246.
9. *O.R.*, XXIV, pt. 1, pp. 576–77.
10. *O.R.*, XXIV, pt. 1, p. 48.

9. BATTLE OF PORT GIBSON

Summary of Principal Events:
April 29–May 1, 1863

April
29–May 1   Sherman's demonstration against Haynes's and Drumgould's Bluffs (Snyder's Mill).

30–May 1   Union landings on east shore of Mississippi River at Bruinsburg.

May
1   Battle of Port Gibson (Thompson's Hill).

For directions to this site, see Part II, Phase 3, Port Gibson.

Report of Maj. Gen. Ulysses S. Grant, USA, Headquarters, Department of the Tennessee, Commanding

Early on the morning of the 1st, I went out, accompanied by members of my staff, and found McClernand with his corps engaging the enemy about 4 miles from Port Gibson. At this point the roads branched in exactly opposite directions, both, however, leading to Port Gibson. The enemy had taken position on both branches, thus dividing, as he fell back, the pursuing forces. The nature of the ground in that part of the country is such that a very small force could retard the progress of a much larger one for many hours. The roads usually run on narrow, elevated ridges, with deep and impenetrable ravines on either side. On the right were the divisions of Hovey, Carr, and [A. J.] Smith, and on the left the division of Osterhaus, of McClernand's corps. The three former succeeded in driving the enemy from position to position back toward Port Gibson steadily all day.

Osterhaus did not, however, move the enemy from the position occupied by him on our left until Logan's division, of McPherson's corps, arrived. McClernand, who was with the right in person, sent repeated messages to me before the arrival of Logan to send Logan's and Quinby's divisions, of McPherson's corps, to him.

I had been on that as well as all other parts of the field, and could not see how they could be used there to advantage. However, as soon as the advance of McPherson's corps (Logan's division) arrived, I sent one brigade to McClernand on the right, and sent one brigade, Brig. Gen. J. E. Smith commanding, to the left, to the assistance of Osterhaus. By the judicious disposition made of this brigade, under the immediate supervision of McPherson and Logan, a position was soon obtained, giving us an advantage which soon drove the enemy from that part of the field, to make no further stand south of Bayou Pierre.

The enemy was here repulsed with a heavy loss in killed, wounded, and prisoners. The repulse of the enemy on our left took place late in the afternoon. He was pursued toward Port Gibson, but night closing in, and the enemy making the appearance of another stand, the troops slept upon their arms until daylight.[1]

Report of Maj. Gen. John A. McClernand, USA

At 4 o'clock [on the afternoon of April 30] all my corps, except the cavalry on the opposite side of the river, took up the line of march, agreeably to instructions from Major-General Grant, for the bluffs, some 3 miles back. Reaching the bluffs some time before sunset, and deeming it important to surprise the enemy if he should be found in the neighborhood of Port Gibson, and, if possible, to prevent him from destroying the bridges over Bayou Pierre on the road leading to Grand Gulf and to Jackson, I determined to push on by a forced march that night as far as practicable.

About 1 o'clock on the morning of May 1, upon approaching Magnolia Church, 13 miles from Bruinsburg and 4 miles from Port Gibson, General Carr's division, leading the advance, was accosted by a light fire from the enemy's infantry, and soon after by the fire of his artillery. Harris' brigade, the command of which had devolved upon Colonel Stone, of the Twenty-second Iowa, . . . was immediately formed in line of battle, Griffiths' and Klauss' batteries brought up, and the enemy's fire briskly replied to and silenced. The division rested upon its arms at Shaifer's plantation during the short remnant of the night.

Coming up about day-dawn in the morning, I learned from a fugitive negro that the two roads diverging at Shaifer's led to Port

Brig. Gen. Peter J. Osterhaus, USA, Commander, Ninth Division, Thirteenth Army Corps (McClernand). (U.S. Army Military History Institute)

Gibson, one to the right by Magnolia Church, and the other to the left, passing near Bayou Pierre, where it is spanned by a rail and earth-road bridge; also that the greatest distance between the roads was only some 2 miles; that the space between, and for miles around, was diversified by fields, thick woods, abrupt hills, and deep ravines, and that the enemy was in force in front and intended to accept battle. I immediately proved the general correctness of this information by further inquiry and by personal reconnaissance, and determined to advance my forces upon the cord of the rude ellipse formed by the roads, resting my reserves back near the forks of the roads.

After the smoke of the previous engagement and the glimmering of the rising sun had ceased to blind our view, I ordered General Osterhaus to move his division on the road to the left, to relieve a detachment of General Carr's division which had been sent to watch the enemy in that direction, and to attack the enemy's right. The object of this movement was to secure whatever direct advantage might result from attacking the enemy's line at a point sup-

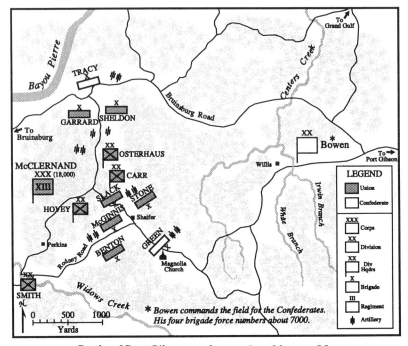

Battle of Port Gibson, early morning, May 1, 1863.

posed to be comparatively weak, and to make a diversion in favor of my right, preparatory to its attack upon the strong force understood to be in its front. The first Brigade of General Osterhaus' division, hastening forward in execution of this order, at 5:30 A.M. encountered the enemy in considerable force a short distance from Shaifer's house. The position of the enemy was a strong one, and he seemed determined to maintain it; yet, after an obstinate struggle for more than an hour, he was forced to yield and seek temporary safety at a greater distance, under cover of ravines and houses.

The splendid practice of Lanphere's and Foster's batteries disabled two of the enemy's guns, which were with difficulty withdrawn, and contributed largely to this success.

Communicating with General Osterhaus, I offered him reenforcements, but his Second Brigade having now come up, he declined them until more urgent occasion should arise. Thus strengthened he pressed forward until insurmountable obstacles in the nature of the ground and its exposure to the fire of the enemy arrested his progress, and proved the impracticability of successful front attack.

It was now 2 P.M., and about this time General J. E. Smith's brigade, of General Logan's division, came up, and attempting to carry the enemy's position by such an attack, failed to do so, thus attesting the correctness of General Osterhaus' admonition upon that point.

A flank movement had been resolved upon by General Osterhaus to accomplish the same object. With the view to deceive the enemy, he caused his right center to be threatened, and, taking advantage of the effect, rapidly moved a strong force toward his extreme right, and personally leading a brilliant charge against it, routed the enemy, taking three pieces of cannon. A detachment of General Smith's brigade joined in the pursuit of the enemy to a point within a half mile of Port Gibson.[2]

THE UNION LEFT

Report of Col. Marcus M. Spiegel, USA, 120th Ohio Infantry, First Brigade, Ninth Division, Thirteenth Army Corps, Army of the Tennessee

About 5 o'clock in the morning we were ordered to advance and take a position on the right of Lanphere's battery, which was accordingly done, under a severe fire of the enemy's shell, in which position we remained about half an hour, when we advanced to the edge of the ravine, and from there were ordered to advance and form a line of battle in a ravine to the extreme left of the division.

Soon after, in conjunction with the One hundred and eighteenth Illinois infantry, we advanced briskly across the open field, taking a position behind a fence fronting the enemy, and in support of the Forty-ninth Indiana, who were deployed as skirmishers on the edge of the woods. Soon thereafter Colonel Keigwin, of the Forty-ninth Indiana, informed me that he had been ordered to the right on a line with his position, and at the same time I received orders to cover the front with my skirmishers and relieve him. I then advanced Companies A, F, and K as skirmishers, and D, I, and B in support.

At 7:30 I was ordered to recall all but one of my companies. I moved, as ordered, to the right, in advance of our line, to relieve the Forty-second Ohio. While passing between our batteries and the position of the Forty-second Ohio, the enemy's shell, grape shot, and bullets flew thick around us, but the brave and gallant boys moved briskly and bravely on, until we arrived in front of the Forty-second Ohio, close to a ravine running parallel with the enemy's strongest position. I then engaged the enemy about twenty minutes, without being able to do him much harm, he being completely under cover on the opposite bank of the ravine.

I then advanced as skirmishers some of the best shots from all the companies down into the ravine, with orders to advance, closely supporting them with the remainder of the regiment, and keeping up a constant fire toward the top of the opposite bank. When nearly down into the ravine, I discovered the exact position of the enemy's advance, toward the left, on the opposite bank. I then charged upon them with the regiment, and quickly drove them from the bank to the knoll, where they rallied and made a stand, which only increased the determination of my brave boys. Rushing up the bank, we drove them pell-mell from behind the knoll, taking 8 prisoners.

When I had obtained possession of the knoll, I did not deem it prudent to pursue them farther, being at least 300 yards in advance of any of our troops, and in danger of meeting the enemy's entire right wing, massed behind a number of old buildings directly in front of me. I deployed my regiment on the knoll, in order to punish the retiring force and hold the position against a formidable attack. As soon as the retiring enemy had rejoined the main body, the attack was renewed with redoubled fierceness and energy, but, meeting with such continued and well-directed volleys from us, he fell back under the cover of the houses again. I then continued to fight the enemy, who was concealed behind logs, fences, and houses, and some perched upon the tops of trees, until my ammunition was beginning to give out and many of the guns were becoming unfit for use, when I was relieved by Col. T. W. Bennett, of the Sixty-ninth Indiana, and ordered to retire. I then fell back to the second ravine in my rear, replenishing the empty cartridge boxes with ammunition from the boxes of the comrades who were killed and wounded.

I remained in that position until late in the afternoon, when, seeing the charge made on the left, I quickly formed my regiment, marching them toward the charging column, in order to support them, if necessary. When, however, the enemy fled in confusion, a glorious victory won, the One Hundred and twentieth had nothing more to do than to exult, cheer, and be merry, and that I assure you was done.[3]

Report of Brig. Gen. John S. Bowen, CSA, Commanding Bowen's Division

On or about April 20, it became evident from the movements of the enemy, then closely watched by Major [Isaac F.] *Harrison* and a portion of my brigade in Louisiana, that he intended to pass below Vicksburg and make his lodgment in Mississippi at or near Grand Gulf. I immediately dispatched for the chief engineer of the department, to confer with him in regard to our position, and also urged the lieutenant-general commanding to send every gun and every man that could be concentrated to my assistance. The engineer officer, after a reconnaissance, fully concurred with me in my idea, that in case they passed my batteries and landed at Bruinsburg or Rodney, I should meet them south of Port Gibson and give them battle; also that it would require from 15,000 to 20,000 men to insure our success.

After the signal failure of the fleet to silence my batteries at Grand Gulf on April 29, and their subsequent passage by them under cover of darkness on the same night, I immediately commenced my dispositions to meet their army on the south side of Bayou Pierre. At the same time my water front was so extended, and presented four such vulnerable points, that nearly the whole division under my command was required to guard it, and left me no hope to fight the enemy on the spot selected unless the promised re-enforcements should reach me in time.

Finding, on the 30th, that Grant's army was crossing the Mississippi and landing at Bruinsburg, near the mouth of Bayou Pierre, I sent out Brigadier-General *Green* with about 450 of his own command (the remainder being posted on Big Black and Bayou Pierre), with a section of the Hudson Battery, and the Sixth Mississippi Regiment (Colonel [Robert] *Lowry's*), to occupy the two roads leading from Bruinsburg to Port Gibson. *Tracy's* brigade, *Stevenson's* division, arrived, jaded from a forced march and without provisions. I ordered them to halt near town, to collect stragglers, cook rations, and after a short rest to report to *Green*, who would point out their position.

During the afternoon I went out in person and established *Green* in his position; returned to Grand Gulf to ascertain what dem-

Maj. Gen. John S. *Bowen*, CSA, Commanding Division, Army of Vicksburg. (U.S. Army Military History Institute)

onstrations were making upon the positions on Big Black, Bayou Pierre, and the river front; received reports of approaches being made on every one, and determined to strengthen the one on Bayou Pierre, as its passage by the enemy would have been extremely disastrous to us. I ordered all the rifled Parrotts (four 10-pounders) and the First Missouri Regiment to this point, then occupied by one regiment of *Green's* brigade and a section of 6-pounders, making about 700 men and six pieces of artillery in all. The Second Missouri was deployed along the river below the batteries to prevent a landing at points beyond the range of our guns.

Two 12-pounder pieces and the Second [First?] Confederate Battalion, under Lieutenant Colonel [George H.] *Forney,* were posted at Winkler's Bluff, to prevent the destruction of the raft and the passage of Big Black River by the gunboats. The First Missouri Cavalry (dismounted) and [Ras.] *Stirman's* battalion, with [W. E.] *Dawson's* battery (four guns), held the position on Big Black known as Thompson's hill, where the enemy had threatened an attack for some days. The remainder of the command . . . was ordered to be ready to move at a moment's notice. . . .

About 1 o'clock in the morning the enemy advanced, drove in *Green's* pickets, and attacked with infantry and artillery. After a sharp contest of an hour and a half, *Green* repulsed him, driving him back toward Bruinsburg.

At sunrise the attack was renewed, and soon the action became general along our entire front. The enemy were gradually extending their lines and threatened completely to envelop us, but the regiments immediately in our front were so repeatedly driven back that their movement was materially delayed. Arriving on the field between 7 and 8 o'clock, and finding our left very much pressed, I called upon the Sixth Mississippi to charge a battery in front of them, to which they nobly responded, and were well seconded by the Twenty-third Alabama, on their right, but not by the Arkansas troops, to their left. We succeeded, however, in forcing them back some distance, and, leaving orders with *Green* to hold the position, I rode back and urged forward *Baldwin's* brigade, then arriving, to his support. I returned just in time to see the position lost, *Green* having been pressed gradually back. Ordering *Baldwin* to take a new line on the Rodney road, I sent *Green* to the right to re-enforce *Tracy,* then severely pressed on the Bayou road. The three reserve regiments from Grand Gulf, with [Henry] *Guibor's* battery and

Landis' section of 24-pounder howitzers, having arrived, one regiment (the Sixth Missouri, Colonel [Eugene] *Erwin*) was sent to the right to reinforce *Green* and *Tracy, Landis'* section placed in *Baldwin's* line (who had no artillery) and the remaining regiments (the Third and Fifth Missouri) moved to the left of the line.

Finding the enemy's right rapidly deploying and occupying a ridge that gave them easy access to the Natchez road, I determined to check their movement, and pushing forward with the Third and Fifth Missouri—detaching them some 300 yards from *Baldwin's* left—we charged their extreme right division, composed of one six-gun battery and twelve regiments of infantry. The first line (four regiments) was routed; the second wavered and gradually gave way; the third held its place, and forced us, after a protracted contest, to retire. This desperate move, carried out with a determination characteristic of the regiments making it, saved us from being flanked and captured, and gave us until sunset to prepare for our retreat.

About 10 A.M., finding that no real attack was to be made on Bayou Pierre or Big Black, I [had] sent for the First Missouri Infantry and First Missouri Cavalry, dismounted. The former regiment arrived in time to cover our retreat over Bayou Pierre and assist in destroying the bridges; the latter (7 miles distant) did not come up until night.

Ammunition was very scarce, especially in *Tracy's* brigade, whose ordnance train had not arrived. Nearly all my field artillery had been left at the points to be guarded around Grand Gulf, and my infantry line was much extended, as may be gleaned from the reports of brigade commanders, showing that companies were sent to re-enforce assailed points where regiments were required.

My returns show the following force engaged:

Part of *Green's* brigade, with Sixth Mississippi and section of Hudson Battery	775
Tracy's brigade and Anderson's battery	1,516
Baldwin's brigade	1,614
Part of *Cockrell's* brigade, with *Guibor's* and section of *Landis'* battery	1,259
Total	5,164

We had thirteen pieces of light artillery. The enemy had landed 30,000 men, and according to their letter-writers nearly all were brought into action during the day. They had certainly five major-generals, including their commander, General Grant, present, showing that the above is no exaggeration of their numbers. My command held this large army in check from daylight until near sundown, often repulsing them, and three times charging and breaking their lines. . . . Our loss . . . is killed, 68; wounded, 380; missing, 384. That of the enemy is estimated in their published accounts at about 2,000 in killed and wounded.[4]

Report of Col. Isham W. Garrott, CSA, Commanding Second Brigade, Stevenson's Division, May 1863

By order of Brigadier-General *Barton*, commanding *Stevenson's* division, nine companies each of the Twentieth, Twenty-third, Thirtieth, and Thirty-first Regiments Alabama Volunteers left camp, near Warrenton, about 7 P.M. on the evening of April 29; crossed the Big Black at Hankinson's Ferry that night, and continued the march next day in the direction of Grand Gulf. When we arrived within 4 miles of the latter place, we were directed to move toward Port Gibson; crossed Bayou Pierre on the suspension bridge between Port Gibson and Grand Gulf, and halted little beyond, where the men, who had been without food all day, obtained raw rations and immediately proceeded to cook them. Before the cooking was done, however, the order to march was given, and the troops proceeded down the bayou to a point 5 or 6 miles in front of Port Gibson, where we were formed in line of battle on the night of the 30th, the brigade having marched 40 miles in twenty-seven hours.

The troops slept on their arms until roused by the fire of artillery on our left about 2 o'clock the next morning, when they promptly fell into line. An officer sent by General *Green* stated to General *Tracy* that General *Green* had sent him to ask at least one regiment and one section of Captain [J. W.] *Johnston's* battery to re-enforce him on the left, strenuously urging that if the left was not sustained the right would be cut off from all chance of retreat, and stating to General *Tracy* that it was General *Green's* opinion that he could not sustain his position on the left fifteen minutes unless re-enforced. General *Tracy* reluctantly ordered the nine companies of the Twenty-third Alabama (then on the field) and two of the four guns of Captain *Johnston's* battery to his relief. This was about sunrise, and before the infantry had become engaged.

The balance of the brigade then on the ground . . . were then placed in the position for battle pointed out by General *Green,* who, as understood, was sent by General *Bowen* to discharge this duty. The battery was placed on the ridge about the center of our line and near some houses. The Thirtieth Alabama was posed on either side of the battery. The left wing of the Twentieth Regiment formed line on their right, stretching out obliquely to the front to a skirt of woods on the east side of the ravine, which is west of the negro houses. Two of the four remaining companies of the Twentieth Regiment were posted at very long intervals, and the other two were deployed as skirmishers to protect our right flank, the distance between the right flank of our little force and Bayou Pierre, which was intended to be protected by these four companies, being not less than 800 yards. The nine companies of the Thirty-first Alabama Regiment were placed in line on Colonel [Charles M.] *Shelley's* left, in a gorge or ravine grown up with reeds, bushes, and some few small trees. The distance between the left flank of this last regiment and the nearest troops on the left was at least 1 mile.

The battle was commenced on the right a little before 7 o'clock in the morning, the enemy first attacking the center of our brigade with artillery and small-arms. The attack was coolly and promptly met by the section of Captain *Johnston's* battery . . . and the Thirtieth Alabama Regiment. The contest here soon became warm and bloody. The battery was in range of the enemy's sharpshooters, and in a short time a number of officers, men, and horses had been killed or wounded.

A little before 8 o'clock our brave and gallant commander, General *Tracy,* fell near the front line, pierced through the breast, and instantly died without uttering a word. The command of the brigade then devolved upon . . . [me], and the fight was continued by our troops with unabated ardor. I knew nothing of the plan of battle except what I had casually learned that morning from General *Tracy.* . . . The enemy was in our front, and I knew of no order to retire. A messenger was immediately sent to the commanding general for instructions, who, on account of the distance to be traveled, did not return until about 11 o'clock, when he brought the order that our position was to be held at all hazards.

In the mean time the fire of the enemy had become much heavier, and the Thirty-first Alabama and the left wing of the Twentieth had become engaged. Skirmishing had also been for some time kept up with the detached companies on the right. Two other pieces of Captain *Johnston's* battery had arrived on the field, and had been ordered to relieve the two which had been placed in position in the morning. Two of the four pieces had by this time been disabled. Lieutenant [Philip] *Peters* and several men had been killed and others had been wounded, and a considerable number of the horses were disabled. Captain *Johnston* had exhibited distinguished gallantry, and his command had bravely stood by their guns; but by 10 o'clock the enemy's fire of artillery and sharpshooters had become so deadly that it seemed impossible for them to remain longer on the field without being sacrificed, and I ordered them to retire, which they did with the only two pieces capable of being carried from the field. The enemy had massed heavy forces in front of our center and of the left wing of the Twentieth Regiment, and they had for some time been receiving a deadly fire. The enemy had even attempted more than once to charge this position in heavy force, but as soon as they emerged from their cover they were repulsed by a deliberate and well-armed fire.

The Forty-sixth Alabama Regiment, belonging to this brigade, after a most exhausting march during the afternoon of the preceding day and night, had arrived on the field by 8 o'clock with about 160 effective men, and formed on the left of the Thirty-first Alabama Regiment.

About 11 o'clock heavy columns of the enemy could be distinctly seen, and it appeared evident that if they could be brought up to make a charge that our slender force would be overwhelmed by vastly superior numbers. The ammunition of the Thirtieth Regiment was now becoming exhausted, and that of the left wing of the Twentieth was growing short. Adjutant [John S.] *Smith*, of the Twentieth Regiment, was then dispatched to Brigadier-General *Bowen* to advise him of our situation, and to ask for instructions and re-enforcements, and that ammunition might be sent us. The general being on a distant part of the field, the adjutant did not return until about 2 o'clock, when he brought the order that our position must be held at all hazards and that re-enforcements would be sent. The enemy had attempted to make, up to this time, several charges on our center, defended by the Thirtieth and left wing of the Twentieth Alabama Regiments, and had been each time heroically repulsed. . . .

Finding that the enemy were advancing in the direction of the skirt of woods to our right and front, Captain [J. McKee] *Gould* and

Lieutenant [J. W.] *Parish,* of the Twentieth Alabama Regiment, with their companies, had been sent forward to prevent their obtaining possession of this wood, and well and bravely did Captain *Gould* and the said companies discharge this duty. Learning after 12 o'clock that these two companies were severely pressed, Captain [R. H.] *Pratt,* of the Twentieth Alabama, with his company, was sent to their support. . . . The enemy's fire on the center not being at all diminished, it became necessary to order one company from the right, which was not so heavily engaged to sustain it. . . . The four companies on the right . . . had resisted all attempts of the enemy to flank us on the right, and after the withdrawal of Captain *Massingale's* company still maintained their ground, but a little after 3 o'clock large bodies of the enemy could be distinctly seen advancing on our slender forces on the right, our center being still heavily pressed.

In the mean time the Sixth Missouri . . . had formed near the left of our brigade, and the Forty-sixth Alabama not yet being engaged, no alternative was left but to be overwhelmed by the masses of the enemy or re-enforce the center and right with that regiment. Five companies were therefore ordered to re-enforce the extreme right, and the other five the center. Colonel [M. L.] *Woods,* being placed in command on the right, this regiment, thus divided, promptly and eagerly advanced to their positions under a galling fire from the enemy. The enemy having now reached the woods near the line on the right, Colonel *Woods,* with half his regiment, was posted at the road a little beyond the gap near the bayou, where embankments furnished good defense against small-arms, and the three companies of the Twentieth Regiment on the right were directed to form there with him, which they promptly did, having retired in good order from their respective former positions, about 200 yards in front of this place. The enemy advanced in great force against this latter position, but Colonel *Woods* and his command bravely met their attack and held them at bay until ordered to retreat. . . .

In order that no means should be spared to resist the advance of the enemy, I sent Adjutant *Smith* to the rear to bring up the two pieces of artillery belonging to Captain *Johnston's* battery, which had been ordered to retire. . . . Adjutant *Smith* found Sergeant [Francis L.] *Obenchain* in command of the two remaining pieces, delivered to him the order, and caused them to be planted on a hill some 600 yards in our rear, and directed that they should be ready for any emergency. Sergeant *Obenchain* . . . promptly brought forward what was left of his command and took position as directed.

Learning . . . that the enemy were about occupying a high hill to the right of our center, from which our men had been driven by an overwhelming force, they were ordered to retire with their commands and take a new and strong position behind the crest of the ridge on which our line of battle had been formed early in the morning so soon as their position became untenable, on account of an enfilade fire of small-arms or artillery. Before this last order was executed, I met Brigadier-General *Green* on the field, explained to him our position, and the orders under which the battle was then raging. He declined to make any change, and stated that he expected to receive an order from General *Bowen* in a short time, and would send it to me. He soon afterward [it being about 5 o'clock] did send an order to retreat by the left flank, which was immediately executed as rapidly as possible.

By this time great numbers of the enemy had advanced into the woods in our front and occupied the high hill before referred to, so that the open ridge over with the Thirtieth and Twentieth Regiments were compelled to pass in falling back was very much exposed to a concentrated fire. . . . Sergeant *Obenchain* and his intrepid comrades, by a cool and skillful fire, greatly assisted in protecting the retreat. . . . The retreat was then conducted in good order some 4 miles over Bayou Pierre and to the ridge on the north side, where the troops went into camp. . . .

Thus for about eleven hours had this most unequal contest continued. Column after column of the enemy had been seen to advance against our line. Several times charges were ordered and attempted, but as soon as the enemy emerged from their cover a deliberate and deadly fire invariably drove them back. . . . There is no doubt that from 12,000 to 15,000 men were engaged during the day with the part of our brigade which took part in this action, while our own number did not exceed 1,400. Our loss was 18 killed, 112 wounded, and 142 missing.[5]

SHAIFER HOUSE

For directions to this site, see Part 2, Phase 3, Stop 3.

Report of Maj. Gen. John A. McClernand, USA (continued)

At 6.15 A.M., when sufficient time had elapsed to allow Osterhaus' first attack to work a diversion in favor of my right, I ordered General Carr to attack the enemy's left. General Benton's brigade promptly moved forward to the right of the main road to Port Gibson. His way lay through woods, ravines, and a light cane-brake; yet he pressed on until he found the enemy drawn up behind the crest of a range of hills intersected by the road. Upon one of these hills, in plain view, stood Magnolia Church. The hostile lines immediately opened on each other, and an obstinate struggle ensued. Meanwhile Stone's brigade moved forward, on and to the left of the road, into an open field, and opened with artillery upon the enemy's left center.

The action was now general, except at the center, where a continuation of fields, extending to the front of my line for more than a mile, separated the antagonists. The enemy had not dared to show himself in these fields, but continued to press my extreme right, with the hope, as I subsequently learned, of crushing it and closing his concave line around me.

General Hovey came up at an opportune moment, and reported his division to be on the ground. I immediately ordered him to form it in two lines near the fork of the two roads, and to hold it there for further orders. About the time it had been thus formed, General Smith's division came up, and General Hovey was ordered to advance his division to the support of General Carr's. In the execution of this order, General McGinnis' brigade moved to the right front, in support of Benton's, encountering the same obstacles that had been overcome by the latter. Colonel Slack's brigade moved by the flank near the main road, and without much difficulty gained its proper position to the left of McGinnis.

During the struggle between Benton's brigade and the enemy, the former had moved to the right to secure its flank, and left a considerable gap between it and Stone's. This gap was immediately closed up by a portion of General Hovey's division upon its arrival upon the ground assigned to it. The enemy's artillery was only 150 yards in front, and was supported by a strong line of infantry, which, it was reported, had just been re-enforced, and was the occasion of the shout of the enemy distinctly heard about this time. . . .

General Hovey ordered a charge, which was most gallantly executed, and resulted in the capture of 400 prisoners, two stand of colors, two 12–pounder howitzers, three caissons, and a considerable quantity of ammunition. A portion of General Carr's division joined in this charge. About this time I heard that Major-General Grant had come up from Bruinsburg, and soon after had

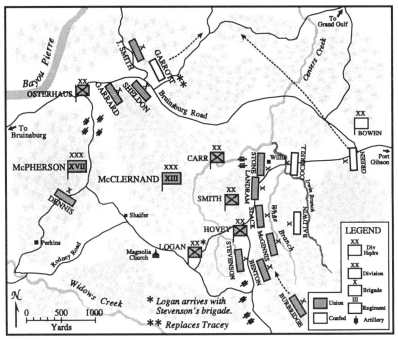

Battle of Port Gibson, late afternoon, May 1, 1863.

the pleasure of meeting him on the field. Determined to press my advantages, I ordered Generals Carr and Hovey to push the enemy with all vigor and celerity. This they did, beating him back over a mile, and frustrating all his endeavors to make an intermediate stand. . . .

General Smith's division came up to Schaiffer's about 7 A.M., and just before General Hovey's moved to the support of General Carr's. The four divisions of my corps were now upon the field, three of them actually engaged. . . . The last immediately moved forward into the fields of Schaiffer's house, and, together with a portion of General Osterhaus's division, held the center, and at the same time formed a reserve.

The second position taken by the enemy on my right front was stronger than the first. It was in a creek bottom [Centers Creek], covered with trees and underbrush, the approach to which was over open fields and ragged and exposed hill-slopes. Having advanced until they had gained a bald ridge overlooking the bottom, Generals Hovey's and Carr's divisions again encountered the enemy's fire. A hot engagement ensued, in the course of which, discovering that the enemy was massing a formidable force on my right front . . . I ordered General Smith to send forward a brigade to support . . . my right flank. Burbridge's brigade rapidly moved forward . . . ; meanwhile General Hovey massed his artillery on the right, and opened a partially enfilading and destructive fire on the enemy. The effect of these combined movements was to force the enemy back upon his center with considerable loss.

Here, with a large concentration of forces, he renewed the attack, directing it against my right center. General Carr met and retaliated it both with infantry and artillery with great vigor. At the same time Landram's brigade, of General Smith's division, re-enforced by a detachment from General Hovey's division, forced its way through cane and underbrush and joined in Carr's attack.

The battle was now transferred from the enemy's left to his center, and after an obstinate struggle he was again beaten back upon the high ridge on the opposite side of the bottom, and within a mile of Port Gibson. General Stevenson's brigade, of General Logan's division, came up in time to assist in consummating this final result. . . .

The battle of Port Gibson, on Bayou Pierre, was one of the most admirably and successfully fought battles in which it has been my lot to participate. . . . If not a decisive battle, it was determinate of the brilliant series of successes that followed. It continued twelve hours, and cost us 803 men killed and wounded.[6]

Report of Brig. Gen. Alvin P. Hovey, USA, Commanding Twelfth Division, Thirteenth Army Corps, Department of the Tennessee

Near 2 o'clock in the morning of May 1, cannonading was heard in our front, which continued for several minutes. The column pressed forward, and at daylight reached [a small tributary of] Center[s] Creek, about 3 miles west of Port Gibson. At this point, at 5:30 A.M., my division was ordered to take position a few hundred yards in advance, upon the right of the road, on the crest of two hills nearly opposite the Shaifer farm-house, at that time the headquarters of Major-General McClernand. The First Brigade [Brig. Gen. G. F. McGinnis] occupied the position in front nearest the enemy's line and at right angles to the road, and the Second Brigade [Col. J. R. Slack] on a similar ridge in the rear of the First. . . . The lines of each brigade were formed under fire from the enemy, who were being engaged by Brigadier-General Benton, to my left and near the center of the line of battle. At this juncture I received orders from Major-General McClernand to hold my division as a reserve until the arrival of the Tenth Division, commanded by Brigadier-General [A. J.] Smith, at which time my whole command was to be in readiness to take part in the action.

On receiving this command I ordered my division to lie down under the cover of the brows of the hills. In less than thirty minutes afterward, General Smith arrived, and the fact was announced to the major-general commanding. In the mean time the brigade under General Benton was engaged in a severe conflict with the enemy upon our left, and gallantly resisting almost overwhelming numbers.

About 7 A.M. an aide from Major-General McClernand came rapidly forward, with orders directing me without the least delay to support General Benton's line. I immediately ordered Brigadier-General McGinnis to march the infantry of the First Brigade in line of battle across a deep and rugged ravine to his support. All concur in describing this ravine as being about 40 rods wide, and filled with vines, cane, deep gulches, and exceedingly difficult of passage. The enemy, no doubt, regarded it as impassable.

As soon as the First Brigade had commenced moving, I ordered the Second Brigade, Colonel Slack commanding, to march by the right flank around the head of the ravine, in support of the forces engaged in the center. They reached their proper position, in line of the division, beyond the ravine, about the same time the left of the First Brigade arrived, the right of the First Brigade being still engaged in working through the tangled vines and underbrush of the ravine. As I rode down the road toward the front and middle of my line, I met Captain Klauss, First Indiana Battery, who had been gallantly fighting the rebel batteries; the field around him and one disabled gun testified to the nature of the conflict. He at once pointed out the position of the rebel battery, the guns of which, with a line of rebel heads in their rear, were plainly visible. I immediately rode down, under cover of the brow of the ravine, to the head of the Second Brigade, where Colonel Slack and Colonel Cameron, of the Thirty-fourth Indiana, were standing. Lieutenant-Colonel Raynor, of the Fifty-sixth Ohio, who had been supporting Captain Klauss' battery, here joined us. Here I attempted to communicate with General McGinnis, who was in the rear of this brigade, but the ground was impassable for my aides on horseback, and my voice could not be heard on account of the noise around him.

I pointed out the battery first to Colonel Cameron, and told him it must be taken. Colonel Slack claimed the honor for his command, but I settled the matter by directing Colonel Cameron, Thirty-fourth Indiana Regiment, to make the charge, and Lieutenant-Colonel Raynor, Fifty-sixth Ohio, to support it. I also directed Colonel Slack to hold his brigade ready to move forward at any instant. The distance of the rebel battery from the point of my attack could not have exceeded 150 yards.

Upon receiving the order to charge, Colonel Cameron commanded his battalion to leap the fence, which, with the Fifty-sixth Ohio, rushed with loud shouts and fixed bayonets, toward the battery. Their advance was met with grape from the rebel battery and a shower of ball from the rebel lines. The fire became intense and concentrated, and both regiments, to shield themselves, fell to the ground, while the fire continued for two or three minutes longer on both sides. At this juncture I gave the command "forward" as loud as I could, and had the gratification of seeing the Thirty-fourth and Fifty-sixth spring to their feet, and, with two companies of the Eleventh Indiana, which I knew by their dress, and several other companies from my division, which I could not then distinguish, rush forward to the charge.

Again the bright bayonets of the Twelfth Division were glittering in the sun; again a wild shout, a shout of triumph, reverberated through the hills. The enemy were beaten back, between 200 and 300 taken prisoner, and 1 stand of colors, 1 12-pounder howitzer, 3 caissons, and 3 six-mule teams, loaded with ammunition, was the reward. . . .

Immediately after the charge . . . several regiments formed on the same ridge in line of battle, and the wildest enthusiasm prevailed as Major-Generals Grant and McClernand rode down our lines. Generals Grant and McClernand commanded me to press the whole line forward immediately and drive the enemy from the field before they could be re-enforced. I gave the command. . . . On reaching the plateau or ridge beyond, our line again received the enemy's fire from a long woody ravine which lay at the base of the ridge. Skirmishers at different points opened a fire upon the enemy for several minutes. Passing through a slight opening in this ravine, Colonel Slack formed the Forty-seventh Indiana and Fifty-sixth Ohio in line of battle and opened fire on the enemy. Being severely pressed, he was subsequently reinforced by the Twenty-fourth Regiment Indiana Volunteers . . . and Twenty-ninth Wisconsin . . . and, after a hot and spirited contest of one hour and a half with about equal numbers, they forced the enemy to retire before them. Here these gallant brigades met with severe loss.

During this contest, and when passing down our lines to the right, I met General McGinnis, who informed me that the enemy were moving on our right, with the probable intention of flanking us. . . . As we passed down the line, my aide . . . discovered a rebel battery moving in the same direction, supported by a large force of infantry, marching partly hidden by the woody ravine. I plainly saw their heavy column advancing. In a few minutes the rebel battery opened on our lines, firing shell and shot from 24 and 12 pounder howitzers. (The shell and shot picked up on the field demonstrated their caliber.) As my infantry were already in close supporting distance, I massed my four batteries on the brow of the ridge, and concentrated their fire into the ravine in the direction of the rebel lines and battery. . . . The fire from my batteries was well directed and continued for over one hour, and drove the rebel battery and infantry from that part of the field.

When the fire from the enemy ceased on the right, General McClernand sent orders to have two regiments move in line of battle from our right through the ravine in which the enemy had been concealed. Colonel Cameron, being on the extreme right at this time, was ordered, in conjunction with one regiment from General Smith's First Brigade, to perform this duty. The length of the ravine was nearly 1 mile, with its width ranging from a few yards to over 100. About equidistant from its ends is a narrow neck, through which the hills and ground beyond are plainly visible. To this neck the regiments . . . marched in line of battle through the ravine, capturing several prisoners. Skirmishers from the Second Brigade continued firing for some time in the upper end of the ravine, above the neck, when the enemy abandoned this part of the field and fled. The firing continued at irregular intervals along the line for some time afterward, but the indications plainly proved that they were only covering a rapid retreat.

Thus ended the battle of Port Gibson, and we slept upon the field 2 miles in advance of the morning's contest.[7]

Report of Brig. Gen. Eugene A. Carr, USA, Commanding Fourteenth Division, Thirteenth Army Corps, Department of the Tennessee

At 1 o'clock on the morning of May 1, my Second Brigade, being in advance, came upon the enemy, strongly posted with artillery, at Magnolia Church, about 12 miles from Bruinsburg and 4 miles from Port Gibson. The enemy opened on the head of the column with artillery, whereupon I formed the brigade in line, brought up the batteries . . . and after firing about two hours drove away and silenced the enemy's guns. In the morning the enemy opened on a road coming in from our left front, when four companies of the Thirty-third Illinois . . . were sent out to check them and hold them at bay till the arrival of General Osterhaus' division, which was assigned to contend with them on that road.

The enemy had returned to his position near Magnolia Church, and at 6:30 in the morning we again attacked him, supported by Hovey's division. I kept the enemy employed with my Second Brigade and the two batteries on the left of and in the road, while I sent the First Brigade, Brig. Gen. William P. Benton commanding, through ravines, canebrake, and timber to the right of the road to press on his left flank. Some of the regiments of General Hovey's division came up, and, with their assistance, the First Brigade charged and routed the enemy, capturing two guns, a stand of colors, some prisoners, and small-arms.

The enemy retreated about 2 miles and took up a new position. In conjunction with the other troops, we pursued and continued fighting him until night, when he retreated across Bayou Pierre, destroying the bridges. . . .

The next day we marched into Port Gibson.[8]

MAGNOLIA CHURCH

For directions to this site, see Part II, Phase 3, Stop 4.

Report of Brig. Gen. Martin E. Green, CSA, Commanding Second Brigade, Bowen's Division, Army of the Mississippi

In the evening of April 29, I received an order from Brigadier-General *Bowen*, commanding, to send a force of 500 beyond Port Gibson, to take position and picket the different roads leading south. I accordingly sent, under command of Colonel [J. E.]

Brig. Gen. Eugene A. Carr, USA, Commander, Fourteenth Division, Thirteenth Army Corps (McClernand). (U.S. Army Military History Institute)

Cravens, that part of his regiment (Twenty-first Arkansas) not on picket, the Fifteenth Arkansas, and Twelfth Battalion Arkansas Infantry (sharpshooters), making in the aggregate a little over 400.

About 1 A.M. on the 30th . . . I received an order from the brigadier-general commanding to proceed at once to Port Gibson and take command of the forces; also stating that the Sixth Mis-sissippi Infantry and Hudson Battery of light artillery would report to me at that place. I accordingly set out for Port Gibson at once, accompanied by my staff, the balance of my brigade being on picket.

Upon reaching Port Gibson, about 3 A.M., I found the command was posted on the Natchez road, about 1½ miles from town. I sent for it and had it marched out on the Rodney road, and took position at the junction of the Rodney and Bruinsburg roads, where I was joined by the Sixth Mississippi and Hudson Battery. After picketing forward on the different roads, I went . . . to reconnoiter the country and choose location for the battle. I went forward several miles examining the different locations, and was best pleased with the one near Union [Magnolia] Church, where the battle was finally fought; but finding the enemy was advancing on both roads, I concluded not to change my position at the junction of the roads until I could get re-enforcements. In the evening General *Bowen* came up and informed me that Brigadier-General *Tracy*, with his brigade, would soon be up. A forward movement was at once decided upon.

General *Bowen* went forward with me and decided to take the position previously selected by myself. General *Bowen* ordered that I should place two or three companies on the Bruinsburg road and the main force on the Rodney road; but after General *Bowen* left me, a scout that I had sent out returned and informed me that the enemy were advancing in force on both roads. This information caused me to change the disposition of the troops, and instead of two or three companies I sent General *Tracy's* entire brigade on the Bruinsburg road, I taking position on the Rodney road near Union [Magnolia] Church, throwing pickets to the front about a mile, and forming my line on the crest of a hill running diagonally across the road, throwing out skirmishers, and ordering the men to sleep on their arms and be ready for action at a moment's warning.

About 12:30 o'clock the pickets were driven in by the enemy. Soon the skirmishers . . . became engaged, and in a few moments a six-gun battery of the enemy opened upon us, to which the Hudson Battery replied, the enemy still continuing to advance slowly. At times the musketry was very warm, extending the whole length of our line. The Hudson Battery, though in very warm place, succeeded in driving the enemy's battery from its position. This, however, was soon replaced by another, which opened upon us with great fury. Our battery replied with signal success, though the enemy's shells and balls fell thick around them, wounding many; yet they stood by their guns and kept up a regular fire. After three hours' hard fighting, the enemy ceased firing and withdrew a short distance, we still holding our position.

At daylight the enemy could be seen reconnoitering in force in every direction, but out of gun-shot range. Between 6 and 7 o'clock the enemy's skirmishers again moved forward and engaged mine. This soon brought on a general engagement by both artillery and infantry. The enemy were pressing heavily upon me, and the ammunition of the Hudson Battery having been expended, I sent to General *Tracy* for re-enforcements. He sent me the Twenty-third Alabama Infantry and a section of *Anderson's* battery (12 pounders). This was about 8:30 o'clock in the morning. The re-enforcements came up under a heavy fire, and took position and fought bravely. We held this position against a force of at least eight to our one, and double our number of pieces of artillery. . . . We were compelled to quit this position about 11 o'clock, the enemy having flanked us with a heavy force on the left. We fell back in order, with but little loss, except the section of *Anderson's* battery. These men had stood manfully to their guns until at least half their number were either killed or wounded, and were compelled to leave their guns for want of teams to bring them off, all their horses except two being killed. As I fell back I met General *Baldwin's* brigade forming on a hill some 1½ miles back. I marched to the rear of General *Baldwin's* brigade, and there received orders to take my command and Colonel [Eugene] *Erwin's* regiment (Sixth Missouri Infantry) to the right wing and re-enforce General *Tracy's* brigade, which I did as speedily as the wearied condition of my men would admit.

On arriving, I found Colonel [I. W.] *Garrott,* in command of *Tracy's* brigade, fighting against greatly superior numbers, and entirely cut off from the balance of the command, and liable to be outflanked at any moment. I threw Colonel *Erwin's* regiment on the left of *Tracy's* brigade, relieving one of Colonel *Garrott's* regiments, which was thrown to the support of his right, and formed my brigade on the left of Colonel *Erwin.* I then ordered them to press the enemy, knowing that unless we could drive him back we must fall back to prevent being cut off, as we were at least 1½ miles in advance of the other portion of the army. Colonel *Erwin* succeeded in driving the enemy in front of him, yet the other portion of the line, although the troops fought hard, could not advance. . . .

I received an order from General *Bowen* to hold my position until near sunset, and by that time, if I could not advance, to retire. Accordingly, after we had fought for some hours in this position, and seeing my right was about being outflanked, and were falling back, I ordered them to face by the left flank and retire from the field, there being a ravine through which we could escape the fire of the enemy. This order, by mistake, was communicated to the right before the left, when it should have been delivered to the left first. I at the same time ordered a section of *Anderson's* battery to open warmly upon the enemy, in order to divert his attention from our movements. This order was obeyed to the letter, and, had it not been for the miscarrying of the order to the infantry, all would have gotten off the field before the enemy could have discovered the move. Colonel Erwin was, however, warmly engaged at the time, and driving the enemy before him, and, not receiving the order in time, came near being surrounded. . . . Colonel *Erwin*, in his advance, recaptured two pieces of artillery that had been captured . . . but the horses having been nearly all killed and he having to fall back at double-quick, was compelled to leave them on the field. . . .

My force when attacked . . . did not exceed 800, and, after being re-enforced by the Twenty-third Alabama, did not exceed 1,100, and with this force I maintained my position against a force of the enemy . . . of at least 7,000 from 12:30 o'clock until about 10:30. My men becoming exhausted, and being outflanked at both flanks, were compelled to fall back. . . . All fought well, and did their duty. All stood at their posts until ordered to leave. . . .

Our loss, without including that of the batteries, Sixth Mississippi, or Twenty-third Alabama, is 222.[9]

Report of Maj. Gen. Ulysses S. Grant, USA, Headquarters, Department of the Tennessee, Commanding

In the morning [2 May] it was found that the enemy had retreated across Bayou Pierre, on the Grand Gulf road, and a brigade of Logan's division was sent to divert his attention, while a floating bridge was being built across Bayou Pierre immediately at Port Gibson. This bridge was completed, 8 miles marched by McPherson's corps to the North Fork of Bayou Pierre, that stream bridged, and the advance of this corps commenced, passing over it at 5 o'clock the following morning. On the 3d, the enemy was pursued to Hankinson's Ferry, with slight skirmishing all day, during which we took quite a number of prisoners, mostly stragglers, from the enemy.

Finding that Grand Gulf had been evacuated, and that the advance of my forces was already 15 miles out from there, and on the road, too, they would have to take to reach either Vicksburg, Jackson, or any intermediate point on the railroad between the two places, I determined not to march them back; but taking a small escort of cavalry, some 15 or 20 men, I went to the Gulf myself, and made the necessary arrangements for changing my base of supplies from Bruinsburg to Grand Gulf.

In moving from Milliken's Bend, the Fifteenth Army Corps, Maj. Gen. W. T. Sherman commanding, was left to be the last to start. To prevent heavy re-enforcements going from Vicksburg to the assistance of the Grand Gulf forces, I directed Sherman to make a demonstration on Haynes' Bluff, and to make all the show possible. From information since received from prisoners captured, this ruse succeeded admirably.[10]

NOTES

1. *O.R.,* XXIV, pt. 1, pp. 48–49.
2. *O.R.,* XXIV, pt. 1, pp. 143–44.
3. *O.R.,* XXIV, pt. 1, pp. 588–89.
4. *O.R.,* XXIV, pt. 1, pp. 663–67.
5. *O.R.,* XXIV, pt. 1, pp. 678–82.
6. *O.R.,* XXIV, pt. 1, pp. 144–46.
7. *O.R.,* XXIV, pt. 1, pp. 601–4.
8. *O.R.,* XXIV, pt. 1, pp. 615–16.
9. *O.R.,* XXIV, pt. 1, pp. 672–74.
10. *O.R.,* XXIV, pt. 1, p. 49.

10. EVOLUTION OF
THE OPERATIONAL PLAN

Summary of Principal Events:
April 6–May 5, 1863

April

16   Passage of the Vicksburg batteries by gunboats and transports.

17–May 2   Grierson's raid.

22   Passage of the Vicksburg and Warrenton batteries by gunboats and transports.

29   Bombardment of Grand Gulf, Mississippi, and passage of the batteries.

29–May 1   Demonstration against Haynes's and Drumgould's Bluffs (Snyder's Mill), Mississippi.

30–May 1   Grant crosses two corps over the Mississippi from Disheroon's plantation to Bruinsburg.

May

1   Battle of Port Gibson.

2   Skirmish on South Fork of Bayou Pierre.

3   Skirmishes on the North Fork of Bayou Pierre, at Willow Springs, Ingraham's Heights, Jones's Cross Roads, Forty Hills, and Hankinson's Ferry, Big Black River, Mississippi.

3   Confederates evacuate Grand Gulf, occupied by Federals.

4   Skirmish at Hankinson's Ferry, Mississippi.

5   Skirmish near Big Sandy Creek, Mississippi.

Grant to Brig. Gen. J. C. Sullivan, Commanding Troops between Milliken's Bend and Smith's Plantation,
May 3, 1863

You will give special attention to the matter of shortening the line of transportation from above Vicksburg to the steamers below.

As soon as the river has fallen sufficiently, you will have a road constructed from Young's point to a landing just below Warrenton, and dispose of your troops accordingly. Everything depends upon the promptitude with which our supplies are forwarded.[1]

Grant to Sherman, Commanding Fifteenth Army Corps, May 3, 1863

My base is now at this place [Grand Gulf], and, in executing your orders for joining me, you will govern yourself accordingly.

I wish you to collect a train of 120 wagons at Milliken's Bend and Perkins' plantation. Send them to Grand Gulf, and there load them with rations, as follows: One hundred thousand pounds of bacon, the balance coffee, sugar, salt, and hard bread. For your own use, on the march from Grand Gulf, you will draw five days' rations, and see that they last five days.

It is unnecessary for me to remind you of the overwhelming importance of celerity in your movements.

On the 1st instant, at 2 A.M., we met the enemy, 11,000 or 12,000 men . . . in a very strong position near Port Gibson, 4 miles south, and engaged them hotly all day, driving them constantly. Our victory was complete. We captured 500 prisoners, four guns, killed General *Tracy* and a large number of the enemy. Our own loss will not exceed 150 killed and 500 wounded. The country is extremely broken, and, therefore, very difficult to operate in.

Yesterday we pushed into Port Gibson by 8 o'clock, to find the enemy gone, and all the bridges across Bayou Pierre destroyed. The bridge was rebuilt, and our troops pushed on to Willow Springs. Found the fine bridge over the north fork of Bayou Pierre destroyed. Repaired it, and by 5 o'clock this morning were in motion again. By 9 we were at Willow Springs, having met the enemy's skirmishers just beyond the bayou. [Brig. Gen. J. A.] Logan is now on the main road from here to Jackson, and McPherson, closely followed by McClernand, on the branch of the same road from Willow Springs.

The enemy is badly beaten, greatly demoralized, and exhausted of ammunition. The road to Vicksburg is open. All we want now are men, ammunition, and hard bread. We can subsist our horses on the country, and obtain considerable supplies for our troops.[2]

Maj. Theodore S. Bowers, Acting Assistant
Adjutant-General, Department of the Tennessee,
to Maj. Gen. Stephen A. Hurlbut, Commanding Sixteenth
Army Corps, Memphis, Tennessee, May 6, 1863

Recent attempts have demonstrated the impossibility of send-ing supplies by the Vicksburg batteries during these moonlight nights. The army is, therefore, dependent upon land transporta-tion for supplies. The distance to be wagoned to a point from which stores can be sent to Grand Gulf by steamboats is 44 miles, and since General Grant has advanced into the interior from Grand Gulf it is feared that, with the present limited land transportation, it will be impossible to keep the army from suffering. The advanc-ing force has only two wagons to a regiment, with which to carry five days' rations, ammunition, and other stores.[3]

Lt. Col. R. Macfeely, Chief Commissar of Subsistence,
to Grant, May 8, 1863

Since the 2d instant [May 2], I have forwarded by wagons to Perkins' plantation and Grand Gulf over 300,000 rations of hard bread, coffee, sugar, and salt, 225,000 rations of salt meat, and 130,000 of soap. The other parts of the ration not being considered essential, only a small amount was sent for issue to hospitals. . . .

I will use every exertion to keep your army supplied. . . . The new road across Young's Point will, I am informed, be placed in good condition in a day or two. There will then be no difficulty in supplying your army. The rations are here, and all that is required are the means of transportation to get them forward.[4]

Grant to Sherman, May 9, 1863

I do not calculate upon the possibility of supplying the army with full rations from Grand Gulf. I know it will be impossible with-out constructing additional roads. What I do expect, however, is to get up what rations of hard bread, coffee, and salt we can, and make the country furnish the balance. We started from Bruinsburg with an average of about two days' rations, and received no more from our own supplies for some days. Abundance was found in the mean time. Some corn meal, bacon, and vegetables were found, and an abundance of beef and mutton.

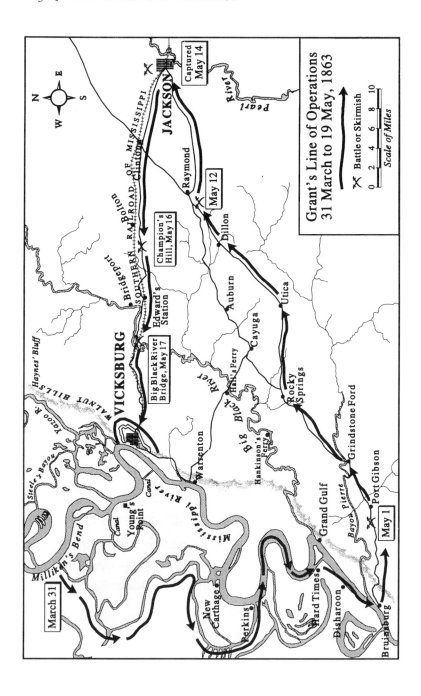

Grant's Line of Operations
31 March to 19 May, 1863

Maj. Gen. Henry W. Halleck, USA, the Union army's general in chief during the Vicksburg campaign. As Lincoln's senior military adviser, he directed field operations from headquarters in Washington. His influence on Grant's Vicksburg campaign was minimal.

A delay would give the enemy time to re-enforce and fortify. If Blair [Maj. Gen. F. P. Blair Jr., commanding Second Division, Fifteenth Corps] were up now, I believe we could be in Vicksburg in seven days. The command here has an average of about three days' rations, which could be made to last that time. You are in a country where the troops have already lived off the people for some days, and may find provisions more scarce, but as we get upon new soil they are more abundant, particularly in corn and cattle.[5]

Henry W. Halleck, General in Chief, to Grant, May 11, 1863

If possible, the forces of yourself and of General Banks should be united between Vicksburg and Port Hudson, so as to attack these places separately with the combined forces. The same thing has been urged upon General Banks.[6]

Report of Maj. Gen. Ulysses S. Grant, USA, Headquarters, Department of the Tennessee, Commanding

It had been my intention, up to the time of crossing the Mississippi River, to collect all my forces at Grand Gulf, and get on hand a good supply of provisions and ordnance stores before moving, and in the mean time to detach an army corps to co-operate with General Banks on Port Hudson, and effect a junction of our forces.

About this time I received letter from General Banks, giving his position west of the Mississippi River, and stating that he could return to Baton Rouge by May 10; that by the reduction of Port Hudson he could join me with 12,000 men.

I learned about the same time that troops were expected at Jackson from the Southern cities, with General *Beauregard* in command. To delay until May 10, and for the reduction of Port Hudson after that, the accession of 12,000 men would not leave me relatively so strong as to move promptly with what I had. Information received from day to day of the movements of the enemy also impelled me to the course pursued.

While lying at Hankinson's Ferry waiting for wagons, supplies, and Sherman's corps, which had come forward in the mean time, demonstrations were made, successfully, I believe, to induce the enemy to think that route and the one by Hall's Ferry, above, were

Maj. Gen. Nathaniel P. Banks, USA, Commander, Department of the Gulf.
(U.S. Army Military History Institute)

objects of much solicitude to me. Reconnaissances were made to the west side of the Big Black to within 6 miles of Warrenton.[7]

Narrative of Maj. Gen. Ulysses S. Grant, USA (continued)

When I reached Grand Gulf May 3d I had not been with my baggage since the 27th of April and consequently had no change of underclothing, no meal except such as I could pick up sometimes at other headquarters, and no tent to cover me. The first thing I did was to get a bath, borrow some fresh underclothing from one of the naval officers and get a good meal on the flag-ship. Then I wrote letters to the general-in-chief informing him of our present position, dispatches to be telegraphed from Cairo, orders to General Sullivan commanding above Vicksburg, and gave orders to all my corps commanders. About twelve o'clock at night I was through with my work and started for Hankinson's ferry, arriving there before daylight.

While at Grand Gulf I heard from Banks, who was on the Red River, and who said that he could not be at Port Hudson before the 10th of May and then with only 15,000 men. Up to this time my intention had been to secure Grand Gulf as a base of supplies, detach McClernand's corps to Banks and co-operate with him in the reduction of Port Hudson.

The news from Banks forced upon me a different plan of campaign. . . . To wait for his co-operation would have detained me at least a month. The reinforcements would not have reached ten thousand men after deducting casualties and necessary river guards at all high points close to the river for over three hundred miles. The enemy would have strengthened his position and been reinforced by more men than Banks could have brought.

I therefore determined to move independently of Banks, cut loose from my base, destroy the rebel force in rear of Vicksburg and invest or capture the city.

Grand Gulf was accordingly given up as a base and the authorities at Washington were notified. I knew well that Halleck's caution would lead him to disapprove of this course; but it was the only one that gave any chance of success. The time it would take to communicate with Washington and get a reply would be so great that I could not be interfered with until it was demonstrated whether my plan was practicable. Even Sherman, who afterwards ignored bases of supplies other than what were afforded by the country while marching through four States of the Confederacy with an army more than twice as large as mine at this time, wrote me from Hankinson's ferry, advising me of the impossibility of supplying our army over a single road. He urged me to "stop all troops till your army is partially supplied with wagons, and then act as quick as possible; for this road will be jammed as sure as life." To this I replied: "I do not calculate upon the possibility of supplying the army with full rations from Grand Gulf. I know it will be impossible without constructing additional roads. What I do expect is to get up what rations of hard bread, coffee and salt we can, and make the country furnish the balance."

We started from Bruinsburg with an average of about two days' rations, and received no more from our own supplies for some days; abundance was found in the meantime. A delay would give the enemy time to reinforce and fortify.

McClernand's and McPherson's commands were kept substantially as they were on the night of the 2d, awaiting supplies sufficient to give them three days' rations in haversacks. Beef, mutton, poultry and forage were found in abundance. Quite a quantity of bacon and molasses was also secured from the country, but bread and coffee could not be obtained in quantity sufficient for all the men. Every plantation, however, had a run of stone, propelled by mule power, to grind corn for the owners and their slaves. All these were kept running while we were stopping, day and night, and when we were marching, during the night, at all plantations covered by the troops. But the product was taken by the troops nearest by, so that the majority of the command had to go without bread until a new base was established on the Yazoo above Vicksburg.

While the troops were awaiting the arrival of rations I ordered reconnoissances made by McClernand and McPherson, with the view of leading the enemy to believe that we intended to cross the Big Black and attack the city at once.

On the 6th Sherman arrived at Grand Gulf and crossed his command that night and the next day. Three days' rations had been brought up from Grand Gulf for the advanced troops and were issued. Orders were given for a forward movement the next day. Sherman was directed to order up Blair, who had been left behind to guard the road from Milliken's Bend to Hard Times with two brigades.

The quartermaster at Young's Point was ordered to send two hundred wagons with Blair, and the commissary was to load them with hard bread, coffee, sugar, salt and one hundred thousand pounds of salt meat.

On the 3d, Hurlbut, who had been left at Memphis, was ordered to send four regiments from his command to Milliken's

Bend to relieve Blair's division, and on the 5th he was ordered to send Lauman's division in addition, the latter to join the army in the field. The four regiments were to be taken from troops near the river so that there would be no delay.[8]

THE CONFEDERATES REACT

Lt. Gen. John C. Pemberton to President Jefferson Davis, May 2, 1863

You know the country about Port Gibson and approaches to Vicksburg and Jackson. General *Bowen,* after maintaining his position below Bayou Pierre until night against overwhelming odds, informed me at 5:30 P.M. that he was compelled to fall back to this side of Bayou Pierre. Telegraphic communications ceased, and have not heard from him since. About 3,500 re-enforcements are *en route* to him; General Loring goes with them.

Enemy is also evidently re-enforcing heavily. I shall concentrate all the troops I can, but distances are great. Unless very large re-enforcements are sent here, I think Port Hudson and Grand Gulf should be evacuated, and the whole force concentrated for defense of Vicksburg and Jackson. It will require at least 6,000 cavalry to prevent heavy raids and to keep railroad communications, on which our supplies depend. Vicksburg and Port Hudson have each about thirty days' subsistence at present. I am holding the country from Snyder's Mill to Bayou Pierre. A large force, which I have no means of meeting, is reported advancing from LaGrange and Corinth.[9]

J. A. Seddon, Secretary of War, to Pemberton, May 2, 1863

Your dispatch received by the President. Heavy re-enforcements will be sent from General Beauregard's command [Department of South Carolina and Georgia]. Will telegraph farther intelligence in the next twenty-four hours.[10]

Gen. Pierce G. T. Beauregard, Department of South Carolina and Georgia, Commanding, to Pemberton, May 5, 1863

I send *Gist's* and *Walker's* brigades (best troops) and two batteries. Keep them together, if practicable, under *Gist;* they will go by Selma and Mobile. Give all assistance possible.[11]

Gen. Joseph E. Johnston to Pemberton, May 2, 1863

Enemy reported falling back. *Forrest* moving west. Cavalry instructed to operate in Mississippi. Let General *Ruggles* communicate with him. If Grant crosses, unite all your troops to beat him. Success will give back what was abandoned to win it.[12]

Pemberton to Brig. Gen. Adams Jackson, May 2, 1863

Arm the 600 exchanged prisoners. Withdraw the guards from Big Black Bridge [*sic*] and other points on Mississippi Central Railroad between Jackson and Grenada, and send them all at once to Vicksburg.[13]

Brig. Gen. John S. Bowen to Pemberton, May 2, 1863

Generals Grant, McClernand, Stevenson, McPherson, Smith and Osterhaus are in Port Gibson. They know of our forces and prospects; they know we expect *Loring* and ammunition.[14]

Pemberton to Commanding Officer or Quartermaster, Edward's Depot, May 2, 1863

Send this dispatch immediately to General *Loring* or *Tilghman;* show it to commander of troops on way if he overtakes them:

General *Bowen* is represented as having fallen back to Grand Gulf, and road is open to enemy. Generals *Loring* and *Tilghman* must be on the lookout for him, and if necessary fall back across Big Black.[15]

Pemberton to Maj. Gen. Simon B. Buckner, Mobile, May 2, 1863

You must assist me in defending Mobile and Ohio Railroad. I have to send all the troops I can raise to aid General *Bowen*.[16]

Buckner to Pemberton, May 2, 1863

I telegraphed you five days ago that all my infantry had been sent to Tennessee; and a few companies of cavalry and an artillery regiment are my only troops to cover Mobile. I will send most of my cavalry to aid [Brig. Gen. A.] *Buford* [at Meridian]. Mobile is now exposed. Should an enemy appear, my orders are to look to you for re-enforcements. I am asking troops from *Beauregard* to guard this point and re-enforce *Loring*.[17]

Brig. Gen. A. Buford to Pemberton, May 2, 1863

Have just received a dispatch . . . stating that . . . the enemy were moving forward in overwhelming numbers. I must have re-enforcements. . . . Have called on citizens to arm themselves.[18]

NOTES

1. *O.R.*, XXIV, pt. 3, p. 268.
2. *O.R.*, XXIV, pt. 3, pp. 268–69.
3. *O.R.*, XXIV, pt. 3, p. 275.
4. *O.R.*, XXIV, pt. 3, pp. 281–82.
5. *O.R.*, XXIV, pt. 3, pp. 285–86.
6. *O.R.*, XXIV, pt. 1, p. 37.
7. *O.R.*, XXIV, pt. 1, pp. 49–50.
8. Ulysses S. Grant, *Personal Memoirs*, 2 vols. (New York: Charles L. Webster, 1885), 1:490–94.
9. *O.R.*, XXIV, pt. 3, pp. 814–15.
10. *O.R.*, XXIV, pt. 3, p. 815.
11. *O.R.*, XIV, p. 926.
12. *O.R.*, XXIV, pt. 3, p. 815.
13. *O.R.*, XXIV, pt. 3, p. 815.
14. *O.R.*, XXIV, pt. 3, p. 815.
15. *O.R.*, XXIV, pt. 3, p. 815.
16. *O.R.*, XXIV, pt. 3, p. 816.
17. *O.R.*, XXIV, pt. 3, p. 817.
18. *O.R.*, XXIV, pt. 3, p. 817.

11. GRANT'S INDIRECT APPROACH

Summary of Principal Events:
May 12–14, 1863

May

12   Engagement at Raymond, Mississippi.
           Skirmish at Greenville, Mississippi.

13   Skirmishes at Mississippi Springs and at Baldwin's and
           Hall's Ferries, Mississippi.

14   Engagement at Jackson, Mississippi.

Report of Maj. Gen. Ulysses S. Grant, USA, Headquarters, Department of the Tennessee, Commanding

On May 7, an advance was ordered, McPherson's corps keeping the road nearest Big Black River, to Rocky Springs, McClernand's corps keeping the ridge road from Willow Springs, and Sherman following with his corps divided on the two roads. All the ferries were closely guarded until our troops were well advanced. It was my intention here to hug the Big Black River as closely as possible, with McClernand's and Sherman's corps, and get them to the railroad at some place between Edwards Station and Bolton. McPherson was to move by way of Utica to Raymond, and from there into Jackson, destroying the railroad, telegraph, public stores, etc., and push west to rejoin the main force.

Orders were given to McPherson accordingly. Sherman was moved forward on the Edwards Station road, crossing Fourteen-Mile creek at Dillon's plantation; McClernand was moved across the same creek farther west, sending one division of his corps by the Baldwin's Ferry road as far as the river. At the crossings of Fourteen-Mile Creek both McClernand and Sherman had considerable skirmishing with the enemy to get possession of the crossings.

McPherson met the enemy near Raymond.[1]

Maj. Gen. James B. McPherson, USA, Commander, Seventeenth Army Corps. (U.S. Army Military History Institute)

Report of Maj. Gen. James B. McPherson, USA, Commanding Seventeenth Army Corps, May 12, 1863

We met the enemy, about 6,000 strong, commanded by Briga-dier-General *Gregg*, at a point 2½ miles west of this place [Raymond], where they were posted and fully prepared to receive us. After a sharp and severe contest of about three hours' duration, in which Major-General Logan's division was chiefly engaged, the enemy were driven back and retreated precipitately, passing out of this town on the Jackson road, Edwards Depot road, and Gallatin road.

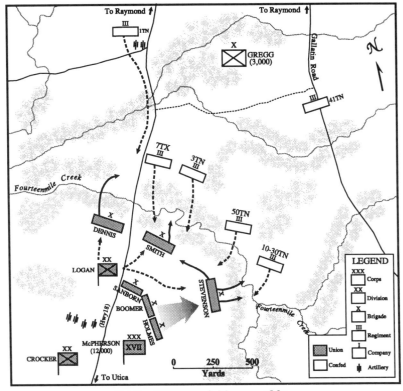

Battle of Raymond, May 12, 1863.

The rough and impracticable nature of the country, filled with ravines and dense undergrowth, prevented anything like an effective use of artillery or a very rapid pursuit. Our loss has been pretty severe in General John E. Smith's and General Dennis' brigades, though I think 250 will cover the total killed, wounded and missing. The loss of the enemy is fully as heavy, if not more so than ours.[2]

BATTLE OF RAYMOND

For directions to this site, see Part II, Phase 3, Stop 5.

Report of Brig. Gen. John E. Smith, USA, Commanding First Brigade, Third [Logan's] Division, Seventeenth Army Corps

[On May 4] in pursuance of orders from Major-General McPherson, I moved toward Grand Gulf, and reached the intersection of the main road from Grand Gulf to Vicksburg, where I received orders to join the division, moving toward Hankinson's Ferry, on the Big Black. I arrived there, after a fatiguing march of 19 miles, at 11 P.M.

Bivouacked near Hankinson's Ferry three days, giving the men ample time to rest and clean themselves, which they needed very much after the severe marches in the heat and dust, which at times was suffocating. Nearly one-third of the command at this time had no shoes, having worn them out on the march, and in consequence were very foot-sore. This, together with their want of supplies, which at times were very short, were subjects of pleasantries with the men, who consoled themselves with the prospect of a fight every other day to make amends for their privations.

In compliance with orders, when about 3 miles from Raymond, about 10 A.M. of the 12th, I formed in line on the right of the road, moving the Thirty-first Illinois by the flank to protect the right of the brigade, and throwing forward to the right and front a heavy line of skirmishers. The enemy's advance were discovered posted in a ravine, protected by the dense timber and undergrowth, and also by a branch of Fourteen-Mile Creek—at times a considerable stream with steep banks—but now with only about 2½ feet of water, and affording an excellent cover for the enemy. With all these advantages of position in his favor, our skirmishers advanced steadily to the attack, the line also advancing as follows: the Twenty-third Indiana on the right, the Forty-fifth Illinois, the One hundred and twenty-fourth Illinois, and the Twentieth Illinois. The Thirty-first Illinois was still marching by the flank on the right through the woods.

The Twenty-third Indiana, being in advance of the line, were suddenly attacked by the unseen foe. Lieutenant-Colonel Davis, finding his command exposed without support, withdrew, and formed on the right of the Twentieth Illinois. The enemy, rushing forward, encountered the Forty-fifth Illinois, thinking they were alone, and attempted to cut them off, but Colonel McCook of the Thirty-first, had, unperceived by the enemy, moved upon their flank and opened fire upon them with such effect that they were driven from the right, and massed their forces in the center, evidently endeavoring to cut through, but here they were opposed by the Twentieth Illinois . . . on the left of the brigade, and the Twentieth Ohio on the right of the Second, who maintained their positions under a galling fire nearly two hours. . . .

The line from the Twentieth Ohio, on the right of the Second Brigade, to my right, now the Thirty-first Illinois, sustained the attack of the whole of the enemy's forces. The line was ordered forward and charged, which they did handsomely, completely routing the enemy, who fled precipitately through Raymond, leaving their dead and wounded on the field. General *Gregg* sent in a verbal request, under a flag of truce, for permission to carry off his wounded, which was not granted. I was now ordered to form column by regiments and move to Raymond as rapidly as possible. Arriving there, we were halted.[3]

Report of Brig. Gen. John D. Stevenson, USA, Commanding Third Brigade, Third Division, Seventh Corps

On the morning of the 12th of May . . . the Third Brigade being in the rear of the column, I received orders to move forward with all possible dispatch, as the enemy were in force in our immediate front. I caused the command to move with alacrity, coming up to the crest of a hill in full view of the field, where, by order of Major-General McPherson, I deployed the command in double lines as a reserve, the Seventh Missouri, Eighty-first Illinois, and Thirty-second Ohio being present, the Eighth Illinois being detailed as rear guard.

I immediately ordered up the Eighth Illinois to the front. The enemy making determined resistance to our advancing lines, and indicating a disposition to flank our right, I was ordered to take position on the right of our line, to check the movement of the enemy. Whilst engaged in executing the command, I received orders from Major-General Logan to send one regiment . . . to take position on the right of the First Brigade. I immediately ordered the Eighty-first Illinois to take position. Soon afterward I received a second order . . . to send to the extreme left another regiment of my command, as the enemy were pressing at that point in force and with great determination. The Eighth Illinois Regiment . . . having arrived on the ground, was immediately sent to the point indicated. I then ordered the Seventh Missouri . . . to take position on the right of the Eighty-first Illinois. I held the Thirty-second Ohio . . . in its original position on the extreme right. Each of these movements was made with skirmishers properly deployed.

On the extreme right, where I was in person, the enemy made a demonstration as if for a flank movement, with a heavy line of skirmishers, which was soon driven back by the skirmishers in front of the Thirty-second Ohio. . . . In the mean time the fight raged with great fierceness on the left and center. The Eighth Illinois . . . charged the advancing line of the enemy . . . and at the point of the bayonet dislodged them from a strong position from which they had poured a most destructive fire upon our lines. Soon the whole line advanced, and the enemy was driven from the position. . . .

The Seventh Missouri . . . failing to unite with the Eighty-first Illinois on the left, advanced through a dense thicket to an open field in front. The regiment, being at the base of a hill held by the enemy, resolutely advanced to take possession of the hill, and, whilst under a most terrific fire, was ordered by the commanding officer to retreat, and retired in great disorder and with heavy loss, the enemy in their front consisting of at least three regiments. Learning that the regiment had broken, I immediately preceded to that part of the field, rallied the regiment, the enemy falling in and forming a new line.

Captain Wiles, of the pioneer corps, having come upon the field with his gallant company and, desiring to share the work and dangers of the field, I placed him with his command on the left of the Seventh Missouri. At this time Major-General McPherson, having strengthened the right with two regiments of General Crocker's division . . . I advanced the entire line on the right, the enemy retiring rapidly before the advancing lines. I pushed my advance until we were in possession of the town of Raymond, the enemy being in full retreat by different roads in the direction of Jackson. . . .

On the night of the 12th we bivouacked in the outskirts of . . . Raymond, and early morning moved toward Jackson . . . bivouacking for the night at Clinton.[4]

Report of Brig. Gen. John Gregg, CSA, Commanding Confederate forces

While in camp 2 miles east of Jackson, Miss., at 3 A.M. on the 11th ... I received a dispatch from the lieutenant-general commanding, directing me to move my brigade promptly to Raymond, and I was directed to use Wirt *Adams'* cavalry, at Raymond, for advanced pickets.

By 5 o'clock the entire brigade was on the march, and at 4 P.M. we were at camp near Raymond. Upon my arrival I found the people in great consternation, being under the impression that the enemy were advancing from Port Gibson. I found none of Colonel *Adams'* cavalry except a single sergeant and 4 men. There was a small State company, under the command of Captain *Hall,* who were, as I was informed, scouting in the direction of Port Gibson. I immediately sent forward Sergeant *Miles* and 4 men to put themselves in communication with Captain *Hall,* and bring me what information of the enemy's movements could be obtained. I also placed strong infantry pickets on the road leading out southwardly and to the west.

In the mean time I had dispatched Colonel *Adams* to move his command to Raymond, unless otherwise ordered by Lieutenant-General *Pemberton,* his command being at Edwards Depot. During the night Captain [W. R.] *Luckett,* with a squadron of 50 men, reported to me and informed me that, having been ordered by Colonel *Adams* to picket the road leading from Raymond to Port Gibson and communicate with me, he had attempted to pass directly from Edwards Depot to the road below, without passing through Raymond, but had met the enemy at Dillon's, 9 miles distant from Raymond, and, being unable to pass, had returned. Fearing that it might be the purpose of the enemy to travel some one of the roads leading northeasterly into the road from Raymond to Jackson, and thus intercept my line of retreat, I ordered Captain [W. S.] *Yerger,* who had now come up and assumed command of the squadron, to picket all these roads, and give me early information of the enemy's movements in that direction.

Early next morning I was informed by couriers from Captain *Hall* that the enemy were advancing rapidly by the road from Utica. Owing to the smallness of the mounted force (Captain *Hall* having but 40 men, and these mostly youths from the neighborhood),

I was unable to ascertain anything concerning the strength of the enemy. A dispatch from the lieutenant-general commanding intimated that the purpose of the enemy was supposed to be an advance upon Edwards Depot, and I inferred from it that it was possible that the force in front of me was a brigade on a marauding excursion. I was strengthened in this opinion by my scouts, who reported that the force they had seen was about 2,500 or 3,000. It was absolutely necessary for me to await their coming, or to fall back without knowing whether the force of the enemy was superior or inferior to my own.

The enemy moved up rapidly, and commenced an artillery fire upon my picket post at 10 o'clock.

In the mean time I had moved the Seventh Texas Regiment . . . to support the picket at the junction of the Port Gibson and Utica roads, and had moved the Fiftieth Tennessee Regiment . . . out on the Lower Gallatin road, and ordered out the Tenth and Thirtieth Tennessee Regiments, consolidated . . . to support it. I also ordered up the Third Tennessee Regiment . . . a half mile out, and placed it in position between the roads.

A single field, dotted with spots of timber, separated the Lower Gallatin and Utica roads, and the main force of the enemy was on the latter road. Finding that I would necessarily be driven into town by his artillery unless I moved up nearer, and believing from the evidence I had that his force was a single brigade, I made my dispositions to capture it. I moved the Fiftieth, Tenth, and Thirtieth Tennessee across a portion of the field into the timber, to fall upon the enemy in rear of his battery, with instructions that they were to approach the enemy as near as possible and wait an attack by our right. I placed Captain [H. M.] *Bledsoe,* with his three pieces of artillery, on the road leading to Utica and Port Gibson, near their junction, directing him to select the most commanding position. Near the artillery I posted the First Tennessee Battalion.

I then ordered up the Third Tennessee into the open field to the right of the Tenth and Thirtieth Tennessee, and the Seventh Texas I moved by the left flank behind some timber to the right of the Third Tennessee. I then sent back an order to the Forty-first Tennessee . . . to move . . . to the position just before occupied by the Third Tennessee. I then ordered forward both the Seventh Texas and Third Tennessee into the timber behind which the enemy battery was posted, the enemy's skirmishers having already been firing upon them from that wood. Skirmishers being advanced, they moved forward in gallant style and hardly lost a man until they entered the timber. The enemy was drawn up in two lines, but both lines were scattered immediately and fell back in a few minutes, but the enemy continued to re-enforce with fresh troops. The firing of musketry was rapid and continuous for more than two hours, and in that time I learned from Colonel *Beaumont* that no attack was made by the Fiftieth because of the immense force which extended back in the wood as far as he could see and because the enemy were advancing a large force on his left flank.

Owing to the failure of the Fiftieth, Tenth, and Thirtieth Tennessee to attack, the enemy were enabled to place a force upon the left flank of the Third Tennessee. I immediately ordered up the Forty-first to relieve the left of the Third Tennessee. Colonel [R.] *Farquharson* moved up in good order and took position promptly. By this time the superior force of the enemy had driven back the Seventh Texas and Third Tennessee, after great loss from both these regiments. Their retreat was protected by the Forty-first Tennessee, and the enemy having moved up on the left of our line . . . and engaged the Tenth, Thirtieth, and Fiftieth Tennessee, the Forty-first also acted as a support to them. . . .

Receiving a dispatch at this time from Colonel *Adams* stating that the enemy had a large supporting force advancing, I ordered all the regiments to withdraw, which was effected in admirable order. Captain *Bledsoe,* with his artillery . . . continued during the whole day to keep back the enemy from advancing either through the open field or by the road, and I have reason to think did great execution among his lines. . . .

The losses . . . were severe. . . . The aggregate of killed in the brigade was 73; wounded, 229, missing, 204. . . . Our aggregate engaged was 2,500.[5]

ENGAGEMENT AT JACKSON, MISSISSIPPI, MAY 14, 1863

Report of Maj. Gen. Ulysses S. Grant, USA (*continued*)

On the night of May 12, after orders had been given for the corps of McClernand and Sherman to march toward the railroad by parallel roads, the former in the direction of Edwards Station and the latter to a point on the railroad between Edwards Station and Bolton, the order was changed, and both were directed to move toward Raymond. This was in consequence of the enemy

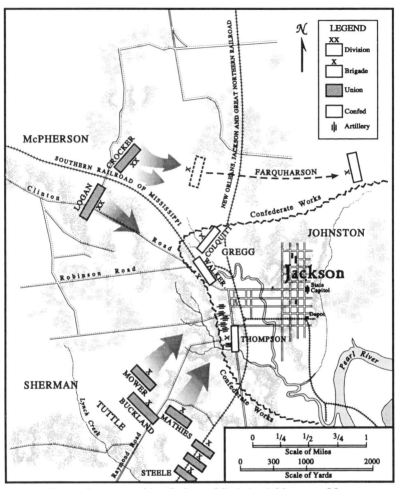

Union forces attacking Jackson, Mississippi, May 14, 1863.

having retreated toward Jackson after his defeat at Raymond, and of information that re-enforcements were daily arriving at Jackson, and that General Joe *Johnston* was hourly expected there to take command in person. I therefore determined to make sure of that place and leave no enemy in my rear.

McPherson moved on the 13th to Clinton, destroyed the railroad and telegraph, and captured some important dispatches from General *Pemberton* to General *Gregg,* who had commanded the day before in the battle of Raymond. Sherman moved to a parallel position on the Mississippi Springs and Jackson road. McClernand moved to a point near Raymond.

The next day Sherman and McPherson moved their entire force toward Jackson. The rain fell in torrents all the night before and continued until about noon of that day, making the roads at first slippery and then miry. Notwithstanding, the troops marched in excellent order, without straggling and in the best of spirits, about 14 miles, and engaged the enemy about 12 m. [noon] near Jackson. McClernand occupied Clinton with one division, Mississippi Springs with another, Raymond with a third, and had his fourth division and Blair's division, of Sherman's corps, with a wagon train, still in the rear near New Auburn, while McArthur, with one brigade of his division, of McPherson's corps, was moving toward Raymond on the Utica road. It was not the intention to move these forces any nearer Jackson, but to have them in a position where they would be in supporting distance if the resistance at Jackson should prove more obstinate than there seemed reason to expect.

The enemy marched out the bulk of his force on the Clinton road, and engaged McPherson's corps about 2½ miles from the city. A small force of artillery and infantry took a strong position in front of Sherman, about the same distance out. By a determined advance of our skirmishers, these latter were soon driven within their rifle-pits, just outside the city. It was impossible to ascertain the strength of the enemy at this part of the line in time to justify an immediate assault; consequently McPherson's two divisions engaged the main bulk of the rebel garrison at Jackson without further aid than the moral support given them by the knowledge the enemy had of a force to the south side of the city and the few infantry and artillery of the enemy posted there to impede Sherman's progress.

Sherman soon discovered the weakness of the enemy by sending a reconnoitering party to his right, which also had the effect of causing the enemy to retreat from this part of his line. A few of the artillerists, however, remained in their places, firing upon Sherman's troops until the last moment, evidently instructed to do so, with the expectation of being captured in the end.

On entering the city it was found that the main body of the enemy had retreated north after a heavy engagement of more than two hours with McPherson's corps, in which he [the enemy] was badly beaten. He was pursued until near night, but without further damage to him.

During that evening I learned that General *Johnston,* as soon as he had satisfied himself that Jackson was to be attacked, had ordered *Pemberton* peremptorily to march out from the direction of Vicksburg and attack our rear. Availing myself of this information, I immediately issued orders to McClernand, and Blair of Sherman's corps, to face their troops toward Bolton, with a view to reaching Edwards Station, marching on different roads converging near Bolton. These troops were admirably located for such a move. McPherson was ordered to retrace his steps early in the morning of the 15th on the Clinton road. Sherman was left in Jackson to destroy the railroads, bridges, factories, workshops, arsenals, and everything valuable for the support of the enemy. This was accomplished in the most effectual manner.[6]

Report of Maj. Gen. William T. Sherman, USA, Fifteenth Army Corps

General Grant . . . was with my column at the time and . . . we heard that the enemy had met General McPherson near Raymond and was defeated.

Next morning we marched to Raymond and passed on to Mississippi Springs, where we surprised a cavalry picket, capturing them; and on the following day, . . . May 14, pushed on to Jackson by the lower road, McPherson's corps following the Clinton road. We communicated during the night so as to arrive at Jackson about the same time.

During the day it rained in torrents, and the roads, which had been very dusty, became equally muddy; but we pushed on, and about 10 A.M. were within 3 miles of Jackson. Then we heard the guns of McPherson to the left, and our cavalry advance reported an enemy to our front, at a small bridge at the foot of the ridge, along which the road we traveled led.

The enemy opened on us briskly with a battery. Hastily reconnoitering the position, I ordered Mower's and Matthies' brigades, of Tuttle's division, to deploy forward to the right and left of the road, and Buckland's to close up. Waterhouse's and Spoor's batteries were placed on commanding ground and soon silenced the enemy's guns, when he retired about half a mile into the skirt of woods in front of the intrenchments at Jackson. Mower's brigade followed him up, and he soon took refuge behind the intrenchments.

The stream, owing to its precipitous banks, could only be passed on the bridge, which the enemy did not attempt to destroy, and forming the troops in similar order beyond the bridge, only that Mower's brigade, from the course he took in following the enemy, occupied the ground to the left of the road and Matthies' brigade to the right, the two batteries in the center, and Buckland's brigade in reserve.

As we emerged from the woods, to our front and as far to the left as we could see, appeared a line of intrenchments, and the enemy kept up a pretty brisk fire with artillery from the points that enfiladed our road. In order to ascertain the nature of the flanks of this line of intrenchments, I directed Captain Pitzman, acting engineer, to take a regiment of the reserve, namely, the Ninety-fifth Ohio, and make a detour to the right to see what was there. While he was gone, Steele's division closed up. About 1 P.M. Captain Pitzman returned, reporting that he had found the enemy's intrenchments abandoned at the point where they crossed the railroad, and he had left the Ninety-fifth Ohio there in possession. I at once ordered General Steele to lead his whole division into Jackson by that route, and as soon as I heard the cheers of his men, Tuttle's division was ordered in by the main road. The enemy's infantry had escaped to the north by the Canton road, but we captured about 250 prisoners with all the enemy's artillery (eighteen guns) with much ammunition and valuable public stores.

Disposing the troops on the outskirts of the town, in obedience to a summons from General Grant, I met him and General McPherson at the hotel near the State-house, and received orders to at once occupy the line of rifle-pits, and on the following day to destroy effectually the railroad tracks in and about Jackson, and all the property belonging to the enemy. Accordingly, on the morning of May 15, Steele's division was set to work to destroy the railroad and property to the south and east, including Pearl River Bridge, and Tuttle's division that to the north and west. This work of destruction was well accomplished, and Jackson, as a railroad center or Government depot of stores and military factories, can be of little use to the enemy for six months.

The railroads were destroyed by burning the ties and warping the iron. I estimate the destruction of the roads 4 miles east of Jackson, 3 south, 3 north, and 10 west.

In Jackson the arsenal buildings, the Government foundry, the gun-carriage establishment, including the carriages for two complete six-gun batteries, stable, carpenter, and paint shops were destroyed. The penitentiary was burned, I think, by some convicts who had been set free by the Confederate authorities; also a very valuable cotton factory. This factory was the property of the Messrs. Greene, who made strong appeals, based on the fact that it gave employment to very many females and poor families, and that, although it had woven cloth for the enemy, its principal use was in weaving cloth for the people; but I decided that machinery of that kind could so easily be converted into hostile uses that the United States could better afford to compensate the Messrs. Greene for their property, and feed the poor families thus thrown out of employment, than to spare the property. I therefore assured all such families if want should force them they might come to the river, where we would feed them till they could find employment or seek refuge in some more peaceful land. Other buildings were destroyed in Jackson by some mischievous soldiers (who could not be detected) which was not justified by the rules of war, including the Catholic church and Confederate hotel—the former resulting from accidental circumstances and the latter from malice.

General Mower occupied the town with his brigade and two companies of cavalry, and maintained as much order as he could among the mass of soldiers and camp-followers that thronged the place during our short stay there; yet many acts of pillage occurred that I regret, arising from the effect of some bad rum found concealed in the stores of the town.[7]

THE CONFEDERATE REACTION

Report of Brig. Gen. John Gregg, CSA, Commanding at Jackson

It being evident that the Federal forces advancing upon Jackson were very large, General [J. E.] *Johnston* instructed me that the city would be evacuated, and that I should take command of the troops and hold the enemy in check until Brig. Gen. John *Adams* should have prepared his train and set out upon our line of retreat—the Canton road.

Pursuant to this, at 3 A.M. I ordered Col. P. H. *Colquitt*, commanding brigade, to move his troops 3 miles toward Clinton, and myself proceeded toward Clinton and instructed him at what point on the road he was to post his command. I also ordered Brigadier-General *Walker* to move his brigade to within easy supporting distance of Colonel *Colquitt*, and remain until it became necessary to render his assistance in order to prevent Colonel *Colquitt's* being forced back.

As a large force of the enemy (since learned to have been Sherman's corps) was approaching by the road from Mississippi Springs, I ordered Colonel [A. P.] *Thompson*, of the Third Kentucky Mounted Infantry, to take position on this road 2 miles from Jackson, and also ordered out to his support the battalion of sharpshooters . . . belonging to Brigadier-General *Walker's* brigade, and Captain [A.] *Martin's* battery, belonging to the same brigade. Colonel [R.] *Farquharson*, commanding the brigade formerly commanded by myself, was ordered to march out on the Clinton road 2½ miles, and thence move by the right flank across the open field toward the Livingston road, and whenever within sight of the enemy make such demonstrations as might impress him with the idea that it was our intention to fall upon his left flank.

At 9 A.M. the enemy came up by the Clinton road and commenced the attack. In a few minutes after, the attack was made by the force on the road from Mississippi Springs. Owing to the well directed fire from Captain [J. A.] *Hoskin's* battery, and the fire of Colonel *Colquitt's* skirmishers, as well, I think, as the fact that Colonel *Farquharson* showed his command in line of battle on the hills to Colonel *Colquitt's* right, the advance of the enemy was very cautious and slow. His movement by the road from Mississippi Springs was retarded in the same spirited manner.

The fighting continued on both roads between the batteries (Captain *Martin's* being well served on the road from Mississippi Springs) and the skirmishers until near 2 o'clock, when I received notice that the trains were already on their way. I immediately ordered the entire force to withdraw, which was done in excellent order, our troops not having permitted the enemy to press them back at any point until the order was given.

The utmost good order prevailed, and during the fight the troops engaged . . . behaved with the most determined coolness and courage. Brigadier-General *Walker's* and Colonel *Colquitt's* commands moved through the streets of Jackson and came into their proper places from the different roads without interference with the movements of each other. Colonel *Thompson*, with his mounted infantry and Captain [T. M.] *Nelson's* company of cavalry, brought up the rear. Colonel *Farquharson,* by my order, proceeded obliquely across from the Clinton to the Canton road and fell into the column at his proper place. . . . I have from reliable sources that the enemy's loss was 400 in killed and wounded. Our loss in killed, wounded, and missing was 200.[8]

Report of Gen. Joseph E. Johnston, CSA, Department of Tennessee

Neither my orders nor my health permitted me to visit Mississippi after March 12, until the time when I took direct charge of that department. From the time of my arrival at Tullahoma until April 14, General *Pemberton's* reports, all by telegraph, indicated that the efforts of the enemy would be against General *Bragg* rather than himself, and looked to the abandonment of his attempts on Vicksburg.

In that of April 13, he says: "I am satisfied Rosecrans will be reenforced from Grant's army. Shall I order troops to Tullahoma?"*

On April 17, General *Pemberton* telegraphed the return of Grant and the resumption of the operations against Vicksburg.

On April 29, he telegraphed: "The enemy is at Hard Times in large force, with barges and transports, indicating a purpose to attack Grand Gulf with a view to Vicksburg." He also reported "heavy firing at Grand Gulf. The enemy shelling our batteries both above and below."

On May 1, he telegraphed; "A furious battle has been going on since daylight just below Port Gibson. . . . Enemy can cross all his army from Hard Times to Bruinsburg. I should have large reinforcements. Enemy's movements threaten Jackson, and, if successful, cut off Vicksburg and Port Hudson."

I at once urged him to concentrate and to attack Grant immediately on his landing, and on the next day I sent the following dispatch to him: "If Grant crosses, unite all your troops to beat him.

---

*Editors' note: In subsequent reports written between *Johnston* and *Pemberton,* they *selectively* quote from one another's messages to justify their respective actions. Each interprets events in a way that reflects most favorably on his own actions to the detriment of the other. The reports from which these telegraph messages are quoted were all written after the fall of Vicksburg. A careful reading of these messages reveals subtle differences which reinforce each commander's interpretation of events, shifting the burden of responsibility—and blame—for the fall of Vicksburg.

Success will give back what was abandoned to win it." I telegraphed to you [J. A. Seddon, Secretary of War] on the 1st: "General Pemberton calls for large re-enforcements. They cannot be sent from here without giving up Tennessee. Can one or two brigades be sent from the east?" On the 7th, I again asked for re-enforcements for Mississippi.

I received no further report of the battle of Port Gibson, and on the 5th asked General *Pemberton,* "What is the result and where is Grant's army?" I received no answer and gained no additional information in relation to either subject until I reached the Department of Mississippi, in obedience to my orders of May 9.

There, on May 13, I received a dispatch from General *Pemberton,* dated Vicksburg, May 12, asking for re-enforcements, as the enemy in large force was moving from the Mississippi south of the Big Black, apparently toward Edwards Depot, "which will be the battle-field if I can forward sufficient force, leaving troops enough to secure the safety of this place."

Before my arrival at Jackson, Grant had beaten General *Bowen* at Port Gibson, made good the landing of his army, occupied Grand Gulf, and was marching upon the Jackson and Vicksburg Railroad.

On reaching Jackson, on the night of May 13, I found there the brigades of *Gregg* and *Walker,* reported at 6,000; learned from General *Gregg* that *Maxey's* brigade was expected to arrive from Port Hudson the next day; that General *Pemberton's* forces, except the garrison of Port Hudson (5,000) and of Vicksburg, were at Edwards Depot, the general's headquarters at Bovina; that four divisions of the enemy, under Sherman, occupied Clinton, 10 miles west of Jackson, between Edwards Depot and ourselves. I was aware that re-enforcements were on their way from the east, and that the advance of those under General *Gist* would probably arrive the next day, and, with *Maxey's* brigade, swell my force to about 11,000.

Upon this information, I sent to General *Pemberton* on the same night (13th) a dispatch, informing him of my arrival and of the occupation of Clinton by a portion of Grant's army; urging the importance of re-establishing communications, and ordering him to come up, if practicable, on Sherman's rear at once, and adding: "To beat such a detachment would be of immense value; the troops here could cooperate; all the strength you can quickly assemble should be brought; time is all-important."

On Thursday, May 14, the enemy advanced by the Raymond and Clinton roads upon Jackson. The resistance made by the brigades of *Gregg* and *Walker* gave sufficient time for the removal of the public stores, and at 2 P.M. we retreated by the Canton road, from which alone we could form a junction with General *Pemberton*. After marching 6 miles the troops encamped.[9]

Report of Lt. Gen. John C. Pemberton, CSA (continued)

The repulse of General *Bowen* at Port Gibson, and our consequent withdrawal to the north bank of the Big Black, rendered it necessary that I should as rapidly as possible concentrate my whole force for the defense of Vicksburg from an attack in the rear by Grant's army, which was hourly swelling its numbers. Orders, therefore, were immediately transmitted to the officers in command at Grenada, Columbus, and Jackson to move all available forces to Vicksburg as rapidly as possible.

On the morning of the 3d, two of the enemy's barges, loaded with hospital and commissary stores, were destroyed in attempting to pass the batteries at Vicksburg.

On the 5th, I telegraphed General *Johnston* that "Six thousand cavalry should be used to keep my communications open, and that the enemy advancing on me was double what I could bring into the field." To the honorable Secretary of War I sent the following telegram . . . [on] May 6: "General *Beauregard* sends but two brigades, perhaps not 5,000 men. This is a very insufficient number. The stake is a great one. I can see nothing so important."

On the 7th, the President notified me that all the assistance in his power to send should be forwarded, and that it was deemed necessary to hold Port Hudson as a means of keeping up our communications with the Trans-Mississippi Department. Major-General *Gardner,* who, with Brigadier-General *Maxey* and 5,000 men, had previously been ordered to Jackson to re-enforce this army, was immediately directed to send *Maxey*'s brigade rapidly forward, and to return himself with 2,000 men to Port Hudson, and hold the place at all hazards.

On the 7th, indications rendered it probable that the enemy would make a raid on Jackson. The staff departments, therefore, and all valuable stores, were ordered to be removed east.

In the mean time my troops were so disposed as to occupy the Warrenton and Hall's Ferry road, which afforded great facilities for concentration; and various positions on the Baldwin's Ferry road, and from thence between Bovina and Edwards Depot, each division being in good supporting distance of the other. Colonel [T. N.] *Waul*, commanding Fort Pemberton, was directed to leave a garrison of 300 men at that place, and proceed with the remainder of his force to Snyder's Mill.

On the 10th, information was received from a scouting party that visited Cayuga and Utica, where the enemy had recently been, that his cavalry force was about 2,000, and that he was supposed to be moving on Vicksburg. My dispositions were made accordingly, and every effort was used to collect all the cavalry possible. Such as could be obtained were placed under the command of Col. Wirt *Adams*, who was directed to harass the enemy on his line of march, cut his communications wherever practicable, patrol the country thoroughly, and to keep Brigadier-General *Gregg* (who had just arrived with his brigade from Port Hudson and was then at Raymond) fully advised of the enemy's movements.

On the 11th, Brig. Gen. John *Adams*, commanding at Jackson, was ordered to hurry forward, as fast as they could arrive, the troops from South Carolina, to re-enforce Brigadier-General *Gregg* at Raymond. At this time information was received from Brigadier-General *Tilghman* that the enemy was in force opposite Baldwin's Ferry, and *Gregg* was notified accordingly, and informed that the enemy's movements were apparently toward the Big Black Bridge, and not, as had been supposed, against Jackson.

On the 12th, the following was addressed to Major-General *Stevenson:*

> From information received, it is evident the enemy is advancing in force on Edwards Depot and Big Black Bridge; hot skirmishing has been going on all the morning, and the enemy are at Fourteen-Mile Creek. You must move up with your whole division to the support of *Loring* and *Bowen* at the bridge, leaving *Baldwin's* and *Moore's* brigades to protect your right.

In consequence of this formation, Brigadier-General *Gregg* was ordered not to attack the enemy until he was engaged at Edwards or the bridge, but to be ready to fall on his rear or flank at any moment, and to be particularly cautious not to allow himself to be flanked or taken in the rear. Thus it will be seen that every measure had been taken to protect Edwards Depot and Big Black Bridge, and, by offering or accepting battle, to endeavor to preserve my communications with the east.

At this juncture, however, the battle of Raymond was fought by a large body of the enemy's forces and one brigade of our troops under the command of Brigadier-General *Gregg*. I have received no official report of that affair, and hence cannot say how it was fought or by whom the engagement was brought on. . . . The command was withdrawn in good order, and retired to Jackson. . . .

On the 12th, the following telegram was sent to General J. E. *Johnston:*

> The enemy is apparently moving his heavy force toward Edwards Depot, on the Southern Railroad; with my limited force I will do all I can to meet him. That will be the battle-field if I can carry forward sufficient force, leaving troops enough to secure the safety of . . . Vicksburg. Re-enforcements are arriving very slowly, only 1,500 having arrived as yet. I urgently ask that more be sent; also that 3,000 cavalry be at once sent to operate on this line. I urge this as a positive necessity. The enemy largely outnumber me, and I am obliged to hold back a large force at the ferries on Big Black lest he cross and take this place. I am also compelled to keep considerable force on either flank of Vicksburg out of supporting distance.

On the evening of the 12th I moved my headquarters to Bovina, to be nearer the scene of active operations. The command arrived at Edwards Depot on the 13th, and was placed in position, covering all the approaches from the south and east, in the following order: *Bowen* on the right, *Loring* in the center, and *Stevenson* on the left. This position was occupied from the night of the 13th until the morning of the 15th.

On the 13th, the following dispatch was sent to General *Johnston:*

> General *Forney* reports from Vicksburg this morning four transports loaded with troops arrived at Young's Point this morning. Five regiments and a battery passed down by Brown and Johnston's. Wagon trains continue to pass back and forth. My re-enforcements will be very small and arrive very slowly. If possible, Port Hudson should also be re-enforced. I have been forced to draw largely from there. I have no major-general to command brigades arriving in Jackson. I am in position with eight brigades near Edwards Depot.

On the morning of the 14th, while on my way to Edwards Depot from Bovina, I received the following dispatch, dated May 13, from General *Johnston,* then at Jackson.

I have lately arrived, and learn that Major-General Sherman is between us, with four divisions at Clinton. It is important to re-establish communications that you may be reenforced. if practicable, come up in his rear at once. To beat such a detachment would be of immense value. The troops here could co-operate. All the strength you can quickly assemble should be brought. Time is all-important.

I immediately replied. . . .

I move at once with whole available force (about 16,000) from Edwards Depot, leaving *Vaughn's* brigade (about 1,500) at Big Black Bridge. *Tilghman's* brigade (1,500), now at Baldwin's Ferry, I have ordered to bring up the rear of my column; he will be, however, from 15 to 20 miles behind it. Baldwin's Ferry will be left necessarily unprotected. To hold Vicksburg are *Smith's* and *Forney's* divisions, extending from Snyder's Mill to Warrenton, numbering 7,500 men. The men have been marching several days, are much fatigued, and I fear will straggle very much. In directing this move, I do not think you fully comprehend the position that Vicksburg will be left in, but I comply at once with your order.

The "detachment" General *Johnston* speaks of in his communication consisted of four divisions of the enemy, constituting an entire army corps, numerically greater than my whole available force in the field; besides, the enemy had at least an equal force to the south, on my right flank, which would be nearer to Vicksburg than myself in case I should make the movement proposed. I had, moreover, positive information that he [the enemy] was daily increasing his strength. I also learned on reaching Edwards Depot that one division of the enemy (A. J. Smith's) was at or near Dillon's. This confirmed me in the opinion, previously expressed, that the movement indicated by General *Johnston* was extremely hazardous.

I accordingly called a council of war of all the general officers present, and placing the subject before them (including General *Johnston's* dispatch) in every view in which it appeared to me, asked their opinions respectively. A majority . . . expressed themselves favorable to the movement indicated by General *Johnston*. The others, including Major-Generals *Loring* and *Stevenson,* preferred a movement by which the army might attempt to cut off the enemy's supplies from the Mississippi River. My own views were strongly expressed as unfavorable to any advance which would separate me farther from Vicksburg, which was my base. I did not, however, see fit to put my own judgment and opinions so far in opposition as to prevent a movement altogether, but believing the only possibility of success to be in the plan of cutting the enemy's communications, it was adopted, and the following dispatch was addressed to General *Johnston.*

> Edwards Depot, May 14, 1863
>
> I shall move as early to-morrow morning as practicable with a column of 17,000 men to Dillon's, situated on the main road leading from Raymond to Port Gibson, 7½ miles below Raymond and 9½ miles from Edwards Depot. The object is to cut the enemy's communications and to force him to attack me, as I do not consider my force sufficient to justify an attack on the enemy in position or to attempt to cut my way to Jackson. At this point your nearest communication would be through Raymond. I wish very much I could join my re-enforcements.
>
> Whether it will be most practicable for the re-enforcements to come by Raymond (leaving it to the right if the march cannot be made through Raymond) or to move them west along the line of railroad (leaving it to the left and south of the line of march) to Bolton Depot, or some other point west of it, you must determine. In either movement I should be advised as to the time and road, so that co-operation may be had to enable the re-enforcements to come through. I send you a map of the country, which will furnish you with a correct view of the roads and localities. . . .

A continuous and heavy rain had made Baker's Creek impassable by the ordinary ford on the main Raymond road, where the country bridge had been washed away by previous freshets. In consequence of this the march was delayed for several hours, but the water not falling sufficiently to make the creek fordable, the column was directed by the Clinton road, on which there was a good bridge, and, after passing the creek upward of 1½ miles, was filed to the right along a neighborhood road so as to strike the Raymond road about 3½ miles from Edwards Depot. The march was continued until the head of the column had passed Mrs. Elliston's house, where it was halted, and the troops bivouacked in order of march. I made my headquarters at Mrs. Elliston's, where I found Major-General *Loring* had also established his.

The divisions of Generals *Stevenson* and *Bowen* having been on the march until past midnight, and the men considerably fatigued—desiring also to receive reports of reconnaissances made in my front before preceding farther—I did not issue orders to continue the movement at an early hour the following morning.

Immediately on my arrival at Mrs. Elliston's on the night of the 15th, I sent for Col. Wirt *Adams,* commanding the cavalry, and gave him the necessary instructions for picketing all approaches in my front, and directed him to send out scouting parties to discover the enemy's whereabouts. I also made strenuous efforts to effect the same object through citizens, but without success. . . .

On the morning of the 16th, at about 6:30 o'clock, Colonel Wirt *Adams* reported to me that his pickets were skirmishing with the enemy on the Raymond road some distance in our front. While in conversation with him, a courier arrived and handed me the following dispatch from General *Johnston:*

> Our being compelled to leave Jackson makes your plan impracticable. The only mode by which we can unite is by your moving directly to Clinton, informing me, that we may move to that point with about 6,000 troops. I have no means of estimating enemy's force at Jackson. The principal officers here differ very widely, and I fear he will fortify if time is left him. Let me hear from you immediately. General *Maxey* was ordered back to Brookhaven. You probably have time to make him join you. Do so before he has time to move away.

I immediately directed a countermarch . . . for the purpose of returning to Edwards Depot to take the Brownsville road, and thence to proceed toward Clinton by a route north of the railroad. A written reply to General *Johnston*'s instructions, in which I notified him . . . of the route I should take, was dispatched in haste. . . .

Just as this reverse movement commenced, the enemy drove in Colonel *Adams'* cavalry pickets, and opened with artillery at long range on the head of my column on the Raymond road. Not knowing whether this was an attack in force or simply an armed recon-naissance . . . I directed the continuance of the movement, giving the necessary instructions for securing the safety of the wagon train. The demonstrations of the enemy soon becoming more serious, orders were sent to division commanders to form in line of battle.[10]

NOTES

1. *O.R.*, XXIV, pt. 1, p. 50.
2. *O.R.*, XXIV, pt. 1, p. 704.
3. *O.R.*, XXIV, pt. 1, pp. 707–8.
4. *O.R.*, XXIV, pt. 1, pp. 716–17.
5. *O.R.*, XXIV, pt. 1, pp. 737–38.
6. *O.R.*, XXIV, pt. 1, pp. 50–51.
7. *O.R.*, XXIV, pt. 1, pp. 753–54.
8. *O.R.*, XXIV, pt. 1, pp. 785–86.
9. *O.R.*, XXIV, pt. 1, pp. 238–41.
10. *O.R.*, XXIV, pt. 1, pp. 259–63.

12. THE BATTLE OF CHAMPION HILL

Summary of Principal Events:
May 12–16, 1863

May

12   Engagement at Raymond, Mississippi.

14   Engagement at Jackson, Mississippi.

15   Advance of Union forces to Clinton, Mississippi.

16   Battle of Champion Hill.

Report of Maj. Gen. Ulysses S. Grant, USA, Headquarters,
Department of the Tennessee, Commanding

On the afternoon of the 15th, I proceeded as far west as
Clinton. . . . On reaching Clinton, at 4.45 P.M., I ordered
McClernand to move his command early the next morning toward
Edwards Depot, marching so as to feel the enemy if he encountered him, but not to bring on a general engagement unless he
was confident he was able to defeat him; and also to order Blair
[commanding Second Division, Fifteenth Army Corps] to move
with him.

About 5 o'clock on the morning of the 16th, two men, em-
ployes [*sic*] on the Jackson and Vicksburg Railroad, who had passed
through *Pemberton's* army the night before, were brought to my
headquarters. They stated *Pemberton's* force to consist of about
eighty regiments, with ten batteries of artillery, and that the whole
force was estimated by the enemy at about 25,000 men. From them
I also learned the positions being taken up by the enemy, and his
intention of attacking our rear.

I had determined to leave one division of Sherman's corps one
day longer in Jackson, but this information determined me to bring
his entire command up at once, and I accordingly dispatched him
at 5:30 A.M. to move with all possible speed until he came up with

the main force near Bolton. My dispatch reached him at 7:10 A.M., and his advance division was in motion in one hour from that time. A dispatch was sent to Blair at the same time to push forward his division in the direction of Edwards Station with all possible dispatch. McClernand was directed to establish communication between Blair and Osterhaus, of his corps, and keep it up, moving the former to the support of the latter. McPherson was ordered forward at 5:45 A.M. to join McClernand, and Lieutenant-Colonel Wilson, of my staff, was sent forward to communicate the information received, and with verbal instructions to McClernand as to the disposition of his forces.

At an early hour I left for the advance, and, on arriving at the crossing of the Vicksburg and Jackson Railroad with the road from Raymond to Bolton, I found McPherson's advance and his pioneer corps engaged in rebuilding a bridge on the former road that had been destroyed by the cavalry of Osterhaus' division that had gone into Bolton the night before. The train of Hovey's division was at a halt, and blocked up the road from farther advance on the Vicksburg road. I ordered all quartermasters and wagon-masters to draw their teams to one side and make room for the passage of troops. McPherson was brought up by this road.

Passing to the front, I found Hovey's division, of the Thirteenth Army Corps, at a halt, with our skirmishers and the enemy's pickets near each other. Hovey was bringing his troops into line ready for battle, and could have brought on an engagement at any moment. The enemy had taken up a very strong position on a narrow ridge, his left resting on a height where the road makes a sharp turn to the left, approaching Vicksburg. The top of the ridge and the precipitous hillside to the left of the road are covered by a dense forest and undergrowth. To the right of the road the timber extends a short distance down the hill, and then opens into cultivated fields on a gentle slope and into a valley, extending for a considerable distance. On the road and into the wooded ravine and hillside Hovey's division was disposed for the attack. McPherson's two divisions—all of his corps with him . . . —were thrown to the right of the road (properly speaking, the enemy's rear), but I would not permit an attack to be commenced by our troops until I could hear from McClernand, who was advancing with four divisions, two of them on a road intersecting the Jackson road about 1 mile from where the troops above described were placed, and about the center of the enemy's

Brig. Gen. Alvin P. Hovey, USA, Commander, Twelfth Division, Thirteenth Army Corps (McClernand). (U.S. Army Military History Institute)

line; the other two divisions on a road still [farther] north, and nearly the same distance off.

I soon heard from McClernand through members of his staff and my own, whom I had sent to him early in the morning, and found that by the nearest practicable route of communication he was 2½ miles distant. I sent several successive messages to him to push forward with all rapidity. There had been continuous firing between Hovey's skirmishers and the rebel advance, which by 11 o'clock had grown into a battle. For some time this division bore the brunt of the conflict; but finding the enemy too strong for them, at the instance of Hovey, I directed first one and then a second brigade from Crocker's division to re-enforce him.

All this time Logan's division was working upon the enemy's left and rear, and weakened his front attack most wonderfully. The troops here opposing us evidently far outnumbered ours. Expecting McClernand momentarily with four divisions, including Blair's, I never felt a doubt of the result. He did not arrive, however, until the enemy had been driven from the field, after a terrible contest of hours, with a heavy loss of killed, wounded, and prisoners, and a number of pieces of artillery.

It was found afterward that the Vicksburg road, after following the ridge in a southerly direction for about 1 mile, and to where it intersected one of the Raymond roads, turns almost to the west, down the hill and across the valley in which Logan was operating on the rear of the enemy. One brigade of Logan's division had, unconscious of this important fact, penetrated nearly to this road, and compelled the enemy to retreat to prevent capture. As it was, much of his artillery and *Loring's* division of his army were cut off, besides the prisoners captured.

On the call of Hovey for more re-enforcements just before the rout of the enemy commenced, I ordered McPherson to move what troops he could by a left flank around to the enemy's front. Logan rode up at this time, and told me that if Hovey could make another dash at the enemy, he could come up from where he then was and capture the greater part of their force. I immediately rode forward and found the troops that had been so gallantly engaged for so many hours were withdrawn from their advanced position, and were filling their cartridge boxes. I directed them to use all dispatch, and push forward as soon as possible, explaining to them the position of Logan's division. Proceeding still farther forward, expecting every moment to see the enemy, and reaching what had been his line, I found he was retreating.

Arriving at the Raymond road, I saw to my left and on the next ridge a column of troops, which proved to be Carr's division, and McClernand with it in person; and to the left of Carr, Osterhaus' division soon afterward appeared, with his skirmishers well in advance. I sent word to Osterhaus that the enemy was in full retreat and to push up with all haste. The situation was soon explained, after which I ordered Carr to pursue with all speed to Black River, and cross it if he could and to Osterhaus to follow. Some of McPherson's troops had already got into the road in advance; but having marched and engaged the enemy all day, they were fatigued and gave the road to Carr, who continued the pursuit until after dark, capturing a train of cars loaded with commissary and ordnance stores and other property. . . .

The battle of Champion's Hill, or Baker's Creek, was fought mainly by Hovey's division, of McClernand's corps, and Logan's and Quinby's division (the latter commanded by Brig. Gen. M. M. Crocker), of McPherson's corps.[1]

ACTIONS ON THE UNION RIGHT—CHAMPION HILL

For directions to this site, see Part II, Phase 3, Stop 6.

Report of Maj. Gen. John A. McClernand, USA, Commanding Thirteenth Army Corps

During the evening of the 15th [May], I received a dispatch from Major General Grant, advising me that the entire force of the enemy at Vicksburg had probably crossed the Big Black and taken position at Edwards Station, and ordering me to feel the enemy without bringing on a general engagement, and to notify General Blair what to do. . . . Orders were issued to commanders of divisions to move forward on the following morning.

General Smith moved forward on the southern [Raymond to Edwards] road at 5 A.M. on the 16th, followed and supported by General Blair; General Osterhaus on the middle [Billy Fields] road at 6 o'clock, followed and supported by General Carr, and General Hovey at the same hour on the northern [Champion Hill] road. The starting of different divisions at different hours was in consequence of the difference in the distances they had to march, and was designed to secure a parallel advance of the different columns. Each division was instructed to keep up communication with . . . those next to it.

Believing that General Hovey's division needed support, I sent a dispatch on the 15th to Major-General Grant, requesting that General McPherson's corps, then arrived in rear of General Hovey, should also move forward, and early on the morning of the 16th I rode over to General McPherson's headquarters and suggested the same thing, urging, among other things, that if his corps should not be needed as a support, it might, in the event I should beat the enemy, fall upon his flank and rear and cut him off. Assurances altogether satisfactory were given by the general, and I felt confi-

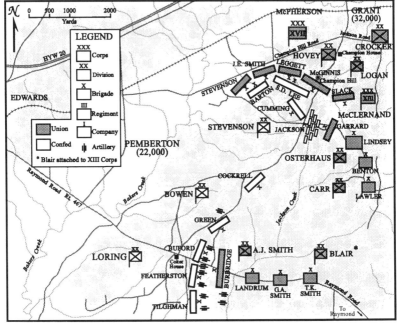

Battle of Champion Hill, midmorning, May 16, 1863.

dent of our superiority on the right. I went forward with the center, formed by Osterhaus and Carr.

At 7:30 A.M., when my whole line had approached within some 5 miles of Edwards Station, General Smith's division, on my left, encountered the enemy's skirmishers, who retired. A half mile farther on they encountered the fire of the enemy's artillery, which was briskly replied to until it ceased.

At the moment these demonstrations commenced, there was strong reason to believe (corroborated by subsequent information) that the enemy was moving in large force on the Raymond road, with the hope of turning my left flank and gaining my rear; but the sudden appearance of my forces in that direction foiled the design and threw his right back in some confusion toward his center and left.

Hearing the report of artillery on the left, General Osterhaus pushed forward through a broad field to a thick wood, which covered a seeming chaos of abrupt hills and yawning ravines. From the skirt of this wood he drove a line of skirmishers, and, continuing his advance until he discovered the enemy in strong force, commenced feeling him. Early notifying Major-Generals Grant and McPherson of what had transpired on the left, I requested the latter to co-operate with my forces on the right, and directed General Hovey to advance promptly but carefully.

At 9:45 A.M. I received a dispatch from General Hovey, informing me that he had found the enemy strongly posted in front; that General McPherson's corps was behind him, that his right flank would probably encounter severe resistance, and inquiring whether he should bring on the impending battle.

My whole command was not about 4 miles from Edwards Station, and immediately informing Major-General Grant, whom I understood to be on the field, of the position of affairs, I inquired whether General McPherson could not move forward to the support of General Hovey, and whether I should bring on a general engagement. A dispatch from the general, dated 12:35 P.M., came, directing me to throw forward skirmishers as soon as my forces were in hand; to feel and attack the enemy in force, if opportunity occurred and informing me that he was with Hovey and McPherson, and would see that they fully cooperated.

Meanwhile, a line of skirmishers had connected Generals Osterhaus' and Smith's divisions, closing up the narrow space between them. General Blair had moved a brigade farther to the right, to support the skirmishers and the proximate flanks of Osterhaus and Smith. General Ransom's brigade, of the Seventeenth Army Corps, had been ordered to hasten up from the neighborhood of Raymond, and skirmishing along my left and center, particularly the latter, was quite brisk.

These measures in part had been taken in compliance with Major-General Grant's orders, based on information, of which he had advised me, that the enemy was in greatest strength in front of my center and left, and might turn my left flank and gain my rear. This doubtless . . . had been the tendency of the enemy early in the morning, but had been counteracted by General Smith's operations. Later information was brought by an aide-de-camp of General Smith, and communicated by me to Major-General Grant, of the absence at that time of the danger he apprehended.

Instantly upon the receipt of Major-General Grant's order to attack, I hastened to do so, ordering Generals Smith and Osterhaus to "attack the enemy vigorously and press for victory," General Blair to support the former and General Carr the latter, holding Lawler's brigade in reserve.

At 10 A.M. General Hovey resumed his advance, and, approaching in plain view of the enemy, disposed his forces for battle along a skirt of wood and across the road of his approach. General McGinnis' brigade was formed on the right, and Colonel Slack's on the left. General Logan's division, of General McPherson's corps, was between the railroad and my right, and about half a mile from the latter.[2]

Report of Brig. Gen. Alvin P. Hovey, USA, Commanding Twelfth Division, Thirteenth Army Corps

During the morning I had thrown forward a part of my escort, under First Lieut. James L. Carey, First Indiana Cavalry, to make reconnaissances in front of the advance guard and skirmishers of General McGinnis' brigade. On arriving near Champion's Hill, about 10 A.M., he discovered the enemy posted on the crest of the hill, with a battery of four guns in the woods near the road, and on the highest point for many miles around. At the time I was marching between the First and Second Brigades, so as to be ready for an attack on either flank. I immediately rode forward and ordered General McGinnis to form his brigade in two lines, three regiments being in advance and two in the reserve. Before my arrival, General McGinnis had formed his three advanced regiments in line of battle, and had thrown out skirmishers in the front and flank of his command.

The second Brigade, Col. James R. Slack, commanding, was immediately formed on the left of the First Brigade, two regiments in advance and two in reserve. Skirmishers were at once sent forward, covering my entire front, and had advanced to within sight of the enemy's battery. They were directed not to bring on the action until we were entirely ready.

At this point I attempted to communicate with Brigadier-General Osterhaus, but my messengers, not knowing the country nor his exact locality, were unable to find his division. In the mean time Major General Grant had arrived, and with him Major-General McPherson with his command.

Before proceeding further, it is necessary that the topography of the field should be described. Midway, or Champion's Hill, is equidistant from Jackson and Vicksburg, and is near the Midway

Station, on the Vicksburg and Jackson Railroad. It is a high promontory, some 60 or 70 feet above the common level of the country, and covered with woods, the Vicksburg and Clinton road
leading over the crest. To the right and northwest of this hill are
undulating fields, and on the left a woody tangled ravine, through
which troops might pass with great difficulty.

About half a mile from this point of the hill General McPherson formed his line of battle in the open field, facing toward the
side of the hill, a distance from the hill of about 400 yards, his front
and the main front of my division being nearly at right angles. As
my division ascended the hill, its line conformed to the shape and
became crescent-like, with the concave toward the hill.

As soon as General McPherson's line was ready . . . about 10:30
A.M., I ordered General McGinnis and Colonel Slack to press their
skirmishers forward up the hill, and follow them firmly with their
respective brigades. In a few minutes the fire opened briskly along
the whole line, from my extreme left to the right of the forces
engaged under Major-General McPherson, and at 11 o'clock the
battle opened hotly all along the line.

The contest here continued for an hour by my forces. For over
600 yards up the hill my division gallantly drove the enemy . . .
capturing 11 guns and over 300 prisoners, under fire. The Eleventh Indiana . . . and Twenty-ninth Wisconsin . . . captured the four
guns on the brow of the hill, at the point of the bayonet. Colonel
Bringhurst with the Forty-sixth Indiana gallantly drove the enemy
from two guns on the right of the Road, and Colonel Byam, with
his brave and eager Twenty-fourth Iowa, charged a battery of five
guns on the left of the road, driving the enemy away, killing gunners and horses and capturing several prisoners. At this time General McGinnis requested me to permit him to take one section of
the Sixteenth Ohio Battery . . . up the hill. The section was taken
up, and after . . . firing 16 rounds was withdrawn, the danger of
capture being imminent. . . .

In the mean time the enemy, being rallied under cover of the
woods, poured down the road in great numbers upon the position
occupied by my forces. Seeing from the character of the ground
that my division was likely to be severely pressed, as the enemy
would not dare advance on the open ground before General
McPherson, who had handled them roughly on the right, I ordered
our captured guns to be sent down the hill. A short time afterward
I received a request to send support to General McGinnis, on the

right. At this time my whole division, including reserves, had for more than one hour been actively engaged, and my only hope of support was from other commands. Brigadier-General Quinby's division, commanded by General Crocker, was near at hand, and had not yet been under fire. I sent to them for support, but being unknown to the officers of that command, considerable delay (not less than half an hour) ensued, and I was compelled to resort to Major General Grant to procure the order for their aid. Colonel Boomer, commanding Third Brigade, of Quinby's division, on receiving the command from General Grant, came gallantly up the hill; Colonel Holmes, with two small regiments . . . soon followed. The entire force sent amounted to about 2,000 men.

My division in the mean time had been compelled to yield ground before overwhelming numbers. Slowly and stubbornly they fell back, contesting with death every inch of the field they had won. Colonel Boomer and Colonel Holmes gallantly and heroically rushed with their commands into the conflict, but the enemy had massed his forces, and slowly pressed our whole line with re-enforcements backward to a point near the brow of the hill. Here a stubborn stand was made.

The irregularity of our line of battle had previously prevented me from using artillery in enfilading the enemy's line, but as our forces were compelled to fall slowly back, the lines became marked and distinct, and about 2:30 P.M. I could easily perceive, by the sound of fire-arms and through the woods, the position of the respective armies. I at once ordered the First Missouri Battery . . . and the Sixteenth Ohio Battery . . . to take position in an open field, beyond a slight mound on my right, in advance of, and with parallel ranges of their guns with, my lines. About the same time Captain Dillon's Wisconsin battery was put in position. . . . Through the rebel ranks these batteries hurled an incessant shower of shot and shell, entirely enfilading the rebel columns.

The fire was terrific for several minutes, and the cheers from our men on the brow of the hill told of the success. The enemy gave back and our forces . . . drove them again over the ground which had been hotly contested for the third time during the day, five more of the eleven guns not taken down the hill falling a second time into our possession.

I cannot think of this bloody hill without sadness and pride. Sadness for the great loss of my true and gallant men; pride for the heroic bravery they displayed. . . . It was, after the conflict, literally the hill of death; men, horses, cannon, and the *debris* of an army lay scattered in wild confusion. Hundreds of the gallant Twelfth Division were cold in death or writhing in pain, and, with large numbers of Quinby's gallant boys, lay dead, dying, or wounded, intermixed with our fallen foe. This ended the battle of Champion's Hill at about 3 P.M., and our heroes slept upon the field with the dead and dying around them.

I never saw fighting like this. The loss of my division, on this field alone, was nearly one-third of the forces engaged.[3]

Report of Brig. Gen. George F. McGinnis, USA, Twelfth Division, Thirteenth Army Corps

We left our encampment, near Bolton, at 7 A.M. on the 16th instant, and moved toward Edwards Depot, at which point the enemy were supposed to be in force. Receiving an order from Brigadier-General Hovey to advance rapidly and cautiously (a portion of Company C, First Indiana Cavalry, being ordered to the front by General Hovey, with instructions to scour the country and report any appearance of an enemy), I ordered forward three companies of the Twenty-fourth Indiana Infantry as an advance guard and deployed two companies of the Forty-sixth Indiana Infantry as flankers on either side of the road. After advancing about 5 miles and arriving near the foot of Champion's Hill, I was informed by the cavalry advance that they had discovered one of the enemy's batteries in position on the road, and about 800 yards in front of us. My command was immediately halted and formed in line of battle, skirmishers thrown out in front and on both flanks, and a messenger dispatched to inform General Hovey of the position of affairs.

After halting some time and seeing no signs of the enemy, and fearing that there might be some mistake in regard to the battery, I determined to satisfy myself by personal observation, and under direction of Sergt. David Wilsey, of Company C, First Indiana Cavalry, who had been in the advance, moved up the road some 600 yards, to a point from which could be distinctly seen one section of artillery. Several of the cavalry occupied a position in the neighborhood and informed me that they had fired several shots at the battery without exciting a reply.

Being satisfied, I returned to my command. In a short time our cavalry began to fall back slowly, and in the course of an hour

I received orders from General Hovey to advance my line and feel the enemy. The order to advance was given, and almost immediately sharp and rapid firing was commenced between the skirmishers. . . . The whole line having advanced about 500 yards, the rebel battery opened upon us with volley after volley of grape and canister. The men were ordered to lie down until we had time to inform ourselves more accurately in regard to the enemy's position and the nature of the ground over which we had to move. . . .

After a short halt, another advance was ordered. The whole line moved forward, with bayonets fixed, slowly, cautiously, and in excellent order, and when within about 75 yards of the battery every gun was opened upon us and every man went to the ground. As soon as the volley of grape and canister had passed over us, the order was given to charge, when the whole line moved forward as one man, and so suddenly and apparently so unexpected to the rebels was the movement, that, after a desperate conflict of five minutes, in which bayonets and butts of muskets were freely used, the battery of four guns was in our possession, and a whole brigade in support was fleeing before us, and a large number of them taken prisoners. The Forty-sixth Indiana was immediately ordered upon the left; they moved up in gallant style, double-quick, and, almost before they knew it, had driven the rebels from a three-gun battery in their immediate front.

The rebels were driven about 600 yards when, being strongly re-enforced, they turned upon us and made a most determined stand. At this point occurred one of the most obstinate and murderous conflicts of the war. For half an hour each side took their turn in driving and being driven. Seeing that we were largely outnumbered, having every confidence in the valor of the First Brigade, and yet fearing they would be overwhelmed, I started messengers to General Hovey, informing him of the state of affairs and asking for assistance. I at the same time ordered the captured artillery to be hauled off by hand. Two pieces were thus hauled off, and others spiked, so as to render them useless to the enemy in case they should recapture them.

With the consent of General Hovey, I had ordered up one section of the Sixteenth Ohio Battery, under Capt. J. A. Mitchell. . . . He advanced well to the front, and after pouring a few effective shots into the enemy, he saw that his pieces were in danger of being captured should he remain longer in that position, when he gave the command "limber to the rear," which was his last order, as at that moment he received a mortal wound. . . . In the meantime the contest went on. In reply to my third message for assistance, I was informed that a brigade would be sent us soon. . . .

Having driven the enemy before us, and fought over the same ground three different times, after having been engaged in a continual conflict for nearly three hours, our ammunition being nearly exhausted, many of the men being entirely out, having fired 80 rounds, and relying upon what they could get from the boxes of the dead and wounded, and being overwhelmed by numbers, the First Brigade began to fall back . . . in good order, step by step, contesting every inch of ground. As we neared the ground upon which the batteries had been captured, and from which the enemy had been driven in the morning, just as it appeared to every one that the guns would again fall into the hands of the rebels, we were greeted by the shouts of the long-promised re-enforcements, and one brigade, under command of Colonel Boomer, came looming over the hill, immediately followed by another. . . . They passed down the line to the front and went gallantly into action.[4]

Narrative of Maj. Gen. Ulysses S. Grant, USA (continued)

The battle of Champion's Hill lasted about four hours, hard fighting, preceded by two or three hours of skirmishing, some of which almost rose to the dignity of battle. Every man of Hovey's division and of McPherson's two divisions was engaged during the battle. No other part of my command was engaged at all. . . .

Osterhaus's and A. J. Smith's divisions had encountered the rebel advanced pickets as early as half-past seven. Their positions were admirable for advancing upon the enemy's line.

McClernand, with two divisions, was within a few miles of the battlefield long before noon, and in easy hearing. I sent him repeated orders by staff officers fully competent to explain to him the situation. These traversed the wood separating us, without escort, and directed him to push forward; but he did not come. It is true, in front of McClernand there was a small force of the enemy and posted in a good position behind a ravine obstructing his advance; but if he had moved to the right by the road my staff officers had followed, the enemy must either have fallen back or been cut off. Instead of this he sent orders to Hovey, who belonged to his corps, to join on to his right flank. Hovey was bearing the brunt of the battle at the time. To obey the order he would have

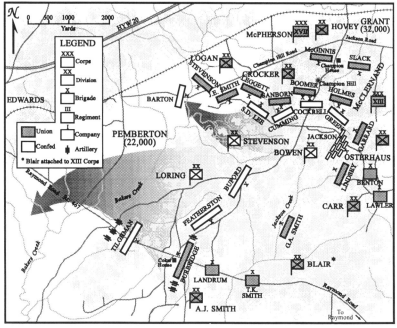

Battle of Champion Hill, late afternoon, May 16, 1863.

had to pull out from the front of the enemy and march back as far as McClernand had to advance to get into battle, and substantially over the same ground. Of course I did not permit Hovey to obey the order of his intermediate superior.[5]

THE OTHER SIDE OF THE HILL

Report of Lt. Gen. John C. Pemberton, USA (continued)

The demonstrations of the enemy soon becoming more serious, orders were sent to division commanders to form in line of battle on the cross-road from the Clinton to the Raymond road, *Loring* on the right, *Bowen* in the center, and *Stevenson* on the left.

Major-General *Stevenson* was instructed to make the necessary dispositions for the protection of the trains then on the Clinton road and crossing Baker's Creek. The line of battle was quickly formed, without any interference on the part of the enemy. The position selected was naturally a strong one, and all approaches from the front well covered. A short time after the formation of the line, *Loring's* division was thrown back so as to cover the military road, it being reported that the enemy had appeared in that direction. The enemy made his first demonstration on our right, but after a lively artillery duel for an hour or more, this attack was relinquished, and a large force was thrown against our left, where skirmishing became heavy about 10 o'clock, and the battle began in earnest along *Stevenson's* entire front about noon.

Just at this time a column of the enemy were seen moving in front of our center toward the right. [John C.] *Landis'* battery, of *Bowen's* division, opened upon and soon broke this column, and compelled it to retire. I then directed Major-General *Loring* to move forward and crush the enemy in his front, and . . . General *Bowen* to co-operate with him in the movement.

Immediately on the receipt of my message, General *Bowen* rode up and announced his readiness to execute his part of the movement as soon as Major-General *Loring* should advance [astride the Raymond road]. No movement was made by Major-General *Loring*, he informing me that the enemy was too strongly posted to be attacked, but that he would seize the first opportunity to assault, if one should offer. The enemy still making strenuous efforts to turn Major-General *Stevenson's* left flank, compelled him to make a similar movement toward the left, thus extending his own line and making a gap between his and *Bowen's* divisions. General *Bowen* was ordered to keep this interval closed, and the same instructions were sent to General *Loring* in reference to the interval between his and General *Bowen's* division.

General *Stevenson* having informed me that unless re-enforced he would be unable to resist the heavy and repeated attacks along his whole line, *Bowen* was ordered to send one brigade to his assistance, which was promptly brought forward under Col. F. M. *Cockrell*, and in a very short time his remaining brigade, under the command of Brig Gen. Martin E. *Green*, was put in, and the two together . . . charged the enemy and for the time turned the tide of battle in our favor. . . .

The enemy still continued to move troops from his left to his right, thus increasing his vastly superior forces against *Stevenson's* and *Bowen's* divisions. Feeling assured that there was no important force in his front, I dispatched several staff officers in rapid succession to Major-General *Loring*, ordering him to move all but one brigade (*Tilghman's*, which was directed to hold the Raymond road and cover the bridge and ford at Baker's Creek) to the left as rapidly as possible. To the first of these messages, sent about 2 P.M., answer was returned by Major-General *Loring* that the enemy was in strong force in his front, and endeavoring to flank him. Hearing no firing on the right, I repeated my orders, . . . explained to him the condition of affairs on the left, and directed him to put his two left brigades into the fight as soon as possible. In the transmission of these various messages . . . over a distance of more than a mile, much valuable time was necessarily consumed, which the enemy did not fail to take advantage of.

About 4 P.M. a part of *Stevenson's* division broke badly and fell back in great disorder, but were partially rallied by the strenuous exertions of myself and staff, and put back under their own officers into the fight, but observing that large numbers of men were abandoning the field on *Stevenson's* left, deserting their comrades . . . I rode up to General *Stevenson,* and informing him that I had repeatedly ordered two brigades of General *Loring's* division to his assistance . . . asked him whether he could hold his position. He replied that he could not; that he was fighting from 60,000 to 80,000 men. I then told him I would endeavor myself to find General *Loring* and hasten him up. . . . I presently met Brigadier-General *Buford's* brigade, of *Loring's* division, on the march and in rear of the right of *Bowen's* division.

Colonel *Cockrell* . . . having in person some time previously urgently asked for re-enforcements, which . . . I was then unable to give him, one regiment of *Buford's* brigade was detached at once and directed to his support; the remainder of *Buford's* brigade was moved as rapidly as possible to the assistance of General *Stevenson.*

Finding that the enemy's vastly superior numbers were pressing all my forces engaged steadily back into old fields, where all advantages of position would be in his favor, I felt it to be too late to save the day, even should Brigadier-General *Featherston's* brigade, of General *Loring's* division, come up immediately. I could, however, learn nothing of General *Loring's* whereabouts; several of my staff were in search of him, but it was not until after General *Bowen* had personally informed me that he could not hold his position longer, and . . . I had ordered the retreat that General *Loring,* with *Featherston's* brigade, moving—as I subsequently learned—by a country road which was considerably longer than the direct route, reached the position on the left . . . [at] Champion's Hill, where he was forming line of battle when he received my order to cover the retreat.

Had the movement in support of the left been promptly made when first ordered . . . I might have maintained my position, and it is possible the enemy might have been driven back, though his vastly superior and constantly increasing numbers would have rendered it necessary to withdraw during the night to save my communications with Vicksburg.[6]

Report of Maj. Gen. Carter L. Stevenson, CSA, Commanding Division

At about 5 P.M., on May 15, the division, being the rear of our army, left its position in line of battle near Edwards Depot, with the view of cutting the enemy's line of communication with his depot of supplies and forcing him to give us battle on our own ground. We reached the head of the column in bivouac on the Raymond road at 3 o'clock, and there halted for the night.

At sunrise I was summoned to appear at headquarters, where I was informed by the lieutenant-general commanding [*Pemberton*] that he had received instructions from General *Johnston* to join him near Canton as soon as possible, and that he had decided to move at once, in pursuance thereto, toward Brownsville, on the north of the railroad, by the route as far as the railroad by which we had advanced the previous night. He directed me to move the trains as rapidly as possible to a point at least 3 miles and left of the road in such a manner as would afford an uninterrupted passage to the infantry and artillery.

I immediately caused the trains to be turned, and, in charge of my Fourth Brigade (Colonel [A. W.] *Reynolds*), to be moved rapidly to the rear, in accordance with the instructions I had received. Colonel *Reynolds* was directed to place one regiment in front of the train and to form the remainder of his brigade in line of battle, covering the Clinton and Raymond roads, there to remain until relieved by the next brigade in his rear. It was intended to hold these roads by the brigades as they successively arrived until the passage of the entire army could be effected. The success of this movement depending mainly on the speedy relief of the road from the obstruction caused by the presence of the train, I dispatched two of my staff officers . . . to superintend the operations of those in charge of the train. About 9:30 A.M. . . . [Major J. W. *Anderson*] reported that the road was open, the trains having been placed as ordered, and free for the passage of the troops. This fact I immediately communicated to the lieutenant-general commanding.

About 9 A.M. *Lee* relieved *Reynolds* on the Raymond and Clinton roads, and in a very short time his skirmishers were engaged by those of the enemy. A brisk skirmish of about three-quarters of an hour developed our position to the enemy, who at once changed his direction by the right flank, with a view of turning our left. My three brigades (the fourth, Colonel *Reynolds,* having moved off with the train), were immediately drawn up in order of battle, *Barton* on the right, *Cumming* in the center, and *Lee* on the left. . . . The line of the march was a cross-road from the Clinton to the Raymond road, intersecting the former nearly at right angles. It was at this fork that my left rested. The enemy, in columns of divisions, moved steadily around our left, forcing it to change direction to correspond, and their movement was so rapid as to keep my line (a single one) in constant motion by the left flank. Of this fact I informed the lieutenant-general commanding, and from time to time every apparent increase of force or additional movements by the enemy was promptly reported.

Finding that they were about to concentrate on the left with the larger part of their force, still moving a column to the flank, as I had no reserve, I moved General *Barton* (my right brigade) by the rear to the extreme left. At the time this order was given the lieutenant-general commanding was notified of the fact, and was informed that the enemy had massed a large force on the left, which would doubtless be the main point of attack.

My line had now been moved to the left, until two regiments of the center, now the right . . . occupied the Raymond and Clinton roads, with an interval of 300 yards between them and the remainder of their brigades. This separation was necessary to protect the right and rear of the new line, now threatened by these roads. . . . My line . . . was necessarily single, irregular, divided, and without reserves. Under the supposition that the army was to move forward in pursuance of the instructions given in the morning, this ground was not reconnoitered with a view to taking up a position for battle until we were on the move facing the enemy.

At about 10:30 A.M. a division of the enemy, in column of brigades, attacked *Lee* and *Cumming.* They were handsomely met and forced back some distance, when they were re-enforced, apparently by about three divisions, two of which moved forward to the attack and the third continued its march to the left, with the view of forcing it.

The enemy now made a vigorous attack in three lines upon the whole front. They were bravely met, and for a long time the unequal conflict was maintained with stubborn resolution. But this could not last. Six thousand five hundred men could not hold permanently in check four divisions, numbering, from their own statements, about 25,000 men; and finally, crushed by overwhelming number, my right gave way and was pressed back upon the two regiments covering the Clinton and Raymond roads, where they were in part rallied. Encouraged by this success, the enemy redoubled his efforts and pressed with the utmost vigor along my line, forcing it back.

At this time (about 2:30 P.M.) *Bowen*'s division of Missouri and Arkansas troops, General *Green* on the right and Colonel [F. M.] *Cockrell* on the left, arrived, gallantly charged the enemy, supported on the left by a portion of *Cumming*'s and *Lee*'s brigades, and drove them back beyond the original line.

In the mean time the enemy had continued his movement to our left, and fell upon *Barton* in overwhelming numbers. He charged them gallantly, but was forced back, and the enemy, following up his advantage, cut him off entirely from the rest of the division. It was here that the lamented Major [J. W.] *Anderson,* my chief of artillery, fell, in the fearless discharge of his duty. . . . Here, too, the gallant *Ridley,* refusing to leave his guns, single-handed and alone fought until he fell, pierced with six shots, winning even from his enemies the highest tribute of admiration.

Nothing could protect the artillery horses from the deadly fire of the enemy. Almost all were killed, and along my whole line the pieces, though fought with a desperation on the part of both officers and men . . . almost all fell into the hands of the enemy. In this manner the guns of *Corput*'s and *Johnston*'s batteries and *Waddell*'s section were lost. Double-shotted, they were fired until in many instances the swarms of the enemy were in among them. Officers and men stood by them to the very latest moment they could. . . . On the extreme right the guns under the immediate command of Captain *Waddell* were fought and lost in the same manner, but retaken by the Missourians. This brave officer, assisted by Lieut. G. D. *Wise,* ordnance officer, fought one of them with his own hands until *Bowen,* too, retired.

Early in the day the Forty-second Regiment of Georgia Volunteers (of *Barton*'s brigade) had been sent to hold the bridge over

Baker's Creek. Barton now moved up to this point, held it for a time, and finally crossed and took up position near Edwards Depot, which he held until nearly dark. Here he was joined by many officers and men of *Cumming's* brigade, who, when driven from their position by the overwhelming numbers of the enemy, had retired by the same route he took.

The two regiments of *Cumming's* brigade which I have before mentioned were kept on the Clinton and Raymond roads; and, thus separated from their brigade, joined *Green's* brigade of *Bowen's* division in the charge upon the enemy, and remained with them until they retired. When re-enforced by *Bowen's* division and the enemy were being driven, I informed the lieutenant general of the fact, and asked that *Loring's* division might be sent up at once.

The attack of *Bowen's* division . . . was made about 2:30 P.M. During the attack of the Missourians, and when the enemy were pressing back our left, thus re-enforced, I met the lieutenant-general on the field, and stated to him that unless *Loring's* division was brought up we could not hold the field. He replied that it had been repeatedly ordered to come forward, and that he would go in person and hasten their movement.

About 4 P.M. *Buford's* brigade, of *Loring's* division, arrived, but not until the enemy had taken possession of the Raymond road and turned upon him two captured batteries. Several pieces of *Withers'* artillery from a ridge nearly opposite opened a brisk fire and soon silenced them. About this time I received orders from the lieutenant-general commanding to withdraw the troops in order to Big Black Bridge.[7]

ACTIONS ALONG THE MIDDLE ROAD

Report of Brig. Gen. Peter J. Osterhaus, USA, Ninth Division, Thirteenth Army Corps

All reports and information obtained . . . confirmed the fact that large bodies of rebel forces were within a few miles of us and prepared to give us battle. They were formed east of Edwards Station, defending all the roads converging at that important railroad station.

In order to take up the position assigned to me . . . by the general commanding the army corps, I left Bolton, marching back on the Raymond road about 3 miles, where I took a road [Billy Fields Road] branching off there for Edwards Station, and bivouacked on the same ground which the enemy's cavalry had just left. Cavalry vedettes and patrols thrown forward developed the enemy in immediate vicinity. His pickets fell back, but a large body of mounted infantry appeared soon after and pressed into the line of my infantry pickets. . . . After a lively engagement the enemy's forces retired and left us without further annoyance for that evening.

The plan of attack for the next morning placed me in the center of our line; General Hovey, Twelfth Division, on my right, on the direct Bolton and Edwards Station road; General Smith, Tenth Division, on my left, on the Raymond and Edwards Station road; and General Carr, Fourteenth Division, following me as reserve on the same road I was marching up.

I left camp on the morning of May 16, precisely at 6 o'clock, with all those safeguards in front and flank which the enemy's vicinity rendered indispensable. Captain Campbell, who had the advance, pushed vigorously forward. By 7:30 o'clock the report of cannon on my left was heard, and cavalry patrols which I had sent out in that direction reported that General Smith had engaged the enemy on the Raymond road. In order to co-operate with him, I advanced rapidly to a point where the road leaves the open fields and enters a very broken section of timbered land, behind which the enemy was formed, apparently in very strong numbers. . . . The casualties on May 1 and the garrisoning of Raymond [had] reduced my division [to] 2,386 infantry, 218 artillery, [and] 100 cavalry. . . .

With this force of 2,704 men, I entered upon one of the most difficult terrains for the passage of troops which can be imagined. A chaos of ravines and narrow hills, sloping very abruptly into sink-hole-like valleys, diverge in all directions. All is covered densely by trees and brush, except the public road, which winds its track in *bizarre* [sic] curves, and follows the hills and valleys, without permitting at any point an open view of more than 50 or 100 yards. This very broken terrain has, on the south side of the road, a general tendency to slope off, being about 1 mile wide. It terminates at a narrow little creek. Passing over this stream, the land becomes smoother again, and opens on large fields, which extend all across from the creek to the road direct from Raymond to Edwards Station, on which General Smith's division was marching. The space between the road occupied by me and the Bolton and Edwards Station road, on my right, on which General Hovey's division was advancing, is . . . utterly impracticable for any military movements, except in a dispersed and loosely connected line of skirmishers.

From General Hovey's division I was about 1 mile off, while General Smith's column was at least 4 miles separated from me to my left and to the rear. His progress was checked more vehemently than that of General Hovey's and my own.

To the First Brigade, General Garrard commanding, I gave the order to advance. Only one section of Lanphere's battery I took along with the brigade, as there was hardly any prospect for artillery to be used on the ground before us.

To prepare against any attack by the enemy on my flank, or his breaking out from any point which in this very difficult terrain might have escaped my notice, I deployed the Second Brigade, with two sections of the Seventh Michigan Battery and the First Wisconsin Battery, on an open and commanding ridge in the field which the advancing First Brigade was leaving behind.

The Third Illinois, commanded by Captain Campbell, led the way carefully, and, supported by the skirmishers of the Seventh Kentucky, we advanced into the timber and against the enemy, who had again selected one of his favorite positions in the brush to give us battle. The ground now became so rough that I had to withdraw the cavalry . . . and afterward employed it in finding my connections with General Smith on my left, and in watching the enemy's movements toward that flank of my position. I have derived a great deal of good from the captain's zeal.

The Seventh Kentucky, with the Forty-ninth Indiana Infantry and one section of Lanphere's battery, formed the advance, and, driving the enemy's skirmishers from one ravine to another, they advanced slowly against his main position, about 1 mile beyond the position occupied by the Second Brigade in the field. I found a comparatively good range for the section of artillery, and concluded to place it in battery there, supported by two companies of infantry, and keeping them in readiness for any emergency, the pieces loaded with canister, in order to secure a rallying point in case my advancing infantry had to fall back.

The Seventh Kentucky on the right and the Forty-ninth Indiana on the left of the road advanced about 1 mile beyond this section of artillery, when the fire and resistance of the enemy became very fierce. I dispatched immediately the Sixty-ninth Indiana and One hundred and eighteenth Illinois infantry to deploy on the left of the road to re-enforce these regiments. Gallantly the line so strengthened advanced, forcing several of the enemy's positions by their impetuous charges up and down the hills.

By this time General Hovey was also engaged, and apparently the main forces of the enemy were concentrated against his and my positions. The artillery played heavily upon us, but without any injury to the troops, the very broken ground and thick timber exposing them only to very short range of infantry.

We advanced until we came to a clearing again in the timber. Here the road on which General Hovey was advancing runs into the road I was fighting on, and here the enemy made a most desperate attempt to prevent the junction of the divisions. We could see his columns advancing in great numbers, and I considered it prudent to strengthen my line by adding the Forty-second Ohio Infantry to the First Brigade, and the One hundred and fourteenth Ohio Infantry (both of the Second Brigade) to support the artillery (one section) in *lieu* of two companies of the Forty-ninth Indiana, which I ordered to join their regiment in front.

Fearing the enemy might try to benefit by the open ground on my left flank . . . and the backward position of General Smith, I made a reconnaissance in that direction and found large numbers of . . . infantry and artillery massed on a commanding elevation [*Loring's* division], apparently in expectation of General Smith's attack. Occasionally the enemy threw shell in the direction of their march.

In order to secure my flank and co-operate with General Smith, I ordered Colonel Lindsey, with the two remaining regiments of his brigade (Sixteenth Ohio and Twenty-second Kentucky Infantry) to take a position in the edge of the timber and open fire against the enemy's position. These two regiments were by no means adequate to repel or resist the numerous force of the enemy, and I therefore applied to Major-General McClernand for re-enforcements from General Carr's division, which was in my rear and on the ground occupied until lately by the Second Brigade. A regiment was ordered to the support of Colonel Lindsey, and this excellent officer deployed his line and attacked the enemy vigorously. Debouching from the timber, he charged the retreating infantry to the very muzzle of the battery covering them.

The promised support was not yet on hand to follow up this attack; therefore the colonel ordered his regiments to fall back into the timber again and await re-enforcements. I . . . take great pleasure to commend the action of that meritorious officer. The direction of the enemy's retreat on that flank was such that he fell (rather unexpectedly to both parties) on the left of the First Brigade, which was advancing and fighting on the main road under General Garrard. Though I had advised this officer of the operations on the left, the information could not be communicated in time to the troops on his left, therefore the appearance of the enemy on their flank stopped for some time the advance of our troops.

General McClernand, who saw the effect of this presumed flank attack, immediately strengthened General Garrard's position by two regiments of General Carr's division. At the same time General Lawler's brigade (also of General Carr's division) was ordered to support Colonel Lindsey. The enemy, becoming convinced of the small force under the colonel, had opened a raking artillery fire on him. A few rounds from General Lawler's artillery were enough to silence his guns and compel him to remove them to safer quarters. Thus strengthened on all sides, the whole line advanced, and after a short but very brisk fire the enemy, already nearly broken by the severe assaults made by my troops, yielded his position.

The main army of the enemy made for Big Black River Railroad Bridge, but a large body of his right wing tried to make good its retreat in another direction. They were perseveringly followed by Colonel Lindsey and General Smith, whose division fell in with Colonel Lindsey's brigade during the pursuit. Thousands of the enemy were found scattered everywhere and fell into our hands as prisoners of war. In one instance, Colonel Lindsey, with the Sixteenth Ohio and Twenty-second Kentucky Infantry alone took more prisoners than the whole number of his brigade combined; also a number of cannon and small arms became ours. We pressed the enemy to Edwards Station, where our army corps bivouacked for the night.[8]

Report of Brig. Gen. Alfred Cumming, CSA, Commanding Third Brigade, Stevenson's Division

The brigade line was established on a succession of slight ridges overlooking a clear field. Strong parties of skirmishers were at once thrown out beyond this field, with directions to penetrate the woods on the other side and engage and hold in check those of the enemy. This they did. . . . Shortly after these dispositions were made, word was sent me by General [S. D.] Lee that, in consequence of the passage of the enemy toward his left, he was extending his line in that direction, coupled with the request that I would move by the flank to preserve the interval between us. The major-general (present with me) directed this to be done, and I moved on the required distance. After making two or more of such moves, (my left having by this time crossed the Raymond road), I was informed by the major-general that *Lee* had bent the left of his line toward the rear, the two branches making an angle more or less obtuse, and was directed to accord my movements with his.

Having sent forward an officer of my staff to notify the officer commanding the skirmishers of the change of direction of the line, and to direct him to make their movements to correspond, I at once proceeded from the center to the extreme left of my brigade, to superintend the change. The directions [orders] . . . were communicated to the officers in command of the skirmishers, but owing to the distance of this line in advance, the inability in a wooded country of determining the point at which the change of direction should be made, and especially to the fact that they were unable to keep up communication with the skirmishers of *Lee's* brigade, they were unable to follow up the movement, and later in the day were forced, after a gallant contest, in which they suffered severely, to retire toward the right.

In its movement by the left flank the brigade had entered a wood rather open for the first few hundred yards, but gradually becoming denser. Arrived at the point where the brigade on my left had filed to the left, it was found that the angle formed by the two branches of the line was nearly a right angle. Here my left regiment (the Thirty-ninth Georgia) was promptly turned into the new direction. The whole of this regiment and four companies of the next [Thirty-fourth Georgia] had succeeded in getting upon what may be termed the second front of the square, when the halting of *Lee's* brigade necessitated the same on my part.

It should here be stated that the three left regiments . . . had each three companies at the front as skirmishers, in addition to which the Thirty-fourth and Thirty-sixth had each one company absent on detached service, thus leaving only six companies of these regiments in line. A halt having been made . . . and the two sides of the square faced outward, notice was at this moment given me that *Lee* (whose brigade was concealed from my observation by the density of the wood) was moving forward. I immediately advanced the second front, with a view to keep abreast with the supposed movement.

The brigade had advanced but a few paces when I was informed that the reported movement by *Lee* had not been made. A halt was at once called, and the line, somewhat disordered as the broken and wooded character of the ground traversed, rectified. In this position the second front of the brigade was drawn up on a succession of ridges and knolls heavily timbered, beyond which, at a distance generally of about 50 yards, the ground fell off abruptly.

While thus engaged in rectifying the line, the battle broke upon us, and without previous intimation received, the skirmishers having been unable . . . to keep pace with the movement of the line, and being no longer interposed between it and the enemy, though of this I was not informed until afterward. Favored by the broken and wooded character of the locality, the enemy advanced two very full regiments (the Seventh and Eleventh Illinois) upon that portion of my line forming what I have termed its second front. Each of these regiments would seem to have been formed into a double column, occupying a half regimental front, and their whole line to have extended from the point of the angle to about the right of the Thirty-ninth Georgia.

Approaching unseen to within a distance of less than 50 yards, the enemy poured in a very heavy and destructive volley, which was at once replied to with effect. About the same moment the enemy appeared in front of and opened fire upon the first front of my line (a brisk and effective fire), but not so near and destructive as that on the second front. On this (second) front the portions of the regiments engaged held for time their position against the greatly superior force of the enemy. . . . But apprised now of the exact position occupied by a section of Captain *Johnston's* battery . . . the enemy's right regiment, by an oblique movement, placed itself in rear of the regiment already confronting the Thirty-fourth Georgia, and the two united bore down upon this regiment and the right of the Thirty-ninth. The position of the Thirty-fourth Georgia on the new direction was unable to withstand the charge of so overpowering a force, and it, together with the right (Thirty-ninth Georgia), was compelled to give way. Throwing myself at the point at which the break had been made, efforts were made to rally the broken line; but the enemy having obtained possession of the batteries and following up closely their advantage, these efforts proved unsuccessful and the whole of the second front fell back.

By this retrograde movement, the right of the Thirty-fourth Georgia and the Thirty-sixth Georgia Regiments, which had in the mean time been engaged with the enemy in their front, were uncovered, and the colonel of the latter, . . . finding that the enemy had penetrated in his rear as far as his colors, gave the order to fall back. This regiment was rallied and held its position . . . advancing in its front, till, threatened with being flanked on its right, it was again compelled to fall back to a new position. In a similar manner the two right regiments . . . were compelled in succession, by the uncovering of their left and the pressure of the enemy on their front, to fall back, which they did, holding the enemy in check at various points when they were able to make a stand. . . . With these operations ends . . . the first phase of the battle so far as concerns this brigade.

Barton's brigade, originally on my right, had in the mean time been moved toward the extreme left, thus leaving my right entirely exposed. This compelled the two right regiments, when they finally fell back, to proceed as far as the farm house in front of our first position before commencing their reorganization. The other regiments of the brigade fell back and reformed on the Raymond road. . . . Here portions of my three left regiments were rallied, together with portions of one or more of *Lee's* regiments, and a line was formed along this road. While engaged in forming this line we were not pressed by the enemy, who would seem to have been similarly occupied.

About this time a Missouri brigade approached the battle-field from the right, and went in on the ground previously occupied by the extreme right of my brigade. As soon as they had completed their reorganization, the Fifty-seventh Georgia Regiment and . . . the Fifty sixth . . . accompanied this movement, and went in on the right of the Missourians. These regiments here hotly engaged the enemy, and, particularly in the movement which drove him for a time, advanced considerably beyond the line on which they had first encountered him in the morning. They only withdrew on the general order being given to this effect.

The three regiments which formed on the Raymond road as their second line having been brought into some kind of order, and *Barton's* brigade, on the left, having gone in and engaged the enemy, these regiments immediately . . . advanced into the wood in their front and formed abreast with *Barton,* engaging the enemy on ground near that originally held by *Lee.*

The contest here was sharp and severe for a time, but of short duration. The enemy flushed with his previous success, and in number much superior to ours, drove our men apparently along the whole division front; slowly at first, afterwards more rapidly, till on reaching the road the fight became precipitate. . . . Scattered bands of them crossed the road in close pursuit of the fugitives. After this it became impossible to rally them again, though strenuous efforts were made to do so several hundred yards from the road. . . . The flight was continued toward the lower bridge over Baker's creek, at which point the greater portion of the army crossed. Crossing with several members of my staff and officers of artillery at a point between the bridges, I repaired to the upper bridge and reported to General *Barton*. . . . Remaining there until nearly sunset, the bridge was then destroyed, or partially so, and we fell back toward Edwards Depot.

Here, with portions of two brigades assembled, the enemy's advance was held in check till the train was destroyed and the army had nearly passed the depot by the other road. We then continued the retreat unmolested to the other side of Big Black. . . .

The brigade went into action about 2,500 strong. Its losses are killed, 142; wounded, 314; missing, 539; total, 995. . . . This brigade took no part in the battle of Big Black.[9]

ACTIONS ON THE UNION LEFT—THE RAYMOND ROAD

For directions to this site, see Part II, Phase 3, Stop 7.

Report of Brig. Gen. Stephen G. Burbridge, USA, Commanding First Brigade, Tenth Division, Thirteenth Corps

At daylight on the 16th, we marched out on the Vicksburg road toward Edwards Station, my brigade being in the advance. About 6 miles out from Raymond we came upon the enemy's pickets, when our line of battle was quickly formed, with heavy skirmishing parties in front. The batteries were thrown into position and shelled the enemy's forces very successfully. We skirmished along gradually, driving the enemy before us, while our main force followed along the road until we reached a watercourse, across which the bridge had been broken down by the retreating enemy.

Finding the enemy was in retreat but a short distance ahead, and apprehending they might avail themselves of some prominent hills, from which they could sweep the plain we were in, I pushed my brigade rapidly ahead until the skirmishers began to find it a hot contest, and as we rose to the crest of the hill [I] had abundant reason to congratulate myself upon my speed, as the enemy had rallied and planted their battery on the second hill, not having had time to form on the first. They poured in a most terrific fire of shot, shell, grape and canister, but my men were well protected by the crest of the hill, and my sharpshooters kept the enemy so much annoyed they had to abandon some of their guns. After repeated application to General Smith for re-enforcements, both of infantry and artillery, I finally succeeded in obtaining the Nineteenth Kentucky and Seventy-seventh Illinois, of Colonel Landram's brigade, who were ready and impatiently awaiting orders to move forward. I also obtained four guns of the Seventeenth Ohio battery, which had been preceded by part of the Chicago Mercantile Battery, both of which did admiral execution.

Receiving orders from General Smith through one of his staff to halt, I did so, holding the position I had gained. It was my conviction at the time, confirmed by all I have learned since, that, properly supported by General Blair's division, we could have captured the whole rebel force opposed to us, and reached Edwards Station before sunset. From prisoners taken the next day, we learned that after the loss of General [L.] *Tilghman,* who was killed by a shot from our batteries, they had attempted to run off their artillery; but, failing to do so, abandoned it, since which time we have obtained the guns, twelve pieces. Also the whole rebel force retreated in great disorder, it being impossible for the officers to again form their men into line.

The night after the battle the men lay upon their arms, hourly expecting an attack. The night passed quietly, however, and at daylight we moved on in line of battle, but soon had abundant evidence that the rebels had skedaddled most hurriedly, leaving arms, ammunition, etc., strewn by the roadside. Forming again in column, we moved on through Edwards Station without further interruption.

As we approached Big Black River, heavy firing became very audible.[10]

Report of Maj. Gen. William W. Loring, CSA, Commanding Division

It was determined by the general to move at 8 o'clock in the morning (15th instant) [May 15], the army intending to cross

Baker's Creek at a ford, which was prevented by its swollen condition. It was, however, put in motion about 3 or 4 P.M., crossing the creek upon a bridge a short distance above the ford. A map was furnished marking the road upon which the army was to march, my division being in the advance. After moving 4 or 5 miles, we were joined by Major [Samuel H.] *Lockett,* chief engineer, who directed the column to take a cross-road leading to Mrs. Ellison's house, on the middle Raymond road. At this place the army was to have encamped, it having been discovered that the road which it was intended the entire force should follow was wrongly laid down upon the map furnished.

About dark my division reached Mrs. Ellison's, and found a great scarcity of water. This information was at once communicated to General *Pemberton,* so that he might make some other disposition of the forces which were following. After dark it fortunately happened that the other divisions were still upon the road leading from the bridge and encamped along it in their line of march. It was still more fortunate that my command was upon the middle Raymond road which led immediately to the ford at which the army was to have crossed in the morning.

Upon this road the enemy was in large force within a few miles of my camp. Being satisfied of this from prisoners taken and from observations of several of my staff sent in advance, very large picket forces were placed in my front, rear, and right flank. Completing my dispositions, I soon after met General *Pemberton,* to whom information of the near proximity of the enemy in large force was given. Additional information was subsequently given him, establishing the fact that he [the enemy] was in our immediate front.

This was the condition of things until 7 or 8 o'clock next morning (16th), when the general informed us that he had a note from General *Johnston,* advising a junction with him in the direction of Brownsville, his force having fallen back from Jackson. This necessitated a movement toward Edwards Depot. The general then gave an order for the train, which had not come up, to retrace its steps.

Pending this, it is said the enemy was in line of battle preparing to attack us. Moving rapidly upon my pickets, he opened a brisk cannonade. I suggested to General *Pemberton* that the sooner he formed a line of battle the better, as the enemy would very soon be upon us. He at first directed me to form *Tilghman's* brigade in

Maj. Gen. William W. *Loring,* CSA, Commanding Division, Army of
Vicksburg. (U.S. Army Military History Institute)

a line of battle upon the ground it then occupied, but soon thought it untenable, and ordered it, with *Featherston's* and *Buford's* brigades (my whole division), into a line of battle on a ridge about three-quarters of a mile in the rear and across a small creek.

This line was almost immediately changed for a ridge still farther back, where my artillery was advantageously posted on both sides of the road, the field to the front being entirely open as far as Mrs. Ellison's house. He also directed the division to occupy the road and the country to the right of it, and in orders conveyed to me at different times during the day he instructed me to hold my position, not attacking the enemy unless he attempted to outflank us. *Bowen's* command was extended so as to join mine on the road. Soon a series of orders came, specifically and with great particularity, for two of my brigades to move to the left, closing the line as often as *Bowen* moved, and we in this manner followed him.

During this time I received an order to retire, also one to advance, both of which were countermanded. My whole division, including reserves, was strung out in line of battle, mostly in thick timber. The enemy during these movements remained steadily in front in heavy force, being, apparently, a full corps, occupying a series of ridges, wooded, and commanding each other, forming naturally a very strong if not impregnable position, throwing forward a heavy line of skirmishers, and showing every indication of an attack in force upon my position, both in front and upon the right flank. General *Bowen* also informed me that he thought the enemy was moving to the right.

While these movements were going on (all of which were brought to the general's attention), desultory firing was heard on the extreme left, and General *Bowen* was summarily ordered in that direction, without warning either to myself or to General *Buford,* commanding a brigade of my division next to him. Not long after, I was ordered to send a brigade to the left, and General *Buford* went at double-quick. While passing *Bowen,* two regiments were detached and went into the fight with that command, *Buford* continuing on to the left. In half to three-quarters of an hour one brigade was ordered to be left on the road, and the other to be taken by myself to the left. This was most earnestly requested to be done by Colonel [W. T.] *Withers,* in command of the artillery, who feared the capture of his guns. He tells me that he was gratified in being able to state that my force arrived sooner than he expected, and in time to save his artillery. But for our prompt arrival, every piece would have been lost, as the whole sustaining force had, except a few bold skirmishers, been driven back.

Upon the approach of [W. S.] *Featherston's* brigade, in rapid march, a considerable force of the retreating army having been rallied behind him, the enemy, who was advancing upon the artillery, fell back in great disorder, Colonel *Withers* pouring in a most destructive fire upon him. It was here that we witnessed a scene ever to be remembered, when the gallant *Withers* and his brave men, with their fine park of artillery, stood unflinchingly amid a shower of shot and shell the approach of an enemy in overwhelming force, after his supports had been driven back, and trusting that a succoring command would arrive in time to save his batteries, and displaying a degree of courage and determination that calls for the most unqualified admiration.

Upon my arrival upon this part of the field, I found the whole country on both sides of the road covered with the fleeing of our army, in many cases in large squads, and, as there was no one endeavoring to rally or direct them, I at once placed my escort under an efficient officer of my staff, with orders to gather up the stragglers and those in retreat away from the road. This duty was performed with great energy and success.

It was also determined that under these circumstances it was necessary, in order to save large numbers of men and guns, as well as to be able, in case the emergency should arise, to retire the army in safety and good order to the ford over Baker's Creek, along the only road open to it, that a vigorous and well-directed attack should be made upon the enemy.

At this moment I met General *Lee* and Colonel *Withers*, and was satisfied, from information obtained from them, that by such an attack upon the enemy's right during the panic which had befallen his center we could overwhelm it, retrieve the day, certainly cut him off from the bridge on our extreme left (of which it was highly important we should hold possession), and save our scattered forces. Dispositions were at once made for the attack, in which General *Lee* lent a cordial and able assistance. This fine officer, with General [M. E.] *Green* and portions of their gallant brigades, we found fighting the enemy where all others, except the brave *Withers*, had been driven back, and contesting every step of the enemy's advancing columns, *Green* declaring he never would have been driven back but for the fact that he had not a cartridge left.

While thus engaged, I received an order for the forces to fall back, and my assistant adjutant-general, who had been dispatched to General *Pemberton* for orders, returned stating that the general said that the movement must not be made; that I must order a retreat and bring up the rear. Officers were immediately sent to advise those not yet informed to retire, and as rapidly as possible, in the direction of the ford, that being the only road left open. As soon as the enemy realized that we were leaving the field, he rallied and moved forward in heavy force.

In the mean time *Featherston's* brigade was put into position to protect the rear of the retreating forces and to cover the falling back of *Buford's* brigade. This duty was ably and gallantly executed. This latter brigade (*Buford's*) about this time met a charge of the enemy (infantry, cavalry, and artillery), and repulsed him in splendid style with great slaughter, the heavy fighting being done by the Twelfth Louisiana, a large regiment. . . .

During this time *Tilghman,* who had been left with his brigade upon the other road, almost immediately after our parting, met a terrible assault of the enemy, and when we rejoined him was carrying on a deadly and most gallant fight. With less than 1,400 effective men he was attacked by from 6,000 to 8,000 of the enemy with a fine park of artillery; but being advantageously posted, he not only held him in check, but repulsed him on several occasions, and thus kept open the only line of retreat left to the army. The bold stand of this brigade . . . saved a large portion of the army. . . .

I had some time before this sent an adjutant to General *Pemberton* and subsequently another to ascertain how his retreating forces were progressing, but having left the field it was impossible to communicate with him. The officer on his return informed me that he had met General *Bowen* at the ford, who had requested him to say to me "For God's sake, hold your position until sundown and save the army." He could hold the ford and the bridge was safe.

I had scarcely received this message when General *Bowen* sent me a written communication, stating that the enemy had crossed the bridge and had outflanked him; that he had been compelled precipitately to fall back, and that I must do my best to save my division. I also received a note from Lieut. Col. Jacob *Thompson* to the same import.

We at once made a movement toward the ford, there being no other road of retreat. There being none on my left that I could use, and being wholly unacquainted with the country—my only guide having been taken by General *Pemberton* to direct him to Big Black Bridge—my first determination was to force my way through by the ford, and rode rapidly to reconnoiter. Arriving there, it was found that our troops were gone, some of whom having been driven back upon us. The enemy's skirmishers were advancing, and a heavy force occupied the commanding ridge across the creek, his artillery playing upon the crossing. The enemy upon our right flank and rear had been re-enforced, so that we were enveloped upon three sides, leaving no road to move upon. Not far from my place of observation I met Dr. Williamson, a highly respectable gentleman of Edwards Depot, who said he knew the whole country, and thought he could take me to a ford on Baker's Creek, 3 or 4 miles below.

By this time darkness was approaching. I at once decided upon this move. By a well-concerted movement we eluded the enemy upon three sides, and to his astonishment made our flank march from between his forces across the fields to a given point in the woods skirting Baker's Creek. The night being dark and the trail a blind one, it was found impossible to get through by following the creek. It was then determined to move across to another road and reach the ford in that direction. My command, being compelled to move back upon the ground where the battle was fought, passed the enemy's camp-fires, and at times our small parties were near enough to hear them. The unused plantation roads upon which we moved were in such bad condition as to render it impossible to carry our artillery over them, and we were obliged to destroy that which we had with our commands, bringing the horses and harnesses with us, the balance having gone with the army into Vicksburg. Soon after striking the timber we discovered Edwards Depot and Withers' gin-house on fire, which convinced us that our forces had passed those points; but as we were led to believe that we could reach the lower ford in 3 or 4 miles, it was hoped that we could pass in between Edwards Depot and Big Black Bridge and rejoin the army. Instead of 3 or 4 miles it was 10 or 12 miles before my command reached the lower Raymond road which led to the ford, and it then was after midnight.

My guide informed us that it was impossible to guide the division to Big Black Bridge with the enemy in possession of Edwards Depot, which we were convinced he had held for several hours, but referred us to a gentleman by the name of Vaughan, who lived within 1 mile of the road. I went to his house and brought him to the column to consult with my generals, and proposed that he should take us to Big Black River. He declared that it was impassable, as all the lower fords over Baker's Creek were swimming, and that to Big Black Bridge he could not take us without moving through the enemy's lines at Edwards Depot. He also informed us that a large force of the enemy had that day passed his house. It was known that the enemy had troops at all ferries over Big Black below the mouth of Baker's Creek, and that the river was a deep and difficult stream to cross. The condition of the command was also taken into consideration, being without artillery, with but few rounds of cartridges; having no implements for immediate construction of a bridge or ferry; our entire train having gone into Vicksburg, and being without supplies of any kind; also the distance to the river was so great that it would have been impossible to have reached it until late next day, when the enemy was sure to have been posted to prevent crossing.

After a full consultation with my brigadiers, all of us were of the opinion that it was impossible to attempt the passage of Big Black at any point, and in doing so the entire division would certainly be lost. Subsequent events have fully shown that we were right in this determination. It was then determined to force the rear of the enemy between Raymond and Utica.

On the evening of the 17th, my command after a hard march reached Crystal Springs, a village on the New Orleans and Jackson Railroad, 25 miles south of Jackson.

On the 19th, [I] reached Jackson with my entire division ... and immediately reported to General *Johnston,* who expressed his gratification that my command had safely arrived.[11]

NOTES

1. *O.R.,* XXIV, pt. 1, pp. 51–53.
2. *O.R.,* XXIV, pt. 1, pp. 148–50.
3. *O.R.,* XXIV, pt. 2, pp. 41–44.
4. *O.R.,* XXIV, pt. 2, pp. 48–50.

5. Ulysses S. Grant, *Personal Memoirs,* 2 vols. (New York: Charles L. Webster, 1885), 1:518–19.

6. *O.R.,* XXIV, pt. 1, pp. 263–64.

7. *O.R.,* XXIV, pt. 2, pp. 93–96.

8. *O.R.,* XXIV, pt. 2, pp. 13–16.

9. *O.R.,* XXIV, pt. 2, pp. 103–7.

10. *O.R.,* XXIV, pt. 2, pp. 31–32.

11. *O.R.,* XXIV, pt. 2, pp. 75–78.

13. GENERALS AT ODDS

Summary of Principal Events:
May 16–July 23, 1863

May
16   Battle of Champion Hill.
17   Engagement at Big Black River bridge.
19–July 4   Siege of Vicksburg.

BATTLE OF THE BIG BLACK

For directions to this site, see Part II, Phase 3, Stop 8.

Report of Lt. Gen. John C. Pemberton, CSA (continued)

On reaching the ford and bridge at Baker's Creek, I directed Brigadier-General *Bowen* to take position with his division on the west bank, and to hold the crossing until *Loring*'s division, which was directed to bring up the rear, had effected the passage. I then proceeded at once to the intrenched line covering the wagon and railroad bridges over the Big Black, to make the necessary arrangements for holding that point during the passage of the river. . . . The entire train of the army . . . was crossed without loss.

On reaching the line of intrenchments occupied by Brigadier-General *Vaughn*'s brigade of East Tennesseeans (*Smith*'s division), he was instructed by myself in person to man the trenches from the railroad to the left, his artillery to remain as then posted, and all wagons to cross the river at once. Special instructions were left with Lieut. J. H. *Morrison*, aide-de-camp, to be delivered to Generals *Loring, Stevenson,* and *Bowen,* as they should arrive, and were delivered to all except General *Loring,* as follows:

General *Stevenson*'s division to cross the river and proceed to Mount Alban.

General *Loring*'s to cross and occupy the west bank.

Brigadier-General *Bowen's* division . . . was directed to occupy the trenches to the right and left of *Vaughn's*, and his artillery to be parked, that it might be available for any point of the lines most threatened.

General *Stevenson's* division, arriving very late in the night, did not move beyond Bovina, and I awaited in vain intelligence of the approach of General *Loring*. It was necessary to hold the position to enable him to cross the river, should the enemy . . . follow him closely up.

For this purpose alone I continued the troops in position until it was too late to withdraw them under cover of night. I then determined not to abandon so strong a front while there was yet a hope of his arrival. . . .

The Big Black River, where it is crossed by the railroad bridge, makes a bend somewhat in the shape of a horseshoe. Across this horseshoe, at its narrowest part, a line of rifle-pits had been constructed, making an excellent cover for infantry, and at proper intervals dispositions were made for field artillery. The line of pits ran nearly north and south, and was about 1 mile in length. North of and for a considerable distance south of the railroad, and of the dirt road to Edwards Depot, nearly parallel with it, extended a bayou, which in itself opposed a serious obstacle to an assault upon the pits. This line abutted north on the river and south upon a cypress-brake, which spread itself nearly to the bank of the river.

In addition to the railroad bridge, which I had caused to be floored for the passage even of artillery and wagons, the steamer *Dot,* from which the machinery had been taken, was converted into a bridge by placing her fore and aft across the river. Between the works and the bridge, about three-quarters of a mile, the country was open, being either old or cultivated fields, affording no cover should the troops be driven from the trenches. East and west of the railroad the topographical features of the country over which the enemy must necessarily pass were similar to those above described; but north of the railroad and about 300 yards in front of the rifle-pits a copse of wood extended from the road to the river.

Our line was manned on the right by the gallant *Cockrell's* Missouri brigade, the extreme left by Brigadier-General *Green's* Missouri and Arkansas men (both of *Bowen's* division), and the center

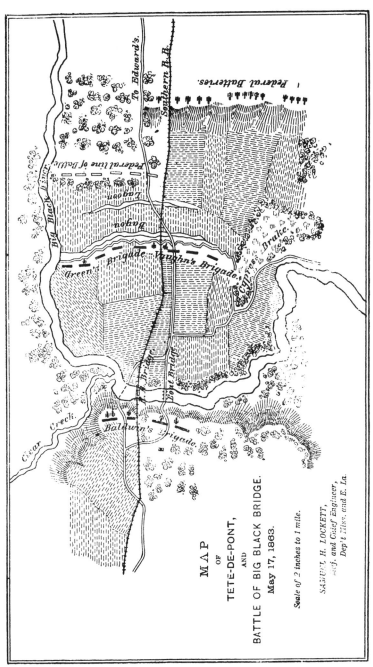

MAP
OF
TETE-DE-PONT,
AND
BATTLE OF BIG BLACK BRIDGE.
May 17, 1863.

Scale of 2 inches to 1 mile.

SAMUEL H. LOCKETT,
Maj. and Chief Engineer,
Dep't Miss. and E. La.

Sketch map of the Confederate position at Big Black River bridge, May 17, 1863. (O.R., XXIV, pt. 2, p. 72) by Brigadier-General *Vaughn's* brigade of East Tennesseeans, in all about 4,000 men—as many as could be advantageously employed in defending the line—with about twenty pieces of field artillery. So strong was the position, that my greatest, almost only, apprehension, was a flank movement by Bridgeport or Baldwin's Ferry [about four miles north and eight miles south, respectively, of the Big Black River Bridge position], which would have endangered my communications with Vicksburg.[1]

Report of Gen. Joseph E. Johnston, CSA

On May 17, I marched 15 miles in the direction of [Clinton]. . . . In the afternoon a letter was brought from . . . [*Pemberton*], dated Bovina, May 17:

> I notified you on the morning of the 14th of the receipt of your instructions to move and attack the enemy toward Clinton. I deemed the movement very hazardous, preferring to remain in position behind the Big Black and near to Vicksburg. I called a council of war, composed of all the general officers. . . . A majority . . . expressed themselves favorable to the movement. . . . The others, including Major-General *Loring* and *Stevenson,* preferred a movement by which this army might endeavor to cut off the enemy's supplies from the Mississippi. My own views were expressed as unfavorable to any movement which would remove me from my base, which . . . is Vicksburg. I did not, however, see fit to place my own judgment and opinions so far in opposition as to prevent the movement altogether, but believing the only possibility of success to be the plan . . . of cutting off the enemy's supplies, I directed all my disposable force, say 17,000, toward Raymond or Dillons.

It also contained intelligence of his engagement with the enemy on the 16th near Baker's Creek [Champion's Hill] . . . and of his having been compelled to withdraw, with heavy loss, to Big Black Bridge. He further expressed apprehension that he would be compelled to fall back from this point, and represented that, if so, his position on Snyder's mill would be untenable. . . . [Later that] . . . night I was informed that General *Pemberton* had fallen back to Vicksburg.[2]

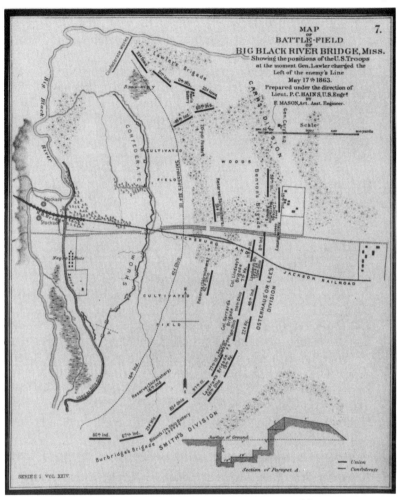

Union dispositions at Big Black River bridge, May 17, 1863. (*Atlas to Accompany the Official Records of the Union and Confederate Armies,* plate XXXVII, no. 7)

Report of Maj. Gen. Ulysses S. Grant, USA, Headquarters, Department of the Tennessee, Commanding

At daylight on the 17th, the pursuit was renewed, with McClernand's corps in the advance. The enemy was found strongly posted on both sides of the Black River. At this point on Black River the bluffs extend to the water's edge on the west bank. On the east side is an open, cultivated bottom of nearly 1 mile in width, surrounded by a bayou of stagnant water, from 2 to 3 feet in depth and from 10 to 20 feet in width, from the river above the railroad to the river below. Following the inside line of this bayou, the enemy had constructed rifle-pits, with the bayou to serve as a ditch on the outside and immediately in front of them. Carr's division occupied the right in investing this place, and Lawler's brigade the right of his division.

After a few hours' skirmishing, Lawler discovered that by moving a portion of his brigade under cover of the river bank he could get a position from which that place could be successfully assaulted, and ordered a charge accordingly. Notwithstanding the level ground over which a portion of his troops had to pass without cover, and the great obstacle of the ditch in front of the enemy's works, the charge was gallantly and successfully made, and in a few minutes the entire garrison, with seventeen pieces of artillery, were the trophies of this brilliant and daring movement. The enemy on the west bank of the river immediately set fire to the railroad bridge and retreated, thus cutting off all chance of escape for any portion of his forces remaining on the east bank.

Sherman by this time had reached Bridgeport, on Black River, above. The only pontoon train with the expedition was with him. By the morning of the 18th, he had crossed the river, and was ready to march on Walnut Hills [north of Vicksburg]. McClernand and McPherson built floating bridges during the night, and had them ready for crossing their commands by 8 A.M. of the 18th.[3]

Report of Brig. Gen. Michael K. Lawler, USA, Commanding Second Brigade, Fourteenth Division

On the morning of the 17th, by 3:30 A.M. Carr's division was again on the road in pursuit of the enemy, Benton's brigade having the advance.

We came upon the enemy at Big Black Bridge, strongly posted behind skillfully constructed rifle-pits, extending across a neck of land formed by the Big Black River, his flanks well protected by this stream, and having in his front, in addition to the rifle-pits, a bayou filled with brush and fallen trees. This, combined with the fact that there were cleared fields of from 400 to 600 yards in width along his whole front from bend to bend of the stream, rendered

Photo of the battlefield at Big Black River bridge. (U.S. Army Military History Institute)

his position really formidable and difficult of approach, subjecting a clearing party, it would seem, to almost certain destruction at the commencement of the contest.

To support Benton's brigade, orders were received to form the brigade in two lines on both sides of the road, the artillery in the center. Shortly afterward I received orders to change position, and by an oblique movement to the right occupy the ground on the right of Benton's brigade, and meet a movement the enemy were reported to be making in that direction with a view to flank us.

This order having been executed, I was instructed by the brigadier-general commanding the division to move forward slowly and cautiously with my command, and develop and press back, if possible, the enemy's left.

Accordingly, I ordered Col. C. L. Harris, Eleventh Wisconsin Volunteers, who held the left of our new position, to move his regiment forward through the woods in his front, his skirmishers

Brig. Gen. Michael K. Lawler, USA, Commander, Second Brigade, Fourteenth Division (Carr), Thirteenth Army Corps (McClernand). (U.S. Army Military History Institute)

covering his advance, and the Twenty-third Iowa, Colonel Kinsman, to follow him at a distance of 100 yards as a support. At the same time I advanced the Twenty-first Iowa Volunteers . . . into the cleared field skirting Big Black River, with instructions to move forward on a line with the Eleventh Wisconsin. The Peoria Battery was left in position on the rising ground in the edge of the field, and the Twenty-second Iowa in rear as a reserve and support.

Meanwhile there had commenced a spirited artillery engagement between the battery of Benton's brigade and the enemy's cannon in position behind their work. The skirmishers of the First Brigade were actively engaged, and those of the Eleventh Wisconsin Volunteers, which . . . advanced steadily forward through the timber to the field in front of the enemy's works, and distant from them about 400 yards. Here I ordered it to halt, and move down to the right through the field skirting the river, and take position in the woods and brush lining this stream. This movement Colonel Harris promptly executed, reaching the position designated without serious loss, though exposed to a heavy fire from the enemy's sharpshooters.

The Twenty-third Iowa, Colonel Kinsman, having come up after the Eleventh Wisconsin, was ordered to make a similar movement to the right, and to move up under cover of the river bank and take position on the right of the Eleventh Wisconsin and as close as possible to the enemy's works, and the Twenty-first Iowa, Colonel Merrill, to take position on the bank between these two regiments. I also directed the Peoria Battery to take position in the open field in front of the left of the enemy and to open an enfilading fire on their center batteries, with which the battery of Benton's brigade was engaged. At the same time the Twenty-second Iowa, Colonel Stone, was ordered to move forward on the left of the field to within supporting distance. These orders were quickly responded to, and the position thus occupied by the brigade continued to be held without material variation.

During the greater part of the forenoon heavy but ineffectual musketry firing was kept up by the enemy upon my men, briskly responded to by our sharpshooters. Late in the afternoon, finding it impossible to press farther forward along the river bank toward the enemy, as I had intended, Colonel Kinsman, Twenty-third Iowa Volunteers, proposed to charge at once the enemy's works and drive them out at the point of the bayonet, and asked my consent. . . .

Foreseeing that a charge by a single regiment, unsustained by the whole line, against fortifications as formidable as those in his front, could hardly be successful, at the same time I gave my consent to his daring proposition I determined that there should be a simultaneous movement on the part of my whole command. Accordingly, the Twenty-first Iowa Volunteers, Colonel Merrill, was ordered to charge with the Twenty-third, the Eleventh Wisconsin . . . following close upon them as a support, and the Twenty-second Iowa . . . which had in the mean time crossed the field and taken position on the river bank on the right of the Eleventh Wisconsin—were ordered to move out into the field and act as a reserve force. Two guns of the Peoria Battery and one 20-pounder Parrott, belonging to the First Wisconsin Battery, were in position in the field, actively at work upon the enemy and doing good service. In addition, orders had been sent to the Forty-ninth and Sixty-ninth Indiana Volunteers—two regiments which had been sent from Osterhaus' division to my support early in the forenoon—to send forward at once two companies as skirmishers to attract the attention of the enemy from the movement on the right, and as soon as the charge should be commenced to move promptly forward to its support. Orders were further given that the men should reserve their fire until upon the rebel works.

Finally the regiments that were to lead the charge were formed, with bayonets fixed, in the edge of the woods on the river bank. All things being in readiness, the command "forward" was given by Colonel Kinsman, and at once his noble regiment sprang forward to the works. The Twenty-first . . . moved at the same instant, the Eleventh Wisconsin . . . closely following. Through a terrible fire of musketry from the enemy in front and a galling fire from his sharpshooters on the right, these brave men dashed bravely on. Kinsman fell, dangerously wounded, before half the distance was accomplished. Struggling to his feet, he staggered a few paces to the front, cheered forward his men, and fell again, this time to rise no more, pierced through by a second ball. Colonel Merrill, the brave commander of the Twenty-first Iowa, fell, wounded, early in the charge. . . .

Immediately Lieutenant-Colonel Glasgow placed himself at the head of the Twenty-third, and Major Van Anda led on the Twenty-first. Undismayed by the loss of their colonels and by the perfect hail-storm of bullet poured into them with destructive effect, the men of the Twenty-third and Twenty-first Iowa and the Eleventh Wisconsin Volunteers pressed onward, nearer and nearer, to the rebel works, over the open field, 500 yards, under a wasting fire, and up to the edge of the bayou. Halting here only long enough to pour into the enemy a deadly volley, they dashed forward through the bayou, filled with water, fallen timber, and brush, on to the rebel works with the shout of victors, driving the enemy in with confusion from their breastworks and rifle-pits, and entering in triumph the rebel stronghold.

Hurrying forward the Forty-ninth and Sixty-ninth Indiana and Twenty-second Iowa Volunteers, I sent the two Indiana regiments to the support of my left, and ordered the Iowa regiment to move against the extreme left of the enemy's works, where they, several hundred strong, still held out, while the Eleventh Wisconsin Volunteers was directed to occupy the ground between the enemy and the bridge and thus cut off their retreat.

The movement was successful. The rebels broke and fled before the Twenty-second Iowa, and fell an easy prey into the hands of the Eleventh Wisconsin Volunteers. Those of the rebels who were not captured hastened to make good their retreat over the bridge. As the result of this successful charge, we may with justice claim that it gave our army entire possession of the enemy's extended lines of works, and with them their field artillery (eighteen pieces in all), a large quantity of ammunition, thousands of small arms, and 3,000 prisoners. . . . Our brigade . . . captured 1,460 small-arms, several hundred accouterments . . . 1,120 prisoners, and 4 stand of colors. . . . More men were captured by my brigade than I had men in the charge; but this brilliant success was not accomplished without considerable loss; 14 killed and 185 wounded in the space of three minutes, the time occupied in reaching the enemy's works, attest the severity of the fire. . . .

The remainder of the 17th . . . and the day after the battle was spent in collecting up the arms and accouterments left on the battlefield by the enemy, in taking care of our wounded, burying our dead and in recruiting our broken ranks. The Twenty-third Iowa Volunteers, which had borne so distinguished a part and suffered so severely in the charge, was placed as a guard over the captured prisoners, and, by order of Maj. Gen. U. S. Grant, has since gone north with them.[4]

BIG BLACK TO VICKSBURG

Report of Lt. Gen. John C. Pemberton, CSA (continued)

Early on the morning of the 17th, the enemy opened his artillery at long range, and very soon pressed forward with infantry into the copse of wood north of the railroad. About the same time he opened on Colonel *Cockrell's* position with two batteries, and advanced a line of skirmishers, throwing forward a column of infantry, which was quickly driven back by our batteries. Pretty heavy skirmishing was for a while kept up along our whole line, but presently the enemy, who had massed a large force in the woods immediately north of the railroad, advanced at a run with loud cheers. Our troops in their front did not remain to receive them, but broke and fled precipitately. One portion of the line being broken, it very soon became a matter of *sauvre qui peut* [every man for himself].

I shall only add . . . that a strong position, with an ample force of infantry and artillery to hold it, was shamefully abandoned almost without resistance. The troops occupying the center did not do their duty. With an almost impassable bayou between ourselves and the enemy, they fled before the enemy had reached that obstacle. . . . Colonel *Cockrell* says in his official report:

> After a lively skirmish fire had been kept up for some time along our whole front, I saw the line between the railroad and first skirt of timber north of the railroad beginning to give way and then running in disorder. I watched this disorderly falling back a few minutes, when I saw that the enemy had possession of the trenches north of the railroad and were rapidly advancing toward the bridge—our only crossing and way of escape—the enemy now being nearer this crossing than my line. I therefore ordered the brigade to fall back, and moving rapidly, gained the bridge, crossed over, and reformed on the west bank of the river north of the railroad. . . .

In this precipitate retreat but little order was observed, the object with all being to reach the bridge as rapidly as possible. Many were unable to do so, but effected their escape by swimming the river. Some were drowned in the attempt; a considerable number, unable to swim, and others too timid to expose themselves to the fire of the enemy by an effort to escape, remained in the trenches and were made prisoners. . . .

Major *Lockett,* chief engineer, was instructed to fire both bridges after seeing that all the troops had crossed. This was effectually accomplished under his personal supervision. The guns in position were ample for the defense, but the infantry failing to support them, they were abandoned. Such as were not in position were safely brought from the field, placed in battery on the bluff on the west bank, and, with others already established and a sufficient force of infantry, held the advancing columns of the enemy effectually in check.

It had become painfully apparent . . . that the *morale* of my army was not such as to justify an attempt to hold the line of the Big Black River. Not only was it greatly weakened by the absence of General *Loring's* division, but also by the large number of stragglers, who, having abandoned their commands, were already making their way into Vicksburg.

The enemy, by flank movements on my left by Bridgeport and on my right by Baldwin's or other ferries, might reach Vicksburg almost simultaneously with myself, or perhaps interpose a heavy force between me and that city. Under these circumstances nothing remained but to retire the army within the defenses of Vicksburg, and to endeavor as speedily as possible to reorganize the depressed and discomfited troops. Orders were accordingly issued at 10 A.M., and Major-General *Stevenson* directed to conduct the retreat, which was executed without haste and in good order. I myself proceeded at once to Vicksburg to prepare for its defense.

I think it due to myself . . . to state emphatically that the advance movement of the army from Edwards Depot on the afternoon of May 15 was made against my judgment, in opposition to my previously expressed intentions, and to the subversion of my matured plans. In one contingency alone I had determined to move toward Jackson; the safety of Vicksburg was of paramount importance; under no circumstances could I abandon my communications with it. A sufficient force must also be left to defend the river front of the city, the approaches by Chickasaw Bayou, by Snyder's Mill, and Warrenton against a *coup de main.* My effective aggregate did not exceed 28,000. At least 8,000 would be required for these purposes; it would also be necessary to hold the bridges across the Big Black, on the line of the Southern Railroad. With these deductions my movable army might reach 18,500 . . . as the maximum.

In the event, therefore, of the enemy advancing with his whole force east of the Mississippi River against Jackson, my communications by the shortest line being open would have enabled me to move upon his rear. General *Johnston's* forces and my own might have formed a junction or have attacked simultaneously in front and rear. But I did not think it would be wise to attempt to execute this plan until the arrival of expected re-enforcements at or near Jackson. Hence I received General *Johnston's* instructions on the morning of the 14th to move to Clinton with all the force I could quickly collect with great regret; and . . . in the presence of one or more of my staff officers I remarked in substance: "Such a movement will be suicidal."

Nevertheless, notifying General *Johnston* of the fact, I took measures for an advance movement at once; not, it is true directly toward Clinton, but in the only direction which, from my knowledge of the circumstances surrounding me, I thought offered a possibility of success. Had I moved directly to Clinton, the enemy would not have given me battle in front, but would have interposed a force greater than my own between me and Vicksburg. . . .

About 7 A.M. on the 16th I received . . . instructions from General *Johnston* . . . which reiterated the previous instructions.

I had in no measure changed my views . . . but I no longer felt at liberty to deviate from General *Johnston's* positive orders. He had been made aware of my views and did not sustain them. The order of march was at once reversed, but the army was hardly in motion before it became necessary to form line of battle to meet the greatly superior forces of the enemy. About 6 P.M. on the 16th, while on the retreat, the following communication [from Gen. *Johnston*] was handed to me:

Camp, Seven Miles from Jackson
May 14, 1863

General: The body of troops mentioned in my note of last night compelled Brigadier-General *Gregg* and his command to evacuate Jackson about noon today. The necessity of taking the Canton road at right angles to that upon which the enemy approaches, prevented an obstinate defense. A body of troops, reported this morning to have reached Raymond last night, advanced at the same time from that direction. Prisoners say that it was McPherson's corps . . . which marched from Clinton. I have no certain information of the other; both skirmished very cautiously. Telegrams were dispatched when the enemy was near, directing General *Gist* to assemble the approaching troops at a point 40 or 50 miles from Jackson, and General *Maxey* to return to his wagons and provide for the security of his brigade . . . by joining General *Gist.* That body of troops will be able, I hope, to prevent the enemy in Jackson from drawing provisions from the east, and this one may be able to keep him from the country toward Panola.

Can he supply himself from the Mississippi? Can you not cut him off from it; and, above all, should he be compelled to fall back for want of supplies, beat him? As soon as the re-enforcements are all up, they must be united to the rest of the army. I am anxious to see a force assembled that may be able to inflict a heavy blow upon the enemy. Would it not be better to place the forces to support Vicksburg between General *Loring* and that place, and merely observe the ferries, so that you might unite if opportunity to fight presented itself? General *Gregg* will move toward Canton tomorrow. If prisoners tell the truth, the force at Jackson must be half of Grant's army. It would decide the campaign to beat it, which can only be done by concentrating, especially when the remainder of the eastern troops arrive; they are to be 12,000 to 13,000.

Most respectfully, . . .

J. E. *Johnston*

It will be observed that General *Johnston's* letter of the 15th, which caused me to reverse my column, with a view of marching to Clinton, was received before the retreat commenced, and about eleven hours earlier than the one of the 14th, just presented. I know nothing of the causes which produced this result, but I respectfully invite attention to the fact that in this letter of the 14th General *Johnston* suggests the very movement which I had made, and for the purpose I had indicated. After expressing the hope that certain dispositions made by himself might prevent the enemy from drawing provisions from the east or from the country toward Panola, he says:

Can he supply himself from the Mississippi? Can you not cut him off from it; and, above all, should he be compelled to fall back for want of supplies, beat him?

I have introduced General *Johnston's* letter entire, that the context, as well as that portion to which I have particularly called attention, may be considered. I had resisted the popular clamor for an advance, which began from the moment the enemy set his polluting foot upon the eastern bank of the Mississippi River. I had resisted the universal sentiment, I believe of the army—I know of my general officers—in its favor, and yielded only to the orders of my superior. I was not invited by General *Johnston* to submit my plans to him for his consideration; it is, therefore, unnecessary now to speak of them.

One of the immediate results of the retreat from Big Black was the necessity of abandoning our defenses on the Yazoo at Snyder's Mill. That position and the line of Chickasaw Bayou were no longer tenable. All stores that could be transported were ordered to be sent into Vicksburg as rapidly as possible; the rest, including heavy guns, to be destroyed.

There was at this time a large quantity of corn (probably 25,000 or 30,000 bushels) on boats, much of which might have been brought in had it been possible to furnish the necessary wagons. The boats were sent up the river. Two companies were directed to remain at Snyder's Mill, making a show of force until the approach of the enemy by land should compel them to retire. To them was intrusted the duty of forwarding all stores possible and of destroying the remainder. This detachment rejoined its command in Vicksburg on the morning of the 18th.

Every precaution was taken to guard the important approaches to the city by *Forney's* and *Smiths'* divisions, while the troops which had been engaged in the battles of the 16th and 17th were bivouacked in rear of the intrenchments. During these battles, the troops of Major-General *Forney's* division were disposed as follows:

Brigadier-General *Hébert's* brigade occupied the line along the Yazoo River from Haynes' Bluff to the Mississippi, including the approaches by Chickasaw Bayou;

Brigadier-General [J. C.] *Moore's* brigade, with the Mississippi State troops (under General [John V.] *Harris*) attached (about 600), guarded the river front at Warrenton and the approaches from the lower ferries on Big Black River;

Brigadier-General [F. A.] *Shoup's* brigade, of Major General *Smith's* division, guarded the river front of the city;

Brigadier-General [W. E.] *Baldwin's* brigade, with [T. N.] *Waul's* Legion attached, guarded the approaches to the city from the Hall's Ferry road around to the railroad bridge on the Big

Black, [and] the heavy artillery at the batteries on the river front under Colonel [Edward] *Higgins.*

Brigadier-General *Moore's* brigade was drawn in at once from Warrenton and placed in the intrenchments on either side of the Baldwin's Ferry road. Brigadier-General *Hébert's* brigade arrived before daylight on the 18th, bringing with it all the light pieces, and, in addition, two 20-pounder Parrotts and a Whitworth gun. This brigade immediately occupied the intrenchments on both sides of the Jackson road.

On the morning of the 18th, the troops were disposed from right to left, as follows: Major-General *Stevenson's* division of four brigades occupied the line from the Warrenton road, including a portion of the river front, to the railroad, a distance of about 5 miles; Major-General *Forney,* with two brigades, the line between the railroad and the Graveyard road, about 2 miles, and Major-General *Smith,* with three brigades (the Mississippi State troops) and a small detachment from *Loring's* division, the line from the Graveyard road to the river front on the north, about 1¼ miles. Brigadier-General *Bowen's* division was held in reserve to strengthen any portion of the line most threatened, and *Waul's* Texas Legion (about 500) was in reserve, especially to support the right of *Moore's* or the left of *Lee's* brigades.

On the entire line about one hundred and two pieces of artillery, of different caliber, principally field, were placed in position at such points as were deemed most suitable to the character of the gun, changes of location being made when occasion called for it. An engineer officer, under the supervision of Major *Lockett,* chief engineer of the department, was assigned to each division, with an assistant to each brigade commander. Daily reports were made through the proper channel to Major *Lockett* of the operations of the engineer department and of the progress of the enemy's works. Major *Lockett* thus kept me constantly informed of all important changes, making himself a daily report. Instructions had been given from Bovina that all cattle, sheep, and hogs belonging to private parties, and likely to fall into the hands of the enemy, should be driven within our lines. A large amount of fresh meat was secured in this way. The same instructions were given in regard to corn, and all disposable wagons applied to this end.

On the 18th, Col. Wirt *Adams,* who had been previously directed to cross to the west bank of the Big Black with all his cavalry, was notified that Snyder's Mill would be abandoned, and that he was expected to operate on the flank and rear of the enemy, with the view of cutting off his supplies in that direction. Colonel *Adams'* force was, however, very inadequate to this purpose.

During the night of the 17th, nothing of importance occurred. Most of the artillery was speedily placed in position on the lines, and immediate measures were taken to arm all men who had either unavoidably lost or who had thrown away their arms on the retreat.

General *Johnston* was notified on the 17th of the result of the battles of Baker's Creek [Champion Hill] and Big Black, and informed that I had in consequence been compelled to evacuate Snyder's Mill.

About noon of May 18, while engaged in an inspection of the intrenchments with Major *Lockett,* my chief engineer, and several of my general officers, the enemy was reported to be advancing by the Jackson road. Just at this moment the following communication was received by courier:

Camp, between Livingston and Brownsville
May 17, 1863
Lieutenant-General *Pemberton:*

Your dispatch of today by Captain [Thomas] *Henderson* was received. If Haynes' Bluff is untenable, Vicksburg is of no value and cannot be held. If, therefore, you are invested in Vicksburg, you must ultimately surrender. Under such circumstances, instead of losing both troops and place, we must, if possible, save the troops. If it is not too late, evacuate Vicksburg and its dependencies, and march to the northeast.

J. E. *Johnston*

The evacuation of Vicksburg! It meant the loss of the valuable stores and munitions of war collected for its defense; the fall of Port Hudson; the surrender of the Mississippi River, and the severance of the Confederacy. These were mighty interests which, had I deemed the evacuation practicable in the sense in which I interpreted General *Johnston's* instructions, might well have made me hesitate to execute them. I believed it to be in my power to hold Vicksburg. I knew and appreciated the earnest desire of the Government and of the people that it should be held. I knew, perhaps better than any other individual, under all the circumstances, its capacity for defense. As long ago as February 17 last, in a letter addressed to His Excellency the President, I had suggested the possibility of the investment of Vicksburg by land and water, and for that reason the necessity of ample supplies of ammunition as well as of subsistence to stand a siege. My application met his favorable consideration, and additional ammunition was ordered. With proper economy of subsistence and ordnance stores, I knew that I could stand a siege. I had a firm reliance on the desire of the President and of General *Johnston* to do all that could be done to raise a siege. I felt that every effort would be made, and I believed it would be successful.

With these convictions on my own mind, I immediately summoned a council of war composed of all my general officers. I laid before them General *Johnston's* communication, but desired them to confine the expression of their opinions to the question of practicability. Having obtained their views, the following communication was addressed to General *Johnston*. . . .

Vicksburg, May 18, 1863

I have the honor to acknowledge the receipt of your communication, in reply to mine. . . . In a subsequent letter of the same date . . . I informed you that the men had failed to hold the trenches at Big Black Bridge, and that, as a consequence, Snyder's Mill was directed to be abandoned. On the receipt of your communication, I immediately assembled a council of war of the general officers of this command, and having laid your instructions before them, asked the free expression of their opinion as to the practicability of carrying them out.

The opinion was unanimously expressed that it was impossible to withdraw the army from this position with such *morale* and material as to be of further service to the Confederacy. While the council of war was assembled, the guns of the enemy opened on the works, and it was at the same time reported that they were crossing the Yazoo River at Brandon's Ferry, above Snyder's Mill.

I have decided to hold Vicksburg as long as is possible, with the firm hope that the Government may yet be able to assist me in keeping this obstruction to the enemy's free navigation of the Mississippi River. I still conceive it to be the most important point in the Confederacy.

The development of the intrenched line from the extreme right of Major-General *Stevenson*'s position to the left of Major General *Smith*'s was about 8 miles, the shortest defensible line of which the topography of the country admitted. The plan was submitted to me immediately after I assumed command of the Department of Mississippi and Eastern Louisiana, in the latter part of October, 1862; was approved, and ordered to be carried out with the utmost dispatch. Similar instructions were about the same time given for fortifying the strong position at Snyder's Mill, and the land defenses of Port Hudson were also ordered to be commenced at once.

The line of defense around the city of Vicksburg consisted . . . of a system of detached works (redans, lunettes, and redoubts) on the prominent and commanding points, with the usual profile of raised field works, connected in most cases by rifle-pits. To man the entire line, I was able to bring into the trenches about eighteen thousand five hundred muskets, but it was absolutely necessary to keep a reserve always ready to re-enforce any point heavily threatened.

It became indispensable, therefore, to reduce the number in the trenches to the minimum capable of holding them until a reserve could come to their aid. It was also necessary that the reserve should be composed of troops among the best and most reliable. Accordingly, *Bowen*'s division (about 2,400) and *Waul*'s Texas Legion (about 500) were designated for that purpose, thus reducing the force in the trenches to little over 15,500 men. The Legion was on the 18th assigned as a reserve to *Forney*'s division, and was held in rear of Brigadier-General *Moore*'s right, but on the evening of the 19th was transferred to *Stevenson*'s division, and during the remainder of the siege was held in rear of Brigadier-General *Lee*'s brigade, occupying one of the most exposed and important positions on the whole line.

On the night of the 17th, and during the 18th, Major-General *Smith,* misapprehending my instructions given him immediately after my return from the Big Black, had occupied an outer line of defense on the range of hills north of the Fort Hill road. This line had undoubtedly some advantages; it was within 600 yards of the inner line, and partially commanded one of our most important river batteries. I considered, however, that the increased length which would necessarily be given to the whole line of defense, the intervening valley, and other objections to its occupation more than counterbalanced the advantages; the troops and artillery were, therefore, on the night of the 18th silently and safely withdrawn, and General *Smith's* division occupied the inner line during the remainder of the siege. The enemy, however, had made during the day a demonstration with artillery and infantry on his position, and early on the morning of the 19th he occupied the abandoned heights. During the day there was constant and heavy skirmishing along the left of our center on the Graveyard road, accompanied with brisk artillery fire. In the afternoon the enemy made a charge on *Smith's* right and *Forney's* left, but was severely repulsed. . . . Later their sharpshooters and artillery opened heavily on the Jackson and Baldwin's Ferry road.

A courier was dispatched with the following telegram to the President:

> We are occupying the trenches around Vicksburg. The enemy is investing it, and will probably attempt an assault. Our men have considerably recovered their morale, but unless a large force is sent at once to relieve it, Vicksburg before long must fall. I have used every effort to prevent all this, but in vain.[5]

Report of Gen. Joseph E. Johnston, CSA (continued)

On Monday, May 18, General *Pemberton* informed me by letter, dated . . . May 17, that he had retired within the line of intrenchments around Vicksburg, having been attacked and forced back from Big Black Bridge, and that he had ordered Haynes' Bluff to be abandoned. His letter concluded: "I greatly regret that I felt compelled to make the advance beyond Big Black, which has proved so disastrous in its results." It will be remembered that General *Pemberton* expected that Edwards Depot would be the battle-field before I reached Jackson . . . and that his army, before he received any orders from me, was 7 or 8 miles east of the Big Black, near Edwards Depot.

On May 19, General *Pemberton's* reply . . . to my communication of the 17th, was brought me near Vernon, where I had gone with the troops under my command for the purpose of effecting a junction with him in the event of his evacuating Vicksburg, as I had ordered. . . . He advised me that he had "assembled a council of war of the general officers of his command, and . . . the opinion was unanimously expressed that it was impossible to withdraw the army from this position with such morale and material as to be of further service to the Confederacy." . . . I replied, "I am trying to gather a force which may attempt to relieve you. Hold out."

The same day I sent orders to Major-General *Gardner* to evacuate Port Hudson. I then determined, by easy marches, to re-establish my line between Jackson and Canton, as the junction of the two commands had become impossible.

On May 20 and 21, I was joined by the brigades of Generals *Gist, Ector,* and *McNair.* The division of General *Loring,* cut off from General *Pemberton* in the battle of Baker's Creek [Champion Hill], reached Jackson on the 20th, and General *Maxey,* with his brigade, on the 23d.

By June 4, the army had, in addition to these, been re-enforced by the brigade of General [N. G.] *Evans,* the division of General *Breckinridge,* and the division of cavalry, numbering 2,800, commanded by Brig. Gen. W. *Jackson.*

Small as was this force (about 24,000 infantry and artillery, not one-third that of the enemy), it was deficient in artillery, in ammunition for all arms, and field transportation, and could not be moved upon that enemy (already intrenching his large force) with any hope of success. The draught upon the country had so far reduced the number of horses and mules, that it was not until late in June that draught animals could be procured from distant points for the artillery and trains.

There was no want of commissary supplies in the department, but the limited transportation caused a deficiency for a moving army.

On May 23, I received a dispatch from Major-General *Gardner,* dated Port Hudson, May 21, informing me that the enemy was about to cross at Bayou Sara; that the whole force from Baton Rouge was in his front, and asking to be re-enforced. On this, my orders for the evacuation of Port Hudson were repeated, and he was informed:

> You cannot be re-enforced. Do not allow yourself to be invested. At every risk save the troops, and, if practicable, move in this direction.

This dispatch did not reach General *Gardner,* Port Hudson being then invested.[6]

Report of Maj. Samuel H. Lockett, CSA, Chief Engineer for Vicksburg

Our army fell back to the city on Sunday, May 17, and were put in the trenches in the following order, viz: Major-General *Stevenson* occupied the line included between the railroad and the Warrenton road, on the south, General *Forney* the line between the railroad and the Graveyard road, and General *Smith* the line from the Graveyard road to the river front, on the north.

On the 18th, I made a careful examination of the entire line, and made the following dispositions of the engineer officers under my command, to facilitate the operations of strengthening and repairing the works: Captain [Powhatan] [brackets in original] *Robinson*, Engineers, was assigned to the line commanded by Major-General *Stevenson*, and had under him, as assistants . . . Captain J. J. *Conway*, Twentieth Mississippi, detailed assistant engineer; Actg. Lieut. A. W. *Gloster*, assistant engineer; Actg. Lieut. R. R. *Southard*, assistant engineer; Capt. James M. *Couper*, commissary Fourteenth [Twentieth] [brackets in original] Mississippi, acting assistant engineer; Mr. B. H. *Saunders*, office assistant.

Capt. D. *Wintter*, commanding company of sappers and miners, was assigned to the line commanded by Major-Generals *Forney* and *Smith*, and had under him as assistants . . . First Lieut. E. *McMahon*, company sappers and miners; Second Lieut. F. *Gillooly*, company sappers and miners; Capt. James [T.] [brackets in original] *Hogane*, acting assistant engineer; Actg. Lieut. S. McD. *Vernon*, assistant engineer, and Acting Lieut. P. J. *Blessing*.

Lieut. [in original] William O. *Flynn*, of Captain *Wintter's* company, was ordered to report for engineer duty to Col. E. *Higgins*, commanding the heavy artillery.

This arrangement gave to each brigade one immediate assistant, whose duty it was to report directly to the brigade commander, and to each division an engineer to take general control.

Lieut. George *Donnellan*, engineer, Provisional Army Confederate States, I kept in my office to take charge of the procuring and distribution of materials. Mr. H. Ginder was employed as draughtsman and Mr. G. C. Brower as clerk.

The working force under my control was . . . twenty-six sappers and miners, of Captain *Wintter's* company; 8 detailed mechanics and foreman; 4 overseers for negroes; 72 negroes hired, 20 being sick; 3 four-mule teams, 25 yoke of draught oxen.

An accurate return of the intrenching tools was never obtained, from the fact that they were always employed and so much scattered. The number, however, was not far from 500 of all kinds.

The work on the lines was generally done by fatigue parties detailed from each command to work within the limits of its own line.

The line of defense around the city of Vicksburg consisted . . . of a system of detached works (redans, lunettes, and redoubts) on the prominent and commanding points, with the usual profile of raised field-works, connected, in most cases, by rifle-pits. These works, having been made during the fall and winter of last year, were considerably weakened by washing, and needed strengthening and repairing. Fatigue parties were immediately set to work making these repairs and completing the connection of rifle-pits from work to work.

On the night of May 17, and the morning of the 18th, all the field guns, Parrott guns, and siege pieces at our disposal were put in position on the line, and platforms and embrasures prepared for them.[7]

Narrative of Maj. Samuel H. Lockett, CSA, Chief Engineer of the Vicksburg Defenses (continued)

The morning of the 18th found us with 102 guns ready for service on the rear line. Some portions of our front were protected by *abatis* of fallen trees and entanglements of telegraph wire. The river batteries were still strong and intact, having lost none of their sea-coast guns.

The troops were placed in position as I had recommended. . . . Early on May 18th the Federal forces appeared on the Jackson and Graveyard roads, which were covered by a part of General M. L. *Smith's* division, posted as skirmishers and pickets outside our main lines. The Federals were held in check, so that during the night General *Smith* had no difficulty in withdrawing his forces within the main line of defense. The next day, when the Federals discovered that the Confederates were gone from their position of the evening before, they came forward rapidly and took that position, with shout and cheer, and soon after rushed upon the main line of defense, apparently with perfect confidence that there would be another "walk over" such as they had had two days before at Big Black bridge.

But this time they struck a rock in General *Shoup*'s brigade, which met them with so heavy and well-directed a fire that they were compelled to fall back. A second time they came forward in greater numbers and with more boldness and determination, but with even more fatal results. They were repulsed with great loss, leaving five stand of colors close to our lines and the ground being strewn with their dead and wounded. These assaults extended from *Shoup*'s position toward our right so as to include a part of *Forney*'s division. Thus they were met by troops which had not been in any of the recent disastrous engagements and were not in the least demoralized. These men stood to their arms like true soldiers, and helped to restore the *morale* of our army.[8]

NOTES

1. *O.R.,* XXIV, pt. 1, pp. 265–67.
2. *O.R.,* XXIV, pt. 2, pp. 241–42.
3. *O.R.,* XXIV, pt. 1, pp. 53–54.
4. *O.R.,* XXIV, pt. 2, pp. 135–39.
5. *O.R.,* XXIV, pt. 1, pp. 265–74.
6. *O.R.,* XXIV, pt. 1, pp. 241–42.
7. *O.R.,* XXIV, pt. 2, pp. 329–30.
8. Samuel H. Lockett, "The Defense of Vicksburg," in *Battles and Leaders of the Civil War,* 4 vols., ed. Robert U. Johnson and Clarence C. Buel (New York: Century, 1884), 3:488–89.

14. THE SIEGE

Summary of Principal Events:
May 19–July 4, 1863

May
19   First Union assault on Vicksburg.
22   Second Union assault on Vicksburg.
23–July 4   Siege of Vicksburg.
27   Engagement between USS *Cincinnati* and the Vicksburg batteries; the *Cincinnati* is sunk.

June
3–17   Transfer of Ninth Army Corps from Kentucky to vicinity of Vicksburg.
5   Maj. Gen. John G. Parke, USA, resumes command of the Ninth Army Corps.
19   Maj. Gen. E. O. C. Ord supersedes Maj. Gen. McClernand in command of Thirteenth Army Corps.
25   Federals detonate a mine under Third Louisana Redan. Assault following up the blast is repulsed.

July
4   Vicksburg surrenders.

Editors' note: The following chapter provides an overview of the siege operations. A detailed tactical discussion of the siege along with directions to the various points of interest along the lines may be found in Part III of this book.

THE INITIAL UNION ASSAULT

Report of Maj. Gen. Ulysses S. Grant, USA, Headquarters, Department of the Tennessee, Commanding

Sherman by this time [May 17] had reached Bridgeport, on Black River, above. The only pontoon train with the expedition was with him. By the morning of the 18th, he had crossed the river, and was ready to march on Walnut Hills [on the north side of Vicksburg]. McClernand and McPherson built floating bridges during the night, and had them ready for crossing their commands by 8 A.M. of the 18th.

The march was commenced by Sherman at an early hour by the Bridgeport and Vicksburg road, turning to the right when within 3½ miles of Vicksburg, to get possession of Walnut Hills and the Yazoo River. This was successfully accomplished before the night of the 18th. McPherson crossed Big Black River above the Jackson road and came into the same road with Sherman, but to his rear. He arrived after night-fall with his advance to where Sherman turned to the right. McClernand moved by the Jackson and Vicksburg road to Mount Albans, and there turned to the left, to get into Baldwin's Ferry road. By this disposition the three army corps covered all the ground their strength would admit of, and by the morning of the 19th the investment of Vicksburg was made as complete as could be by the forces at my command.

During the day there was continuous skirmishing, and I was not without hope of carrying the enemy's works. Relying upon the demoralization of the enemy, in consequence of repeated defeats outside of Vicksburg, I ordered a general assault at 2 P.M. on this day. The Fifteenth Army Corps [Sherman], from having arrived in front of the enemy's works in time on the 18th to get a good position, were enabled to make a vigorous assault. The Thirteenth [McClernand] and Seventeenth [McPherson] Army Corps succeeded no further than to gain advanced positions covered from the fire of the enemy.[1]

Report of Maj. Gen. Francis P. Blair Jr., USA, Commanding Second Division, Fifteenth Army Corps

About midnight of the 18th, the Third Brigade of my division, commanded by Brig. Gen. Hugh Ewing, joined me before the works of Vicksburg, having marched from Grand Gulf (by Raymond) . . . a distance of 85 miles, in three days. . . . [His] brigade was assigned position on the right of my division, his right resting on the left of General Steele's division (First Division, Fifteenth Army Corps). His left connected closely with the right of my First Brigade, commanded by Col. Giles A. Smith, who held the center of my line and occupied the ground in front of the stockade near the bastion [Stockade Redan], which commands the Graveyard Road. The Second Brigade, Col. Thomas Kilby Smith commanding, held the left of my line, the right resting on the left of the First Brigade, and its line of battle extending across the Graveyard Road.

During the morning of the 19th, the entire line of skirmishers of my division was pushed forward, with a view of obtaining a closer position and of reconnoitering the ground.

At 2 P.M. the signal was given for an assualt, and my whole division dashed forward, and, wherever the nature of the ground was not insuperable, reached the enemy's intrenchments, and in several instances planted our flags upon his works. Two regiments of General Ewing's brigade, the Fourth Virginia and Forty-seventh Ohio, succeeded in approaching very near the enemy's works. The Thirteenth U.S. Infantry, Capt. E. C. Washington, and One hundred and sixteenth Illinois Volunteer Infantry, Col. N. W. Tupper, of the First Brigade . . . pushed forward to the bastion. The One hundred and twenty-seventh Illinois Volunteer Infantry, Col. Hamilton N. Eldridge, and Eighty-third Indiana Volunteer Infantry, Col. Benjamin J. Spooner, of the Second Brigade . . . also succeeded in reaching the same ground, but the heavy fire of the enemy, who, not being pressed in any other quarter, were strongly re-enforced in our front, made it utterly impossible for them to make a lodgement in the works. They held their positions, however, with the utmost tenacity until night, when they withdrew.[2]

Report of Brig. Gen. Peter J. Osterhaus, USA, Commanding Ninth Division, Thirteenth Army Corps

The Thirteenth Army Corps . . . reached the road leading from Hall's Ferry to Vicksburg. On this avenue we approached the city, and at nightfall we came within sight of its extensive fortifications. Numerous flags floating over the works proved that the persisting leaders of the enemy would try a last attempt to rally their men to fight again, and to save, if possible, the stronghold of rebeldom on the Mississippi River. We bivouacked on a very narrow little creek, about 2 miles from the line of fortifications.

Orders received on May 19 placed the Thirteenth Army Corps on the left wing of the army, which prepared to invest the city. My division was to form the extreme left, and General [A. J.] Smith's the right of our first line, while General Carr, deploying his divi-

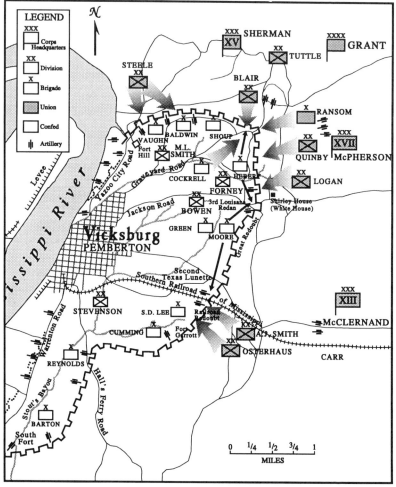

Union assaults on Vicksburg, May 19, 1863.

sions in the center of us, took the second line. Such were our instructions. . . .

I at once proceeded to make . . . a reconnaissance of the grounds which were to be the field of operations for the Ninth Division. At the little creek we had bivouacked on, the ground on the left of the road rises gradually, and, forming a plateau sloping from west to east, is converted into fields planted with corn. At the west end of the plateau it abruptly sinks into a deep valley again.

At the margin of this valley the plateau reaches its highest elevation, and runs almost parallel and on the same lead with that ridge in front (west) which the enemy had covered with his fortifications.

The distance between the plateau and the fortifications does not exceed 1,500 yards, but the interval is very broken indeed. The main figures of this intermediate ground are two ridges running almost parallel with the fortified line and with the west side of the plateau, but hardly on any point high enough to mask these from each other. The ridges are very steep, creating three narrow valleys, in each one of which is a small running stream. These hills and valleys are . . . variously intersected by cross valleys and gorges, making a passage over them very difficult. To go straight forward over them with artillery is out of the question, except by pulling them up and down by hand; though on the south end of that section of terrain where the . . . three valleys converge, the slopes appeared to offer some practicability for military movements, and I was informed that I could find there a plantation road which connected the Hall's Ferry and the Warrenton and Vicksburg roads.

The main Baldwin's Ferry road, on which the Thirteenth Army Corps was approaching, turns on the highest ridge of the plateau to the right, and, following the undulations of the ground, enters the line of the enemy's fortifications in front of the position assigned to General Smith's division. . . . I ordered my division to advance in the following order:

The First Brigade, under General [A. L.] Lee, deployed into line of battle to the edge of the valley (west end of the plateau), with one section of 20–pounder Parrotts . . . on the right, and two sections of the same on the left. The Second Brigade, under Col. D. W. Lindsey, deployed into line, by battalions in mass, in the rear of the First Brigade. Being placed on the extreme left, I ordered a strong line of pickets thrown out on that flank, supported by the left battalion of the Second Brigade, in order to prevent any surprise from that side, Lanphere's battery was kept in reserve, supported by the cavalry. The right section of Foster's battery was opened by 10 o'clock on a battery in front of General Smith, where we could see a party of the rebels at work. The distance was at least 1,500 yards, but the projectiles from these superior guns reached the object and dispersed the working party.

All the forts in my front were fully manned, and a number of guns were in view, but they did not fire even when Foster's battery, on the left of . . . Lee's brigade, to find the range, threw several shells among them. Their guns remained silent. I ordered General Lee to advance his line into the valley, leaving only a support to the batteries, and, as far as he found no resistance with skirmishers, feeling the way carefully.

The general descended into the valley and marched up the next ridge, passed the next valley, and was debouching from a small strip of timber in order to ascend the second line of hills. Here his troops came in view of the enemy, who then opened with shot and shell, though without doing any injury. The general halted under the shelter of the many ravines. Colonel Lindsey's brigade followed this forward movement, under orders to support and strengthen any part of General Lee's line if necessary.

Shortly before this, I received orders from corps headquarters [McClernand] to prepare everything for a general assault at 2 P.M. After having advised my brigade commanders of this order, Captain Lanphere's battery was brought forward to support the assault, and unlimbered on an eminence on the left of Foster's battery. Both batteries were to open fire on the enemy's works and wherever he should show himself. The forward movement of the infantry had left the batteries without an effective support in case of a flank attack, and I therefore ordered Captain Campbell's cavalry to proceed on the plantation road . . . leading to Warrenton and Hall's Ferry, scour all the country south, and apprise me of anything that might transpire in that direction.

At 2 o'clock all the batteries fired three volleys, and the infantry began the advance. They climbed the steep hills before them in most brilliant style, and marched over the brow of the ridge through a most raking fire.

The extremely irregular ground and the situation of the objects of attack made the direction of the advance of the First Brigade bear to the left, and, of course, it created a gap in the line of attack between mine and General Smith's command, on my right. Under my orders . . . Colonel Lindsey . . . at once inserted his brigade in this opening, and the whole division now advanced steadily and gallantly against a most fearful fire from the enemy's rifle-pits and batteries, which commanded (mostly by cross-fire) every hill, every ravine, gully, and gorge leading to the fortifications.

Many a brave man sank down under the hail-storm of iron and lead, and among them . . . General A. L. Lee, who, so shortly connected with the division, had shown so many military virtues, was wounded; but the victors at Port Gibson, Champion's Hill, and Big Black River marched forward and held the ground gained. They came within 300 or 350 yards of the enemy's works, and, availing themselves of every swell and nook of the ground, opened now on their part a murderous fire, compelling the rebel gunners very soon to leave their guns. . . .

The artillery . . . supported movements of the infantry with a well-directed fire; but in order to bring the batteries to a more effective range, I selected a hill at least 500 yards nearer the rebel works for a battery, and at once ordered one section of Lanphere's battery to be brought forward. The pieces had to be drawn up the very steep hill by hand, and as soon as one piece was in position it was opened on by the enemy.

The feasibility of establishing a battery on the steep hill being thus demonstrated, I ordered a breastwork to be built during the night on the same spot for two sections of Lanphere's battery. I laid the faces of this work out so that we could rake every battery in our front.

After nightfall a strong force of sharpshooters and reserves were detailed to occupy and hold the ground gained by our first attack on Vicksburg. . . . In the early part of the morning the infantry had formed again in their respective places they occupied yesterday, but behind the line of sharpshooters, who kept up a very lively fire . . . in the rifle-pits.[3]

THE SECOND UNION ASSAULT

Report of Maj. Gen. Ulysses S. Grant, USA (continued)

The 20th and 21st were spent in perfecting communications with our supplies. Most of the troops had been marching and fighting battles for twenty days, on an average of about five days' rations drawn from the commissary department. Though they had not suffered from short rations up to this time, the want of bread to accompany the other rations was beginning to be much felt.

On the 21st, my arrangements for drawing supplies of every description being complete, I determined to make another effort to carry Vicksburg by assault. There were many reasons . . . to adopt this course. I believed an assault from the position gained by this time could be made successfully. It was known that *Johnston* was at Canton with the force taken by him from Jackson, re-enforced by

Lithograph portraying the Union assault on May 22. (Frank Leslie's *The American Soldier in the Civil War*)

other troops from the east, and that more were daily reaching him. With the force I then had, a short time must have enabled him to attack me in the rear, and possibly succeeded in raising the siege.

Possession of Vicksburg at that time would have enabled me to have turned upon *Johnston* and driven him from the State, and possessed myself of all the railroads and practical military highways, thus effectually securing to ourselves all territory west of the Tombigbee, and this before the season was too far advanced for campaigning in this latitude. It would have saved the Government sending large re-enforcements, much needed elsewhere; and, finally, the troops themselves were impatient to possess Vicksburg, and would not have worked in the trenches with the same zeal, believing it unnecessary, that they did after their failure to carry the enemy's works.

Accordingly, on the 21st orders were issued for a general assault on the whole line, to commence at 10 A.M. on the 22d. All the corps commanders set their time by mine, that there should be no difference between them in movement of assault. Promptly at the hour designated the three army corps then in front of the enemy's works commenced the assault. I had taken a commanding position near McPherson's front, and from which I could see all the advancing columns from his corps and a part of each of Sherman's and McClernand's. A portion of the commands of each succeeded in planting their flags on the outer slopes of the enemy's bastions, and maintained them there until night.

Each corps had many more men than could possibly be used in the assault over such ground as intervened between them and the enemy. More men could only avail in case of breaking through the enemy's line or in repelling a *sortie*. The assault was gallant in the extreme on the part of all the troops, but the enemy's position was too strong, both naturally and artificially, to be taken in that way. At every point assaulted, and at all of them at the same time, the enemy was able to show all the force his works would cover.

The assault failed, I regret to say, with much loss on our side in killed and wounded, but without weakening the confidence of the troops in their ability to ultimately succeed. No troops succeeded in entering any of the enemy's works with the exception of Sergeant [Joseph E.] Griffith, of the Twenty [second] Iowa Volunteers, and some 11 privates of the same regiment. Of these none returned, except the sergeant and possibly 1 man. The work entered by him, from its position, could give us no practical advantage unless others to the right and left of it were carried and held at the same time.

About 12 M. [noon] I received a dispatch from McClernand that he was hard pressed at several points, in reply to which I directed him to re-enforce the points . . . from such troops as he had that were not engaged. I then rode around to Sherman, and had just reached there when I received a second dispatch from McClernand, stating positively and unequivocally that he was in possession of and still held two of the enemy's forts; that the American flag then waved over them, and asking me to have Sherman and McPherson to make a diversion in his favor. This dispatch I showed to Sherman, who immediately ordered a renewal of the assault on his front. I also sent an answer to McClernand, directing him to order up McArthur to his assistance, and started immediately to the position I had just left on McPherson's line, to convey to him the information from McClernand by this last dispatch, that he might make the diversion requested. Before reaching McPherson, I met a messenger with a third dispatch from McClernand. . . .

> General: We have gained the enemy's intrenchments at several points, but are brought to a stand. I have sent word to McArthur to re-enforce me if he can. Would it not be best to concentrate the whole or a part of his command on this point.
>
> P.S. I have received your dispatch. My troops are all engaged, and I cannot withdraw any to re-enforce others.

The position occupied by me during most of the time of the assault gave me a better opportunity of seeing what was going on in front of the Thirteenth Army Corps than I believed it possible for the commander of it to have. I could not see his possession of forts, nor necessity for re-enforcements, as represented in his dispatches, up to the time I left it . . . between 12 M. and 1 P.M., and I expressed doubts of their correctness, which . . . the facts subsequently, but too late, confirmed. At the time I could not disregard his reiterated statements, for they might possibly be true; and that no possible opportunity of carrying the enemy's stronghold should be allowed to escape through fault of mine, I ordered Quinby's division, which was all of McPherson's corps then present but four brigades, to report to McClernand, and notified him of the order. I showed his dispatches to McPherson, as I had to Sherman, to satisfy him of the necessity of an active diversion on their part to

Maj. Gen. John A. McClernand, USA, Commander, Thirteenth Corps, Army of the Tennessee. (U.S. Army Military History Institute)

hold as much force in their fronts as possible. The diversion was promptly and vigorously made, and resulted in the increase of our mortality list fully 50 per cent, without advancing our position or giving us other advantages.

About 3:50 P.M. I received McClernand's fourth dispatch. . . . I have received your dispatch in regard to General

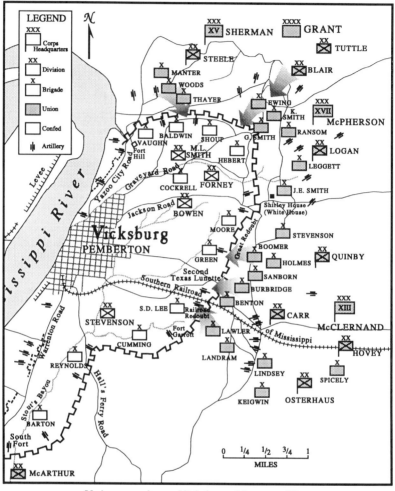

Union assaults on Vicksburg, May 22, 1863.

Quinby's division. As soon as they arrive I will press the enemy with all possible speed, and doubt not I will force my way through. I have lost no ground. My men are in two of the enemy's forts, but they are commanded by rifle-pits in the rear. Several prisoners have been taken, who intimate that the rear is strong. At this moment I am hard pressed.

The assault of this day proved the qualities of the soldiers of this army. Without entire success, and with a heavy loss, there was

no murmuring or complaining; no falling back, nor other evidence
of demoralization.

After the failure of the 22d, I determined upon a regular siege.[4]

THE SIEGE

Grant to Maj. Gen. Henry W. Halleck, May 22, 1863

Vicksburg is now completely invested. I have possession of
Haynes' Bluff and the Yazoo; consequently have supplies. To-day
an attempt was made to carry the city by assault, but was not entirely successful. We hold possession, however, of two of the
enemy's forts, and have skirmishers close under all of them. Our
loss was not severe.

The nature of the ground about Vicksburg is such that it can
only be taken by a siege. It is entirely safe to us in time, I would say
one week, if the enemy do not send a large army upon my rear.
With the railroad destroyed to beyond Pearl River, I do not see
the hope that the enemy can entertain of such belief.[5]

Grant to Halleck, May 24, 1863

My troops are now disposed with the right (Sherman's corps)
resting on the Mississippi, where the bluff strikes the water, we
having the first crest and the upper of the enemy's water batteries.
McClernand is on the left with his corps, his right having about
one brigade north of the railroad, the rest south of it. One division occupies the roads leading south and southeast from the city.
The position is as strong by nature as can possibly be conceived
of, and is well fortified. The garrison the enemy have to defend it
I have no means of knowing, but their force is variously estimated
from 10,000 to 20,000.

I attempted to carry the place by storm on the 22d, but was
unsuccessful. Our troops were not repulsed from any point, but
simply failed to enter the works of the enemy. At several points
they got up to the parapets of the enemy's forts, and planted their
flags on the outer slope of the embankments. . . . The assault was
made simultaneously by the three army corps at 10 P.M. The loss
on our side was not very heavy at first, but receiving repeated dispatches from General McClernand, saying that he was hard pressed
on his right and left and calling for re-enforcements, I gave him

306] THE VICKSBURG CAMPAIGN

all of McPherson's corps but four brigades, and caused Sherman to press the enemy on our right, which caused us to double our losses for the day. The whole loss . . . will probably reach 1,500 killed and wounded.

General McClernand's dispatches misled me as to the real state of facts, and caused much of this loss. He is entirely unfit for the position of corps commander, both on the march and on the battle-field. Looking after his corps gives me more labor and infinitely more uneasiness than all the remainder of my department.

The enemy are now undoubtedly in our grasp. The fall of Vicksburg and the capture of most of the garrison can only be a question of time. I hear a great deal of the enemy bringing a large force from the east to effect a raising of the siege. They may attempt something of the kind, but I do not see how they can do it. The railroad is effectually destroyed at Jackson, so that it will take thirty days to repair it. This will leave a march of 50 miles over which the enemy will have to subsist an army, and bring their ordnance stores with teams. My position is so strong that I could hold out for several days against a vastly superior force. I do not see how the enemy could possibly maintain a long attack under these circumstances. I will keep a close watch on the enemy, however.

There is now a force at Calhoun Station, about 6 miles north of Canton, on the Mississippi Central Railroad. This is the force that escaped from Jackson, augmented by a few thousand men from the coast cities, intended to re-enforce the latter place before the attack, but failed to reach in time.[6]

Grant to Halleck, May 25, 1863

There is evidence of a force collecting near Big Black River, north-east of here about 30 miles. I have ordered all the force that can be spared from West Tennessee, and communicated with General Banks, asking him to come with all the force he can. I can manage the force in Vicksburg and an attacking force on the rear of 30,000, but may have more to contend against. Vicksburg will have to be reduced by regular siege. My effective force here is about 50,000, and can be increased 10,000 more from my own command.[7]

Grant to Halleck, May 29, 1863

The enemy under *Johnston* is collecting a large force to attack me and rescue the garrison of Vicksburg. I have had my cavalry and six brigades of infantry out looking after them, and they confirm the report of a large force being collected at Canton. The number is reported to be 45,000, but may not be so large. If Banks does not come to my assistance, I must be re-enforced from elsewhere. I will avoid a surprise and do the best I can with all the means at hand.[8]

President Abraham Lincoln to Grant, June 2, 1863

Are you in communication with General Banks? Is he coming toward you or going farther off? Is there or has there been anything to hinder his coming directly to you by water from Alexandria?[9]

Halleck to Grant, June 2, 1863

Yours of the 29th received. I will do all I can to assist you. I have sent dispatch after dispatch to General Banks to join you. Why he does not I cannot understand. His separate operation upon Port Hudson is in direct violation of his instructions. If possible, send him this dispatch. My last dispatch from him was May 4.[10]

Grant to Halleck, June 3, 1863

The approaches are gradually nearing the enemy's fortifications. Five days more should plant our batteries on their parapets.

Johnston is still collecting troops at Canton and Jackson. Some are coming over the railroad, and all the country is joining his standard. The destruction of the enemy's artillery and ordnance stores was so complete that all these must be brought in from a distance.

I sent a large force up between the Yazoo and Big Black Rivers. Forage, beef, and bacon were found in great abundance. The forage and bacon were destroyed by our troops and the stock brought to camp. I am now placing all my spare force on the narrowest part of land between the two rivers, about 45 miles northeast, with the cavalry watching all the crossings of Big Black River. We shell the town a little every day, and keep the enemy constantly on the alert. We but seldom lose a man now. The best of health and spirits prevail among the troops.[11]

Grant to Lincoln, June 8, 1863
(Received June 10—9:10 P.M.)

I send by mail letter from General Banks, of June 4. I am in communication with him. He has Port Hudson closely invested.[12]

Grant to Halleck, June 8, 1863

Vicksburg is closely invested. I have a spare force of about 30,000 men with which to repel anything from the rear. This includes all I have ordered from West Tennessee. *Johnston* is concentrating a force at Canton, and now has a portion of it west of Big Black River. My troops have been north as far as Satartia, and on the ridge back of that point there is no force yet. I will make a waste of all the country I can between the two rivers. I am fortifying Haynes' Bluff, and will defend the line from here to that point at all hazards.[13]

Grant to Halleck, June 8, 1863

It is reported that three divisions have left *Bragg's* army to join *Johnston. Breckinridge* is known to have arrived.[14]

Grant to Halleck, June 11, 1863

Re-enforcements other than from my own command are beginning to arrive. There is every indication that they may be required. The enemy occupy Yazoo City and Canton, with an entire division of cavalry on the ridge between the two rivers. I am fortifying Haynes' Bluff, and will have a garrison there of 13,000 men, besides the ability to throw an equal amount more there in case of an attack, and still keep up the investment of Vicksburg. [General] Kirby *Smith* is showing signs of working to this side of the river, either to operate against General Banks or myself. He may find difficulty in crossing the river, but the great number of bayous and little lakes within a short distance of shore in this region afford such facilities for concealing boats that the means of crossing an army may still be left to the rebels; particularly may this be the case about Natchez. I now fear trouble on the opposite side of the river, between Lake Providence and Milliken's Bend.[15]

Grant to Halleck, June 11, 1863

I have reliable information from the entire interior of the South. *Johnston* has been re-enforced by 3,000 troops from Mobile and other parts of Georgia; by [J. P.] *McCown's* and *Breckinridge's* divisions (9,000 men) and 4,000 of *Forrest's* cavalry, from *Bragg's* army; 9,000 men from Charleston, and 2,200 from Port Hudson. Orders were sent the very day General Banks invested Port Hudson, to evacuate it. Garrison there now 8,000. [R. E.] *Lee's* army [of Northern Virginia] has not been reduced; *Bragg's* force now 46,000 infantry and artillery and 15,000 cavalry. Everything not required for daily use has been removed to Atlanta, Ga. His army can fall back to Bristol or Chattanooga at a moment's notice, which places, it is thought, he can hold, and spare 25,000 troops. Mobile and Savannah are now almost entirely without garrisons, farther than men to manage large guns. No troops are left in the interior to send to any place. All further re-enforcements will have to come from one of the great armies. There are about 32,000 men west of the Mississippi, exclusive of the troops in Texas. Orders were sent them one week ago by *Johnston.* The purpose of the order not known. [General F. J.] Herron has arrived here, and troops from Burnside looked for tomorrow.[16]

Halleck to Grant, June 12, 1863

I hope you fully appreciate the importance of time in the reduction of Vicksburg. The large re-enforcements sent to you have opened Missouri and Kentucky to rebel raids. The siege should be pushed night and day with all possible dispatch.[17]

Grant to Halleck, June 18, 1863

Everything progresses well here. *Johnston's* forces are at Yazoo City, Benton, Brownsville, and Clinton. I am fortifying Haynes' Bluff to make my position certain, but believe I could go out with force enough to drive the rebels from between the two rivers. Deserters come out daily. All report rations short. We scarcely ever lose a man now. Health and condition of troops most excellent.[18]

Grant to Halleck, June 19, 1863

I have found it necessary to relieve Major-General McClernand, particularly at this time, for his publication of a congratulatory address calculated to create dissension and ill-feeling in the army. I should have relieved him long since for general unfitness for his position. Major General Ord is appointed to his place, subject to the approval of the President.[19]

Grant to Halleck, June 26, 1863

Yesterday a mine was sprung under the enemy's most commanding fort [Third Louisana Redan], producing a crater sufficient to hold two regiments of infantry. Our men took immediate possession, and still hold it. The fight for it has been incessant, and thus far we have not been able to establish batteries in the breach. Expect to succeed.

Joe *Johnston* has removed east of the Big Black. His movements are mysterious, and may be intended to cover a movement from his rear into East or West Tennessee, or upon Banks. I have General Sherman out near his front on the Big Black with a large force watching him. I will use every effort to learn any move *Johnston* may make, and send troops from here to counteract any change he may make, if I can.[20]

Grant to Halleck, June 27, 1863

Joe *Johnston* has postponed his attack until he can receive 10,000 re-enforcements, now on their way from *Bragg's* army. They are expected early next week. I feel strong enough against this increase, and do not despair of having Vicksburg before they arrive. This latter, however, I may be disappointed in. I may have to abandon protection to the leased plantations from here to Lake Providence, to resist a threat from Kirby *Smith's* troops. The location of these leased plantations was most unfortunate, and against my judgment. I wanted them put north of the White River.[21]

THE CONFEDERATE DEFENSE

Narrative of Maj. Samuel H. Lockett, CSA, Chief Engineer of the Vicksburg Defenses (continued)

The 20th and 21st of May were occupied by the Federal forces in completing their line, at an average distance of about eight hundred yards from our works. The Confederates utilized the time in putting up traverses against enfilade fires, and in making covered approaches from the camps in rear to the line of works. Many a man and officer had already been picked off by the quick-sighted Federal sharp-shooters, while passing along our lines or between them and the cooking-camps. It took several days for our men to learn the caution necessary to protect themselves.

On the 22d of May the gun-boats moved up within range and opened fire upon the river front. At the same time several dense columns of troops assaulted our lines in the rear. These assaults covered the right of General *Smith*'s position, where General *Shoup*'s brigade was posted, the whole of General *Forney*'s front, and that of Stephen D. *Lee*'s brigade of *Stevenson*'s division.

The assaults were made with great determination and admirable courage by the Federal soldiers. Once, twice, three times they came forward and recoiled from the deadly fire poured upon them by the Confederates, who were now thoroughly restored to their old-time confidence and aroused to an enthusiastic determination to hold their lines. Every assault was repulsed with terrible loss to the attacking parties.

At two points on the line—on General *Forney*'s and General S. D. *Lee*'s front—the Federals obtained a lodgment and planted their colors on our parapet; but the brave fellows paid for their success by being either killed or captured and having their colors fall into our hands. On General *Lee*'s line they even succeeded in capturing one of our detached works and drove out the men who held it. But it was retaken in a few minutes by a charge of *Waul*'s Legion, led by Colonel *Pettus* of Alabama.

The losses on both sides were severe; several thousand men, estimated by us at 3,500, were left dead and wounded between the lines. On the 25th the Federal dead and some of their wounded in the fight of the 22d were still in our front and close to our lines. The dead had become offensive and the living were suffering fearful agonies. General *Pemberton,* therefore, under a flag of truce, sent a note to General Grant, proposing a cessation of hostilities for two and a half hours, so that the dead and dying men might receive proper attention. This was acceded to by General Grant, and from six o'clock until nearly dark both parties were engaged in performing funeral rites and deeds of mercy to the dead and wounded Federal soldiers.

On this occasion I met General Sherman for the first time. Naturally the officers of both armies took advantage of the truce

Maj. Gen. Martin L. *Smith*, CSA, Commanding Division, Army of Vicksburg. (U.S. Army Military History Institute)

to use their eyes to the best possible advantage. I was on the Jackson road redan, which had been terribly pounded and was the object of constant attention from a battery of heavy guns in its immediate front. The Federals were running toward it in a zigzag approach, and were already in uncomfortable proximity to it.

While standing on the parapet of this work a Federal orderly came up to me and said that General Sherman wished to speak to me. Following the orderly, I reached a group of officers standing some two hundred yards in front of our line. One of these came forward, introduced himself as General Sherman, and said: "I saw that you were an officer by your insignia of rank, and have asked you to meet me, to put into your hands some letters intrusted to me by northern friends of some of your officers and men. I thought this would be a good opportunity to deliver this mail. . . ."

"Yes, General, it would have been very old, indeed, if you had kept it until you brought it into Vicksburg yourself."

"So you think, then," said the general, "I am a very slow mail route."

"Well, rather, when you have to travel by regular approaches, parallels, and zigzags."

"Yes," he said, "that is a slow way of getting into a place, but it is a very sure way, and I was determined to deliver those letters sooner or later."

The general then invited me to take a seat with him on an old log nearby, and thus the rest of the time of the truce was spent in pleasant conversation. In the course of it the general remarked: "You have an admirable position for defense here, and you have taken excellent advantage of the ground." "Yes, General," I replied, "but it is equally as well adapted to offensive operations, and your engineers have not been slow to discover it." To this General Sherman assented. Intentionally or not, his civility certainly prevented me from seeing many other points in our front that I as chief engineer was very anxious to examine.

The truce ended, the sharp-shooters immediately began their work and kept it up until darkness prevented accuracy of aim. Then the pickets of the two armies were posted in front of their respective lines, so near to each other that they whiled away the long hours of the night-watch with social chat. Within our lines the pick and shovel were the weapons of defense until the next morning.[22]

SIEGE OPERATIONS

Reports of Capts. Frederick E. Prime and Cyrus B. Comstock, U.S. Corps of Engineers, Chief Engineers of the Army of the Tennessee

On May 19, the troops . . . invested the city of Vicksburg thoroughly on the northern and eastern sides and incompletely on the south, Sherman's corps occupying the right, McPherson's the center, and McClernand's corps the left. Sherman's corps occupied the same position till near the close of the siege, when a division was moved toward the Big Black River to form part of a covering force against [General J. E.] *Johnston*. McArthur's brigade, of McPherson's corps, was at first posted on the extreme left, resting on the Mississippi, to cover our depots at, and communications with, Warrenton, but was replaced by Lauman's division, brought from Haynes' Bluff, and then took post as reserve to McPherson's corps, in rear of Logan's division, furnishing working parties to assist Ransom and occasionally Logan. Lauman was to have been relieved by Parke's corps, which started for Warrenton for that purpose, and Lauman to take position on the left of Hovey's division, of McClernand's corps, Hovey's front being diminished, as he had too much ground to cover, and Herron, on his arrival, to take post between the two.

This arrangement was altered by Parke's corps going to Haynes' Bluff, Herron's division taking the extreme left on its arrival, and Lauman moving to Hovey's left. The front, covered by Herron's and Lauman's divisions, could not be so well invested as under the previous arrangement, from the diminished number of troops. McClernand's corps was further diminished by Osterhaus' division being withdrawn from Hovey's left and sent to guard the crossings of the Big Black by the railroad and Jackson road. This doubled the front covered by Hovey.

At the close of the siege the position of the troops investing the city·was, from our right, first, Sherman's corps, diminished by a division; second, McPherson's, diminished by a division; third, McClernand's (now Ord's) corps, also diminished by a division; fourth, Lauman's division; fifth, Herron's division.

The investment was close only after the arrival of Herron's division, being previously weak from the weakness of our force, and was made on the northern instead of the southern side of the city—first, to be near our depot of supplies at Chickasaw Bayou, on the Yazoo River, and to cover that depot; secondly, to be in such a position that a relieving force could not by a rapid movement effect a junction with the garrison of the city before we could attack that force.

At the beginning of the siege the enemy's defenses were essentially the same as at its close, making the place an intrenched camp 4 miles long and 2 miles wide, the line of defense not following its windings, being 7 miles long and well adapted to the ground.

Description of Ground

Perhaps the best idea of the ground around Vicksburg may be obtained by supposing that originally a plateau, having from 200 to 300 feet elevation, here reached the Mississippi; that the fine soil . . . has gradually been washed away by rains and streams till the plateau has disappeared, leaving in its place an intricate net-work of ravines and ridges, the latter everywhere sharp, and the former only having level bottoms when their streams become of some size. . . . The soil when cut vertically will remain so for years. For this reason the sides of the smaller and newer ravines were often so steep that their ascent was difficult to a footman unless he aided himself with his hands. The sides of the ravines were usually wooded, but near the enemy's lines the trees had been felled, forming in many places entanglements which under fire were absolutely impassable. At Vicksburg the Mississippi runs nearly south, and the streams which enter from the east run southwest. One such stream enters the river 5 miles below the city, and the dividing ridge which separates two of its branches was that on which the defensive line east of the city was placed. This line on the northern side of the city was on a dividing ridge between two small streams, which enter the Mississippi above Vicksburg.

Description of the Enemy's Line

It may be said, then, that the enemy's line of defense, leaving the river on the north side of the city where the bluff strikes the river, was generally on a dividing ridge . . . as high or higher than the ground in its vicinity; that in two places the line crossed the valleys of small streams, reaching the river bluff again 2 miles

Photo of sections of the Confederate lines around Vicksburg. (U.S. Army Military History Institute)

below the city, at a point where the bluff has receded to a distance of 1 mile from the river, and then following the bluff up the river for a mile, to give fire toward the river or any troops that might attempt an attack from the south by moving up between the bluff and the river along the river bottom. This line was well located for seeing the ravines in its front, and consisted of small works on commanding points, necessarily irregular, from the shape of the ridges on which they were situated; in only one case (that of a redoubt 30 yards square) closed at the gorge; of weak profile placed at distances varying from 75 to 100 yards from each other, and connected by lines of simple trench or rifle-pit.

Vicksburg was, then, rather an intrenched camp than a forti-fied place, owing much of its strength to the difficult ground, obstructed by fallen trees in its front, which rendered rapidity of movement and *ensemble* in an assault impossible.

Reasons for an Assault

On May 22, a general assault was made at 10 A.M. Steele's division, of Sherman's corps attacked on the north side at a point about half way between the river and the northeast angle of the enemy's line; Blair's division, of Sherman's corps, near this angle; McPherson's corps near the Jackson road, and McClernand's corps near the railroad.

These attacks were gallantly made, men from each of the corps reaching the enemy's line, and in one instance entering one of the enemy's works; but the fire both of artillery and musketry from the enemy's line was so heavy, and the loss in moving over the rough and obstructed ground so severe, that the assault failed at all points. The troops took the nearest cover, in some places under the parapet of the enemy's work, on which our flag was flying, and waited for night to enable them to fall back without further exposure to the murderous fire. The question as to the practicability of carrying the place by assault without previous preparation was now settled for men as well as for officers. Before such an assault could again be attempted with a reasonable prospect of success, the enemy's artillery must, so far as practicable, be disabled by our fire, and means used to cover our troops until close to the enemy's work from the fire, long-continued exposure to which had caused the failure of the first assault. Preparations were accordingly made for the construction of batteries, opening trenches, etc., and the siege was commenced.

Engineer Organization

The engineer organization here, as in all our armies, was very deficient, if we judge either from the practice of nations wiser in the art of war than ourselves or from results. Thirty officers of engineers would have found full employment. When the siege commenced there were with the army two engineer officers doing engineer duty. Superintendence at any particular point was impossible, without neglecting the more important general superintendence of the whole line. A few officers had been detailed, either from a list of additional aides-de-camp or from the line, for engineer duty; these were assigned to the head-quarters of corps or divisions. Several divisions had pioneer companies attached to them; these were used as engineer soldiers in the construction of gabions, fascines, in building batteries, and in saps, and, notwithstanding their rawness at first, toward the close of the siege became in some divisions very effective.*

With so deficient an engineer organization was the siege to be carried on; more engineer officers could not be obtained, so that the rate of progress of an approach or even its position, often depended on the energy and engineering skill of the division or brigade commander who furnished the working party for it.

Approaches

The following were the principal approaches made during the siege ... [and] derived their names from the brigade or division commanders who furnished the guards and working parties. The 2nd of these was along what was called the Graveyard road; the 5th along the Jackson road; the 6th along the Baldwin's Ferry road; the 7th along the railroad; the 9th on the Hall's Ferry road, and the 10th on the Warrenton road. The 2d, or Ewing's approach, was directed against the northeast angle of the enemy's line, where that line, bending around the ravines at the head of a small stream, takes the form of a bastion [a type of geometrical fieldwork]. This approach, early begun, was the principal one in front of Sherman's corps, and with collateral work was that on which he expended most labor.

On the Jackson road, where it enters the enemy's line of defense, is a commanding hill, quite strongly salient, which had on it a redan for several guns. The ridge along which the Jackson road runs offered fair ground, and along it McPherson pushed his main approach—the one earliest begun and on which his corps did most work. A. J. Smith and Carr pushed approaches toward salient works, called by the Confederates Forts Pulaski and Beauregard, one to the right, the other to the left of the railroad. Hovey's approach on the square redoubt was not begun until late in the siege. The last three approaches were in front of McClernand's (afterward Ord's) corps.

There was another approach begun by Colonels Woods and Mantger to the right of Thayer's, and near the river. After the work

---

Gabions are cylindrical baskets of various dimensions, open at both ends, which were filled with dirt and rocks and used to protect artillery or to protect personnel while digging saps. *Fascines* are long cylindrical bundles of wood used to reinforce earthworks. *Saps* are trenches dug toward enemy positions through which troops can

THE SIEGE [319

Photo of gabions similar to those used by Union troops during the siege of Vicksburg. (U.S. Army Military History Institute)

move with protection until in position to assault enemy fortifications. Henry Lee Scott, *Military Dictionary: Comprising Technical Definitions; Information on Raising and Keeping Troops; Actual Service, Including Makeshift and Improvised Matériel; and Law, Government, Regulations, and Administration Relating to Land Forces* (New York: D. Van Nostrand, 1862), pp. 283, 320, and 544.

had been energetically pushed by these officers, it met a deep ravine, precluding further progress. As the approach would not have
been used in an assault, it has not been mentioned. . . . A brief history of the approaches above mentioned may be of some interest.

Thayer's Approach

This approach commenced near the crest of a ridge, ran
down the slope which was toward the enemy, and then up the
opposite slope of the ravine, toward the ridge on which the salient approach was situated. As it was difficult to defile this approach, blinding [protective measures] was resorted to. Fascines
made of cane were used; these, being placed across the trench,
which was about 6 feet deep, formed a roof which hid the movements of our men, and, where well constructed, was impenetrable
to musket balls. Artillery, of course, would have soon destroyed
it, but the enemy did not use this arm against it. This approach
was sharply resisted by the enemy, who came outside of their line
and had to be driven from the ground . . . before the work could
be pushed forward. When near the salient approach, the officer
in charge . . . thought he heard the enemy's miners at work.
Accordingly, work in the sap was stopped and a mine begun,
which was not yet complete when the place surrendered. This
approach was under the superintendence of Captain [Herman]
Klostermann, who commanded the efficient pioneer company
of Steele's division.

Ewing's Approach

This approach, in front of Blair's division, of Sherman's corps,
consisted in places of two or three approaches (Ewing's, Light-
burn's, and Buckland's), and was the most important one in
Sherman's front. It was pushed forward until the enemy annoyed
the sappers very seriously with grenades and mines, the grenades
being 6 or 12-pounder loaded shells, with short, lighted fuses. We
then resorted to mining, and as the explosion of the enemy's
mines, crushing our first gallery [passageway to main chamber for
placing powder for a mine], had shattered the earth for 30 feet
around, a detour was made to avoid this shaken earth. The mine,
a heavy one, was completed just before the surrender of the place,
but was not charged [loaded]. . . .

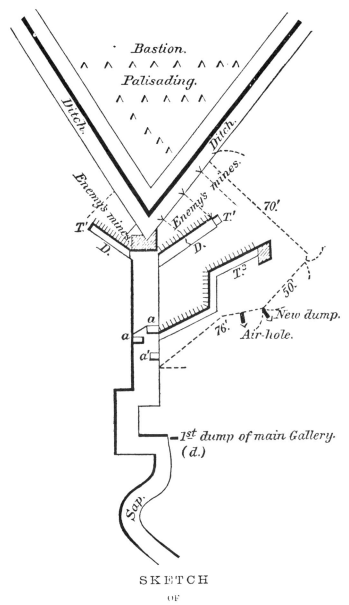

SKETCH

OF

BASTION IN FRONT OF BRIG. GEN. EWING.

Diagram of Ewing's approach.

Giles A. Smith's Approach

This approach was 200 yards to the south of Ewing's, and pushed forward from a ravine parallel at this point to the enemy's line, which gave cover near that line. It was directed on a salient of the enemy's line, and was close to it when the city surrendered. . . .

Ransom's Approach

This approach, in front of McPherson's right, started from the same ravine as the preceding, and at the surrender was close upon the enemy's line. It being in a re-entrant of that line, had to give cover against fire from both flanks, which was quite freely used by the enemy, making the work difficult. This approach would have been very important in an assault, as the ground here in rear of the enemy's line was seen by our artillery, and it would have been difficult for him to mass troops to resist an assault. . . .

Logan's Approach

This was the approach in front of McPherson's corps, on which most work was done. It followed the ridge along which the Jackson road runs, and approached a high, commanding salient, called by us Fort Hill, which, if once in our possession, would have made this part of the enemy's line untenable. The enemy resisted our approach here more strongly than at any other point, burning saprollers, using mines, and throwing grenades. Counter-mines were used by us, one heavy one being fired June 25, destroying a part of the enemy's parapet. An attempt was made to hold the crater, but after heavy loss from the hand-grenades which the enemy threw into it, the attempt was abandoned. Another mine was begun, and was to have been fired when the place was assaulted, but the enemy's miners being heard at work near it, and being feared that they might crush our galleries which were not lined, the mine was loaded and fired July 1, destroying the enemy's parapet at this point and giving a crater 30 feet in diameter, the charge being about 1,800 pounds, a portion of it damaged powder. It was afterward ascertained that this explosion crushed the enemy's galleries and disabled about 25 men—indeed, half a dozen men were thrown into our works.

No attempt was made to occupy this crater, as a similar attempt of June 25 had failed with severe loss.

The enemy's salient here being too high for our men to be able to return the grenades which they threw upon us so freely, and having no Cohorn [*sic*] mortars [a brass twenty-four-pound mortar], Mr. Tresilian, civil assistant engineer, had some wooden mortars made by shrinking iron bands on cylinders of tough wood, and boring them out for 6 or 12 pound shells. These mortars stood firing well, and gave sufficiently good results at 100 or 150 yards distance.

We afterward learned that the enemy, lying closely packed in the salient, suffered severely from this fire. . . .

A. J. Smith's Approach

This approach followed generally the line of the Baldwin's Ferry road, injudiciously leaving it in one place to avoid hard digging. When this approach reached the immediate vicinity of the salient on which it was directed, its progress was much impeded by the enemy's artillery fire, grenades, etc. The enemy also attempted to blow up the sap-roller with a mine, but failed by underestimating the distance and using too feeble a charge. They succeeded in burning one sap-roller by lodging a fire-ball against it. The work, however, was pushed forward, and a mine had been commenced when the place surrendered.

Carr's Approach

This approach, beginning on the railroad, followed its cut for 100 yards, and was directed to a work just to the left of another deep cut. When within 60 yards of the enemy's line, a parallel was made, from which the salient might have been stormed.

On July 4, this approach was within about 10 yards of the enemy's ditch.

Hovey's Approach

This approach, directed on a redoubt, was not begun till late, although the ground gave cover here to within a short distance of the enemy's line.

This was one instance among many where the lack of engineer officers was shown. With a proper number of officers, the ground in all its details would have been thoroughly reconnoitered, and the best positions for approaches chosen, instead of wasting work,

Maj. Gen. Andrew J. Smith, USA, Commander, Tenth Division, Thirteenth Army Corps (McClernand). (U.S. Army Military History Institute)

as in this case, when the best approaches were selected after the siege was half over. . . .

Lauman's Approach

This approach, in front of Lauman's division, was at first begun on a ridge which runs out from the enemy's line 300 yards east of the Hall's Ferry road, and a good deal of work had been expended on it, when it was decided to abandon it for an approach along the Hall's Ferry road, ravines there giving cover within 300 yards of the enemy's line, the approach being directed on a work very salient, and, therefore, weak. The enemy, conscious of this, made repeated sorties, driving off working parties and taking a few prisoners. In one case, June 22, they filled up 50 yards of our trench and began a counter-trench, from which they were driven the following night with some loss.

Herron's Approach

General Herron's division did not arrive till June 11, and the approach of his division along the Warrenton road was slow. Little was done, besides driving in the enemy's pickets and erecting three batteries, till June 24, when a parallel, to cover supports, was begun at 200 yards distance from the enemy's line. The portion proposed was finished and an approach run forward to within 100 yards of a salient of the enemy's line, when the place fell. . . .

Character of the Enemy's Defense

At the assaults of May 19 and 22, the enemy used artillery fire freely. Afterward, as our batteries were built and opened, their artillery fire slackened, until toward the close of the siege it was scarcely used at all, the enemy contenting himself with occasionally running a gun into position, firing two or three rounds, and withdrawing it again as soon as our fire was concentrated on it. A 10-inch mortar was fired a good deal at first from a ravine behind the enemy's line in McPherson's front, and afterward from a work in Herron's front, but did little damage.

On the surrender of the place their artillery was found to be considerably injured; nevertheless, if at almost any point they had put ten or fifteen guns in position, instead of one or two to invite concentration of our fire, they might have seriously delayed our approaches. We attributed during the siege the silence of their artillery to the lack of ammunition, but on the surrender of the place over 40,000 rounds of captured artillery ammunition were reported to the chief of ordnance of General Grant's army. A small portion of this, judiciously used, would have rendered our approach much slower. As it was, we had little besides musketry fire to contend with in the distant approaches and parallels, and even this was used sparingly in comparison with our own, probably from a deficiency of percussion caps. The mines used by the enemy were feeble ones, their charges always light, and rarely doing other damage than making the ground where they had been exploded impracticable for our own, as we did not use gallery frames or sheeting [reinforcing materials for tunnel walls].

Indeed, their active defense was far from being vigorous, the object seeming to be to wait for another assault, losing in the mean time as few men as possible. This indifference to our approach became at some points almost ludicrous. We were accustomed to cover the front of our night working parties by a line of pickets or a covering party, and the enemy, while we were not nearer than 100 yards to their line, would throw out their pickets in front of it.

On one occasion, in front of Ord's corps, our pickets, in being posted, became intermixed with the enemy's, and after some discussion the opposing picket officers arranged their picket lines by mutual compromise, these lines in places not being more than 10 yards apart. . . . As the enemy could have stopped our work by remaining in his lines and firing an occasional volley, the advantage of this arrangement, novel in the art of war, was entirely on our side, and was not interfered with. In Lauman's and Herron's front the enemy was not so courteous; in Lauman's front especially they made sorties several times, resulting in loss of men and retardation of work to ourselves.

Siege Materiel and Works

The larger part of the fascines, gabions, and sap-rollers was prepared by the pioneer companies of the different divisions. Material for the wattling of gabions was abundant, grape-vines being chiefly used, though these made gabions that were inconveniently heavy, from the fact that vines of too large size were taken. Captain Freeman, aide-de-camp, experimented with cane as material for wattling, and found by crushing the joints with a mallet the rest of the cane was split sufficiently to allow it to be woven between the stakes of the gabion and yet be strong, making a good and very neat gabion.

For fascines the cane was largely used, it being found in abundance and making excellent and light work. Some difficulty was experienced at first in making sap-rollers which should be impervious to Minie balls and not too heavy for use on the rough ground over which the saps ran. The difficulty was obviated by Lieutenant Hains, engineers, who caused two barrels to be placed head to head and secured, and the sap-roller to be built up of cane fascines around this hollow core.

The aggregate of our trenches was 12 miles; eighty-nine batteries were constructed during the siege, the guns from those in rear being moved forward as the siege advanced, there being two hundred and twenty guns in position on June 30. . . . These guns were mainly siege or field guns, a few heavy ones, however, being obtained from the Navy, one battery of these guns, on the right, in front of Woods' brigade, being manned and officered by the Navy. These batteries were sometimes constructed under the supervision of the pioneers of the division to which the battery belonged, and sometimes by the officer who was to command the finished work.

The style of the work was very varied, both reveting* and platforms depending on the materials which could be obtained at the time. In some cases they were well and neatly reveted with gabions and fascines, and furnished with substantial plank platforms, while in others reveting of rough boards, rails, or cotton bales was used, and the platforms were made of boards and timber from the nearest barn or cotton-gin house.

From the feebleness of the enemy's artillery fire, our parapets often were not more than 6 or 8 feet thick. In all close batteries the gunners soon found the necessity of keeping the embrasures closed against rifle-balls by plank shutters, sometimes swung from a timber across the top of the embrasure; sometimes merely placed in the embrasure, and moved when firing. Whenever an approach gave opportunity for fire, loop-holes were either formed in the parapet, made by using sand-bags, or in a timber laid along the parapet. These

---

Reveting is the reinforcing of the interior sides and top of the trenches dug as part of the siegeworks (Scott, *Military Dictionary*, pp. 504–9).

Photo of Union siege lines around Vicksburg, showing a parallel and an observation tower known as "Coonskin' Tower." (U.S. Army Military History Institute)

timbers were rarely displaced by the enemy's fire; they would have been dangerous if that artillery fire had been heavy.

In close approaches the sap was reveted with gabions, empty barrels, or with cotton bales, or sometimes left unreveted, it being difficult to prevent the working parties from sinking the sap to the depth of 5 or even 6 feet when the enemy's fire was heavy, and reveting then was unnecessary. Indeed, when the enemy's grenades were most annoying, it was impossible to keep detailed working parties at their posts, and it was necessary to depend on the pioneers already referred to for this dangerous work. The compactness of the alluvial soil making lining for mining galleries unnecessary, these galleries were formed with ease; as mines could not make an easier way into the enemy's line than existed already, their only use was to demoralize the enemy by their explosion at the moment of an assault. Three were completed and several others begun during the siege. More importance was attached to them by officers and men than they deserved.

The labor in the trenches was done by men of the pioneer companies of divisions, by details from the line, or by negroes.

Several of the pioneer companies had negroes attached to them, who had come into our camps. These negroes were paid $10 per month, in accordance with law, and proved to be very efficient laborers when under good supervision.

The labor performed by details from the line, as is usual in such cases, was very light in comparison with that done by the same number of pioneers or negroes. Without the stimulus of danger or pecuniary reward, troops of the line will not work efficiently, especially at night, after the novelty of the labor has worn off. The amount of night work done by a given detail depends very much on the discipline of the command from which it is taken and on the energy of its officers. Under average circumstance, such details do not in a given time accomplish half the work of which they are capable.

The want of officers of engineers has already been referred to, there being at no time more than three on engineer duty. Over a line so extended and ground so rough . . . only a general supervision was possible, and this gave to the siege one of its peculiar characteristics, namely, that many times, at different places, the work that should be done, and the way it should be done, depended on officers, or even on men, without either theoretical or practical knowledge of siege operations, and who had to rely upon their native good sense and ingenuity. Whether a battery was to be constructed by men who had never built one before, a sap-roller made by those who had never heard the name, or a ship's gun-carriage to be built, it was done, and, after a few trials, was well done. But . . . it must be recollected that these powers were shown at the expense of time, and while a relieving force [under *Johnston*] was gathering in our rear. Officers and men had to learn to be engineers while the siege was going on. . . .

Reasons for Another Assault

On July 1 the approaches were in the condition described above. The hand-to-hand character of the fighting now showed that in the closer approaches little farther progress could be made by digging alone; the enemy's works were weak, and at ten different points we could put the heads of regiments under cover within from 5 to 100 yards of his line. The assault would be but little easier if we waited ten days more. . . . Accordingly it was decided to assault on the morning of July 6.

Orders were at once issued to prepare the heads of approaches for the easy debouch of troops, to widen the main ones, so that

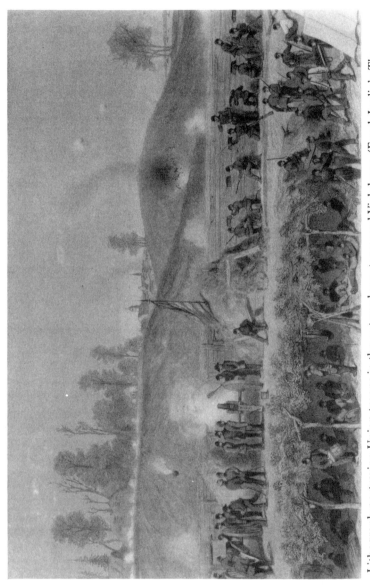

Lithograph portraying Union troops in the entrenchments around Vicksburg. (Frank Leslie's *The American Soldier in the Civil War*)

the troops could move easily by fours and artillery could pass, and to prepare planks and sand-bags, stuffed with pressed cotton, for crossing ditches. These preparations were in progress when the place surrendered, July 4.[23]

THE DEFENSE OF VICKSBURG

Report of Maj. Samuel H. Lockett, CSA, Chief Engineer for Vicksburg (continued)

On the 22d, the enemy's artillery fire was very heavy along their whole line, and a determined assault was made on the Graveyard, Jackson, and Baldwin's Ferry roads, and along the whole of General *Lee's* front on the right of the railroad. A breach was made in the redoubt near the railroad . . . and many other of the raised works were considerably battered. All damages were repaired, however, at night, and the morning of the 23d found our works in as good condition as at the beginning of the enemy operations.

The enemy, being apparently satisfied with their attempts at carrying our works by assault, now commenced their regular approaches, and soon had possession of a line of hills on the main roads, not exceeding 350 yards distance from our salient points. These hills they crowned with heavy batteries and connected as rapidly as possible with their second parallel.

On the 24th, some of the enemy's sappers crept up a ravine to within 40 yards of the work on the Jackson road, and started a sap, apparently with the intention of mining. When they had reached within 20 paces of our work, they were dislodged by hand-grenades, and relinquished this attempt for some time.

On the 25th, the enemy appeared in force on the Warrenton road, and commenced establishing batteries in Gett's field . . . some 600 yards from the advanced redoubt on this road. They also pushed their first parallel on toward our right, and crossed the Hall's Ferry road about 1,000 yards from the advanced redoubt on this road. Their line of circumvallation* was by this completed, and remained unbroken thenceforward. To prevent any approach of the enemy up the river flat, I attempted to construct an *abatis* from the hills to the river, and sent out a working party . . . for that

---

*Earthworks made by besieging forces that face outward to protect the rear from enemy attacks while conducting siege operations (Scott, *Military Dictionary*, p. 160).

purpose. The guard for the working party was driven in after a skirmish and the capture of 100 of the enemy. The work was not accomplished. On this day rifle-pits were started along the river front to connect the line of land defenses on the right with the heavy batteries.

Along the rear line the engineers were engaged in general repairs, strengthening the parapets, extending the rifle-pits, placing obstructions in front of the exposed points, consisting of *abatis*, palisades [wooden walls, generally on top of earthworks], ditches, and entanglements of pickets and telegraph wire. Sandbag loop-holes were also made along the whole line to protect our sharpshooters. These sand-bags were made from tent-flies and old tents turned over to me by the quartermaster's department, and from the same source I obtained a supply of material during the whole siege. A 32-pounder was moved from the river front and mounted on the left of General *Smith's* line, a new battery for three guns started in rear of General [S. D.] *Lee's*, and a new battery for two guns built on the left of General [J. C.] *Moore's*.

On the night of the 26th, the usual work of repairs and improvements went on; the rifle-pits on the river front were pushed ahead; the battery in rear of General *Lee* was finished, and a 30-pounder Parrott put in position. On this night the enemy for the first time fired on our working parties, and wounded a lieutenant commanding a fatigue party.

On the 27th, the enemy attacked our river front with their gunboats, without, however, doing any serious damage. They were driven off, and the *Cincinnati* sunk by the upper battery. This battery was protected by traverses from an enfilade fire from the enemy's sharpshooters on the hills across Mint Spring Bayou.

On the 28th, the usual repairs and improvements continued along the whole line: a new battery made in rear of the line left of Hall's Ferry road; the new battery in rear of General *Lee* improved and "Whistling Dick" (an 18-pounder rifled piece) put in position, and a new battery started in rear of General *Moore's* center, but the working party was driven off by the enemy's sharpshooters, and the work stopped.

On the 30th, but little work was done on the line under Captain *Robinson's* charge, excepting along General *Lee's* front, and during the whole siege our works, from Fort Garrott to the right, were but little injured, the enemy being kept at a considerable distance by a line of pickets kept in protected places along the ridge in front of our main line, excepting on the Hall's Ferry road. Captain *Wintter* and his assistants were kept constantly busy putting obstructions on the Yazoo Valley and other roads, repairing the embrasures of batteries, and thickening the parapets, which had begun to show the effects of the enemy's continual battering. The new battery in rear of General *Moore's* center was commenced by running a covered approach to the position selected. On this day I also started a number of excavations on the Baldwin's Ferry road, in a deep cut, for the purpose of scattering our ammunition, which was much exposed to the enemy's fire at the depot magazine. These excavations were put under the charge of Mr. *Ginder,* with a working force of 25 negroes from the jail-gang, and were finished in about a week.

On the 31st, works of repair continued along the whole line; the new works continued, and a breach in the redan on the left of Jackson road filled up and parapet repaired with sand-bags.

From June 1 to the 4th there was no variation in the engineer operations. By the 4th, the enemy had succeeded in establishing a third line of parallels not exceeding 150 yards from our salient works, and then commenced several double saps against the following works, viz. the stockade redan, on the Graveyard road; the Third Louisiana redan, on the left of Jackson's road; and the lunette on right of Baldwin's Ferry road. I had some thundering barrels and loaded shells prepared to be placed in these and all other exposed works, to be used in case of an assault. The stockade redan and the stockade on its left beginning to suffer a good deal from the enemy's artillery, a new line of rifle-pits was started in front of the stockade, and the ditch of the redan was prepared for riflemen, to give a double line at this point.

The enemy continued their saps against this and that of the Third Louisiana without much interruption until the night of the 8th, when their sap-roller was burned by firing pieces of port-fire[*] and cotton-balls steeped in turpentine into it from muskets. Their sappers were thus exposed, and forced to retire and recommence their operations with another roller some distance back. In spite of all our attempts to stop them, the enemy steadily approached with these saps until the night of the 13th, when they had reached

---

[*]A composition of niter, sulphur, and granular powder that was driven into a case of strong paper and used to ignite artillery charges prior to the invention of the friction-primer (Scott, *Military Dictionary*, p. 466).

within 60 feet of the stockade redan and within 40 yards of the Third Louisiana, and showed very evidently their intention to attack these salients by mining. I accordingly ordered counter-mines to be started from the ditch of the former to oppose their progress. The latter work having no ditch, other arrangements had to be made. This work had also become considerably battered by this time, and the old parapets were nearly gone. A new one was accordingly made a few feet in rear of the first, and the main body of the work was still preserved entire, and our men protected from the enemy's fire.

On the night of the 13th, a 10-inch mortar was placed in position in rear of General *Moore's* center, and a 20-pounder Parrott in rear of General *Green's* left.

On the night of the 14th, a new series of rifle-pits was begun, running along a couple of spurs in the rear, so as to envelop the stockade and its redan, as a precaution against the contingency of the enemy's carrying this point by assault, or rendering it untenable by his mining operations.

On the 15th, I discovered that the saps against the lunette on the right of the Baldwin's Ferry road were making rapid progress, and also the one against the railroad redoubt. Countermines were immediately ordered and commenced from the ditches of these works.

From this time till the end of the siege the main efforts of the enemy were directed against these salient works, viz: The stockade redan, the Third Louisiana redan, the lunette on the Baldwin's Ferry road, the railroad redoubt, and Fort Garrott, on General Lee's right, and later against the work on the Hall's Ferry road, against all of which they ran regular double saps, and our principal operations consisted in endeavors to impede their progress, and in preparations to meet them when practicable by countermining. Retrenchments were also made in rear of all the threatened points, to provide against the possibility of the enemy's being successful in their attempts. The rest of the line other than the works mentioned above was but little damaged, and was easily kept in repair by fatigue parties working at night. The Third Louisiana redan, being on a very narrow ridge, had no exterior ditch, and I found it impossible to get in its front to start a counter-mine without exposing our sappers to a terrible fire from the enemy's sharpshooters and batteries, not more than 150 yards distant. A shaft was accordingly started from the inside of the work, but before it was completed the enemy had succeeded in getting under the parapet and had prepared their mine under the salient.

This mine was exploded on the 25th instant [June 25], but did no material damage, as a parapet had been made to meet such an event some 15 feet back of the salient. Five or six men engaged in sinking a shaft were buried by this explosion. An attempt was made to assault the work immediately after the explosion, but our men, having good cover behind the new parapet, repulsed the assailants with considerable slaughter.

On the night of the same day two of our mines in front of the stockade redan were exploded, and completely destroyed the enemy's sap-roller, filled up their sap, and two parallels they had started to envelop the redan. Our mines were about 35 feet from the counterscarp of the redan, and the enemy's sap-roller was several paces within this distance, so that they received the full effect of our explosion. The charge in one mine was 45 pounds, in the other 80, with the chambers 8 feet under ground. On this same night a 9-inch Dahlgren gun was put in position in rear of General *Moore's* center, to counterbatter the enemy's heavy works on the Jackson road, and the 10-inch mortar was removed to the Warrenton road.

On the 28th, we sprang another mine in front of the lunette on the Baldwin's Ferry road, but unfortunately the explosion was premature, and the enemy's sap was hardly near enough to be much injured. Their sap-roller was, however, burned at night by fire-balls, their sappers driven away, and their progress materially interfered with. A new mine was immediately started and was soon ready for explosion.

On the 30th, the enemy succeeded again in getting under the Third Louisiana redan, and had covered the entrance to their gallery with a timber shelter, to protect their sappers from our hand grenades. To destroy this, I had a barrel containing 125 pounds of powder rolled over the parapet and exploded with a time-fuse of fifteen seconds. The effect of the explosion was very severe, and fragments of sap-rollers, gabions, and pieces of timber were thrown into the air, and, I think, some of the enemy's sappers must have been burned and smothered.

They continued their operations, however, and established another line on July 1, and exploded it about 1.30 P.M. The charge must have been enormous, as the crater made was at least 20 feet deep, 30 feet across in one direction and 50 in another. The earth upheaved was thrown many yards around, but little of it falling back into the crater. I learned from the enemy's engineer that they had 1,500 pounds [of] powder in this mine. The original faces of the redan were almost completely destroyed, and the explosive effect extended to a parapet I had made across the gorge of the work, making in it almost a practicable breach for an assault. No assault was attempted, however, and I went to work immediately to repair damages as well as possible. . . .

To give some idea of the difficulties attending this work, I will state that the enemy had two 9-inch Dahlgrens, several heavy Parrotts and field pieces, and a Cohorn mortar playing upon this redan, in addition to as heavy a fire of musketry as I ever witnessed, to be so long continued. In the course of one hour that I remained in the work at least a dozen of its garrison were killed or wounded by the mortar alone. On the same night one of the enemy's sap-rollers on the right of the Jackson road was burned and their sappers driven off by hand-grenades.

On the night of the 2d, Captain Robinson exploded one of his mines in front of the railroad redoubt, but with little effect, the explosion being premature. On this night we had prepared the following mines, viz: One in front of the work on Hall's Ferry road; two in front of Fort Garrott; two on Baldwin's Ferry road; one on right of Jackson road; two in front of small redan on General *Green's* left, and three on General *Shoup's* line, all of which would have been ready for the enemy by the time he came within the limits of their effects. These mines contained from 100 to 125 pounds powder, and were at an average depth of between 6 and 9 feet under the surface of the earth. The flag of truce, however, on the 3d, stopped all operations on both sides, and the efficiency of our preparations were not tested. . . .

In concluding this report, I beg leave to all the attention of the lieutenant-general commanding to the fact that no one was called upon to perform more arduous and continuous duty than the engineer officers and their assistants, and none more steadily and cheerfully endured all that their duty imposed upon them.[24]

JOINT OPERATIONS DURING THE SIEGE

Narrative of Adm. David D. Porter, USN

As soon as the Army appeared, driving the Confederates into Vicksburg, all the gun-boats below the city were ordered up to attack the batteries, which fire was kept up for three hours. At midnight the fire was reopened and directed to all points where it might be possible to harass the enemy's troops, and it was continued all night. The Confederates must have had an uncomfortable time of it, after marching and fighting all day with little hope of rest within their trenches. Shot and shells were whistling about them and every now and then a fire broke out in the city, threatening destruction to their stores and munitions of war.

The admiral ordered up the army transports with stores and provisions, which the Union forces were glad to get that day before sunset.

The works at Haynes' Bluff were found to be very formidable—far too much so to have been taken by our Army; or from the water side. . . . As soon as the Confederates had evacuated Haynes' Bluff, and all the rafts which blocked the river above had been removed, Lieutenant-Commander Walker, in the *DeKalb,* was sent up the Yazoo River with a sufficient force to destroy all the works at Yazoo City. . . . The expedition returned down the river, having fully accomplished all they went for. . . . The Confederates now lost all hope of being able to build rams or any other vessels on the tributaries of the Mississippi. . . .

On the evening of the 21st of May, Admiral Porter received a communication from General Grant to the effect that he intended to make a general attack upon the Confederate works at Vicksburg at 10 A.M. the next day. He had closely invested the enemy's works and was so near that he thought he could get inside. The admiral was requested to attack on the water side, and shell all the batteries from 9:30 to 10:30 A.M. to annoy the garrison and draw off as many as possible from the trenches.

In the meantime the Admiral with the *Benton, Tuscumbia, Carondelet,* and *Mound City* opened on the hill batteries and silenced them one after another, and the *Mound City* had the honor of disabling the heaviest gun the enemy had mounted, called "Whistling Dick," a gun that had hitherto defied the best marksmen.

The Confederates did not stand to their guns this day as they had been accustomed to do. They were receiving a heavy fire in the rear as well as in front, and the shriek of the shells from the army field-pieces, as they fell by the hundred in the Confederate works, could be heard down on the water amid the roar of the heavy cannon. The batteries one after another were silenced as the gunboats, firing bow and broadside guns, moved upon them, until they came to the 13 gun battery in front of the city.

This battery was commanded by Colonel *Higgins* (formerly a lieutenant in the US. Navy). . . . He felt called upon to show his old naval friends that he would not flinch from his post no matter what force was brought against him. But the water was high (nearly level with the banks) and the gunboats were *above* the enemy's water batteries. . . . They had nothing but this one battery to engage their attention, as all the others had been silenced. This was the hottest fire the gun-boats had yet been under . . . [and] went on for two hours and a quarter when it was quite time, according to rule, that the enemy should abandon his post, but he still held on. . . . Colonel *Higgins* was left master of the field.

The gun-boats had done what was required of them by General Grant, and more. He asked an hour's attack to annoy the garrison, while his Army assaulted in the rear; they fought the batteries for two hours and a half. . . . The gunboats kept up their attack until the 27th, when there was a lull for a time.

There was still work for the Navy to do in the Yazoo, while General Grant was starving the Confederates out in Vicksburg. . . .

A short summary of the work done by the Navy during the last forty days of the siege . . . will assure those who served at this critical period in the Navy, that they are not forgotten. . . . The mortar boats were kept at work for forty days, night and day, throwing shells into every part of Vicksburg and its works, some of them even reaching the trenches in the rear of the city. . . . Five 8-inch, four 9-inch, two 42-pounder rifled guns and four 32-pounder shell guns were landed at different points during the siege at the request of the officers commanding divisions, or of General Grant, and whenever officers and men could be spared from the fleet they were sent on shore to work the guns. . . .

The banks of the Mississippi were so watchfully guarded from Vicksburg to Cairo that the army transports went through with troops and stores, for a distance of about 450 miles, without molestation. The marine brigade, under Brigadier-General Ellet, was constantly landing along the river to break up guerilla warfare. Without a watchful eye on the Mississippi on the part of the Navy, the operations of the Army would have been often interrupted. Only one Army steamer was disabled during the siege operations.[25]

NOTES

1. *O.R.*, XXIV, pt. 1, p. 54.
2. *O.R.*, XXIV, pt. 2, p. 257.
3. *O.R.*, XXIV, pt. 2, pp. 17–19.
4. *O.R.*, XXIV, pt. 1, pp. 54–56.
5. *O.R.*, XXIV, pt. 1, p. 37.
6. *O.R.*, XXIV, pt. 1, pp. 37–38.
7. *O.R.*, XXIV, pt. 1, p. 39.
8. *O.R.*, XXIV, pt. 1, p. 40.
9. *O.R.*, XXIV, pt. 1, p. 40.
10. *O.R.*, XXIV, pt. 1, p. 40.
11. *O.R.*, XXIV, pt. 1, pp. 40–41.
12. *O.R.*, XXIV, pt. 1, p. 41.
13. *O.R.*, XXIV, pt. 1, p. 41.
14. *O.R.*, XXIV, pt. 1, p. 41.
15. *O.R.*, XXIV, pt. 1, p. 42.
16. *O.R.*, XXIV, pt. 1, p. 42.
17. *O.R.*, XXIV, pt. 1, p. 42.
18. *O.R.*, XXIV, pt. 1, p. 43.
19. *O.R.*, XXIV, pt. 1, p. 43.
20. *O.R.*, XXIV, pt. 1, p. 43.
21. *O.R.*, XXIV, pt. 1, pp. 43–44.
22. Samuel H. Lockett, "The Defense of Vicksburg," in *Battles and Leaders of the Civil War*, 4 vols., ed. Robert U. Johnson and Clarence C. Buel (New York: Century, 1884), 3:489–90.
23. *O.R.*, XXIV, pt. 2, pp. 168–77.
24. *O.R.*, XXIV, pt. 2, pp. 329–35.
25. David D. Porter, *The Naval History of the Civil War* (Boston: Sherman Publishing, 1886), pp. 320–26.

15. THE FALL OF VICKSBURG

Summary of Principal Events:
May 23–July 5, 1863

May	
23–July 4	Siege operations.
June	
25	Mine exploded under Third Louisiana Redan.
July	
1	Second mine exploded under Third Louisiana Redan.
2	Confederate subordinate commanders recommend *Pemberton* surrender Vicksburg.
4	Vicksburg surrenders.
5	Union forces turn to push *Johnston* out of Mississippi.

Report of Gen. Joseph E. Johnston, CSA (continued)

About May 24, the enemy made such demonstrations above the Big Black and toward Yazoo City, that I sent *Walker's* division to Yazoo City, with orders to fortify it, and, the demonstrations being renewed, placed *Loring's* division within supporting distance of *Walker's*, and in person took post at Canton.

Dispatches arrived from General *Pemberton,* dated Vicksburg, May 20 and 21. In that of the 20th he stated that the enemy had assaulted his intrenched lines the day before and were repulsed with heavy loss. He estimated their force at not less than 60,000, and asked that musket-caps [percussion caps] be sent, they being the main necessity. He concluded: "An army will be necessary to save Vicksburg, and that quickly. Will it be sent?" On the 21st, he wrote:

> The men credit and are encouraged by a report that you are near with a large force. They are fighting in good spirits and their organization is complete.

Caps were sent as fast as they arrived.

On May 29, I sent a dispatch to General *Pemberton* . . .

> I am too weak to save Vicksburg; can do no more than attempt to save you and your garrison. It will be impossible to extricate you unless you co-operate and we make mutually supporting movements. Communicate your plans and suggestions if possible.

The receipt of this was acknowledged in a communication dated Vicksburg, June 3, in which General *Pemberton* says: "We can get no information from outside as to your position or strength, and very little in regard to the enemy."

In a dispatch dated June 20, I said that General [Richard] *Taylor* had intended to attack the enemy opposite Port Hudson on the night of the 15th, and attempt to send cattle across the river. The want of field transportation rendered any movement for the relief of Port Hudson impossible had a march in that direction been advisable; but such a march would have enabled Grant (who had now completed his strong lines around Vicksburg) to have cut my line of communication and destroyed my army, and from the moment that I put my troops to march in that direction, the whole of Middle and Northern Mississippi would have been open to the enemy. . . .

On June 4, I told the Secretary of War, in answer to his call for my plans, that my only plan was to relieve Vicksburg, and my force was far too small for the purpose.

On June 10, I told him I had not at my disposal half the troops necessary.

On the 12th, I said to him:

> To take from *Bragg* a force which would make this army fit to oppose Grant would involve yielding Tennessee. It is for the Government to decide between this State and Tennessee.

On the 14th, I sent General *Pemberton* the following:

> All that we can attempt to do is to save you and your garrison. To do this, exact co-operation is indispensable. By fighting the enemy simultaneously at the same points of his line, you may be extricated. Our joint forces cannot raise the siege of Vicksburg. My communications with the rear can best be preserved by operating north of railroad. Inform me as soon as

possible what points will suit you best. . . . General [Richard] *Taylor*, with 8,000 men, will endeavor to open communications with you from Richmond [Louisiana].

To this communication General *Pemberton* replied, June 21, recommending me to move north of the railroad toward Vicksburg, to keep the enemy attracted to that side, and stating that he would himself move at the proper time by the Warrenton road, crossing the Big Black at Hankinson's Ferry; that "the other roads are too strongly intrenched and the enemy in too heavy force for a reasonable prospect of success," unless I could compel him to abandon his communications by Snyder's [Mill].

On the 15th, I expressed to the Department the opinion that without some great blunder of the enemy we could not hold both Mississippi and Tennessee, and that I considered saving Vicksburg hopeless.

On the 18th, I said:

> Grant's position, naturally very strong, is intrenched and protected by powerful artillery and the roads obstructed. His re-enforcements have been at least equal to my whole force. The Big Black covers him from attack, and would cut off our retreat if defeated.

On June 22, in reply to a dispatch from General *Pemberton* of the 15th, in which he said that, though living on greatly reduced rations, he had sufficient for twenty days, I informed him that General *Taylor* had been sent by General E. K. *Smith* to co-operate with him from the west bank of the Mississippi, and that in a day or two I would try to make a diversion in his favor, and, if possible, open communications, adding—

> I fear my force is too small to effect the latter. I have only two-thirds of the force you told Messenger *Saunders* to state to me as the least with which I ought to make an attempt. Scouts report the enemy fortifying toward us and the roads blocked.

A day or two after this, a dispatch was brought me from General *Pemberton,* dated June 22, suggesting that I should make to Grant "propositions to pass this army out, with all its arms and equipages," renewing his hope of my being able, by force of arms, to act with him, and expressing the opinion that he could hold out for fifteen days longer. To this dispatch I replied June 27, informing him that General E. K. *Smith's* troops had fallen back to Delhi, and that I had urged him to assume the direct command, and continued:

> The determined spirit you manifest, and his expected co-operation, encourage me to hope that something may yet be done to save Vicksburg and to postpone both of the modes suggested of merely extricating the garrison. Negotiations with Grant for the relief of the garrison, should they become necessary, must be made by you. It would be a confession of weakness on my part, which I ought not to make, to propose them. When it becomes necessary to make terms, they may be considered as made under my authority.

On June 29, field transportation and other supplies having been obtained, the army marched toward the Big Black, and on the evening of July 1 encamped between Brownsville and the river.

Reconnaissances, which occupied the 2d and 3d, convinced me that attack north of the railroad was impracticable. I determined, therefore, to make the examinations necessary for the attempt south of the railroad; thinking, from what was already known, that the chance for success was much better there, although the consequences of defeat might be more disastrous.

On the night of the 3d, a messenger was sent to General *Pemberton* with information that an attempt to create a diversion would be made to enable him to cut his way out, and that I hoped to attack the enemy about the 7th.

On the 5th, however, we learned [of] the fall of Vicksburg, and therefore fell back to Jackson.[1]

Report of Lt. Gen. John C. Pemberton, CSA *(continued)*

Late in the afternoon of the 25th, the enemy exploded his first mine under the parapet of General *Forney's* works. . . . From this time until the 1st [of July] nothing of moment occurred. On that day, however, the enemy sprung another mine on the right of the Jackson road. . . . Our engineers were kept constantly and busily emloyed in countermining on different portions of the line. About this time, our stock of bacon having been almost exhausted, the experiment of using mule meat as a substitute was tried, it being issued only to those who desired to use it, and I am gratified to say it was found by both officers and men not only nutritious, but very palatable, and every way preferable to poor beef. . . .

On July 1, I felt satisfied that the time had arrived when it was necessary either to evacuate the city and cut my way out or to capitulate upon the best attainable terms. My own inclination led me to favor the former. With this view, therefore, I addressed to my division commanders . . . the following communication: "Unless the siege of Vicksburg is raised or supplies are thrown in, it will become necessary very shortly to evacuate the place. I see no prospect of the former, and there are many great, if not insuperable obstacles in the way of the latter. You are, therefore, requested to inform me with as little delay as possible as to the condition of your troops, and their ability to make the marches and undergo the fatigues necessary to accomplish a successful evacuation. You will, of course, use the utmost discretion while informing yourself through your subordinates upon all points tending to a clear elucidation of the subjects of my inquiry."

The next day I received a reply from each of these officers.[2]

Maj. Gen. Carter L. Stevenson, CSA, Commanding Division, to Pemberton, July 2, 1863

My men are very cheerful, but from long confinement in the trenches and short rations are necessarily much enfeebled, and a considerable number would be unable to make the march and undergo the fatigues which would probably be necessary in a successful evacuation of this city. If pressed by the enemy, and it should be necessary to place the Big Black in our rear in one march, the chances are that a considerable number of those now in the trenches could not succeed. I believe, however, that most of them, rather than be captured, would exert themselves to the utmost to accomplish it.[3]

Maj. Gen. John H. Forney, CSA, to Pemberton, July 2, 1863

I concur in the unanimous opinion of the brigade and regimental commanders, that the physical condition and health of our men are not sufficiently good to enable them to accomplish successfully the evacuation. The spirit of the men is still, however, unshaken, and I am satisfied they will cheerfully continue to bear the fatigues and privations of the siege.[4]

Maj. Gen. Carter L. *Stevenson*, CSA, Commanding Division, Army of Vicksburg. (U.S. Army Military History Institute)

Maj. Gen. Martin L. Smith, CSA, to Pemberton, July 2, 1863

Your note of yesterday desires of me a reply on two points, viz: The condition of my troops, and their ability to make the marches and undergo the fatigue necessary to a successful evacuation of this place. The length of the marches and the amount of fatigue necessary to a successful evacuation not being indicated, I confine myself to giving the following information and opinions.

There are about 3,000 men in my division, including State troops, in a condition to undertake a march of 8 or 10 miles a day in this weather, if there is an opportunity of resting at intervals. Out of these 3,000, only about 2,000 are considered reliable in case we are strong opposed and much harrassed. A secret evacuation I consider almost impossible, on account of the temper of many in my command, who would, of necessity, be left behind, not to mention their natural timidity when left alone, which would induce them to at once get into communication with the enemy for their own fancied safety. I would really expect the enemy to become aware of the movement before my command had cleared the right of our line.

It is proper to mention that the 2,000 alluded to have suffered severely in the loss of field officers during the siege; and while their individual bravery remains the same, they will be more readily thrown into confusion from want of officers to handle them, if forced to halt and go through any formation to oppose an enemy. In other words, while under the impression that the troops will to-day resist an assault as obstinately, or perhaps more so, as when they first manned the trenches, I do not think they would do as well out of them and in the field.

I believe that General *Johnston* either has or will fight Grant, and my hope has been that he would be successful and in time to relieve us. At present, however, I see no chance of timely relief from him, and his dispatches have never indicated a hope of being able to raise the siege. Under these circumstances, I deem it best to propose terms of capitulation before forced to do so from want of provisions.[5]

Maj. Gen. John S. Bowen, CSA, to Pemberton, July 2, 1863

My men are in as good, if not better spirits, than any others in the line, and able to stand as much fatigue, yet I do not consider them capable (physically) of enduring the hardships incident to such an undertaking. Forty-five days' incessant duty day and night, with short rations, the wear of both mind and body incident to our situation, has had a marked effect upon them, and I am satisfied they cannot give battle and march over 10 or 12 miles in the same day. In view of the fact that General *Johnston* has never held out the slightest hope to us that the siege could be raised; that his demonstration in our favor to relieve this exhausted garrison would of necessity be sufficient to raise it, I see no alternative but to endeavor to rescue the command by making terms with the enemy.

Under the most favorable circumstances, were we to cut our way out, we could not, in my opinion, save two-thirds of our present effective strength. No provision could be made for our wounded who fell in the attempt, or those we leave behind in the hospitals, and our army would reach General *Johnston* (if we should get through) a mere handful of broken-down stragglers.

I would therefore recommend that an immediate proposition be made to capitulate. If accepted, we get everything we have any right to hope for; if rejected, we can still hold out stubbornly for some days, and our enemy may make the proposal to us. When our rations are exhausted, or nearly so, we may accept a surrender with the condition of a general parole instead of imprisonment for the command. If the offer is made at once, we have a better chance of making terms than when we have only one day's resistance in store in case of a refusal. The proposition coming from us, if rejected, will make our men determined to fight to the last; theirs, on the contrary, will feel that after Vicksburg has been offered, their blood is shed to gratify a mere vindictive feeling against its garrison, whose only fault has been the noble defense they have made, and I believe that numbers of the enemy have still enough manhood to admire our courage and determination and urge liberal terms of capitulation.[6]

Report of Lt. Gen. John C. Pemberton, CSA (continued)

So far as I know, not a solitary brigade or regimental commander favored the scheme of cutting out, and only two, whose views were presented to me, intimated the possibility of making more than one-half of their commands available for that purpose.

With this unanimous opinion of my officers against the practicability of a successful evacuation, and no relief from General *Johnston,* a surrender with or without terms was the only alternative left me.[7]

THE SURRENDER

Grant to Maj. Gen. Henry W. Halleck,
July 4, 1863—10:30 A.M.

The enemy surrendered this morning. The only terms allowed is their parole as prisoners of war. This I regarded as of great advantage to us at this juncture. It saves probably several days in the captured town; leaves troops and transports ready for immediate service. General Sherman, with a large force, will face immediately on *Johnston* and drive him from the State. I will send troops to the relief of General Banks, and return the Ninth Corps to General Burnside.[8]

Narrative of Charles A. Dana, Assistant Secretary of War

On the morning of Friday, July 3d, a soldier appeared on the Confederate line, in McPherson's front, bearing a flag of truce. General A. J. Smith was sent to meet this man, who proved to be . . . General J. S. *Bowen.* He bore a letter from *Pemberton* addressed to Grant. The letter was taken to headquarters, where it was read by the general and its contents were made known to the staff. It was a request for an armistice to arrange terms for the capitulation of Vicksburg. To this end *Pemberton* asked that three commissioners be appointed to meet a like number to be named by himself. Grant immediately wrote this reply:

> The useless effusion of blood you propose stopping by this course can be ended at any time you may choose by an unconditional surrender of the city and garrison. Men who have shown so much endurance and courage . . . will always challenge the respect of an adversary, and I can assure you will be treated with all the respect due to prisoners of war.
>
> I do not favor the proposition of appointing commissioners to arrange terms of capitulation, because I have no terms other than those indicated above.

Bowen . . . who had been received by A. J. Smith, expressed a strong desire to converse with General Grant. While declining this, Grant requested Smith to say to *Bowen* that if General *Pemberton* desired to see him an interview would be granted between the lines in McPherson's front at any hour in the afternoon which *Pemberton*

Lithograph of the meeting between Grant and Pemberton, July 3, 1863.
(*Harper's Pictorial History of the Civil War*)

might appoint. After *Bowen's* departure a message was soon sent
back to Smith, accepting the proposal for an interview, and ap-
pointing three o'clock as the hour. Grant was there with his staff
and with Generals Ord, McPherson, Logan, and A. J. Smith.
Sherman was not present, being with his command watching Joe
Johnston, and ready to spring upon the latter as soon as *Pemberton*
was captured. *Pemberton* came late, attended by General *Bowen* and
Colonel L. M. *Montgomery.*

It must have been a bitter moment for the Confederate chief-
tain. *Pemberton* was a Northern man, a Pennsylvanian by birth, from
which State he was appointed to West Point. . . . In the old army
he fell under the spell of the influence of Jefferson *Davis,* whose
close friend he was. *Davis* appears to have thought *Pemberton* was a
military genius, for he was jumped almost at a stroke, without much
previous service, to be a lieutenant general, and the defense of
the Mississippi was given over to his charge. His dispositions
throughout the entire campaign, after Grant crossed at Bruinsburg, were weak, and he was easily overcome, although his troops
fought well. As Joe *Johnston* truthfully remarks in his *Narrative,*
Pemberton did not understand Grant's warfare at all. Penned up and

finally compelled to surrender a vital post and a great army . . . an almost irremediable disaster to his cause, *Pemberton* not only suffered the usual pangs of defeat, but he was doubly humiliated by the knowledge that he would be suspected and accused of treachery by his adopted brethren, and that the result would be used by the enemies of *Davis*, whose favorite he was, to undermine the Confederate administration. As the events proved, it was indeed a great blow to *Davis's* hold upon the people of the South. These things must have passed through *Pemberton's* mind as he faced Grant for this final settlement of the fate of Vicksburg.

The conversation was held between *Pemberton* and his two officers and Grant, McPherson, and A. J. Smith, the rest of us being seated on the ground nearby.

We could, however, see that *Pemberton* was much excited, and was impatient in his answers to Grant. He insisted that his army be paroled and allowed to march beyond our lines, officers and all, with eight days' rations, drawn from their own stores, officers to retain their private property and body servants. Grant heard what *Pemberton* had to say, and left him at the end of an hour and a half, saying that he would send in his ultimatum in writing before evening; to this *Pemberton* promised to reply before night, hostilities to cease in the meantime.

Grant then conferred at his headquarters with his corps and division commanders, all of whom, except Steele, who advised unconditional surrender, favored a plan proposed by McPherson, and finally adopted by Grant. The argument against the plan was one of feeling only. In its favor it was urged that it would at once not only tend to the demoralization of the enemy, but also release Grant's whole army for offensive operations against Joe *Johnston* and Port Hudson, while to guard and transport so many prisoners would require a great portion of our army's strength. Keeping the prisoners would also absorb all our steamboat transportation, while paroling them would leave it free to move our troops. Paroling would also save us an enormous expenditure.

After long consideration, General Grant reluctantly gave way to these reasons, and at six o'clock in the afternoon he sent a letter by the hands of General Logan and Lieutenant-Colonel Wilson, in which he stated as terms that, as soon as rolls could be made out and paroles signed by officers and men, *Pemberton* would be allowed to march out of our lines, the officers taking with them their side-arms and clothing, and the field, staff, and cavalry officers one horse each. The rank and file were to retain all their clothing, but no other property. If these conditions were accepted, any amount of rations deemed necessary was to be taken from the stores they had, besides the necessary cooking utensils. Thirty wagons also, counting two two-horse or mule teams as one, were to be allowed to transport such articles as could not be carried along. The same conditions were allowed to all sick and wounded officers and soldiers as fast as they became able to travel. . . .

It was not till a little before peep of day that the reply was furnished. In the main the terms were accepted, but *Pemberton* proposed as amendments:

> At 10 A.M. to-morrow I propose to evacuate the works in and around Vicksburg, and to surrender the city and garrison under my command by marching out with my colors and arms, stacking them in front of my present lines, after which you will take possession. Officers to retain their side-arms and personal property, and the rights and property of citizens to be respected.

General Grant immediately replied:

> I can make no stipulations with regard to the treatment of citizens and their private property. . . . The property which officers will be allowed to take with them will be as stated in my proposition of last evening. . . . If you mean by your proposition for each brigade to march to the front of the line now occupied by it, and stack arms at 10 A.M., and then return to the inside and there remain as prisoners until properly paroled, I will make no objection to it. Should no notification be received of your acceptance of my terms by 9 A.M., I shall regard them as having been rejected, and shall act accordingly.

The answer came back promptly, "The terms proposed by you are accepted."

We had a glorious celebration that day. . . . At the appointed hour . . . the surrender was consummated, the Confederate troops marching out and stacking arms in front of their works, while *Pemberton* appeared for a moment with his staff upon the parapet of the central fort. At eleven o'clock Grant entered the city. He was received by *Pemberton* with more marked impertinence than at their former interview. Grant bore it like a philosopher, and in reply treated *Pemberton* with even gentler courtesy and dignity than before.

I rode into Vicksburg at the side of the conqueror, and afterward perambulated among the conquered. The Confederate soldiers were generally more contented even than we were. Now they were going home, they said. They had had enough of the war. The cause of the Confederacy was lost. They wanted to take the oath of allegiance many of them. *I was not surprised to learn a month later that of the twenty-odd thousand well men who were paroled at Vicksburg the greater part had since dispersed* [emphasis added], and I felt sure they could never be got to serve again. The officers, on the other hand, all declared their determination never to give in. They had mostly on that day the look of men who have been crying all night. . . .

I found the buildings of Vicksburg much less damaged than I had expected. Still, there were a good many people living in caves dug in the banks. Naturally the shells did less damage to these vaults than to dwellings. There was a considerable supply of railroad cars in the town, with one or two railroad locomotives in working condition. There was also an unexpected quantity of military supplies. At the end of the first week after our entrance sixty-six thousand stand of small arms had been collected, mainly in good condition, and more were constantly being discovered. They were concealed in caves, as well as in all sorts of buildings. The siege and seacoast guns found exceeded sixty, and the whole captured artillery was above two hundred pieces.

The stores of rebel ammunition also proved to be surprisingly heavy. As Grant expressed it, there was enough to have kept up the defense for six years at the rate they were using it. The stock of army clothing was officially invoiced at five million dollars—Confederate prices. Of sugar, molasses, and salt there was a large quantity, and sixty thousand pounds of bacon were found in one place.

The way in which Grant handled his army at the capitulation of Vicksburg was a splendid example of his energy. As soon as negotiations for the surrender began on the 3d, he sent word to Sherman, at his camp on Bear Creek, to get ready to move against *Johnston*. Sherman always acted on the instant, and that very afternoon he threw bridges across the Big Black. He started his forces over the river on the 4th as soon as he received word that *Pemberton* had accepted Grant's ultimatum. In the meantime Grant had ordered part of Ord's corps, all of Steele's division, and the two divisions of the Ninth Corps . . . at Haynes's Bluff, to be ready to join Sherman as soon as the capitulation was effected. . . . By Sunday night, July 5th, part of Ord's force was across the Big Black and Steele was well up to the river.[9]

Narrative of Sylvanus Cadwallader, a Northern War Correspondent

When last heard from, *Pemberton* was a considerable distance east of Jackson and his army of nearly 30,000 paroled soldiers which marched away with him had dwindled down by sickness, death and desertion, to less than 5,000. The wisdom of Grant's releasing them on parole was thus early proven. Thousands of them declared they would never fight again, and such of them as lived in the territory held by us could never be forced to return. The lists of these paroled prisoners which Rawlins carried with him to Washington, filled a box three feet long, two feet in width, and two feet deep.

It was a very cheap way however of transporting over 30,000 prisoners.[10]

JOINTNESS IN THE CAMPAIGN

Maj. Gen. William T. Sherman to Adm. David D. Porter, July 4, 1863

No event in life could have given me more personal pride or pleasure than to have met you today on the wharf at Vicksburg— a Fourth of July so eloquent in events as to need no words or stimulants to elevate its importance.

I can appreciate the intense satisfaction you must feel at lying before the very monster that has defied us with such deep and malignant hate and seeing your once disunited fleet again a unit; and better still, the chain that made an enclosed sea of a link in the great river broken forever. In so magnificent a result I stop not to count who did it; it is done, and the day of our nation's birth is consecrated and baptized anew in a victory won by the united Navy and Army of our country. God grant that the harmony and mutual respect that exists between our respective commanders and shared by all the true men of the joint service may continue forever and serve to elevate our national character, threatened with shipwreck.

Photo of U.S. Marine Corps troops in dress uniform during the Civil War. (U.S. Army Military History Institute)

Thus I muse as I sit in my solitary camp out in the wood [guarding against *Johnston*], far from the point for which we have jointly striven so long and so well, and though personal curiosity would tempt me to go and see the frowning batteries and sunken pits that have defied us so long and sent to their silent graves so many of [our] early comrades in the enterprise, I feel that other tasks lie before me and time must not be lost. Without casting anchor, and despite the heat and the dust and the drought, I must again go into the bowels of the land to make the conquest of Vicksburg fulfill all the conditions it should in the progress of this war.

Whether success attend my efforts or not, I know that Admiral Porter will ever accord to me the exhibition of a pure and unselfish zeal in the service of our country.

It does seem to me that Port Hudson, without facilities for supplies or interior communication, must soon follow the fate of Vicksburg and leave the river free, and to you the task of preventing any more Vicksburgs or Port Hudsons on the banks of the great inland sea.

Though farther apart, the Navy and the Army will still act in concert, and I assure you I shall never reach the banks of the river or see a gunboat but I will think of Admiral Porter, Captain Breese, and the many elegant and accomplished gentlemen it has been my good fortune to meet on armed or unarmed decks of the Mississippi Squadron.

Congratulating you and the officers and men of your command on the great result in which you have borne so conspicuous a part, I remain as ever,

Your friend and servant,
W. T. Sherman[11]

Narrative of Adm. David D. Porter, USN (continued)

In the history of the world's sieges nothing will be found where more patience was developed, more endurance under privations, or more courage shown, than by the Union forces at the siege of Vicksburg, while on the part of the besieged it was marked by their great fertility of resource in checking almost every movement of ours, and for the long months of suffering and hardship they underwent. . . . If General Grant had never performed any other military act during the war, the capture of Vicksburg alone, with all the circumstances attending the siege, would have entitled him to the highest renown.

I saw myself, at Sevastapol [September 1855], the great strongholds of the Malakoff tower and the Redan the day after they were taken by a combined army of one hundred thousand men; and these strongholds, which have become famous . . . never in any way compared with the defenses of Vicksburg. . . . The hills above, with their frowning tops standing in defiance, were enough to deter a foe without having intrenchments bristling with cannon and manned by the hardiest troops in the Confederacy. . . .

That was a happy Fourth of July when the Confederate flag came down at Vicksburg. . . . When the American flag was hoisted on the ramparts of Vicksburg, my flag-ship and every vessel of the fleet steamed up or down to the levee before the city. We discerned a dust in the distance, and in a few moments General Grant, at the head of nearly all his generals with their staffs, rode up to the gangway, and, dismounting, came on board. That was a happy meeting. . . . I opened all my wine-lockers—which contained only Catawba—on this occasion. It disappeared down the parched throats . . . [and] exilerated [*sic*] that crowd as weak wine never did before.

There was one man there who preserved the same quiet demeanor he always bore . . . and that was General Grant. No one, to see him sitting there with that calm exterior amid all the jollity, and without any staff, would ever have taken him for the great general who had accomplished one of the most stupendous military feats on record. . . . General Grant was the only one . . . who did not touch the simple wine offered him; he contented himself with a cigar.[12]

FALL OF PORT HUDSON

Porter to Grant, July 11, 1863

Port Hudson has surrendered unconditionally on the 9th instant [July 9]. The steamer has just brought the dispatches.[13]

Grant to Maj. Gen. Nathaniel P. Banks, July 11, 1863

It is with pleasure I congratulate you upon your removal of the last obstacle to the free navigation of the Mississippi. This will prove a death to Copperheadism in the Northwest, besides serving to demoralize the enemy. Like arming the negroes, it will act as a two-edged sword, cutting both ways. . . .

I ordered the boats and other articles you required at once, and as many of the boats as can be got ready will go down at the same time with this. I also ordered, on the strength of Colonel Smith's report, about 1,000 men to Natchez, to hold that place for a few days, and to collect the cattle that have been crossing there for the rebel army. I am also sending a force to Yazoo City to gather the heavy guns the rebels have there, and to capture, if possible, the steamers the enemy have in Yazoo River.

Sherman is still out with a very large force after Joe *Johnston,* and cannot well be back under six or seven days. It will be impossible, therefore, for me to send you the forces asked for in your letter until the expiration of that time. . . .

So far as anything I know of being expected from my force, I can spare you an army corps of as good troops as ever trod American soil. . . . When the news of success reached me, I had General Herron's division on board transports, ready to start for Port

Hudson. That news induced me to change their direction to Yazoo City.[14]

SHERMAN AGAINST JOHNSTON

Narrative of Maj. Gen. William T. Sherman, USA (continued)

Vicksburg surrendered, and orders were given for at once attacking General *Johnston*. The Thirteenth Corps (General Ord) was ordered to march rapidly, and cross the Big Black at the railroad-bridge; the Fifteenth [Gen. McPherson] by Messinger's, and the Ninth (General Parkes) by Birdsong's Ferry—all to converge on Bolton. My corps crossed the Big Black during the 5th and 6th of July, and marched for Bolton, where we came in with General Ord's troops; but the Ninth Corps was delayed in crossing at Birdsong's. *Johnston* had received timely notice of *Pemberton's* surrender, and was in full retreat for Jackson.

On the 8th all our troops reached the neighborhood of Clinton. . . . Johnston had marched rapidly, and in retreating had caused cattle, hogs, and sheep to be driven into the ponds of water, and there shot down; so that we had to haul their dead and stinking carcasses out to use the water. On the 10th . . . we had driven the rebel army into Jackson, where it turned at bay behind the intrenchments, which had been enlarged and strengthened since our former visit in May. We closed our lines about Jackson. . . .

On the 11th we pressed close in, and shelled the town from every direction. One of Ord's brigades . . . got too close and was very roughly handled and driven back in disorder. . . . The weather was fearfully hot, but we continued to press the siege day and night, using our artillery pretty freely; and on the morning of July 17th the place was found evacuated. General Steele's division was sent in pursuit as far as Brandon (fourteen miles), but General *Johnston* had carried his army safely off, and pursuit in that hot weather would have been fatal to my command. Reporting the fact to General Grant, he ordered me to return. . . .

The value of the capture of Vicksburg . . . was not measured by the list of prisoners, guns, and small-arms, but by the fact that its possession secured the navigation of the great central river of the continent, bisected fatally the Southern Confederacy, and set the armies which had been used in its conquest free for other purposes; and it so happened that the event coincided as to time with another great victory which crowned our arms far away, at Gettysburg. . . .

The campaign of Vicksburg, in its conception and execution, belonged exclusively to General Grant, not only in the great whole, but in the thousands of its details. I still retain many of his letters and notes, all in his own handwriting, prescribing the routes of march for divisions and detachments, specifying even the amount of food and tools to be carried along. . . . No commanding general of an army ever gave more of his personal attention to details, or wrote so many of his own orders, reports, and letters, as General Grant. His success at Vicksburg justly gave him great fame at home and abroad. The President conferred on him the rank of major-general in the regular army, the highest grade then existing by law; and General McPherson and I shared in his success by receiving similar commissions as brigadier-generals in the regular army.[15]

President Abraham Lincoln to Grant, July 13, 1863

I do not remember that you and I ever met personally. I write this now as a grateful acknowledgment for the almost inestimable service that you have done the country.

I wish to say a word further. When you first reached the vicinity of Vicksburg, I thought you should do, what you finally did—march the troops across the neck, run the batteries with the transports, and thus go below; and I never had any faith, except a general hope that you knew better than I, that the Yazoo Pass expedition, and the like, could succeed. When you got below, and took Port-Gibson, Grand Gulf, and vicinity, I thought you should go down the river and join Gen. Banks; and when you turned Northward East of the Big Black, I feared it was a mistake.

I now wish to make the personal acknowledgment that you were right, and I was wrong.[16]

Yours very truly,
A. Lincoln

NOTES

1. *O.R.,* XXIV, pt. 1, pp. 242–45.
2. *O.R.,* XXIV, pt. 1, pp. 280–81.
3. *O.R.,* XXIV, pt. 2, pp. 345–46.

4. *O.R.*, XXIV, pt. 1, p. 282.

5. *O.R.*, XXIV, pt. 1, p. 282.

6. *O.R.*, XXIV, pt. 1, pp. 282–83.

7. *O.R.*, XXIV, pt. 1, p. 283.

8. *O.R.*, XXIV, pt. 1, p. 44.

9. Charles A. Dana, *Recollections of the Civil War; with the Leaders at Washington and in the Field in the Sixties* (New York: D. Appleton, 1898), pp. 94–101.

10. Sylvanus Cadwallader, *Three Years with Grant, as Recalled by War Correspondent Sylvanus Cadwallader,* ed. Benjamin P. Thomas (New York: Alfred A. Knopf, 1955), p. 125.

11. *O.R.N.*, series 1, XXV, pp. 105–6.

12. David D. Porter, *Incidents and Anecdotes of the Civil War* (New York, D. Appleton, 1885), pp. 200–201.

13. *O.R.*, XXIV, pt. 3, p. 499.

14. *O.R.*, XXIV, pt. 3, pp. 499–500.

15. William T. Sherman, *Memoirs of General William T. Sherman, by Himself,* 2 vols. (New York: Appleton, 1875), 1:359–62.

16. Roy P. Basler, ed., *The Collected Works of Abraham Lincoln,* 9 vols. (New Brunswick, N.J.: Rutgers University Press, 1953) 6:326.

PART II
DRIVING TOUR
OF THE VICKSBURG CAMPAIGN

Grant's Vicksburg campaign was a continuation of an effort begun in the first months of 1862 when Union forces launched their drive to gain control of the Mississippi River. By December 1862, control of the upper and lower Mississippi River had been achieved. In that month, Maj. Gen. Ulysses S. Grant undertook a series of operations that eventually resulted in the capture of the city and garrison of Vicksburg on July 4, 1863.

The operational area of the campaign spanned vast distances, covering nearly the entire state of Mississippi and parts of Tennessee, Louisiana, and Arkansas. Days, not hours, must be allocated to exploring the Vicksburg campaign in all its complexity. If you have only a few hours available in Vicksburg, you will want to spend them at the Visitor Center and driving the siege lines at the Vicksburg National Military Park. Part III of this book provides a guided tour of the siege lines. Should you desire to dedicate the time and explore the campaign in greater detail, Part II divides the campaign into three excursions that can be visited in one or two days, depending upon the amount of time you have available.

All directions assume Vicksburg as the start point. The excursions, or tours, are winter 1862–63 operations, operations to isolate Vicksburg, and operations after the Union army crosses into Mississippi below Vicksburg.

PHASE 1: WINTER 1862–63 OPERATIONS

Drive to the Mississippi State Welcome Center located at Exit 1A off I-20. This will be the start point for directions to this section of the campaign.

At this point the reader may wish to go back and read Part I, "The Strategic Situation."

Directions to Stop 1. **From the Welcome Center, turn left (north) on Washington Street (Business Route 61). Drive 2.7 miles; turn left on Veto Street. Drive 0.3 mile; turn right at the stop sign on Mulberry. This returns you to Washington Street again. Drive 4.3 miles to Chickasaw Road and turn left. Drive 0.5 mile to Chickasaw Lane, turn around there, and retrace your route for 0.1 mile. Pull off the road beside the open field on the right.**

The high ground to your front is Walnut Hills, also known as the bluffs above Chickasaw Bayou, Sherman's initial objective. Confederate infantry and artillery forces occupied fighting positions on the hills and a line of entrenchments along their base. The defenders had cut down trees, sharpening the branches and making obstacles (abatis) to impede the attacking Federal forces. What remains today of Chickasaw Bayou can be seen to your left as you face the Walnut Hills.

STOP 1, CHICKASAW BAYOU

In the fall of 1862, Grant had originally planned a single-thrust attack following the Mississippi Central Railroad south from his base between La Grange and Grand Junction, Tennessee. He initiated this operation on November 4. Confronted by stiffening Confederate opposition and upon learning that Maj. Gen. John A. McClernand had been authorized to recruit and field a force to attack down the Mississippi, Grant changed his plan. He devised a two-pronged attack on Vicksburg designed to seize that city and open the Mississippi River.

Lithograph of the Sixth Missouri Regiment, Blair's Division, Sherman's Corps, during the assault on Chickasaw Bayou. (*Harper's Pictorial History of the Civil War*)

Grant would take the main force and advance south along the Mississippi Central line, a route that would take him into Vicksburg from the east—and thus high-ground—side of the city. The railroad would be the main line of communications, carrying the supplies for the 40,000 men in Grant's command. At the same time, Maj. Gen. William T. Sherman would move a force of nearly 32,000 men down the Mississippi and land on the northwest side of the city. While Grant occupied the main Confederate army, under the command of Lt. Gen. John C. *Pemberton,* along the line of the Tallahatchie and Yalobusha Rivers, Sherman would be able to attack and seize the relatively lightly protected fortifications on the north side of Vicksburg.

Grant's initial advance pushed the Confederate forces back to the Tallahatchie, then the Yalobusha. He moved deliberately, repairing roads and bridges and keeping the rail lines up with his advance for logistic support. His slow pace gave the defenders time to regroup. Grant's infantry finally moved into Holly Springs on November 29 and then pushed on south toward Oxford. On December 20, Grant ordered Sherman to move downriver. That same day, Confederate cavalry commanders, Maj. Gen. Nathan B. *Forrest* and Maj. Gen. Earl *Van Dorn,* raided key Federal bases in northern Mississippi and Tennessee. *Forrest* struck the rail lines near Jackson, Tennessee, while *Van Dorn* attacked Grant's logistics base in Holly Springs, destroying everything that had been stockpiled to support the continued offensive.

Deprived of a logistical base, Grant decided he could not continue toward Vicksburg. The conventional wisdom of that time dictated that a secure base with intervening secure lines of communication was essential for successful operations. As a result, Grant pulled his forces back north to Memphis to rebuild his supply base. As he was pulling back, he ordered his field commanders to make use of all the food and forage to be found in the local countryside to compensate for the supplies lost in the Confederate raids. He quickly discovered that the countryside held abundant supplies and his troops could live off the land with minimal problems. Grant tucked that critical information aside to be used later in the campaign.

Grant tried to inform Sherman of his withdrawal, but the Confederate raiders had cut all the telegraph lines, making direct communication with Sherman impossible. Sherman had heard rumors about the raid on Holly Springs, but since he had not received any change of orders, he proceeded to Vicksburg. He landed his troops on the Yazoo River on December 26, a part of them advancing to where you are now standing. At the time, the river was very high and much of the countryside was under water. While Sherman was trying to get his forces organized for the attack, the defenders, warned by telegraph of the approach of the amphibious force, hastily put the 6,000 men available into the defenses. Eventually, because Grant was no longer occupying Pemberton's main force, the Confederates were able to move nearly 19,000 men into the defenses before the beginning of the Union attack. This maneuver would prove deadly for the attackers, who had to use narrow causeways over the flooded ground to attack the well-entrenched defenders, supported by artillery that commanded the approaches to the Confederate positions.

For detailed readings, see Part I, Chapter 3.

Directions to Grant's Canal. **Drive straight ahead to Business Route 61. At the stop sign, turn right. In 0.1 mile there is a small historical marker addressing the Chickasaw Bayou battle. Retrace your route and return to the Mississippi Welcome Center. From the Welcome Center you will drive across the Mississippi River on the old bridge (U.S. Highway 80) adjacent to the center. Drive 2.1 miles to a sign for Grant's**

Canal. Turn left, then bear to the right. Drive 0.2 mile, under the I-20 bridge, and park.

The canal is on the left. This is the remnant of the canal begun by Brig. Gen. Thomas Williams in the summer of 1862. Grant ordered Sherman's corps to resume efforts on construction of the canal in January 1863. Three months later, plagued by the elements and constant Confederate shelling, the project was abandoned.

STOP 2, GRANT'S CANAL

As Sherman withdrew from the Chickasaw Bayou area to Milliken's Bend, McClernand arrived, brandishing his orders from the president that placed him in command. Sherman returned to commanding his own corps. Noting that supply ships ferrying men and equipment downriver from Memphis were being attacked by Confederates operating from Fort Hindman, also called Arkansas Post, on the Arkansas River, Sherman suggested an expedition to capture the place. McClernand agreed that the threat to the Union line of communications on the Mississippi had to be removed. (See Part I, Chapter 3, "Safeguarding the Line of Communications—Arkansas Post," for a description of this action.)

When Grant discovered McClernand had left the Mississippi and gone up the Arkansas River—and then proposed going deeper into Arkansas after the victory at Arkansas Post—he felt McClernand had strayed too far from his primary objective and ordered him back to the Mississippi. Grant informed Maj. Gen. Henry Halleck, Federal general in chief in Washington, of his concerns about McClernand's fitness for command and his displeasure with the general's performance to date. Halleck supported Grant, authorizing him to relieve McClernand, if required. Because of McClernand's strong political connections (he had been a Democratic congressman from Illinois before the war), Grant opted not to relieve him at the time. Instead, Grant chose to assume command of the operations around Vicksburg himself, thus relegating McClernand to a corps command. Grant arrived at Milliken's Bend on January 28, 1863, and assumed command of all forces in the area on January 30.

Rather than allow his troops to sit idle in winter quarters until spring, Grant decided to conduct a series of peripheral operations aimed at capturing Vicksburg. In these efforts he had little confidence in success, but at a minimum his troops would be kept busy through the winter and would be campaign hardened when spring did arrive. Should one of these operations prove successful, Grant was prepared to send forces to exploit any advantage.

The first of these peripheral operations entailed the continuation of work on the canal begun by Brig. Gen. Thomas Williams, whose brigade accompanied Admiral Farragut's force the previous year when they had moved up from New Orleans. Because of the hairpin turn of the main channel of the Mississippi at Vicksburg, a canal dug across the base of this peninsula would bypass the fortifications at Vicksburg. This was backbreaking labor, done under difficult conditions due to heavier than normal rains throughout the winter. The canal was dug wide enough and deep enough to float Rear Adm. David D. Porter's gunboats and transports. But before the protective dam at the north end could be removed to allow the power of the river to complete the job, the Mississippi flooded and washed out the dam, spreading water generally over the countryside instead of scouring the canal as intended. In the meantime, the Confederates had moved artillery to a position from which it could sweep the exit from the canal. On March 27 Grant ordered the canal abandoned.

At the same time the canal was being dug, another attempt to get around Vicksburg was made by trying to get into Lake Providence, north and west of Vicksburg. From the lake a route was sought through the intervening swamps and from there into a series of bayous and small rivers leading into the Red River, well south of Vicksburg. Again, a Union army corps, this one commanded by Maj. Gen. James B. McPherson—an officer with extensive engineering experience from the prewar army—set to work cutting trees and digging channels. This effort continued through February and March, with limited results. Seeing the lack of progress after two months, and the great distance that had to be covered, Grant ordered the work halted.

For detailed readings, see Part I, Chapter 4.

PHASE 2: ISOLATING VICKSBURG

Directions to Mississippi Welcome Center. **Drive back to U.S. Highway 80. Note that the railroad tracks are unguarded where you will cross them; take proper caution. Turn left, drive 2.1 miles, and get back on I-20 East. Drive east, back across the Mississippi River, to Exit 1A. Drive back to the Mississippi Welcome Center and park there.**

As you drive back across the river, you will have an excellent view of the city and its dominating bluffs. From the Welcome Center parking lot, take the walkway crossing over the highway to Navy Circle. Standing in the fortification and facing the river you are looking west. Porter's fleet, approaching from the right, made its run past the gauntlet of Vicksburg's batteries on the night of April 16, 1863.

STOP 1, RUNNING THE BATTERIES/DECEPTION OPERATIONS

Grant had little confidence in the success of any of the peripheral operations. Sometime between January and March 1863, he decided to march his army southward on the west side of the Mississippi and cross over onto the eastern bank, thereby opening a new line of operations. Initially, he discussed his plans with no one. Pivotal to successful execution of the plan was Porter and his Mississippi flotilla. When consulted, Porter assured Grant that it was possible to run past the batteries at Vicksburg, but once done a return upstream would be too hazardous. Sherman was more direct. He implored Grant not to move south but to return to La Grange, Tennessee, or Oxford, Mississippi, and open a proper line of operations, one that would follow the railroad line and permit adequate logistical support.

Undeterred, Grant set his plan in motion on March 29 when he ordered McClernand to put the roads leading from Milliken's Bend to New Carthage, fifteen miles to the south, in good repair. This was no small task, requiring numerous bridges and log corduroy passages to be built through swamps and bayous filled with winter floodwaters. By mid-April, however, McClernand reported that troops and wagons could move to New Carthage.

Grant devised an elaborate deception plan to cover army operations on the west bank of the Mississippi. At Grant's direction, on April 2 Sherman ordered Brig. Gen. Frederick Steele's division to conduct operations north of Vicksburg, threatening Confederate positions along Deer Creek and Black Bayou. [Note: This action is covered in Part II, "Steele's Bayou, Deer Creek, Fort Pemberton Excursion."] *Pemberton* reacted by sending troops from Maj. Gen. Carter L. *Stevenson's* division north to confront Steele.

To further draw *Pemberton's* attention from activities west of the river, Grant ordered Maj. Gen. Stephen A. Hurlbut to launch cavalry raids in eastern Mississippi. Although Hurlbut was permitted to select the officer to lead these raids, Grant strongly recommended Col. Benjamin H. Grierson for the task. Between April 17 and May 2, Grierson's 1,700 troopers, at times moving in as many as five independent columns, covered nearly 600 miles operating between La Grange, Tennessee, and Baton Rouge, Louisiana, causing great consternation throughout Mississippi. At one point, over 20,000 Confederate infantry and cavalry troops were chasing after the Yankee raiders. [See Part I, Chapter 7, and Chapter 8, "The Other Side of the Hill," for more on Grierson's raid.] Although resulting in modest material accomplishments, Grierson's raid admirably succeeded in distracting *Pemberton* during the critical movement of Union forces to the south.

On the night of April 16, the Union fleet steamed past the Vicksburg batteries, suffering surprisingly little damage thanks to Porter's meticulous planning and superb leadership. A week later, another convoy of transports also made the passage. Grant now had waterborne artillery and transport south of Vicksburg.

As Grant concentrated his two corps, McClernand's and McPherson's, at Hard Times, south of New Carthage, on the west bank of the Mississippi, he ordered Sherman to threaten the defenses north of Vicksburg. Taking a small force, including the remaining gunboats north of Vicksburg, on April 29 Sherman conducted a demonstration against Haynes's and Drumgold's Bluffs near Snyder's Mill, north of Vicksburg, to draw attention from the main effort in the vicinity of Grand Gulf. This charade included marching troops overland where they could be seen, then putting them back on the ships and sailing them in view of the Confederates. A force of 5,000 troops, identified to reinforce Brig. Gen. John S. *Bowen* around Port Gibson/Grand Gulf should Grant cross there, was held by *Stevenson* north of Vicksburg. *Stevenson* indicated to *Pemberton* that he felt the feint was south of Vicksburg and that the main attack was from Sherman in the north. *Pemberton* hesitated, and at the critical moment that *Bowen* needed reinforcements at Port Gibson, they were watching Sherman reembark his troops—to sail back to the Mississippi, where Sherman would within the week rejoin Grant on the east side of the river. [See Part I, Chapter 8, "Assault on Grand Gulf," for more detail.]

Grant's ability to conceptualize the total operation, not just the tactical battlefield, meant that he would meet the enemy force with the advantage of both numbers and surprise. He had outgeneraled his opponents.

For detailed readings, see Part I, Chapter 6.

OPTIONAL SITES

At this point, those who desire to visit some of the outlying areas where operations occurred during the winter of 1862–63 may do so. These areas are at some distance from Vicksburg and will entail considerable travel time.

Steele's Bayou, Deer Creek, Fort Pemberton Excursion

The start point for this part of the campaign is the National Park Service Visitor Center. From the Visitor Center, get on I-20 East, drive 1.0 mile, and exit on U.S. Highway 61 Bypass (north). Drive 30.0 miles on U.S. Highway 61 to Mississippi (MS) Route 1. Turn left on MS Route 1 and drive 0.7 mile to the sign for Hill's Plantation (on the right). Park and get out of your car.

STOP 1, STEELE'S BAYOU, BLACK BAYOU, DEER CREEK

Over the winter of 1862–63, Grant kept his forces busy trying a variety of innovative means of getting around Vicksburg without having to pass the city's massed batteries. One of the more audacious plans was suggested by Admiral Porter.

The high ground north of Vicksburg known as Walnut Hills was the key terrain dominating the city's defenses. Sherman had failed in his attempt to capture this high ground in December 1862. In March 1863 Porter proposed flanking the dominating positions at Haynes's Bluffs on the Walnut Hills with naval forces. He believed a way could be found through the maze of rivers, streams, creeks, and bayous that would place his gunboats in a position from which capture of the Confederate positions on Walnut Hills would be possible.

Steaming into the Yazoo River on March 14, Porter's gunboats first made their way into Steele's Bayou, then traveled north to Black Bayou, following it to Deer Creek. Passing into Deer Creek, Porter steamed northward seeking to pass further east using the Rolling Fork River.

Once in the Rolling Fork, he intended to move southward along the Big Sunflower River, bringing his force into the Yazoo upriver and on the flank of the Confederate positions on Walnut Hills.

You are standing at the intersection of Black Bayou and Deer Creek. The bayou was on your left as you drove up to this Stop. Were you to proceed approximately 10 miles farther on MS 1 you would encounter the modern canal that generally follows the trace of Steele's Bayou. The road you came in on was built over the junction of the two bodies of water. Deer Creek proceeds north from its juncture with Black Bayou approximately 13 miles (straight-line distance; farther by the twists and turns of the creek) to the town of Rolling Fork, where it intersects with Rolling Fork River. Hill's Plantation, briefly the site of Sherman's headquarters, was in the grove of trees to the right of the road. Though long since destroyed, the plantation house is described in the historical marker adjacent to the road.

For detailed readings, see Part I, Chapter 5, "Deer Creek."

Return to your car. Drive the 0.7 mile back to U.S. 61. Turn left (north) on U.S. 61 and drive 13.6 miles to Rolling Fork. (You will be driving along and across Deer Creek as you proceed north.) Turn left on MS Route 14. The Rolling Fork River, which leads to the Big Sunflower River, is on your right. Drive 0.2 mile, then turn left on First Street (this is the intersection of Deer Creek and Rolling Fork River— Deer Creek is now filled in here). Drive 0.8 mile to a "T" in the road. Drive straight across the road on the small dirt road running along the cemetery. Stop and park.

STOP 2, DEER CREEK

The tree-choked creek on your left as you parked is Deer Creek. As you look at the creek, you can immediately understand Admiral Porter's difficulties as he struggled to get his steam-powered ironclads through this waterway. His descriptions of Deer Creek in 1863 are very similar to what you see here. It was near this location where Union gunboats were finally stopped by trees felled across the creek and Confederate artillery fire from positions on the creek banks. Stalled and fearing attacks from Confederate infantry, Porter urgently requested Sherman's infantry to come to his aid.

For detailed readings, see Part I, Chapter 5, "Deer Creek."

Get back in your car. Turn right out of the cemetery, drive 0.1 mile, turn right again, and drive 0.2 mile to the yield sign. [Note: the Indian

mound referred to in the readings (Part I, Chapter 5, "Deer Creek") is to the left of the silver-roofed barn, about 400 yards away and across the road.] You are now at U.S. 61. If you turn right, you will be going back to Vicksburg. If you turn left, you can drive to another of the peripheral winter campaign sites, Fort Pemberton, located approximately 75 miles northeast of this location in the vicinity of the junctions of the Tallahatchie, Yalobusha, and Yazoo Rivers, near the town of Greenwood, Mississippi.

Directions to Fort Pemberton. Turn left onto U.S. 61 North. Drive 37.4 miles. Turn right (east) on U.S. 82. Drive 39.6 miles to a sign for Fort Pemberton (which comes after a sign that says "Welcome to Greenwood"). Turn left into the parking area and get out of your car.

STOP 3, FORT PEMBERTON

As you walk into what is left of the fortification you will see a stone historical marker. With your back to the highway and facing the marker, you are looking north. If you walk north to the riverbank and look to your left (up the Tallahatchie River), you will see the sharp bend in the river around which the Union gunboats initially appeared when they attacked the fort. Before leaving this Stop, you may wish to walk back to the highway and note the highway bridge west of the old fortification. This bridge crosses the canal that today connects the Tallahatchie and Yalobusha Rivers, a distance of less than a half mile separating the two.

The Yazoo Pass Expedition

Fort Pemberton was built in February 1862 by Maj. Gen. William *Loring's* Confederates to block the advancing Union force. Anticipating a Union effort to find a way through connecting rivers between the Mississippi River and the Yazoo River, on February 17, 1863, Lieutenant General *Pemberton* sent *Loring* to select a site and construct a fort to deny the Federals access to the northern water routes.

Even as Fort Pemberton was under construction, Grant placed Lt. Col. James H. Wilson, a young West Point engineer (class of 1861), in charge of reopening Yazoo Pass. On February 24, leaving the Mississippi River and passing into Moon Lake, Wilson used black powder charges to breach a levy and clear obstructions, thereby permitting Union gunboats to gain access to the Coldwater River. With great difficulty, being forced to clear much of the route as they progressed, gunboats from Porter's Mississippi Squadron, under the command of Lt. Cmdr. Watson Smith and accompanied by troops under the command of Brig. Gen. Leonard F. Ross, steamed south on the Coldwater toward Greenwood, Mississippi, and Fort Pemberton.

Fort Pemberton, situated between the Tallahatchie and Yazoo Rivers, commanded both waterways and offered good positions for artillery and infantry defenses. *Loring* used cotton bales and dirt to reinforce the natural strength of the position and by March 11 had placed seven artillery pieces, including a thirty-two-pound gun that equaled in size anything on the Union gunboats. Union gunboats attacked the fort without success on three occasions in March and twice in April. At one point, the Federals attempted to flood out the defenders by severing additional levees to the north. A mere two-foot rise in the level of the river would have been sufficient. This effort also failed, and the line of operations was abandoned.

For detailed readings, see Part I, Chapter 5, "Fort Pemberton."

At this point the coverage of the bayou expeditions is concluded. You may proceed back to Vicksburg or whatever destination you desire from here.

PHASE 3: THE UNION ARMY CROSSES INTO MISSISSIPPI: PORT GIBSON TO THE BIG BLACK RIVER BRIDGE

The start point for this excursion is the Mississippi State Welcome Center at Exit 1A off I-20 in Vicksburg. From the Welcome Center parking lot, turn right onto U.S. Highway 61. Drive 0.1 mile and turn left onto I-20 East. Drive 0.6 mile to Exit 1B, U.S. 61 South (toward Natchez). Drive 23.6 miles farther to Mississippi (MS) Route 462. Turn right toward Grand Gulf State Park. Drive 7.5 miles to the entrance to Grand Gulf Military Monument (State Park).

[If you have time, there is a museum here worthy of a visit. In addition to Civil War artifacts and exhibits that explain various aspects of the battle for Grand Gulf and Fort Cobun, the museum has an interesting collection of Civil War wagons and carriages. Unique among the collection is a meticulously restored field ambulance. This utility vehicle was the "jeep" of its day, often appropriated by commanders as a command vehicle. The park itself has emplacements from 1863 (Fort Wade) that are still well preserved. A small fee is charged for entrance to the museum and its exhibits. However, this is not the planned stop for this battlefield guide.]

Turn right out of the park and drive an additional 1.0 mile to Fort Cobun. Follow the main road as it winds through what was once the thriving town of Grand Gulf. Continue driving, bearing right at the "Y" in the road, until the road comes to a dead end in a small parking lot adjacent to Fort Cobun. Park and walk up onto what was the parapet surrounding the fortification.

STOP 1, GRAND GULF

Grant opened a new line of operations on March 31, 1863, when he started moving his troops south of Vicksburg on the Louisiana side of the Mississippi River. First McClernand's and then McPherson's corps moved through the difficult terrain, cut by numerous bayous that had to be bridged by the Union forces. Having assigned but few engineer officers, the flexible western troops soon made themselves expert at bridging the wet expanses of Louisiana bottomland. By April 29 the two Union corps were at Hard Times, Louisiana, prepared to cross to the eastern side of the river. They were joined there by Porter's fleet, which had passed the batteries of Vicksburg on April 16 and 22 (see Part I, Chapter 6).

Originally, Grant intended to land his force at Grand Gulf, then a well-known Mississippi River port. To do that, he planned to have Porter's fleet neutralize or defeat the Confederate batteries located where you now stand, Fort Cobun, and at Fort Wade, in the state park. The modern visitor should understand that the Mississippi River in 1863 ran directly under the parapets where you now stand. The backwater lake you see at the foot of the fort today was the main channel in 1863. Once Porter's gunboats had neutalized the forts, Grant's army would cross the river and land, using transports that had come down the river.

Fort Cobun's defenses were commanded by Brig. Gen. John S. *Bowen*. *Bowen* had approximately 4,000 soldiers available for defending the fortifications in the vicinity of Grand Gulf. Reinforcements from Vicksburg had been promised but were delayed in arriving as a direct result of Grant's operational deception activities. *Pemberton* was reacting to Grierson's cavalry raid (see Part I, Chapter 7) plus the danger posed by Sherman's corps, left north of Vicksburg to threaten that approach.

Pemberton hesitated in sending additional forces to Grand Gulf because he was uncertain where Grant's main effort would fall. However, *Bowen's* defenders would prove themselves more than a match for the Union gunboats. Finding himself unable to pound Forts Cobun and Wade into submission, Grant was forced to find another crossing site.

For detailed readings, see Part I, Chapter 8, "The Other Side of the Hill."

Directions to Port Gibson. **Return to your car and drive back 4.9 miles along the same route you came in on. You will take the right fork at a "Y" in the road. This road, Oil Mill, leads to Port Gibson. From this turn, drive another 3.3 miles into the center of Port Gibson. You will come to a stop sign with the courthouse on the left and the county administration building on the right. Turn right at the stop**

sign and drive 0.1 mile. At the third light, turn right on Carrol Street (you will see a small marker referring to the campaign on the corner), then bear left at the fork (you will see a small brown sign that directs you toward Point Lookout). From the turn it is 4.3 miles to Point Lookout. Turn right into Point Lookout, overlooking Bayou Pierre, and park.

STOP 2, BRUINSBURG/POINT LOOKOUT

When Porter's gunboats were unable to neutralize the Confederate batteries at Grand Gulf, Grant had to find another landing site for his troops. On April 29 a Union reconnaissance party found a good landing site at Bruinsburg, just a short distance downstream from Grand Gulf. Grant immediately directed McClernand to Bruinsburg, and by daybreak on April 30, McClernand's entire corps had landed and was marching toward Port Gibson. Before the end of the day, two brigades of the lead division (Logan's) of McPherson's corps had closed on the eastern bank of the Mississippi River. As he consolidated his position on the east bank, Grant sent orders to Sherman directing him to cease his deception operations on the Yazoo River north of Vicksburg and move his corps to join the main army.

Upon reaching the east bank of the Mississippi, McClernand started toward Port Gibson on the Rodney Road. Before nightfall, Union troops clashed with the Confederates in the dark near the Shaifer House (Stop 4), thus setting the stage for the Battle of Port Gibson, also known as the Battle of Thompson's Hill. McClernand ordered Brigadier General Osterhaus to advance his division toward Port Gibson at first light on May 1 along a connecting plantation road toward the Bruinsburg Road (the road to your front). As his lead units marched up the road in the early morning, they ran into Brig. Gen. Edward *Tracy*'s brigade of *Bowen*'s Confederate defenders, occupying the position where you are now located. McClernand's other three divisions moved southeast along the Rodney Road. Their actions—occurring at the same time as the fighting here—are covered at Stop 3.

For details, see Part I, Chapter 8, "Sherman's Division," and Chapter 9, "Battle of Port Gibson."

Directions to Shaifer House. Get back in your car and turn left onto the Bruinsburg–Port Gibson Road. Drive 3.0 miles to a "Y" in the road. Make a sharp right (the turn is somewhat hard to see—it is just past the new Magnolia Church). Drive 1.3 miles farther and bear to the right onto a gravel road. Then drive 1.4 miles and pull in at the Shaifer House. Park and move up to the vicinity of the house. [Note: The terrain you have just driven through is an excellent example of the type of soil (loess) and the deep ravines typical of this entire area—in 1863 and today.]

STOP 3, SHAIFER HOUSE

During the night of April 30–May 1, Brig. Gen. Martin *Green* had moved up to the vicinity of the Shaifer House to determine if the Federal troops were indeed advancing on this route. He was in the process of calming the terrified women of the Shaifer family when the crash of muskets announced the arrival of the lead elements of the Union force.

After the initial skirmish, the Union commanders decided to wait for daylight before attacking with the divisions of Carr, Hovey, and A. J. Smith. Despite their numerical superiority, the difficult terrain again caused problems for the Union forces as they attempted to deploy. By this time General *Bowen* was on the scene and realized he had the bulk of Grant's army in front of him. He sent aides to bring up every Confederate soldier who could be spared as the Union forces began their attack about 8:00 A.M.

For detailed readings, see Part I, Chapter 9, "Shaifer House."

Directions to Magnolia Church. Return to your car. Turn around and retrace the route over which you came. Drive 0.4 mile to the old Magnolia Church site. Pull over here.

STOP 4, MAGNOLIA CHURCH

At Magnolia Church *Green*'s men attempted to halt the attacking Union force but eventually were forced back toward Port Gibson. As this fighting was taking place, the Union attack at Lookout Point (Stop 2), aided by the initial elements of McPherson's XVII Corps sent by Grant to reinforce Osterhaus's division, began driving back the Confederate defenders. The Confederates were forced to retreat behind Bayou Pierre and, by the following morning, *Bowen*'s force was gone. This action not only caused the loss of Port Gibson but also forced *Bowen* to withdraw his troops from Grand Gulf to avoid capture. Grant was now firmly established on the eastern bank of the Mississippi River.

For detailed readings, see Part I, Chapter 9, "Magnolia Church."

Continue to drive for 1.1 miles to the hardtop road. [Note: At 0.6 mile you will cross Willow Creek, site of another intense fight where the Confederates again tried to stop the Union advance on the afternoon of May 1.] Continue on the hardtop an additional 1.2 miles until you reach a stop sign. Turn right and drive 1.3 miles back into Port Gibson. At the second light, turn left onto U.S. 61 North. Drive 0.7 mile north across the Pierre Bayou bridge and turn right onto MS Route 18. Drive 42.5 miles. Just before reaching Fourteenmile Creek, there is a historical marker. Pull off the highway (taking great care because of the traffic) near this marker.

STOP 5, BATTLE OF RAYMOND

Following his success at Port Gibson, Grant had to make some very difficult decisions. His original plan, approved by General Halleck and President Lincoln in Washington, was to send a corps south to assist Maj. Gen. Nathaniel Banks, commander of Federal forces in New Orleans, to seize Port Hudson, the other bastion besides Vicksburg blocking the Mississippi. As Grant prepared to execute this action, he got word from Banks that he would not be able to support an attack on Port Hudson until May 10 and then with only 15,000 men—far fewer than Grant had anticipated. Grant concluded that he would lose a month to reorganization and inactivity in trying to take Port Hudson, a month that the Confederates could use to recover from the precarious position in which they now found themselves.

Grant then made one of the most daring and significant decisions of the entire war. He determined to move on Confederate forces reported to be at Jackson, Mississippi, with the intention of preventing them from reinforcing *Pemberton's* garrison at Vicksburg. Once this force was neutralized, Grant could march unhindered on Vicksburg. The army would carry its own rations and obtain whatever else was required by foraging off the land. Grant's experience from the previous December convinced him of the feasibility of this plan. At the same time, a tenuous line of communications extending from Bruinsburg to the rear of the army was intended to carry ammunition, coffee, salt, and hardtack. Confidently, Grant was prepared to go forward even if this line should be cut. The corps of McClernand and McPherson were ordered to proceed at once for Jackson.

Pemberton, in the meantime, had his own dilemma. He had no idea what Grant was planning. Sherman was still north of Vicksburg and thus threatened the city from that direction. *Pemberton* called for reinforcements from General Joseph *Johnston,* who was in Tullahoma, Tennessee. *Johnston* had none to give him but told *Pemberton* that he must concentrate his force and defeat Grant if and when he established his army on the east bank of the Mississippi. At the same time, President Jefferson *Davis* was writing to *Pemberton* urging him not to allow Vicksburg to be taken, whatever else Grant did. *Pemberton,* caught between conflicting guidance, tried to do a little of both. He dispatched 20,000 men to defeat Grant's army while maintaining another 10,000 within the defenses of Vicksburg.

For detailed readings, see Part I, Chapter 10.

Pemberton expected Grant to head directly for Vicksburg from the Port Gibson area, so Grant sent Sherman's corps, which came across the river landing at Grand Gulf, to move toward the Big Black River— on the route to Vicksburg—as part of his operational deception plan. In the meantime, he ordered McPherson's corps to move as quickly as possible on Jackson to cut the railroad and scatter any Confederate forces in the vicinity of the state capital. Grant wanted to be certain he prevented *Pemberton* from linking up with the army Joe *Johnston* was moving toward Vicksburg.

As McPherson's troops moved toward Jackson, a brigade of about 2,500 Confederates, commanded by Brig. Gen. John *Gregg,* moved into the town of Raymond (located about two miles from where you are now standing). Because he had received information from *Pemberton* that the main Union army was moving toward Vicksburg and was nearing the Big Black River (Sherman's deception), *Gregg* thought the Union troops moving toward him were a small flank detachment. He planned to attack and roll up that flank, thus forcing the Union army to pull back to their bases around Grand Gulf. McPherson's veterans had other ideas—even if it took some hard fighting.

For detailed readings, see Part I, Chapter 11, "Battle of Raymond."

Directions to Champion Hill. **Return to your car and continue for 0.2 mile, then turn left toward Raymond. Drive 1.9 miles. At the stop sign (before the water tower) turn left on MS Route 467 (Raymond-Bolton Road). Drive 1.4 miles (you will pass the courthouse on the right). At the "Y" in the road, turn right toward Bolton (at the yield sign). Drive another 5.7 miles. Turn left on Champion Hill Road (do not cross the railroad tracks). Drive 4.4 miles farther. Pull over to the side of the road as best you can (there is no good parking area here). Look to the left (south) from the open area in which you are parked. The hill you see is Champion's Hill.**

STOP 6, CHAMPION HILL (Also known as the Battle of Bakers Creek)

Following the fighting at Raymond on May 12, 1863, *Gregg's* Confederates withdrew to Jackson, Mississippi, where they joined forces with General Joseph E. *Johnston. Johnston* arrived in Jackson on May 13 expecting to take command of an assembled force of 12,000 soldiers. However, when he learned that McPherson's and Sherman's corps, over 20,000 men, were approaching, he determined to fall back to the north rather than risk another defeat similar to Raymond. *Gregg* was ordered to defend Jackson until the supply trains could be safely removed from the city, then follow.

On the morning of May 14, McPherson's veterans approached Jackson in a pouring rain that mired the roads. Greatly outnumbering the Confederate forces in artillery and infantry, Union forces compelled the Confederate defenders to withdraw and abandon the city in order to preserve their forces. Union troops poured into Jackson and immediately set to work destroying its manufacturing capabilities in order to deny those resources to the Confederacy.

For detailed readings, see Part I, Chapter 11, "Engagement at Jackson, Mississippi, May 14, 1863," and "The Confederate Reaction."

With *Johnston's* forces compelled to withdraw to the east, Grant could now turn to his main objective, the capture of Vicksburg. Informed by a spy of the Confederate plan to attack the Union rear as the Federal army dealt with Jackson, Grant ordered McClernand and McPherson to advance on the Confederates in the vicinity of Edwards, while Sherman completed the destruction of all military-related concerns in Jackson. McClernand's corps advanced along the Raymond and Middle Roads, while McPherson's corps moved along the Jackson Road on the north.

You are currently standing on an extension of the Jackson Road built in the 1920s. In 1863, the Jackson Road turned south and ran over the top of Champion Hill, in the vicinity of Champion House, owned by Lt. Sid *Champion,* then serving with *Pemberton's* army. The Champion Hill Missionary Baptist Church, which is private property, sits near the former site of Champion House.

At about 7:00 A.M. on May 16, A. J. Smith's Union division made initial contact in the south, along the Raymond Road. The Confederate positions extended south from Champion Hill, which was lightly outposted, along the ridge running southwest in front of Bakers Creek. Using to good advantage a strong natural defensive position, *Pemberton*

Lithograph of the attack on Champion Hill by the Twenty-fourth Indiana Regiment, Hovey's Division. (*The Soldier in Our Civil War: A Pictorial History of the Conflict, 1861–1865*)

sought to defeat the Federal forces advancing up the Raymond and Middle Roads. However, he did not realize that Grant's forces also were moving west on the Jackson Road until pickets reported that the Confederate left was in danger of being turned by Logan's division. Acting on their own initiative, *Pemberton's* subordinates, especially S. D. *Lee,* ordered a hurried shift of units to meet this threat, and the critical battle of the Vicksburg campaign began to unfold.

For detailed readings, see Part I, Chapter 12, "The Battle of Champion Hill."

Now drive straight ahead for 2.5 miles to a "T" in the road. Turn left on Buck Reed Road. Drive 1.6 miles to another "T" and turn left onto MS Route 476. Drive 1.5 miles and turn right on Adams Lane, at the sign for Cal-Maine Foods. Pull into the Coker House parking area.

The Coker House was built around 1852 by H. B. Coker. During the battle of Champion Hill it was used as a field hospital by both Union and Confederate soldiers. Currently, it is being restored by the Jackson Civil War Roundtable.

STOP 7, THE SOUTH WING OF
THE CHAMPION HILL BATTLE

To the north along the Middle Road, Osterhaus's and Carr's divisions were relatively inactive in the absence of distinct orders from McClernand to drive home an attack. As a result, *Pemberton* shifted forces away from this sector to counterattack Hovey's and Logan's divisions. *Bowen's* division pushed back the Federals almost to the Champion House before Union reinforcements, sent forward by Grant, again turned the tide.

At about 2:30 P.M., McClernand finally ordered Osterhaus to attack in the center, hitting the gap created when the Confederates pulled out to counterattack the threat from the north flank. Only *Loring's* division, located in the vicinity where you are now, could influence the action. *Pemberton* ordered *Loring* to attack. He hesitated, seeing huge numbers of blue-coated infantry to his front (from A. J. Smith's and Francis Blair's divisions), which even though they were not attacking were content to carry on an artillery duel at this time. By the time *Loring* did start to move, it was too late for the defenders. The forces on Champion Hill broke, and *Pemberton* ordered a retreat.

The Union forces on the north cut the Jackson Road leading to the bridge over Bakers Creek, leaving the entire Confederate army with one route of escape across the creek—the Raymond Road bridge and ford. *Pemberton* ordered all forces to retreat except the brigade of Brig. Gen. Lloyd *Tilghman,* which was ordered to hold its position at all costs until the Confederates could safely escape. *Tilghman* was one of the last casualties of the battle, killed by an artillery round as he held his position.

In the meantime, the remainder of *Loring's* division, south of the main Southern force and finally moving to counterattack the crossroads of the Middle Road and Jackson Road, found itself cut off from the escape route. Throughout the night, *Loring's* units tried to find a way to cross the flooded Bakers Creek, but every possible crossing was held by Union troops. *Loring* finally moved off to the south and eventually marched a roundabout route back to Jackson, where he rejoined *Johnston's* army, while the rest of *Pemberton's* army retreated to the Big Black River.

For detailed readings, see Part I, Chapter 12, "Actions on the Union Left—The Raymond Road."

From the Coker House, turn left onto MS Route 467 and drive 3.1 miles into Edwards. (Note: At 0.2 mile from the Coker House you will

see a monument erected at the site where Confederate Brig. Gen. Lloyd Tighlman was killed during the battle.) As you enter Edwards, MS 467 splits; follow it to the left for an additional 0.4 mile. At the stop sign, turn right on Moriah Street for 0.2 mile. At the stop sign turn left on Vicksburg Street (Old Highway 80) and drive 4.4 miles. Turn left into an unmarked gravel lane leading into the fields and park. Exercise special caution as you park and stand on the edge of the road to observe the Big Black River battlefield. The road is narrow with no shoulder, and traffic tends to be heavy at times.

STOP 8, ENGAGEMENT AT THE BIG BLACK RIVER BRIDGE

As you stand on the road and face the direction you were driving, you are facing west. The Big Black River bridge is approximately a mile farther to the west down the road. Confederate positions extended along a line running north and south about one-half mile west from where you are standing, with both flanks loosely anchored on the river as it looped around the fields.

Battle of the Big Black River Bridge

Six miles west of Champion Hill was the Big Black River, over which *Pemberton* had to move to get back to Vicksburg. Uncertain of *Loring's* fate and in the belief that he was moving to join *Pemberton,* the Confederate army commander resolved to hold a line at the Big Black River. Designated to defend the approaches to the bridge was a Tennessee brigade under Brig. Gen. John *Vaughn,* newly arrived and not suffering from the exhaustion of the defeat at Champion Hill. *Vaughn's* troops occupied earthworks in the area that had been dug the previous month in response to Grierson's raid. The remainder of *Bowen's* division added their weight to the defenses as they arrived. The exhausted units from the Champion's Hill battle moved to the west side of the river. The position was strong, with a reinforced parapet of logs, cotton bales, and dirt, fronted in places by abatis and water barriers. Eighteen artillery pieces were placed into the defenses to sweep the open low ground, making this position even more formidable.

The Union troops were in pursuit at 3:30 A.M. on May 17, a mark of the discipline and esprit of the army. At daybreak, the lead units of Carr's division of McClernand's corps made contact with *Pemberton's* force. After some initial skirmishing, the Union pressed home the attack.

For detailed readings, see Part I, Chapter 13, "Battle of the Big Black" and "Big Black to Vicksburg."

After seeing the defenses crumble at the Big Black, *Pemberton* pulled his forces back into the entrenchments of Vicksburg.

For detailed readings, see Part I, Chapter 13, "Big Black to Vicksburg."

Get back in your car and turn left (west) on Old Highway 80 and drive 3.2 miles to Bovina. At the stop sign turn right and drive 0.1 mile, and then left 0.2 mile to the junction of I-20. At this point you may proceed to Vicksburg or continue on your way. This ends this portion of the campaign.

PART III
DRIVING TOUR OF
THE VICKSBURG SIEGE LINES

This portion of the Vicksburg campaign will begin at the National Park Service (NPS) Visitor Center in Vicksburg, off Exit 4B of I-20.

The start point for this part of the campaign is the Memorial Arch just beyond the entrance ticket station. As you enter the military park, en route to the first Stop, you will be driving along a section of the Union siege lines. Later in your tour you will cover this section of the line in greater detail.

Drive for 1.0 mile along the one-way road as designated by the Park Service. Turn left on Pemberton Avenue and drive 0.3 mile across the area between the Union and Confederate lines (which should give you an appreciation for what the Union attackers had to cross). At the yield sign, you must turn left onto Confederate Avenue because of the one-way road. Drive 0.2 mile; you will pull into a parking area at the Confederate Great Redoubt (National Park Service [NPS] Stop 11). Get out of your car and climb past the Louisiana Monument to a gray NPS map on its far side.

STOP 1, THE CONFEDERATE DEFENSES—
THE GREAT REDOUBT

The siege part of the Vicksburg campaign will be covered by looking first at the Confederate defenses and then how Grant chose to attack them. This approach is different from the manner in which the National Park Service covers the siege. The NPS tour is designed to move people through the battlefield park in the most efficient manner possible while still giving the necessary details of the actions. In this battlefield guide, the Confederate defense will be covered first because they were in place first. Then the discussion will detail the Union actions to capture the Confederate siegeworks, ranging from Grant's initial quick thrust to the tedious process of digging trenchworks to reduce the defenses.

Initially, Confederate defenses were oriented toward the Mississippi River and the areas north of the city, from which the Union was most likely to attack. Recall that the first overland attempt on Vicksburg came from the northwest with Sherman's attack on Walnut

Print of a scene depicting siege operations at Vicksburg. (U.S. Army Military History Institute)

Hills across Chickasaw Bayou in December 1862. Over time, the Southern defenders expanded their defensive positions until they extended from the north to the south of the city, defending from an attack from any direction. The eastern defenses, facing the direction from which Grant's army was now approaching, were located on good terrain and consisted of dug-in rifle pits running between forts, all with log embrasures that included head logs to protect the defending infantry. In all, *Pemberton* had nearly 30,000 troops to defend the city.

The Confederate defenders of Vicksburg had experienced a series of stinging defeats as Grant's army closed in. From Grand Gulf and Port Gibson to the defense of the Big Black River bridge, Union forces had repeatedly overwhelmed the smaller Confederate forces, driving them back within the defenses at Vicksburg. Although *Pemberton* believed in the strength of the defensive positions he had constructed around the city, he knew only too well that unless a relief force could come to his aid Vicksburg would fall to Grant's army. However, *Pemberton* was determined to hold out as long as possible, hoping that President Davis would send help or that some change in Union strategy or in the Yankee leadership might miraculously save Vicksburg. As long as the city held out, the North's domination of the Mississippi and the splitting up of the Confederacy could be prevented.

Grant's army, victorious in nearly every battle or skirmish since crossing the Mississippi, approached the defenses of Vicksburg confident that a determined assault would carry the lines. After two attempts to force the lines failed, on May 19 and 22, 1863, Grant laid siege to the city. The Federals had sufficient soldiers both to besiege the city and defend against any relief attempts by *Johnston* moving against Grant's rear. Grant's plan is discussed in the readings that follow.

The Great Redoubt, where you are now standing, was built, along with the Third Louisiana Redan (Stop 7), to protect Vicksburg from attack down the Jackson Road. The Union attack on May 22 struck this area in great strength. Brig. Gen. John D. Stevenson's brigade of McPherson's corps got into the ditch fronting the redoubt before finally being repulsed with heavy losses. Today, the terrain in this area looks very different from how it appeared in 1863. All the trees in the area had been cut down and used in building the fortifications, forming obstructions, or for firewood.

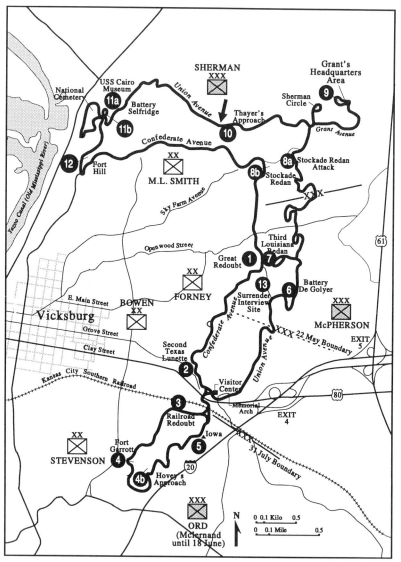

Map showing the location of Stops on the driving tour of the siege lines.

Report of Maj. Gen. John H. Forney, CSA, Commanding Division

On the morning of May 17, while the main body of the army was falling back to the intrenchments around Vicksburg, ... in pursuance of instructions from the lieutenant-general commanding, [I] directed General *Hébert* to prepare to evacuate the post of Snyder's Mill and to hurry into Vicksburg all commissary stores possible. For this purpose all available wagons were sent to him.

In the afternoon of the same day, I was directed to place my division in the trenches. Accordingly, General *Moore's* brigade was brought at once from its position near Warrenton, and placed in the intrenchments on either side of the Baldwin's Ferry road. General *Hébert* was directed to march his troops to Vicksburg, bringing with him all ordnance and ordnance stores he could; to send up the Yazoo all boats at Haynes' Bluff, with orders that they should be fired rather than allowed to fall into the hands of the enemy; to send mounted men to watch the approaches from Bridgeport and the railroad bridge, and to leave behind, at Snyder's, a few companies to keep up a show of occupation, with orders to destroy the heavy guns and other public property (previously prepared for destruction) whenever it would become evident the place would fall into the possession of the enemy, and then to make the best of their way to Vicksburg, or endeavor to escape across the Yazoo. . . .

The detachment rejoined its command in Vicksburg on the morning of the 18th. General *Hébert* arrived in Vicksburg, with his command, before daylight on the . . . 18th, having succeeded in bringing with him, from Snyder's, besides all the light pieces, two 20-pounder Parrotts and a Whitworth gun. His troops were soon in the intrenchments on either side of the Jackson road. In bringing my troops from their former position, I directed them to drive inside of the fortifications all the beef-cattle, hogs, and sheep that had been collected from the surrounding country, and squads of mounted men had previously been sent out for this purpose.

On May 18, at about 1 P.M., Brigadier-General *Shoup*, of General *Smith's* division, reported the enemy advancing on his position, and, by direction of the lieutenant-general, two of General *Hébert's* regiments were sent from his right to re-enforce his left. The whole of the division (the effective strength of which was about 4,700) was now in the trenches, from the railroad, on the right, to Graveyard road, on the left, a distance of about 2 miles (*Moore* on the right, *Hébert* on the left.) On this line there were twenty-seven pieces of artillery, most of which were field pieces. This number was afterward increased by three or four siege guns placed in rear of my right. Besides my own troops, Colonel *Waul's* Texas Legion was also assigned to me and held in reserve behind *Moore's* brigade. Brigadier-General *Lee's* brigade, of Major-General *Stevenson's* division, was on my immediate right; Brigadier-General *Shoup's* brigade, of Major-General *Smith's* division, on my immediate left.

On the 19th, the enemy made his first assault on my extreme left [Sherman's attack on Stockade Redan] and extending along *Smith's* division. He was several times repulsed, and finally fell back. By this time my entire division front was completely and closely invested. My skirmishers were withdrawn, and skirmishing prohibited (by order), in order to husband ammunition. During the next day the enemy kept up his sharpshooting and artillery fire, but made no assault.

On May 22, he assaulted three points on my line . . . three times on my extreme left and extending to General *Smith's* front, twice on the Jackson road, and twice on Baldwin's Ferry road, at 11 A.M. and 5 P.M. These assaults were made by larger bodies and apparently with greater determination than those of May 19. Colonel *Waul's* Legion had previously been sent to General *Stevenson;* but *Green's* brigade of *Bowen's* division was in reserve behind my right, and assisted in repelling the attack at that point. There were also on this day two Louisiana regiments, of *Smith's* division, in reserve behind my division. The enemy was repulsed in each of his attempts, though he succeeded in getting a few men into our exterior ditches at each point of attack, from which they were, however, driven before night. Hand-grenades were used at each point with good effect. . . . The casualties in my division were 42 killed and 95 wounded. The loss of the enemy must have reached 2,000.

From this time to the close of the siege the enemy kept up an incessant fire of sharpshooting and cannonading, in the mean time planting batteries and continuing his approaches, the main points being the work on the Baldwin's Ferry road, the one on the Jackson road, and a point midway between the Graveyard and Jackson roads. Approaches were also made on my extreme left; but this point was, properly speaking, under the supervision of Major-General *Smith.*

Lithograph depicting the fighting around the explosion of a Union mine on June 25, showing how hand grenades were used by the opposing sides. (*The Soldier in Our Civil War: A Pictorial History of the Conflict, 1861–1865*)

On or about June 2, my line was contracted by closing in to the right, in consequence of its close investment and the reduction of its numbers by casualties, my left now resting midway between the Graveyard and Jackson roads. The approachments at all . . . [of these] points were brought to within easy hand-grenade distance, and mines were pushed forward under the works.[1]

Return to your car and drive south along the one-way road. At 0.4 mile you will see Pemberton's statue on the right. Drive 0.8 mile (0.4 mile past Pemberton's statue). Stop at the parking area on the right (NPS Stop 12).

Walk past the statue of Jefferson Davis to a small plaque describing the Second Texas Lunette. This lunette was on the hill to your front now occupied by a private cemetery. Walk over to the Union markers near the cemetery.

STOP 2, SECOND TEXAS LUNETTE

The Second Texas Lunette, named after the Second Texas Volunteer Infantry that manned the position throughout the siege, was built to defend the Baldwin Ferry Road, which approached Vicksburg from the southeast. In the coordinated Union assault on May 22, McClernand's corps attacked this key position. At the same time, Union troops were attacking the Railroad Redoubt (Stop 3), the Great Redoubt (Stop 1), the Third Louisiana Redan (Stop 6), and the Stockade Redan (Stops 8A and 8B).

The Confederates had ample time to prepare to defend against this assault. The Texans had loaded as many as five rifles per man before the attack began and had half their force along the defensive bulwarks while the other half waited to reload emptied weapons. The Union opened with an intense artillery bombardment lasting several hours. When the infantry assault finally began, the defenders waited until the Federals were almost at the defensive works and then opened a murderous fire. The Yankees fell back, regrouped, attacked again, and then again. Each time they took heavy losses. The attacks lasted until nearly dark but were unsuccessful and resulted in severe casualties. On all fronts the Union lost 3,199 casualties, 502 of whom were killed. The Union casualties are particularly significant considering that the Union commanders could look out across the relatively open space between the two lines and see the more than 3,000 men covering the ground, unlike most battles that were not so easy to observe. This sight had a strong impact on the Union commanders—as it would on you if you saw the same thing where you are now standing. The Confederates lost less than 500 total casualties on May 22.

At this location, Pvt. Thomas H. Higgins of the 99th Illinois Infantry won the Medal of Honor when he carried his regimental colors through the middle of the worst of the firing. Hundreds of defenders shot at him, but he came on, finally carrying the Stars and Stripes over the top of the Confederate works unharmed. Quickly captured, he was searched to find the armored breastplate that the defenders knew he had to be wearing, but they found him wearing nothing other than a blue wool coat over a cotton shirt. His Medal of Honor citation was based in part on testimony from his Confederate opponents.

As the assault portion of the battle ended, the Union settled into siege operations. A series of approach trenches were dug toward the lunette. One of these had approached to within ten yards of the outer ditch fronting the position when the city finally surrendered.

Report of Col. Ashbel Smith, CSA, Second Texas Infantry, Moore's Brigade, Forney's Division

As the forces below Vicksburg fell back into the city, the Second Texas Infantry was moved back, still holding its relative position of advance guard, first to its former bivouac in the rear of Warrenton, and successively into the city of Vicksburg, which it entered on Sunday, May 17. It was first posted on the extreme right of the lines adjoining the Mississippi River. Later in the evening it was moved to a position on our lines between the Baldwin's Ferry road and the Jackson Railroad, occupying its proper place as the right battalion of *Moore's* brigade. Subsequently, the same night, an hour or two after midnight, the men were roused from their bivouac on the ground, and moved out of their brigade position, and changed places with the Forty-second Alabama (a gallant regiment), in order that the Second Texas Infantry might man the fort which commanded the Baldwin's Ferry road at the very point where the road traversed the lines to enter the city. This was the assailable point of our lines; the place of danger; the post of honor; the key of this portion of our works of defense. The other similar point was where the Jackson road crossed our lines to enter the city, and this position, for a similar reason, appears to have been manned by the Third Louisiana Infantry, a most gallant corps.

Reverting to the position occupied by the Second Texas: The ground is so irregularly broken here that it is scarcely possible to give by description a clear notion of its configuration. The center of the position on the lines now occupied by the Second Texas was a fort situated on a projecting swell or *mamelon* of ground well in advance of the general outline of the works. The Baldwin's Ferry road, approaching the fort from the right and front obliquely, came up to its right salient, ran along its front at the foot of the *glacis* [sloped face of an earthwork], and wound round its left flank to enter the city. The rifle-pits connecting with the retired parts of the fort on the right receded very rapidly, to take advantage of the ground. For a like reason there was an interval of upward of 100 yards between the left of the fort and the continuation of the general line of defenses to the left. Through this interval the Baldwin's Ferry road entered the city.

To the front of the fort, and both to its right and left, the earth is most irregularly broken into large and deep valleys, more or less perfectly communicating with each other and affording perfect cover for large bodies of men. Of these valleys there are two important *debouches* [exits] into the road—one . . . with a sharp curve into the road about 35 paces to the right of our right salient; the other . . . by a long, straight valley approaching obliquely and terminating at the road in the interval between the left of the fort and the continuation of our lines to the left. Coming up this latter valley takes the front of the fort in *enfilade* and its right flank and rifle-pits in reverse. Between these two *debouches,* in front of the fort and separated from it by the road, which here runs in a deep trench, is a sharp elevation of the height of the fort, with a rapid declivity from us. Everywhere, from close proximity to our works to an indefinite distance outward, were crests between the irregular system of valleys . . . some of which were more elevated than the fort. These crests, at varying distances from our works of 60 yards to a mile, furnished suitable positions for the enemy's cannon, and protected them and their infantry from our fire as effectually as could have been done by artificial breastworks. In short, for many operations in the progress of attack, the great natural strength of this district, so much vaunted, inured as much to the advantage of the besiegers as of the besieged.

Our fort was an irregular *lunette,* with no flank on the left; or it may be considered a redan with a large *pan coupe* [broken corner], having its left thrown forward and its right retired. Its left having no flank, its interior was exposed to an enfilading and reverse fire from the enemy approaching by the valley, which debouches on its left. Its parapet was about 4½ feet high on the inside, its superior slope about 14 feet thick. It was surrounded by a ditch in front nearly 6 feet deep, with an irregular *glacis* made by the natural slope of the earth to the ferry road. There were two embrasures for cannon, with a traverse between them.

The men of my regiment were stationed as follows: The two right companies occupied the rifle-pits tending off from the right of the fort; the four next companies manned the fort; the four remaining, or left, companies occupied the lines next on our left separated from the fort by the interval of upward of 100 yards, above described. In addition there were, at the commencement of the siege, placed in the fort two detachments, with their guns, from Captain *Tobin's* battery.

The embrasures were subsequently filled up, for reasons which will be hereafter stated. A flank on our left and another traverse were constructed for protection against a fire up the left valley. A ditch 2 feet deep was dug on the inside of the parapet, to enable the men to stand erect without being exposed to the enemy's fire. As the enemy's elongated shot traversed the parapet near its upper slope and killed several men, the parapet was strengthened by adding to its interior slope in some places 2 feet to its thickness.

It was also found necessary to deepen the trenches and strengthen the breastworks of the rifle-pits on the right. I was also obliged to construct covered ways for the purpose of safe communication with the sinks and wells in our rear. And eventually it was deemed prudent to construct a strong line of rifle-pits across the gorge of the fort for the greater security of our rear, and to be used in case our lines should be breached or carried by assault. After all improvements, the interior of the fort was swept within 2 feet of the ground by the enemy's Minies. This did not prevent the men from bivouacking at night, lying flat on the ground; but during the day safety compelled them to seek the protection of the ditches next [to] the parapet and traverses.

In the night of May 17 . . . the Second Texas Infantry took its position on the lines.

The 18th, houses were burned, trees were cut down, and other obstructions were removed, and dispositions made to receive the enemy. In the evening the enemy's pickets were reported on the ferry road, 3 miles in our front.

Early the 19th, I sent forward Captain [William] *Christian* with his company to observe the enemy, and, if need be, to deploy as skirmishers and hold him in check. Soon clouds of the enemy's skirmishers were seen emerging through the woods on the hills some 2 miles distant, and deploying to the right and left. Captain *Christian* met them about half a mile in our front. The skirmish-

ing was heavy. I re-enforced him with Captain [R.] *Debord*'s company, and Major [G. W. L.] *Fly* was ordered to the command of
the detachment. After several hours of skirmishing, the detachment returned about 3 P.M., being obliged to fall back, as both their
flanks were threatened, having been left uncovered by the retiring of our skirmishers of other regiments. In this day's skirmishing we lost two men . . . killed or captured.

All this day . . . [and] the 20th and 21st, heavy black columns
of the enemy, or clouds of dust marking their movements, were
seen pouring through the timber over the hills, taking positions
where they were concealed by the irregularities of the ground.
As these columns came up into position, they opened on us with
cannon and rifled musketry, which increased hour by hour with
their augmenting numbers, until the uproar and rattle was almost
incessant and very grand. We returned the fire fiercely, but the
irregularities of the ground appeared to protect the enemy as effectually as we were sheltered by our breastworks. On the 21st,
our two guns had become disabled; several of the gunners were
killed or wounded. Two guns, with their detachments from another battery . . . were brought into the fort to supply their place.
The investment of the city, as afterward appeared, was this day
completed.

At an early hour of the morning of . . . May 22, the enemy
opened a most furious cannonade and fire of musketry, which were
continued with occasionally varying intensity till 10 A.M. This was
the hour designated in the enemy's orders . . . for a general assault on our lines throughout their entire length. There was a
sudden, sullen silence of the enemy's artillery. Hitherto the positions of the enemy were known only by the flash of their guns
and the clouds of smoke which enveloped their heads. Instanta-
neously—the enemy springing up from the hollows and valleys to
our right and front—the earth was black with their close columns,
and ere Private *Brooks* could well exclaim, "Here they come," they
were surging on within a few paces of the foot of our works. The
assault on the fort and lines of the right of the Second Texas was
made in a column of five regiments, with a regiment front, and
with stormers provided with tools and implements. Dashing forward in good order they were hurled against our works with the
utmost fury and determination. The Second Texas was ready;
standing up boldly on the *banquette* [the step of earth within the
parapet, enabling defenders to fire over the crest], and exposing

their persons to the fire of ten times our numbers, my men received the enemy with a most resolute and murderous fire; my cannon belched canister; my men made the air reel with yells and shouts as they saw the earth strewn with the enemy's dead. One of the enemy's regiments staggered and was thrown into utter confusion. Our men, too, fell thick and fast; the detachment of cannoneers suffered particularly.

The enemy still rushed forward boldly, for, reaching the foot of our works, they were in security. Such was the profile of the works and the configuration of the adjoining ground in front that the fire of the fort could not reach men on the *glacis* or in the road, which was here worn into a trench at its foot. Such, too, was the outline of our lines, my fort being thrown so far in advance of the general outline, and my rifle-pits on my right receding by so obtuse an angle . . . that no portion of my front or left was commanded by any other portion of our lines. . . . I had no flanking arrangements.

This secure position of the enemy would cover some few hundred men, and communicated, at not more than 20 paces distance, with the deep, irregular valley on the right. From this and other more distant positions behind the crests . . . the enemy maintained an incessant and fierce storm of Minies, under cover of which he made several very daring attempts to carry the fort, clambering up in force the external slope of the parapet. As the enemy could not be seen until he should have mounted the superior slope and be ready to dash in, I ordered the front rank next to the parapet to maintain the fire, and placed the rear rank on bended knees, with guns loaded and bayonets fixed and at a charge, ready to receive the enemy, alternating the position of the ranks as their guns became heated. Four paces to the rear I placed a reserve, lying on the ground, with guns loaded and bayonets fixed in like manner. This reserve was obliged to take this recumbent posture, for the central space within the fort was terribly searched by the enemy's Minies through our embrasures. Besides several abortive attempts, there were during this day three notable and most determined movements to sweep over the top of our works and dash with the bayonet into the fort.

The traverses between the two embrasures were made in part with cotton bags; the embrasures were reveted with cotton bags. Early in the day these cotton bags were displaced and uncovered of dirt by the enemy's artillery; the Minie balls playing on them

402] THE VICKSBURG CAMPAIGN

incessantly bowed out the cotton as if from the flue of a gin-stand, and scattered it all over the area of the fort. It was ignited from the muzzles of the enemy's rifles, the air was filled with smoke, and the fire was making its way to the ammunition boxes. The middle of the fort was swept within 2 feet of the ground with Minies.

Accordingly, I ordered men, lying flat on the earth, to brush away with their hands the burning cotton, and thus prevented the ignition and explosion of the ammunition. One of my cannons was disabled and knocked out of battery early in the day. The other could not be depressed so as to reach the enemy at the foot of the works. The detachment was so weakened by the dead, wounded, and missing, that there were scarcely men enough to serve it. It remained idle for several hours. About 2 o'clock I ordered it to be run up into battery and fired. As the last remaining corporal raised himself over the trail to aim, a Minie ball, within 15 inches of the platform, passed through his heart and he rolled over dead.

In one of the furious assaults the enemy mounted the parapet to near its superior slope. Numbers of them were pouring a murderous fire through our right embrasure, amid the smoke of the burning cotton, which enveloped and almost blinded the men in this angle of the fort, and they were apparently on the eve of dashing in. I shouted "Volunteers to clear that embrasure!" Four men sprang to the platform . . . and, discharging their guns within 5 paces of the muzzles of the assailants, hurled them back headlong into the ditch outside. The repulse was decisive. . . . To clear the outside ditch, spherical case was used as hand-grenades . . . with good effect.

After the repulse of this assault . . . about 3 P.M., there was for an hour or more a great slackening of the enemy's fire. He . . . ordered an attack to be made on our left. A heavy column came marching up the valley already described as debouching in the interval on our left.

Early in the day I had observed our exposed condition on this side, and had asked for support from the reserves. It was now at hand and opportunely, for my numbers were so reduced . . . that I could ill spare any considerable body from my front. It was now about 5 P.M. The reserve, some Arkansas and Missouri [troops] under General *Green,* hesitated for a moment. . . . I ordered instantly Captain [J. J.] *McGinnis'* company, which was in the rifle-pits to the right, to march to the left, crossing the gorge of the fort, to their aid, but as this company was coming into position the

Missourians dashed forward, and after half an hour's sharp fighting, they repulsed the enemy most gallantly.

This approach of the enemy's column . . . was the signal for the renewal of his attack in front. The firing was very brisk, but the assault was feeble compared with the fierce onslaughts earlier in the day. . . . As the shades of the night were setting in, the enemy's fire slowly and sullenly slackened. It ceased with the dark, [and] the enemy returned to their covers in the hollows and valleys. . . .

The loss of the enemy . . . was enormous. The ground in our front and along the road, and either side of the road for several hundred yards way to the right, was thickly strewn with their dead. In numbers of instances two and three dead bodies were piled on each other. Along the road for more than 200 yards the bodies lay so thick that one might have walked the whole distance on them without touching the ground. . . . On the 25th, there was a truce for burying the Yankee dead which had not been removed. More than 100 dead bodies . . . were buried. . . .

Failing to carry the city by assault, the enemy applied himself to a siege in regular form, and constructed his earthworks with almost incredible diligence and activity. Cannons placed in battery soon frowned on us from every eminence, and rifle-pits with breastworks bristled everywhere in front of our lines. From the commencement of the siege in form there was a fierce cannonade once, twice, thrice, and even oftener in the twenty-four hours, with occasional shots at irregular intervals; an incessant stream of Minies swept just above the upper slope of our parapet, increasing in strength day after day, as rifle-pit after rifle-pit was constructed. This stream was kept up from dawn till dark, whether any one was seen on our works or not. Let, however, a head appear, and the whir of a hundred Minies instantly hissed around it. This constant firing rendered the position in our rear unsafe. . . .

At different times throughout the siege the enemy made abortive attempts to assault our fort. His men, with a furious rattle of musketry, would spring to the top of their works, as if urged to dash forward, but the prompt response of the rifles of the Second Infantry . . . nipped their eagerness and they dropped back. Occasionally, too, there were movements on the enemy's lines during the night, which led to the suspicion that a night attack was contemplated. This apprehension, and the daily increasing proximity of the enemy's works to our lines, made it prudent to keep a portion of our men (sometimes one-half, sometimes one-third) under arms during the night as well as day. All our men at all times slept on their arms. . . . They were never relieved, but remained at all times at their post [and] the fatigue was very great. They did their duty not only without a murmur, but with gaiety.[2]

Return to your car and drive 0.2 mile. Follow the road to the right (otherwise you will return to the Visitor Center). Drive an additional 0.5 mile and pull into the parking area (NPS Stop 13). Walk up to the redoubt.

STOP 3, RAILROAD REDOUBT

This fort was built to guard the approach to Vicksburg along the line of the Southern Railroad of Mississippi. Here, too, on May 22 the Union assaulted after a nearly four-hour artillery bombardment. Carr's division of McClernand's corps attacked parts of *Stevenson*'s defending Confederate division. Again, the Confederates held their fire until the Yankee attackers were nearly on top of them, then poured a deadly fire that generally stopped the assaults, although remnants of several units planted their colors on the parapet (the earthen outer walls) of the redoubt before being repulsed. The southeast angle of the fort had been crumbled by the intensity of the artillery fire. Sgt. J. E. Griffith, of the Twenty-second Iowa, led twelve men through the gap and into the fort. *Waul*'s Texas Legion along with the Thirtieth Alabama quickly counterattacked, leaving only Griffith alive as he pulled back toward Union lines bringing a dozen prisoners with him. Unable to exploit any of the small breakthroughs, the Union troops, after taking heavy losses, returned to their lines by dark.

Siege operations were then begun against the Railroad Redoubt. Approach trenches were closing on the site when the Southerners surrendered.

Report of Brig. Gen. Michael K. Lawler, USA, Commanding Second Brigade, Fourteenth Division, Thirteenth Corps

Marching early the 19th instant [from the Big Black battle-field] I arrived in the rear of Vicksburg and rejoined the division in the afternoon of that day. During the remainder of the 19th instant and all day of the 20th, my brigade acted as a reserve to the troops of Smith's division, operating against the fortifications of Vicksburg.

Photo of the Confederate Railroad Redoubt at Vicksburg, taken in 1899. (U.S. Army Military History Institute)

At night of the 20th, orders were received to move forward and take the advance, relieving Landram's brigade, of Smith's division, which was quietly and quickly done under cover of the darkness. As soon as I had taken the advance, to protect my ranks from the enemy's sharpshooters rifle-pits were put in course of construction.

This work progressed favorably during the 21st. Two pieces of artillery . . . were also brought up and planted on our right, in line with the pits.

Late in the evening of the 21st, orders were received to charge the enemy's works at 10 A.M. on the 22d . . . this to be a part of a simultaneous movement of our whole army upon the rebel fortifications. . . . By daylight . . . my brigade, consisting of the Eleventh Wisconsin and the Twenty-first and Twenty-second Iowa Volunteers, had moved forward and occupied the ravine immediately in front of and about 100 yards from the rebel fortifications. The Ninety-seventh Illinois, . . . placed temporarily under my command, was stationed in the ravine in the rear of the Eleventh Wisconsin Volunteers. Here they were sheltered by the brow of the hill, on the top and a little to the rear of which the enemy's works were constructed.

This position they continued to occupy without change until the hour (10 A.M.) appointed for the charge arrived. Promptly at the hour my line was formed for the assault, the Twenty-second Iowa . . . occupying the right; the Eleventh Wisconsin . . . the left; with the Twenty-first Iowa . . . supporting the Twenty-second, and the Ninety-seventh Illinois the Eleventh Wisconsin. Colonel Stone led his regiment [Twenty-second Iowa] . . . against the enemy's fort directly in our front; the Eleventh Wisconsin . . . charged toward the rifle-pits to the left of the fort, the two supporting regiments closely following.

As soon as they reached the crest of the hill, a terrible fire from the enemy in front and on both flanks swept the ground and did fearful execution. Officers and men fell on every side, but with a courage that could not be daunted the Twenty-second and Twenty-first Iowa on the right, and the Eleventh Wisconsin and a portion of the Ninety-seventh Illinois on the left, moved upon the enemy's works.

Reaching them, the width and depth of the ditch in front of the works combined with the heavy fire poured into them by the rebels, checked the main advance of the Twenty-second and Twenty-first Iowa. A few brave men, however, leaping into the ditch, clambered up the sides of the fort, rushed into it, engaging in a hand-to-hand conflict with the rebels occupying the outer wing of the fort, overcame them, killing many and compelling the remainder to surrender. Thus a portion of their works were in our position, with the flag of the Twenty-second Iowa planted upon the walls. Those men . . . who did not go into the fort sheltered themselves in the ditch in its front and the gullies washed on the sides of the hill, and opened a vigorous and effective fire upon the rebels.

On the left, the Eleventh Wisconsin Volunteers . . . with portions of the Twenty-second and Twenty-first Iowa . . . which had become detached from their commands, and Ninety-seventh Illinois, succeeded in crossing the brow of the hill, under shelter of which their line had been formed; but, unfortunately, between them and the enemy's pits in their front was a deep and hitherto concealed ravine, filled with *abatis*. Into this Colonel Harris moved with his command [Eleventh Wisconsin], but beyond it, owing partly to the difficulty of the ravine itself, partly to the concentrated fire of the enemy, and partly to a want of sufficient support, he found it impossible to advance. Disposing of his men in the bottom and along the sides of the ravine as best he could, he halted and bravely held his ground.

In the mean time Landram's brigade had moved forward to my support, and as it came up into the ravine the Nineteenth Kentucky was ordered to move over the hill to the assistance of the Eleventh Wisconsin . . . which . . . they promptly did, losing, however, many men in the passage. . . .

The Seventy-seventh Illinois moved up to the right to the support of the Twenty-second and Twenty-first Iowa. Facing the fire of the enemy, they advanced upon the rebel fort and planted their banner on its walls beside those of the Twenty-second Iowa. The One hundred and thirtieth Illinois halted in the ravine as a reserve; but while my command was being strengthened . . . the enemy were not idle. Heavy re-enforcements had been drawn from their right and massed in my front behind their works.

As my men were already much exhausted, and as the re-enforcements sent them were light, farther advance under the circumstances was deemed impracticable, and orders were accordingly issued directing the men of the two brigades to hold the ground already gained . . . with the hope that re-enforcements might soon be forwarded. . . . No re-enforcements, however, could be spared us during the forenoon, and until late in the afternoon our position remained the same as in the morning. All the efforts of the enemy to dislodge or drive us back were unavailing. At sunset, however, a determined rush was made by the rebels to regain possession of their work, which, in consequence of the exhaustion of the men holding it, was successful.

Falling back a few rods from the rebel works until they obtained the protection of the crest of the hill, my men halted and opened such a fire upon the enemy as effectually checked their advance and compelled them to remain close under the protection of their works. A heavy fire was kept up from both sides until dark, when, by mutual consent, it ceased.

At 8 P.M. I received orders to withdraw my men and occupy the same ground I held the evening before the charge, which was promptly done, after bringing off all my wounded, with the exception of those in the ditch immediately under the rebel works.

The loss of the brigade . . . was very heavy. Out of the three regiments . . . 375 were killed, wounded, and missing. . . . All officers and men did their duty nobly.[3]

Return to your car and drive 0.7 mile to the parking area near Fort Garrott (NPS Stop 14). Walk to the Confederate position.

STOP 4A, FORT GARROTT (SQUARE FORT)

According to the precise use of military engineering terms of the day, a *fort* was a structure with four sides. Fort Garrott, named after the commander of the Twentieth Alabama Volunteer Infantry who was killed here by a Union sharpshooter, was one of a number of Confederate forts along the defensive lines. Today's visitor should note that the Confederate defenses did not end at Fort Garrott (even though today the National Military Park does). The defenses stretched on to the south and west all the way to the Mississippi River, nearly three miles from where you now are standing.

Maj. Gen. Carter L. *Stevenson*'s division defended the line here at Fort Garrott, extending to the Mississippi River. Union Brig. Gen. Alvin Hovey commanded the attacking force in this vicinity. Hovey's division did not arrive until May 24, so they did not assault Fort Garrott. Operations against this position consisted of laying siege through the use of extensive trenchworks, which were dug in a zigzag fashion to prevent the defenders from seizing a part of the trench and firing along its length. Re-creations of these entrenchments can still be seen leading up to Fort Garrott. Union siege lines were within 50 feet of the fort when the Confederates surrendered on July 4.

Report of Maj. Gen. Carter L. Stevenson, CSA, Commanding Division, July 29

On the morning of May 18, the positions to be held by each of the different divisions were assigned by the lieutenant-general himself. The portion of the line of defense which was assigned to my division included the river front and the works south of the city from the river to the railroad, a line of about 5 miles in length. *Barton* occupied the river front and the fortifications on the right;.*Reynolds,* those on the right center to the Hall's Ferry road; *Cumming,* the left center, and [S. D.] *Lee,* re-enforced by *Waul*'s Texas Legion, the extreme left. . . .

On the evening of the 18th the enemy made his appearance in front of our lines, and immediately began to push forward his sharpshooters. The number of guns, superiority of range and metal, and exhaustless supply of ammunition, enabled them in

Photo of the Confederate Fort Garrott, taken in 1899. (U.S. Army Military History Institute)

a very short time to plant many batteries in such commanding positions as to damage our works materially, and inflict a very considerable loss among the men.

On the morning of May 22, many indications showed that they contemplated an assault upon the line of General *Lee*. A tremendous artillery fire was opened and kept up for about two hours, while the fire of their large force of sharpshooters was heavy and incessant.

At about 1 P.M. a heavy force moved out to the assault, making a gallant charge. They were allowed to approach unmolested to within good musket range, when every available gun was opened upon them with grape and canister, and the men, rising in the trenches, poured into their ranks volley after volley with so deadly an effect that, leaving the ground literally covered in some places with their dead and wounded, they precipitately retreated.

An angle of one of our redoubts had been breached by their artillery before the assault and rendered untenable. Toward this point, at the time of the repulse of the main body, a party of about

60 of the enemy, under the command of a lieutenant-colonel, made a rush and succeeded in effecting a lodgment in the ditch at the foot of the redoubt and planting two flags on the edge of the parapet. The work was constructed in such a manner that this ditch was commanded by no part of the line, and the only means by which they could be dislodged was to retake the angle by a desperate charge, and either kill or compel the surrender of the whole party by the use of hand-grenades. A call for volunteers for this purpose was made and promptly responded to by Lieut. Col. E. W. *Pettus*, Twentieth Alabama Regiment, and about 40 men of *Waul's* Texas Legion. A more gallant feat than this charge has not illustrated our arms during the war.

The preparations were quietly and quickly made, but the enemy seemed at once to divine our intention, and opened upon the angle a terrible fire of shot, shell, and musketry. Undaunted, this little band, its chivalrous commander at its head, rushed upon the work, and in less time than it requires to describe it, it and the flags were in our possession.

Preparations were then quickly made for the use of hand-grenades, when the enemy in the ditch, being informed of our purpose, immediately surrendered.

From this time forward, although on several occasions their demonstrations seemed to indicate other intentions, the enemy relinquished all idea of assaulting us, and confined himself to the more cautious policy of a system of gradual approaches and mining.

The weakness of our garrison prevented anything like a system of sallies, but from time to time, as opportunities offered, and the enemy effected lodgments too close to our works, they were made with spirit and success. Among them, I may particularize a night sally made under the command of Lieutenant-Colonel [C. S.] *Guyton*, of the Fifty-seventh Georgia Regiment, with a portion of that regiment and of the Forty-third Tennessee. . . . The enemy had entrenched themselves at three different points on and to the left of the Hall's Ferry road. The command sallied out, charged their works with admirable gallantry, and took them, with considerable loss to the enemy, who were in greatly superior force.

On the lines occupied by General *Barton* and Colonel *Reynolds*, the configuration of the ground favoring it, the enemy were prevented from making any close lodgments by a judicious system of picketing and a series of attacks; and although they sometimes succeeded by force of numbers in gaining favorable positions, they were invariably dispossessed by the daring sallies of the garrison. . . .

I cannot find words sufficiently strong to express the pride and gratification afforded me by the dauntless spirit with which officers and men encountered all the dangers, and by the unmurmuring endurance with which they bore up for forty-seven sleepless nights and days, under all the hardships incident to their position. Confined, without a moment's relief from the very day of their entrance into the fortifications to that of the capitulation of the city, to the narrow trenches; exposed without shelter to the broiling sun and drenching rain; subsisting on rations barely sufficient for the support of life; engaged from the earliest dawn till dark, and often during the night, in one ceaseless conflict with the enemy, they neither faltered nor complained, but, ever looking forward with confidence to relief, bore up bravely under every privation—saw their ranks decimated by disease and . . . missiles . . . —with the fortitude that adorns the soldier and the spirit that becomes the patriot who battles in a holy cause.[4]

Report of Brig. Gen. Alvin P. Hovey, USA, Commanding Twelfth Division, Thirteenth Army Corps

My first brigade, commanded by Brigadier-General McGinnis, arrived before the outer works of Vicksburg on the 20th of May. On the 22d, that brigade was ordered by Major-General McClernand to support General Osterhaus' division on the extreme left, in an attack upon the city, which was to be simultaneous along the whole line. I was personally ordered to take charge of the batteries in front of Osterhaus' and my own command. Those placed in battery were Captain Foster's 20-pounder Parrotts, . . . Lanphere's 10 pounder Rodmans . . . and the Second Ohio . . . and Sixteenth Ohio Battery. . . . During the attack these batteries did admirable execution, and fully sustained their part of the charge. The position of the defenses, with *abatis* filling the approaches, prevented General Osterhaus' forces from making a successful charge, and my brigade, supporting his forces, was not seriously engaged. . . .

On the 24th of May, my second brigade . . . arrived from Black River Bridge, having been relieved by Brigadier-General Osterhaus. Colonel Lindsey, of the Ninth Division, with his brigade, was temporarily assigned to my command. At that date I commanded the extreme left of the continuous line of our forces. . . .

Receiving orders on the 23d to prepare for a siege, my forces commenced the work with spirit, and during the whole period prosecuted their labors with success, pressing our rifle-pits to within a few yards of the enemy's fortifications. During this period Capt. George W. Schofield placed his battery (First Missouri) in position, and with much labor succeeded in procuring four 24-pounder siege guns from Haynes' Bluff, which did great execution during the siege.

The strain upon my forces was extreme. For more than forty days they were under constant fire, casualties happening daily in the midst of their camps; men were killed and wounded in their beds, at the table, in the rifle-pits, and yet, during all this long period, there was no murmur, no complaint. They were veterans and determined to succeed.[5]

Return to your car. You will now be departing the Confederate defensive lines and moving around to the Union siege lines. Drive 0.5 mile. Park.

Get out and look west toward Fort Garrott from the position where the Union forces began their siege operations against this part of the line.

STOP 4B, HOVEY'S APPROACH

Siege warfare required extensive engineering effort. You are currently located at the start point for the siege operations against Fort Garrott. The ground between the entrenchments was swept by fires from both sides, rendering conventional forms of assault suicidal. Engineering operations, employing saps, parallels, sap rollers, and all the tactics and technology of siege craft, enabled the attacking force to move inexorably closer to their opponents' lines until eventually they were breached.

Report of Brig. Gen. Alvin P. Hovey, USA (continued)

This approach, directed on a redoubt, was not begun till late, although the ground gave cover here to within a short distance of the enemy's line.

This was one instance among many where the lack of engineer officers was shown. With a proper number of officers, the ground in all its details would have been thoroughly reconnoitered, and the best positions for approaches chosen, instead of wasting work, as in this case, when the best approaches were selected after the siege was half over.[6]

Return to your car. You will now be driving along the Union siege lines that opposed the Confederate entrenchments around Vicksburg. Drive 0.8 mile and park in front of the Iowa Monument. You will see General McClernand's statue directly to your front.

STOP 5, GRANT'S PROBLEMS WITH McCLERNAND

Grant did not care for McClernand. More than a personal dislike, he believed McClernand lacked competence as a general. In January 1863, Grant personally assumed command of the forces in the vicinity of Vicksburg to deny McClernand that role. Later, on two occasions, at Champion Hill and during the assault on the defenses of Vicksburg in May, Grant found fault with McClernand's generalship. Ordinarily, Grant would not have hesitated to remove from command someone in whom he had no confidence, but McClernand had powerful political connections. Finally, as the account below reveals, Grant found the excuse he was looking for to remove McClernand from the command of his corps. Were this episode simply a squabble between two generals, it would not deserve comment, but the insights to be gained from a brief review of the immediate events leading to McClernand's relief are instructive for what they tell us about Grant, his generalship, and his relationship with Halleck and Lincoln.

Report of Maj. Gen. John A. McClernand, USA, Commanding Thirteenth Army Corps

Early on the morning of the 19th [of May], accompanied by my staff, I made a personal reconnaissance to the brow of a long hill overlooking a creek 2 miles from Vicksburg. This hill runs north and south, and conforms very much to the line of Vicksburg's defenses, in plain view on a similar range a mile west. The creek is called Two-Mile Creek because it is only two miles from Vicksburg. . . .

The intervening space between these two ranges consisted of a series of deep hollows separated by narrow ridges, both rising near the enemy's works, and running at angles from them until they are terminated by the narrow valley of Two-Mile Creek. The heads of the hollows were entirely open. Nearer their termination they were covered with a thicket of trees and underbrush. At this time the pickets and skirmishers of the enemy were in this thicket, watchful to discover and obstruct our advance.

The enemy's defenses consist of an extended line of rifle-pits occupied by infantry, covered by a multitude of strong works occupied by artillery, so arranged as to command not only the approaches by the ravines and ridges in front, but each other.

Since 4 A.M. my command had been under orders to be in readiness to move forward and commence the investment of the city. By 6:30 A.M. it came up, and in obedience to my orders formed behind the crest of the hill upon which I had been waiting, General Smith's division on the right of the Vicksburg road; General Osterhaus' on the left, and General Carr's along the base of the hill, as a reserve. Skirmishers were thrown forward, who engaged the enemy's skirmishers, and artillery was opened from the most commanding positions upon the enemy's works, and a body of infantry observed between them and Burbridge's brigade, on my right. In a short time the enemy's skirmishers fell back, and my line advanced across Two-Mile Creek to the hills on the opposite side.

About this time (10:30 A.M.) an order came from Major-General Grant directing corps commanders to gain as close a position as possible to the enemy's works until 2 P.M.; at that hour fire three volleys from all their pieces in position, when a general charge of all the corps along the line should be made.

By 2 o'clock, with great difficulty, my line had gained a half mile, and was within 800 yards of the enemy's works. The ground in front was unexplored and commanded by the enemy's works, yet, at the appointed signal, my infantry went forward under such cover as my artillery could afford, and bravely continued a wasting conflict until they had approached within 500 yards of the enemy's lines, and exhaustion and the lateness of the evening interrupted it. An advance had been made by all the corps, and the ground gained firmly held, but the enemy's works were not carried. . . .

On the 20th, General Hovey brought up Colonel Slack's brigade, of his division, from Champion's Hill, and supported General Osterhaus on the left. General Carr supported General Smith on the right. Lively skirmishing continued during the 20th and 21st, and farther approach to the enemy's works were made where it could be done.

On the evening of the 21st, I received an order of the same date from Major-General Grant, in material part as follows:

> A simultaneous attack will be made to-morrow at 10 A.M. by all the army corps of this army. During to-day army corps commanders will have examined all practicable routes over which troops can possibly pass. They will get into position all the artillery possible, and gain all ground they can with their infantry and skirmishers. At an early hour in the morning a vigorous attack will be commenced by artillery and skirmishers. The infantry, with the exception of reserves and skirmishers, will be placed in columns of platoons, or by a flank, if the ground over which they have to pass will not admit of a greater front, ready to move forward at the hour designated.
>
> Promptly at the hour designated all will start at quick time, with bayonets fixed, and march immediately upon the enemy, without firing a gun until the outer works are carried. Skirmishers will advance as soon as possible after heads of columns pass them, and scale the walls of such works as may confront them.

General Carr's division relieved General Smith's on the same day, and now formed the advance on the right, supported by the latter. On the left, dispositions continued as before. . . . As far as practicable everything was done calculated to insure success.

On the morning of the 22d, I opened with artillery, including three 30, six 20, and six 10-pounder Parrotts . . . and continued a well-directed and effective fire until 10 o'clock, breaching the enemy's works at several points, temporarily silencing his guns and exploding four rebel caissons.

Five minutes before 10 o'clock the bugle sounded the charge, and at 10 o'clock my columns of attack moved forward, and within fifteen minutes Lawler's and Landram's brigades had carried the ditch, slope, and bastion of a fort. . . . Within fifteen minutes . . . Benton's and Burbridge's brigades, fired by the example, rushed forward and carried the ditch and slope of another heavy earthwork. . . . My men never fought more gallantly—nay, desperately. For more than eight long hours they maintained their ground with death-like tenacity. Neither a blazing sun nor the deadly fire of the enemy shook them. Their constancy and valor filled me with admiration. The spectacle is one never to be forgotten. . . .

Meantime Osterhaus' and Hovey's forces, forming the column of assault on the left, pushed forward under a withering fire upon a more extended line until an enfilading fire from a strong redoubt on their left front and physical exhaustion compelled them to take shelter behind a ridge. . . . Alarmed for his safety, and the assault of the corps immediately on my left having failed, the enemy early hastened to mass large numbers from his right and left in my front. Thus re-enforced, he renewed his efforts with increased effect. All my forces were now engaged. . . . Failure and loss of my hard-won advantages became imminent. . . . I requested re-enforcements and notified Major-General Grant of the fact.

At 11 A.M. I informed him that I was hotly engaged; that the enemy was massing upon me from his right and left, and that a vigorous blow by General McPherson would make a diversion in my favor. Again, at 12 m. [noon], that I was in partial possession of two forts, and suggested whether a vigorous push ought not to be made all along our lines. . . . Major General Grant directed me to communicate with General McArthur, to use his forces to the best advantage, and informed me that General Sherman was getting on well. This dispatch was dated at 2 P.M. and came to hand at 3:15 P.M. About the same time I received information that General Quinby's division was coming to my support. . . . I replied that I had lost no ground; that prisoners informed me that the works in which I had made lodgments were commanded by strong defenses in the rear, but that with the divisions promised I doubted not that I would force my way through the hostile lines . . . but obstacles intervened to disappoint. General McArthur's division . . . did not get up until next day. Colonel Boomer's and Sanborn's brigades, of General Quinby's division, much exhausted, came up, but before either of them could be fully applied . . . night set in and terminated the struggle. . . .

About 8 P.M., after ten hours continuous fighting, without food or water, my men withdrew to the nearest shelter and rested for the night, holding by a strong picket most of the ground they had gained.

My loss during this memorable day comprised fully three-fourths of my whole loss before Vicksburg, and was as follows:

	Killed	Wounded	Missing
Osterhaus' division	35	233	1
Smith's division	49	400	36
Hovey's division	42	—	—
Carr's division	109	559	57

TOTAL   1,487[7]

The Relief of McClernand

Charles A. Dana to Hon. Edwin M. Stanton, Secretary of War, June 22, 63, 9 A.M. (Received June 24, 3:35 A.M.)

McClernand last night was relieved of his command and ordered to report to Washington for orders. As the matter may be of some [political] importance, I telegraph the correspondence connected with it. The congratulatory address spoken of in General Grant's first letter is one that first reached here in the *Missouri Democrat* of June 11. In it he [McClernand] claims for himself most of the glory of the campaign; reaffirms that on May 22 he held two rebel forts for several hours, and imputes to other commanders a failure to aid him to keep them and take the city. The letters are as follows:

Grant to McClernand, June 17, 1863

Enclosed I send you what purports to be your congratulatory address to the Thirteenth Army Corps. I would respectfully ask if it is a true copy. If it is not a correct copy, furnish me one by bearer, as required both by regulations and existing orders of the department.

McClernand to Grant

I have just returned. The newspaper slip is a correct copy of my congratulatory Order No. 72. I am prepared to maintain its statements. I regret that my adjutant did not send you a copy promptly as he ought, and I thought he had.

Special Orders No. 164. Headquarters, Department of the Tennessee

IV. Major-General McClernand is hereby relieved from the command of the Thirteenth Army Corps. He will proceed to any point he may select in the State of Illinois, and report by letter to Headquarters of the Army for orders. Maj. Gen. E. O. C. Ord is hereby appointed to the command of the Thirteenth Army Corps subject to the approval of the President. . . .

Though the congratulatory address in question is the occasion of McClernand's removal, it is not its cause, as McClernand intimates when he says incorrectly that General Grant has taken exceptions to this address. That cause, as I understand it, is his repeated disobedience of important orders, his general insubordinate disposition, and his palpable incompetence for the duties of the position. As I learned by private conversation, it was, in General Grant's judgment, also necessary that he should be removed, for the reason, above all, that his relations with other corps commanders rendered it impossible that the chief command of this army should devolve upon him, as it would have done were General Grant disabled, without most pernicious consequences to the cause.[8]

Narrative of Maj. Gen. William T. Sherman, USA (continued)

After our men had been fairly beaten back from off the parapet, and had got cover behind the spurs of ground close up to the rebel works, General Grant came to where I was, on foot, having left his horse some distance to the rear. I pointed out to him the rebel works, admitted that my assault had failed, and he said the result with McPherson and McClernand was about the same. While he was with me, an orderly or staff-officer came and handed him a piece of paper, which he read and handed to me. I think the writing was in pencil, on a loose piece of paper, and was in General McClernand's handwriting, to the effect that "his troops had captured the rebel parapet in his front," that "the flag of the Union waved over the stronghold of Vicksburg," and asking him (General Grant) to give renewed orders to McPherson and Sherman to press their attacks on their respective fronts, lest the enemy should concentrate on him (McClernand).

General Grant said, "I don't believe a word of it"; but I reasoned with him, that this note was official, and must be credited, and I offered to renew the assault at once with new troops. He said he would instantly ride down the line to McClernand's front, and if I did not receive orders to the contrary, by 3 o'clock P.M., I might try it again. Mower's fresh brigade was brought up under cover, and some changes were made in Giles Smith's brigade; and, punctually at 3 P.M., hearing heavy firing down along the line to my left, I ordered the second assault. It was a repetition of the first, equally unsuccessful and bloody. It also transpired that the same thing had occurred with General McPherson, who lost in this second assault some most valuable officers and men, without adequate result; and that General McClernand, instead of having taken any single point of the rebel main parapet, had only taken one or two small outlying *lunettes* open to the rear, where his men were at the mercy of the rebels behind their main parapet, and most of them were actually thus captured.

This affair caused great feeling with us, and severe criticisms on General McClernand, which led finally to his removal from the command of the Thirteenth Corps. . . .

The immediate cause, however, . . . was the publication of a sort of congratulatory order addressed to his troops, first published in St. Louis, in which he claimed that he had actually succeeded in making a lodgment in Vicksburg, but had lost it, owing to the fact that McPherson and Sherman did not fulfill their parts of the general plan of attack.

This was simply untrue. The two several [*sic*] assaults made May 22d, on the lines of Vicksburg, had failed, by reason of the great strength of the position and the determined fighting of its garrison. I have since seen the position at Sevastopol [Crimean War], and without hesitation I declare that at Vicksburg to have been the more difficult of the two.[9]

Return to your car and drive 0.4 mile to a yield sign. Continue 0.1 mile to a stop sign, then another 0.1 mile. You will go past the Visitor Center, back through the Memorial Arch. From the arch drive along the Union siege lines for 1.9 miles to Battery De Golyer. Do not turn on Pemberton Avenue, but continue on. Stop in the parking area at Battery De Golyer (NPS Stop 1).

Lithograph of the position of Waterhouse's Battery (Sherman's Corps) during the siege operations. (Frank Leslie's *Illustrated Famous Leaders and Battle Scenes of the Civil War*)

STOP 6, ARTILLERY IN UNION SIEGE OPERATIONS

Battery De Golyer is typical of the Union artillery emplacements that supported the siege. From this position, a battery fired in support of the May 22 attack on the Great Redoubt (Stop 1). On May 24 Capt. Samuel DeGolyer's Eighth Michigan Light Artillery (six guns) occupied this site. Later, twenty-two guns were moved into this position, the largest concentration of cannon in the Union lines. DeGolyer was killed directing the fire of his battery from this point. Earthworks were built up in front of the artillery to help protect the gunners. Sharpshooters were also assigned to suppress the fire of Confederate riflemen who were inflicting casualties on the gun crews.

Report of Maj. Charles J. Stolbrand, USA,
Second Illinois Light Artillery, Chief of Artillery,
Third Division, Seventh Army Corps

At about 3 o'clock of May 19, I had placed in position the Third Ohio Battery, Capt. W. S. Williams commanding, the Eighth Michigan Battery, Captain Samuel De Golyer commanding, and Battery L, Second Regiment Illinois Light Artillery, Capt. William H. Bolton commanding, at about 2,500 yards distant from the rebel works. The batteries opened fire, and soon thereafter the rebel artillery in their works modified and materially slackened fire. About two hours afterward, having previously reconnoitered the ground and received Major-General Logan's assent, I directed Captain De Golyer's two howitzers to advance about 1,800 yards to the line subsequently occupied by all the light batteries.

Fire was immediately opened with good effect, vigorously though not very effectively replied to by the rebel artillery for a short space of time. At dark, however, these pieces were withdrawn about 500 yards to the rear, owing to the fact that no infantry support came up with the pieces.

In the morning of the 20th, the batteries . . . were all drawn forward to the ground occupied the evening before by the howitzers, and gradually entrenched by earth thrown up in front. Battery D, First Illinois Light Artillery, was, on the 20th, placed in battery within intrenchments near the white [Shirley] house, and performed during the siege valuable and important services at different places and stations in that vicinity.

The siege having been successfully terminated, I cannot but refer with pleasure and gratification to the willingness, endurance, and zeal with which all my subordinates submitted to all the hardships incident thereunto. Throughout, from the captains down to the bugler, the same hearty co-operation met me. . . .

The expenditure of ammunition at the siege has been as follows:

Battery D, First Illinois Light Artillery	5,200	rounds
Battery L, Second Illinois Light Artillery	2,368	"
Battery, Third Ohio	3,521	"
Battery, Eighth Michigan	2,409	"
Total expended	13,498[10]	

Get back in your car and drive o.6 mile. Drive past the Shirley House and park in front of the Third Louisiana Redan. Walk up onto the redan.

From this Confederate defensive position you can look east and see the Shirley House, the only wartime structure still existing in the park. The Shirley House was the start point for Union operations against the Third Louisiana Redan.

STOP 7, THIRD LOUISIANA REDAN

This redan was one of the major defensive positions built to protect Vicksburg from attacks along the Jackson-Vicksburg Road. An attack by John E. Smith's brigade of McPherson's corps down the Jackson Road on May 22 was halted by the intense fire from the Third Louisiana Redan.

Grant determined not to risk any more Union lives in direct assaults against this strong Confederate position. He directed his soldiers to dig mines under the redan, seeking to destroy the integrity of the defensive position by exploding gunpowder charges packed into the mines. The Union trench leading to the redan started at the Shirley House (known as "the white house" to the Union troops) and ended just outside the walls of the redan. From that point a tunnel was dug forty feet under the position. It was filled with 2,200 pounds of black powder. When preparations were completed, Union artillery and infantry were moved into position to assault through the gap that the explosion was expected to make.

At 3 P.M. on June 25 the mine exploded and the Forty-fifth Illinois Infantry led the charge into the redan, supported by nearly 150 cannon. The Confederates had detected the mining operation, however, and had withdrawn to a second position hurriedly prepared behind the original redan on higher defensible terrain. Despite all Federal efforts to hold the redan, the Union troops were unable to dominate the position because they were hampered by the deep crater (forty feet wide and twelve feet deep). They withdrew the next day. A new shaft was dug and its mine detonated on July 1. This mine virtually destroyed the redan, but no infantry assault followed—the losses had been too heavy the first time.

Report of Maj. Gen. John H. Forney, CSA, Commanding Division

The enemy made strenuous efforts to possess himself of the main work on the Jackson road, defended by the Third Louisiana Regiment, the occupation of which by him would necessitate the abandonment of our trenches for a considerable distance to the right and left, as it would give him an enfilade fire either way. Opposite this point he planted a number of heavy siege guns, with which he made a serious breach in the parapet of the redan. The fire of these guns was, however, in a great measure diverted by the fire of a 10-inch mortar, which we had planted close in the rear of our lines. We were only permitted to retain this mortar a few days, when it was again removed to the right and its place supplied by a 9-inch Dahlgren gun, which the enemy disabled the second day after it opened fire.

On June 25, about 5 P.M., the enemy sprung his first mine under the parapet of this work. The explosion effected a breach through which the enemy immediately attempted to charge, but was promptly and gallantly repulsed. The Sixth Missouri Regiment, which had been held in reserve, was on the spot immediately after the explosion, and its commander . . . was instantly killed while attempting to lead a charge over the works. Six men of the Forty-third Mississippi Regiment, who were in a shaft countermining at the time of the explosion, were buried and lost. At dark the enemy had possessed himself of the ditch and slope of the parapet, and our forces retired to an interior line a few feet back. This point was now re-enforced by a part of Colonel [F. M.] *Cockrell's* brigade, of *Bowen's* division, and work was resumed by the enemy and by us, they mining and we countermining, until July 1,

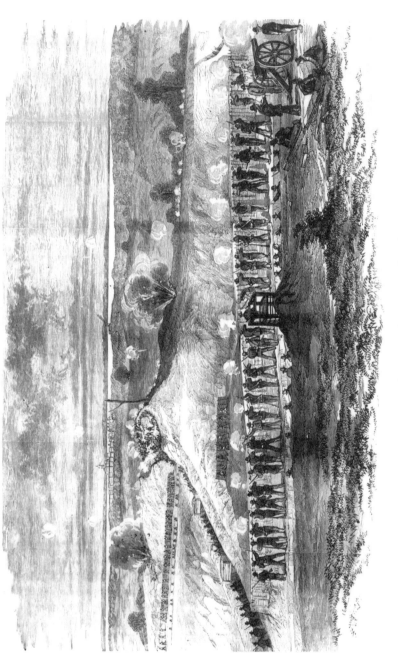

Lithograph of the fight in the crater after the explosion of the mine at the Third Louisiana Redan on June 25. Note the openness of the terrain as depicted by the artist. The Union besiegers could see into the city from their lines. (Frank Leslie's *Illustrated Famous Leaders and Battle Scenes of the Civil War*)

Lithograph depicting the Forty-fifth Illinois, Logan's Division, McPherson's Corps, storming the Third Louisiana Redan along Jackson Road after exploding a large mine on June 25. (Frank Leslie's *The American Soldier in the Civil War*)

at about 1 P.M., when the enemy sprung his second mine, which was much heavier than the first.

The result was the entire demolition of the redan, leaving only an immense chasm where it stood. The greater portion of the earth was thrown toward the enemy, the line of least resistance being in that direction. Our interior line was much injured. Nine men who were countermining were necessarily lost, and a large number of those manning the works were killed and wounded. The enemy, however, made no attempt to charge, seeming satisfied with having materially weakened the position. I understand that the amount of powder used by the enemy in this explosion was one ton.

While all this was taking place on the Jackson road, the enemy was by no means idle at other points. At the work on the Baldwin's Ferry road his sappers had nearly reached the ditch. At this place we sprung a counter-mine, which was unfortunately a little premature.

The artillery, though well served, was of but little advantage to us during the siege. The enemy concentrated a heavy fire, dismounting or disabling gun after gun. To this fire we could make but a feeble response. Ammunition was scarce, and orders forbade its use except against advancing columns of infantry or batteries being planted. The proportionate loss of officers and men of the artillery was unusually great. . . .

The siege . . . was a contest which tried more the endurance and resolution of the men and their company and regimental commanders than the skill of their generals. My men during the siege did . . . their whole duty to the entire satisfaction of their general. . . . The patience with which my troops submitted to the many privations and hardships to which they were subjected, and the unabated courage and cheerfulness which they sustained throughout, are worthy of all praise, and merited a better fortune.

The casualties in my division during the siege were as follows: *Hebert*'s brigade—killed, 203; wounded, 480; *Moore*'s brigade— killed, 72; wounded, 385. Total—killed, 275; wounded, 865.[11]

Report of Brig. Gen. Mortimer D. Leggett, USA, Commanding First Brigade, Third Division, Seventeenth Army Corps

Until the 25th of June, nothing occurred to call the brigade from its regular routine of duties—picketing, sharpshooting, and working the trenches. . . . I lost only an occasional man . . . during the whole time bivouacked within short musket range of the enemy's works.

As the trenches progressed, I advanced my sharpshooters, thus protecting as much as possible those at work in the trenches. After running the main trenches up to the enemy's works, I was ordered to withdraw 15 paces and open a sap to the left, running nearly parallel with the enemy's works. The saps and trenches were constructed under the direction of Captain Hickenlooper, of General McPherson's staff. While in the discharge of this duty, a mine was opened at the mouth of the main trench, penetrating the enemy's fort, known as Fort Hill [Third Louisiana Redan], and on the 25th of June I was ordered to hold my command in readiness to charge and take said Fort Hill as soon as the mine should be sprung, to hold the breach made by the explosion at all hazards, and, if practicable, to charge over and drive the enemy from his works.

At 3:30 . . . my command was in readiness, the Forty-fifth Illinois being in the front, supported by the other regiments of the brigade, and Lieut. H. C. Foster, of the Twenty-third Indiana, with 100 men being placed in the left-hand sap . . . with orders to charge with the Forty-fifth Illinois, provided they attempted to cross the enemy's works. At 4:30 o'clock the mine was sprung, and before the dirt and smoke was cleared away the Forty-fifth Illinois had filled the gap made by the explosion and were pouring deadly volleys into the enemy. As soon as possible, loop-hole timber was placed upon the works for the sharpshooters, but the enemy opened a piece of artillery at very close range on that point, and the splintering timbers killed and wounded more men than did balls, and I ordered the timbers to be removed. Hand-grenades were then freely used by the enemy, which made sad havoc amongst my men, for, being in the crater of the exploded mine, the sides of which were covered by the men, scarcely a grenade was thrown without doing damage, and in most instances horribly mangling those they happened to strike.

The Forty-fifth Illinois, after holding the position and fighting desperately until their guns were too hot for further use, were relieved by the Twentieth Illinois. During this time hand-grenades were freely used on both sides, Private William Lazarus, of Company I, First U.S. Infantry, being detailed to throw them, who, after throwing about twenty, was mortally wounded, after which a detail of 3 men from the same command were detailed for that duty.

The Twentieth Illinois was relieved by the Thirty-first Illinois, and they in turn by the Fifty-sixth Illinois, of the Third Brigade, but their ammunition being bad they were unable to hold the position and were relieved by the Twenty-third Indiana. The Seventeenth Iowa, of the Third Brigade, then relieving the Twenty-third Indiana, and the Thirty-first Illinois relieving them, held the position until daylight, when the Forty-fifth Illinois relieved them and held the position until 10 A.M. of the 28th. . . . [At] 5 P.M. of the same day . . . I received orders to withdraw to the left-hand gap, where I maintained the position until the surrender, . . . when, by order of Major-General Logan, my brigade . . . was honored with the privilege of being the first to enter the garrison, and the flag of the Forty-fifth [Illinois] the first to float over the conquered city.

The troops under my command, though for forty-eight days and nights under a harassing fire of musketry and artillery, and constantly subject to duty the most exhausting and fatiguing, bore their part with a courage and patience and persistent energy never excelled. . . .

It is proper . . . that I should especially name Lieut. J. W. Miller, of the Forty-fifth Illinois, who, as one of my staff, was assigned to the immediate command of the pickets and sharpshooters, and in the discharge of this responsible duty was, during the whole siege, in the most exposed position, almost without sleep or rest, exhibiting a personal courage and physical endurance seldom asked for or found in any officer.[12]

Drive back from the Third Louisiana Redan and turn left at Shirley House. Drive 1.8 miles to the parking area at the site of the attack on Stockade Redan. (Note: At 0.6 mile you will cross over a 1960s road constructed to allow local traffic to bypass the park. The road fronting the Shirley House is the old Jackson-Vicksburg Road.) Park and walk to the Union cannons.

STOP 8A, ATTACK ON THE STOCKADE REDAN

Stockade Redan is the imposing defensive position directly to your front. It was built to guard the avenue of approach along the Graveyard Road. On May 19, Sherman ordered Maj. Gen. Francis Blair's division to attack and seize the redan. Hoping to defeat a demoralized enemy quickly, Blair attacked with the brigades of T. Kilby Smith on the left (south and east) of Old Graveyard Road, Giles Smith on the

Photo of the Stockade Redan, taken in 1899. (U.S. Army Military History Institute)

right (north and west) of the road, and Hugh Ewing on Giles Smith's right (west). Before reaching the redan, all three brigades had to pass through the low ground that you can see to your front. The ground was covered with felled tree branches, placed there to break up the linear attack lines of the Union units.

Kilby Smith's troops, especially the Eighty-third Indiana, reached within a few yards of the eastern face of the redan before being pinned down by intense fire. Giles Smith's attack took heavy losses crossing the ravine under a hail of Confederate fire. The only regular army unit in Blair's division, the First Battalion, Thirteenth U.S. Infantry, was on the left of Giles Smith's force. Ordered to charge the position, the Thirteenth U.S. moved through the maelstrom, losing heavily but gaining a foothold on the face of the redan. Seventeen different soldiers were killed or wounded carrying the regimental colors as the regulars tried to force their way into the redan—but to no avail. The battalion lost 43 percent of its strength in this attack. Its commander, Capt. Edward C. Washington, was killed, and its flag had fifty-six bullet holes shot through it. As a result of this valorous performance,

Sherman authorized the regiment to insert the words "First at Vicksburg" on its regimental colors, a tradition that lives on to this day. Hugh Ewing's brigade, on the right of the division, appeared to be on the verge of success when they, too, were caught in a murderous crossfire and forced to halt and seek cover. At dark, Blair pulled the remnants of his division back to the vicinity where you are now standing, having suffered more than 600 casualties in a few hours (85 percent of the total casualties suffered by Sherman's corps).

On May 22 Sherman again attacked the Stockade Redan. This time, instead of trying to cross the difficult ravine, as had occurred on May 19, he ordered the attack to move down the Graveyard Road, preceded by 150 volunteers carrying logs and timbers to fill in the ditch in front of the redan to make entry by the attackers easier. The volunteers, dubbed "forlorn hope," emerged in front of the redan about 150 yards away as the road curved through a cut from behind the hill that you can see.* The Confederates fired volleys into their column, forcing them to break ranks and seek cover. This choked off the road, and the attack lost all momentum. Less than 1,000 of Sherman's 15,000 men had been committed to the attack, since there was no good avenue to push the remainder into the battle.

Later, after Grant responded to McClernand's plea for supporting attacks by Sherman and McPherson, Sherman sent Mower's brigade of Tuttle's division again down Graveyard Road, with the Eleventh Missouri attacking four abreast in the lead. When that regiment reached the cut that had been the undoing of the earlier attacks, the Confederate defenders again poured intense fire into their ranks. The attack bogged down, and Sherman did not renew it.

Report of Maj. Gen. Francis P. Blair Jr., USA, Commanding Second Division, Fifth Corps

About midnight of . . . [May] 18th, the Third Brigade of my division, commanded by Brig. Gen. Hugh Ewing, joined me before the works of Vicksburg, having marched from Grand Gulf (by Raymond) to this place, a distance of 85 miles, in three days. Gen-

---

*A "forlorn hope" refers to those who volunteer for particularly hazardous duties. Henry Lee Scott, *Military Dictionary: Comprising Technical Definitions; Information on Raising and Keeping Troops; Actual Service, Including Makeshift and Improvised Matériel; and Law, Government, Regulations, and Administration Relating to Land Forces* (New York: D. Van Nostrand, 1861), p. 310.

Maj. Gen. Francis P. Blair Jr., USA, Commander, Second
Division, Fifteenth Army Corps (Sherman). (U.S. Army
Military History Institute)

eral Ewing's brigade was assigned position on the right of my division, his right resting on the left of General Steele's division (First
Division, Fifteenth Army Corps). His left connected closely with
the right of my First Brigade, commanded by Col. Giles A. Smith,
who held the center of my line and occupied the ground in front
of the stockade near the bastion, which commands the Graveyard
road. The Second Brigade, Col. Thomas Kilby Smith commanding, held the left of my line, . . . its line of battle extending across
the Graveyard road.

During the morning of the 19th, the entire line of skirmishers of my division was pushed forward, with a view of obtaining a
closer position and of reconnoitering the ground.

At 2 P.M. the signal was given for an assault, and my whole division dashed forward, and, wherever the nature of the ground was not insuperable, reached the enemy's intrenchments, and in several instances planted our flags upon his works. Two regiments of General Ewing's brigade . . . succeeded in approaching very near the enemy's works. The Thirteenth U.S. Infantry . . . and One hundred and sixteenth Illinois Volunteer Infantry . . . of the First Brigade, Col. Giles A. Smith commanding, pushed forward to the bastion. The One hundred and twenty-seventh Illinois Volunteer Infantry . . . and Eighty-third Indiana Volunteer Infantry . . . of the Second Brigade . . . also succeeded in reaching the same ground, but the heavy fire of the enemy, who, not being pressed in any other quarter, were strongly re-enforced in our front, made it utterly impossible for them to make a lodgment in the works. They held their positions, however, with the utmost tenacity until night, when they withdrew.

The 20th and 21st were employed in skirmishing with the enemy, reconnoitering the ground, and improving our position.

On the 22d, I received an order to renew the assault at 10 o'clock in the morning. I massed my division in the ravine to the left of the Graveyard road, where it debouches upon that road as it passes across the valley immediately in front of the bastion. A volunteer storming party, consisting of 2 officers and 50 men from each brigade of the division, was to lead the assault. General Ewing's brigade and the brigades of Cols. Giles A. Smith and Thomas Kilby Smith were to follow in the order in which they are named, and to charge across the road by the flank.

At the signal the volunteer storming party . . . dashed forward in gallant style and planted the flag of the Union . . . upon the bastion of the enemy. The leading regiment of General Ewing's brigade, the Thirtieth Ohio Volunteers, went forward with equal impetuosity and gallantry, but the next regiment . . . faltered and gave way under the fire of the enemy, which was far from being severe on this regiment, and was, in fact, directed upon the head of the column. The men lay down in the road and behind every inequality of ground which afforded them shelter, and every effort . . . to rally them and urge them forward proved of no avail. . . . Lieut. A. C. Fisk, aide-de-camp to General Hugh Ewing, was conspicuous in his efforts to encourage and animate them to go forward to the assistance of their gallant comrades, who could be seen already upon the very intrenchments of the enemy, and

Sergt. Maj. Louis Sebastian, Thirty-seventh Ohio Volunteer Infantry, went along the whole line of the regiment, exposing himself to the heaviest fire of the enemy, exhorting and remonstrating with the men and urging them forward; but it was all in vain. They refused to move, and remained in the road, blocking the way to the other regiments behind, and I was finally compelled to order the Forty-seventh Ohio and Fourth West Virginia forward by another route, to the left of the road.

These regiments advanced with commendable spirit and alacrity, and reached a position to which most of the Thirtieth Ohio, so long unsupported, had been compelled to recoil and shelter themselves, and which was less than 150 yards from the bastion. I then ordered the brigade of Col. Giles A. Smith forward by the same route, to the left of the road, as that taken by the last two regiments of General Ewing, and as soon as this brigade went forward it was followed up by the brigade of Col. Thomas Kilby Smith; but this route, while it was better covered from the fire of the enemy, led through ravines made almost impassable with *abatis* of fallen timber, and did not admit of anything like a charge. I therefore directed Col. Giles A. Smith to go forward as rapidly as the nature of the ground would admit, and to assault whenever he found it practicable to do so, and directed Col. Thomas Kilby Smith to follow close up and support any movement Col. Giles A. Smith should make. Col. Giles A. Smith pushed forward, following the ravine to the left of the position of General Ewing, and reached a ridge about 100 yards from the enemy's intrenchments.

At this point he found General Ransom, commanding a brigade of the division of General McPherson's corps, who had approached by a ravine from the left of my position, and who, from the nature of the ground, was able to advance his brigade under cover still nearer to the enemy's works than that of Colonel Smith. General Ransom and Colonel Smith communicated with each other, and determined to make a simultaneous assault. It was late in the afternoon before these brigades were able to reach the positions which I have referred to, so difficult and toilsome was the nature of the ground over which they moved, rendered still more so by the *abatis* and artificial entanglement thrown across it by the enemy. Both brigades went forward with a cheer when the signal was given to advance, and the sharpshooters from Ewing's brigade and our artillery opened upon the enemy at the same time with considerable effect; but, after reaching the face of the works of the enemy, they encountered a most fatal and deadly enfilading fire from the enemy's guns on the left, which came crashing through the ranks, while in front they were met by an obstinate resistance from an entrenched foe, and it was found impossible to advance. Both brigades, however, maintained pertinaciously the ground they had won, and Col. Giles A. Smith's brigade still retains it, having fortified the position, and, under orders since given by you, the position has been materially strengthened and advanced. . . .

The active operations of the day were closed by an impetuous assault of the brigade of General Mower, of General Tuttle's division, in your army corps, which rushed forward by the flank on the same road which had been attempted in the morning by the brigade of General H. Ewing. The attack was made with the greatest bravery and impetuosity, and was covered by a tremendous fire from our batteries, and by the sharpshooters of Ewing's and Giles A. Smith's brigades, and its failure only served to prove that it is impossible to carry this position by storm.

I append a recapitulation of the casualties in my command. . . . Killed, 10 officers, 163 enlisted men; Wounded, 65 officers, 643 enlisted men, Missing, 9. Aggregate 890.[13]

You have three options for seeing the remainder of the action at this Stop.

Option 1: You can complete the readings for the Confederate defense of the Stockade Redan (approximately 100 yards away, Stop 8B) where you are now, at Stop 8A.

Option 2: To get the Confederate perspective, you can walk along the Old Graveyard Road to the Stockade Redan, where the Stop 8B readings describe the events.

Option 3: Or you may return to your car and read the Confederate actions at the point where the one-way road takes you to the Stockade Redan. (This guide will tell you when you have returned to that point.)

STOP 8B, DEFENSE OF THE STOCKADE REDAN

The Confederate defenders in the area of the Stockade Redan were not the demoralized and defeated troops that Grant had anticipated. Units of *Hébert*'s brigade of Maj. Gen. John H. *Forney*'s division occupied the south and east side of the defenses there. These troops were fresh and full of fight, having been preparing the Vicksburg defenses while the battles at Champion Hill and Big Black were being fought. The main part of the redan was defended by troops from *Cockrell's* brigade of *Bowen's* division. Although these troops had been at Champion Hill and Big Black and had taken heavy casualties in that fighting, the strong defensive works of the redan added more strength to the already good fighting mettle of the troops in what most considered the best division in *Pemberton's* army—Brig. Gen. John S. *Bowen's* division.

As you look out from the defenses, remember that the trees had been cut down and used as obstacles. Looking at the ground, you can see the natural strength of the position on this difficult terrain, coupled with the efforts of placing abatis (cut trees and branches) to break up Union attack formations. The defenders had sufficient ammunition, spare rifles, other supplies, and good artillery support. *Hébert's* brigade took 87 casualties in the May 19th attack; *Cockrell's* brigade, 70. In the May 22 attack, *Hébert* took 60 casualties; *Cockrell*, 123. The defenders obviously had the better of the two infantry assaults. Siege operations were conducted against the Stockade Redan, like the other parts of the Confederate lines, until the surrender.

Report of Col. Francis M. Cockrell, CSA, Commanding First Brigade, Bowen's Division

On May 18, 1863, began the siege of Vicksburg. On this evening I received an order from General *Bowen* to move out on the Graveyard road to support Major-General *Smith's* division. Reporting to General *Smith*, in obedience to his order I occupied a line on the extreme left, in advance of the main line, afterward occupied during the siege, and was fired upon by the enemy's skirmishers before gaining my position. Skirmishing continued till darkness closed in. This evening I had 1 man killed and 8 men wounded. During the night of the 18th instant, I withdrew in rear of our main line, and remained in reserve, in rear of the right of Brigadier-General *Baldwin's* brigade.

About 2 P.M. (May 19), the enemy massed a large force in front of Brigadier-General *Shoup's* brigade and the left of Brigadier-General *Hébert's*, and the right of Brigadier-General *Baldwin's*, and made a most furious and determined assault. Seeing this concentration of the enemy's forces, I immediately moved the Fifth Missouri Infantry . . . to the support of General *Hébert's* left, and the First Missouri Infantry . . . to the support of line [*sic*] at the stockade between General *Hébert's* left and *Shoup's* right, and the Second Missouri Infantry . . . to the support of the Twenty-seventh Louisiana Regiment on *Shoup's* right, and the Sixth Missouri Infantry . . . to the support of Brigadier-General *Vaughn's* brigade, on the extreme left (then threatened), and held the Third Missouri Infantry . . . in readiness to re-enforce any point. The enemy in large masses, without any regular lines, pressed forward very close to our works, but were soon severely repulsed and driven back in disorder; and every subsequent effort was likewise repulsed.

This brigade, with General *Shoup's* brave Louisianians, had the honor of receiving the first assault of the enemy and repulsing them. . . . The brigade remained near this line up to the 22d. . . . On this day, about 2 P.M., the enemy, preparatory to a charge, moved his whole force as near our lines as could be done, and then made a most desperate and protracted effort to carry our lines by assault. This assault was preceded by a most furious fire from the enemy's numerous batteries, of shell, grape, and canister. The air was literally burdened with hissing missiles of death.

Nobly did the officers and soldiers of this brigade greet every assault . . . with defiant shouts and a deliberately aimed fire, and hurled them back in disorder. The enemy gained the ditch around the redan to the right of the stockade and occupied it for some time. Colonel *Gause*, of the Third Missouri Infantry, procured some fuse-shell, and, using them as hand-grenades, threw them into the ditch, where they exploded, killing and wounding some 22 of the enemy.

This day the brigade lost 28 killed and 95 wounded, the Third Missouri suffering fearfully, losing 12 killed and 52 wounded, having been exposed during the assault to an enfilading and rear fire in the redan, against which there was then no protection or defense.

From this day until June 25, this brigade was held in reserve and ordered from point to point of our whole line, accordingly as different points of the line were threatened or became endangered by the near approach of the enemy.[14]

Report of Brig. Gen. Louis Hébert, CSA, Commanding Brigade, Forney's Division [covering the period May 17–22, 1863]

On May 17 last, I was stationed at Snyder's Mill, on the Yazoo River, in command of the Confederate forces at that point. This position I had occupied since January 2.

On May 17, at 11 A.M., I received orders to prepare to evacuate the place and to send into Vicksburg the commissary stores, and to have driven in all the cattle, hogs, and sheep that could be gathered in the neighboring country. Having but a very small number of wagons and but few mounted men, I . . . commenced carrying out my instructions as far as practicable. At 2:45 P.M. I received orders to send to Vicksburg all ordnance stores and to prepare to spike or destroy the heavy guns. All remaining wagons were loaded with ordnance stores, and Col. Isaac W. *Patton* put to work to prepare the guns for spiking or destruction. Colonel *Patton* was the commander of my heavy artillery. At 5:30 P.M. I received the orders to march my command to Vicksburg, leaving two companies at Snyder's Mill . . . to keep up a show of occupation, and to spike or destroy the guns and . . . remaining stores when the enemy would be discovered approaching the position. At the same time I was ordered to send all our transports and store-boats then at Haynes' Bluff to the Upper Yazoo, above Fort Pemberton. All the boats left in the evening and night, carrying off such stores as were on board at the time. . . .

Having made all arrangements possible under existing circumstances with reference to the post of Snyder's Mill, I moved with my command at 7:30 P.M. by the Valley road to Vicksburg, where I reported myself at 2:30 o'clock on the morning of May 18. I was immediately ordered to the trenches, with instructions to occupy the line commencing with the works on the immediate right of the Jackson road, and extending to the left, so as to occupy the main redan on the Graveyard road. These dispositions were all made by 8 o'clock in the morning. I found in the main redan, on the left of the Jackson road, one 20-pounder Parrott gun, of *Waddell's* artillery, under Lieutenant [T. Jeff.] *Bates.* Early in the day, Col. Isaac W. *Patton* received orders directly from the lieutenant-general commanding to return to Snyder's Mill for the purpose of disposing of the guns and stores left there. These orders relieved Lieutenant-Colonel *Plattsmier* of the charge I had assigned him, and I have therefore no report to make of what was really finally abandoned at Snyder's Mill.

On May 18, soon after my command had been placed in the trenches, the enemy made his appearance in front of my line, pressing forward on the Graveyard road, as if intending an assault. Taking one regiment and one battalion from my right, I sent them to re-enforce my left. . . . At about 3:45 P.M. . . . the enemy opened artillery on the Graveyard road, but no attempt at a charge was made, as had been anticipated. His skirmishers pressed forward, however, and by night our skirmishers (by direction of the lieutenant-general commanding) were drawn into our lines, pickets alone being put out for the night.

By the morning of the 19th, the enemy had planted several batteries along my front, on the Jackson and Graveyard roads, and his strong line of sharpshooters was within easy musket range of our works. He had also commenced his line of works, and, so far as my front was concerned, he may be said to have completed his investment. The peremptory orders to draw in our skirmishers, not to use our artillery except against advancing columns of infantry, or against artillery being placed in battery (all to save ammunition), allowed the enemy to at once make his investment a close one, and to commence his trenches, saps, etc., in close proximity to our works. From that time our entire line became subject to a murderous fire, and nearly every cannon on my line was in time either dismounted or otherwise injured.

At about 10 A.M. on May 19, an attack was made on the Graveyard road, extending along the front of Major-General *Smith's* right and the front of my two regiments and battalion on my left. Seeing the advancing columns, I directed Lieutenant *Bates'* 20-pounder Parrott and a 3-inch rifle piece of the Appeal Battery in the work on the Jackson road to open upon them. This was done with very good effect. The enemy, however, several times pressed on to the assault, but were as often repulsed, notwithstanding the effort of the officers. Before long he fell back discomfited, having suffered severely.

On the 21st and 22d, he rapidly pushed on his works in entrenching, sapping, constructing batteries, etc., under cover of heavy sharpshooting and cannonading.[15]

Report of Brig. Gen. Louis Hébert, CSA, May 21, 1863

Soon after daylight, the enemy opened their batteries and line of sharpshooters, and kept up their fire with rapidity and serious effect during the day, to dark; even since an occasional shot is fired from one of their batteries. Besides undergoing the fire on my brigade front, my extreme right has suffered from the sharpshooters on the left of Brigadier-General *Moore,* and very severely from a battery in [*Moore's*] front. . . . This battery has been very effective against my headquarters.

The enemy's sharpshooters are in close proximity, and their batteries have injured much of our parapets. The two 20-pounder Parrotts remaining on my line have been dismounted, and are unserviceable. One 12-pounder howitzer is disabled, though it may yet fire a few shots. Damages will be repaired as far as practicable tonight.

Casualties.—Killed: Captain *Gomez,* Twenty-third Louisiana Infantry; Captains *Chrisman* and *Tatom,* Thirty-sixth Mississippi, and 3 enlisted men. Wounded: Capt. C. A. *Brusle,* aide-de-camp, and 12 enlisted men.[16]

Report of Brig. Gen. Louis Hébert, CSA, June 19, 1863

I have the honor to report that, for two days before, the enemy had been advancing their works on the Jackson road, under the cover of cotton bales placed on a car, which car was moved along at will. Yesterday I directed Lieutenant-Colonel *Russell,* of the Third Louisiana Regiment, to make an attempt to destroy this cotton, and, if necessary, I would order some volunteers to dash forward and fire the cotton.

The lieutenant-colonel, however, invented a safer and a much simpler course. He procured spirits of turpentine and tow [coarse fibers of hemp and flax], and, wrapping his musket-balls with the same, fired them, with light charges, into the cotton bales. His attempt succeeded admirably. The cotton was soon burning, and our sharpshooters, having been well instructed, prevented the fire from being extinguished or the cotton rolled away. Lieutenant-Colonel *Russell* reports that the car and over twenty bales of cotton on it were destroyed. He says that the car was composed of the platform of a freight railroad car, and the wheels apparently iron. The car was at a distance of some 75 yards from our works when destroyed, at 10 P.M. yesterday. Lieutenant Colonel *Russell* deserves commendation for his success.[17]

Report of Brig. Gen. Louis Hébert, CSA, June 26, 1863

Kept out at the trenches during the entire night, and afflicted today with a fever, I have failed to this time to hand in my usual daily report.

The night of the 24th [of June] passed off with little firing on my line, and no change was visible, except the nearer approach of saps and the addition of newly thrown-up earth at several points.

During the 25th, the enemy continued his labors, but no movements of troops were seen. The skirmishing was as usual. At 5 P.M. rapid musketry firing on our right seemed to indicate an attack on the Baldwin's Ferry road and farther to the right. Up to about 5:30 P.M. there was no indication of a projected attack on the Jackson road.

At that hour the enemy sprang his mine under the main redan, on the left of the road, and advanced to the assault. His attempt was a feeble one, and was easily defeated; but few of his men could be brought to mount the breach, and, with the exception of one officer (supposed to be a field officer, leading the forlorn hope), evinced [no] determination. He mounted the parapet, waved, and called his men forward, but was instantly shot down. After his repulse, the enemy occupied the outer slope of our works, and from there commenced, accompanied by musketry fire, a terrific shower of hand-grenades upon our men. We replied with grenades and sharpshooters, and this species of combat is still going on this morning.

Everything indicates that during the night the enemy did a great deal of work, and is likely to have started new mines. At any rate, he has given shelter in our outer ditch to his men by throwing up sand-bags, etc. He is now in position to appear in our works at any instant. As soon as any indication of an attack became apparent, Col. Eugene *Erwin* moved with his reserve regiment (the Sixth Missouri Infantry) to the line. At the assault, he gallantly attempted to lead some of his men to follow him over the parapet. Whilst on the top he was instantly killed. . . .

After the first charge, the enemy attempted to advance by covering himself with logs and pieces of timber. He was made to fall back several times by the rapid and well-directed fire of a piece of our artillery. . . . He has, however, in the night succeeded in covering his men. . . .

Three regimental flags alone were seen at any time, and it is my belief that the enemy never contemplated but an assault to secure the redan, and there hold. This he undoubtedly thought of doing during the confusion that would exist, as he conceived, in our troops. He was, however, quite mistaken, as the explosion created no dismay or panic among our brave officers and soldiers, and every one was ready for the foe before he appeared.

At the time of the explosion, 6 enlisted men of the Forty-third Mississippi Regiment were at work in the shaft, which our engineers were digging in the redan to meet the enemy's line. These soldiers were necessarily lost. Not another man was injured by the explosion. This is attributable to the shaft in question, which served as a vent upward to the force of the blast, and thus confined the breaking up of the soil to a shorter distance in the direction of the perpendicular of the redan.

At 10 P.M. Col. James *McCown,* with his Fifth Missouri Regiment . . . reported as re-enforcement. He was ordered by me to take position in the ravine, where the Sixth Missouri has been camped, in the rear of the Third Louisiana.[18]

Report of Brig. Gen. Louis Hébert, CSA, July 1, 1863

I have the honor to report that about 1:30 P.M. the enemy sprang another and a larger mine under the main redan of the work on the left of the Jackson road, this time destroying the parapet of the redan. Our interior work is uninjured. The enemy attempted no immediate charge after the blast, but opened a brisk artillery fire. The change occasioned exposes a portion of our troops heretofore protected, and there is necessity of immediate work, both to strengthen our interior line and give more protection to exposed points. Lieutenant *Blessing,* assistant engineer on this portion of the line, was wounded a few hours since. I earnestly ask that some other officer be immediately sent to replace him.[19]

Brig. Gen. Louis Hébert, CSA, to Major-General Forney, CSA, July 2, 1863

In answer to your note of this date, giving copy of a note to you from the lieutenant-general commanding, of yesterday, inquiring "into the condition of the troops, and their ability to make the marches and undergo the fatigues necessary to accomplish a successful evacuation."

I respectfully state that, with the permission granted by your note, I have consulted with and obtained the opinions of my most trustworthy and reliable officers, confidentially placing before them the question of *cutting out.* I asked them if their men were physically able to "make the marches and undergo the fatigues necessary."

Without exception all concurred in one single and positive opinion—*that their men could not fight and march 10 miles in one day;* that even without being harassed by the enemy or having to fight, they could not expect their men to march 15 miles the first day; hundreds would break down or straggle off even before the first lines of the enemy were fairly passed. This inability on the part of the soldiers does not arise from want of spirit, or courage, or willingness to fight, but from real physical disability, occasioned by the men having been so long shut up and cramped up in pits, ditches, etc., in the trenches; many are also in ill-health, who still are able to remain in the works.

The unanimous opinion of my officers I fully concur in, and I unhesitatingly declare that it is my sincere conviction that, so far as my brigade is concerned, it cannot undergo the marches and fatigues of an evacuation. The spirit of my men to fight is unbroken, but their bodies are worn out. Left to their choice to "surrender" or "cut their way out," I have no doubt that a large majority would say "cut out." But the question to my mind for me to answer is not between "surrender" and "cutting out"; it is are my men able to "cut out." My answer is *No!* . . . Most of my brigade are Mississippians, who I am confident will leave the ranks, and, throwing away their arms, make their way home the moment we leave our works. So long as they are fighting for Vicksburg they are as true soldiers as the army has, but they will certainly leave us so soon as we leave Vicksburg. . . . I could not expect to keep together one-tenth of my men a distance of 10 miles.[20]

Return to your car and continue to drive 0.3 mile. Veer right and drive 0.8 mile to Grant's headquarters area. Park near the statue of Grant.

STOP 9, GENERAL GRANT IN COMMAND

Maj. Gen. Ulysses S. Grant moved his headquarters into a small wooden house that stood on this site as soon as he came from the Big Black battle site. The house was located where the Grant statue now stands. As Sherman's troops prepared for the attack on May 22, they requested that Grant move out of the house so that the wood planks and timbers could be used for scaling ladders and ditch bridging materials. Grant used a tent for the remainder of the siege and moved his headquarters into a house in Vicksburg only after the fall of the

city. He spent much of his time in the forward Union positions, sometimes acting as an engineer when one was needed at a particular point
(he was educated and trained at West Point, which qualified him as
an engineer in the army). Grant's twelve-year-old son, Fred, was with
him in his headquarters here—as he had accompanied his father
throughout the Vicksburg campaign.

Narrative of Sylvanus Cadwallader, a Northern War Correspondent (continued)

Grant's headquarters were at a point directly in rear of where
the corps of Sherman and McPherson came together, and about
five miles from the center of the City. The situation was well chosen on a pleasant elevation, in the edge of a strip of timber which
afforded protection from the glaring, burning mid-day sun, made
drainage and sanitary conditions easily secured, and was also near
to a brook of running water kept from pollution. The escort
company was immediately adjoining, and the whole headquarters
encampment was constantly well policed. In the light of after experience it seemed altogether too near the Confederate fortifications for safety. But I do not remember that a single shot or shell
invaded its precincts. There were no "Whitworth" guns in Vicksburg [there was one] to carry destructive bolts from four to six
miles (as frequently occurred at Petersburg), nor were any very
long range guns brought to bear upon us.[21]

Narrative of Maj. Gen. Ulysses S. Grant, USA (continued)

After the unsuccessful assault of the 22d the work of the regular siege began. Sherman occupied the right starting from the river
above Vicksburg, McPherson the centre . . . and McClernand the
left, holding the road south to Warrenton. Lauman's division . . .
was placed on the extreme left of the line.

In the interval between the assaults of the 19th and 22d, roads
had been completed from the Yazoo River and Chickasaw Bayou,
around the rear of the army, to enable us to bring up supplies of
food and ammunition; ground had been selected and cleared on
which the troops were to be encamped, and tents and cooking
utensils were brought up. The troops had been without these from
the time of the Mississippi up to this time.

All was now ready for the pick and spade. Prentiss and Hurlbut were ordered to send forward every man that could be spared. Cavalry especially was wanted to watch the fords along the Big Black, and to observe *Johnston*. I knew that *Johnston* was receiving reinforcements from *Bragg*, who was confronting Rosecrans in Tennessee. Vicksburg was so important to the enemy that I believed he would make the most strenuous efforts to raise the siege, even at the risk of losing ground elsewhere.

My line was more than fifteen miles long, extending from Haines' Bluff to Vicksburg, thence to Warrenton. The line of the enemy was about seven. In addition to this, having an enemy at Canton and Jackson, in our rear, who was being constantly reinforced, we required a second line of defense facing the other way. I had not troops enough under my command to man these. General Halleck appreciated the situation and, without being asked, forwarded reinforcements with all possible dispatch. . . .

The work to be done, to make our position as strong against the enemy as his was against us, was very great. The problem was also complicated by our wanting our line as near that of the enemy as possible. We had but four engineer officers with us. Captain Prime, of the Engineer Corps, was the chief, and the work at the beginning was mainly directed by him. His health soon gave out, when he was succeeded by Captain Comstock, also of the Engineer Corps. To provide assistants on such a long line I directed that all officers who had graduated at West Point, where they had necessarily to study military engineering, should in addition to their other duties assist in the work. . . .

We had no siege guns except six thirty-two pounders, and there were none at the West to draw from. Admiral Porter, however, supplied us with a battery of navy-guns of large calibre, and with these, and the field artillery used in the campaign, the siege began.

The first thing to do was to get the artillery in batteries where they would occupy commanding positions; then establish the camps, under cover from the fire of the enemy but as near up as possible; and then construct rifle-pits and covered ways, to connect the entire command by the shortest route. The enemy did not harass us much while we were constructing our batteries. Probably their artillery ammunition was short; and their infantry was kept down by our sharpshooters, who were always on the alert and ready to fire at a head whenever it showed itself above the rebel works.

In no place were our lines more than six hundred yards from the enemy. It was necessary, therefore, to cover our men by something more than the ordinary parapet. To give additional protection sand bags, bullet-proof, were placed along the tops of the parapets far enough apart to make loop-holes for musketry. On top of these, logs were put. By these means the men were enabled to walk about erect when off duty, without fear of annoyance from sharpshooters. . . .

There were no mortars with the besiegers, except what the navy had in front of the city; but wooden ones were made by taking logs of the toughest wood that could be found, boring them out for six or twelve pound shells, and binding them with strong iron bands. These answered as coehorns, and shells were successfully thrown from them into the trenches of the enemy.

The labor of building the batteries and entrenching was largely done by the pioneers, assisted by negroes who came within our lines and who were paid for their work; but details from the troops had often to be made. The work was pushed forward as rapidly as possible, and when an advanced position was secured and covered from the fire of the enemy the batteries were advanced. By the 30th of June there were two hundred and twenty guns in position, mostly light field-pieces, besides a battery of heavy guns belonging to, manned and commanded by the navy. We were now as strong for defense against the garrison of Vicksburg as they were against us; but I knew that *Johnston* was in our rear, and was receiving constant reinforcements from the east.[22]

Narrative of Bvt. Brig. Gen. Adam Badeau, USA, Military Secretary and Aide-de-Camp to General Sherman

Grant had now about forty thousand men for duty, and on the 23d [after the failed assault of May 22], orders were given for the axe and the shovel to support the bayonet. The hot season was at hand, the troops had already endured many hardships, they were almost altogether unprovided with siege material, so that the difficulties before the . . . army were not only formidable, but peculiar. The engineer organization was especially defective; there were no engineer troops in the entire command, and only four engineer officers, while twenty would have found ample opportunity for all their skill. Several pioneer companies of volunteers were . . . used for engineering purposes, and, although raw at first became effective before the close of the siege. There were no permanent depots of siege materials; spades and picks were kept at the steamboat landing, on the Yazoo, and in the camps near the trenches; gabions and fascines were made as they were needed, by the pioneer companies, or by details of troops from the line. Grant's artillery was simply that used during the campaign, with the addition of a battery of naval guns of larger calibre, loaned him by Admiral Porter. There was nothing like a siege train in all the West, no light mortars, and very few siege-howitzers nearer than Washington; and there was not time to send to northern arsenals for supplies. With such material and means the siege of Vicksburg was begun. . . .

One result of this scarcity of engineers was, that Grant gave more personal attention to the supervision of the siege than he would otherwise have done. His military education fitted him for the duty, and he rode daily around the lines, directing the scientific operations, infusing his spirit into all his subordinates, pressing them on with energy to the completion of their task, and, with unflagging persistency devising and employing every means to bring about the great end to which all labor, and skill, and acquirement was made to tend. . . . At one time every graduate of the Military Academy in Grant's army below the rank of general was on engineer duty. . . .

The aggregate length of the trenches was twelve miles. Eighty-nine batteries were constructed during the siege. . . . On the 30th of June there were in position two hundred and twenty guns, mostly light field-pieces . . . [and] one battery of heavy guns, on the right . . . manned and officered by the navy.

A line of works was . . . constructed from the Yazoo to the Big Black river, quite as strong as those which defended Vicksburg, so that the city was not only circumvallated, but counter-vallated as well. In case of an attack, *Johnston* would have been obliged to assault Grant's rear under the same disadvantages that Grant himself had encountered in attacking Vicksburg. . . .

The engineers were kept constantly and busily employed, mining and counter-mining on different portions of the line. Demonstrations were made by *Johnston,* and some of his dispatches were intercepted, from which it was discovered that he intended immediately to attempt the forcible relief of the garrison. The works on the Big Black, extending from that river to the Yazoo, a distance of eight miles, were strengthened, in anticipation of such a movement. The troops on the west side of the Mississippi also were on the alert, as there was danger that the rebel General, Richard *Taylor,* might move up from Louisiana against them.²³

Drive 0.7 mile back to the main park road. At the "Y" in the road you will see a sign for the USS *Cairo* Museum. From that sign, drive 0.8 mile to the parking area for Thayer's Approach (NPS Stop 6). Park and get out of your car.

STOP 10, SHERMAN'S CORPS IN THE SIEGE

Sherman's corps occupied the northern part of the Union siege lines, at long last occupying the Walnut Hills area that had been his objective in the failed Chickasaw Bayou campaign in December 1862. Other actions of Sherman's corps were covered at Stop 8 (Stockade Redan). This part of Sherman's line was manned by the brigade of Brig. Gen. John M. Thayer, Steele's division. Thayer's troops attacked up the long slope you see to your front on May 19 and 22. Both assaults were repulsed, with 50 casualties on May 19 and 155 casualties on May 22. After those failed attacks, Thayer's troops began digging a trench that started to the rear of where you now are standing. The approach began with a tunnel running through a hill over which today runs the park road. The trench was six feet deep, and the diggers were protected by a "roof," a *fascine* made of bundles of cane cut from nearby thickets. Parts of the original trench are visible on the face of the hill. Thayer's troops were in the process of digging a mine under the Confederate position to blow it up, similar to the actions at the Third Louisiana Redan (Stop 7), when Vicksburg surrendered.

Narrative of Maj. Gen. William T. Sherman, USA (continued)

On the 20th of May General Grant called the three corps commanders together. . . . We compared notes, and agreed that the assault of the day before had failed, by reason of the natural strength of the position, and because we were forced by the nature of the ground to limit our attacks to the strongest parts of the enemy's line, viz. where the three principal roads entered the city. It was not a council of war, but a mere consultation, resulting in orders from General Grant for us to make all possible preparations for a renewed assault on the 22d. . . . I reconnoitred my front thoroughly . . . and concluded to make my real attack at the right flank of the bastion, where the Graveyard road entered the enemy's intrenchments, and at another point in the curtain a hundred yards to its right (our left); also to make a strong demonstration . . . about a mile to our right, toward the river. All our field batteries were put in position, and were covered by good epaulements; the troops were brought forward, in easy support, concealed by the shape of the ground; and to the minute, viz., 10 A.M. of May 22d, the troops sprang to the assault. A small party . . . provided with plank to cross the ditch, advanced at a run, up to the very ditch; the lines of infantry sprang from cover, and advanced rapidly in line of battle. I took a position within two hundred yards of the real parapet, on the off slope of a spur of ground, where by advancing two or three steps I could see every thing. The rebel line, concealed by the parapet, showed no sign of unusual activity, but as our troops came in fair view, the enemy rose behind their parapet and poured a furious fire upon our lines; and, for about two hours, we had a severe and bloody battle, but at every point we were repulsed. . . . The two several assaults . . . had failed, by reason of the great strength of the position and the determined fighting of its garrison. I have since seen the position at Sevastopol, and without hesitation I declare that at Vicksburg to have been the more difficult of the two.

Thereafter our proceedings were all in the nature of a siege. General Grant drew more troops from Memphis, to prolong our general line to the left, so as completely to invest the place on its land-side, while the navy held the river both above and below. . . . By May 31st Vicksburg was completely beleaguered. Good roads were constructed from our camps to the several landing-places on the Yazoo River, to which points our boats brought us ample supplies, so that we were in a splendid condition for a siege. . . . If we could prevent sallies, or relief from the outside, the fate of the garrison of Vicksburg was merely a question of time. . . .

The campaign . . . in its conception and execution, belonged exclusively to General Grant, not only in the great whole, but in the thousands of details. I still retain many of his letters and notes, all in his own handwriting, prescribing the routes of march for divisions and detachments, specifying even the amount of food and tools to be carried along. . . . No commanding general of an army ever gave more of his personal attention to details, or wrote so many of his own orders, reports, and letters, as General Grant.[24]

Return to your car. Drive 1.1 miles to the Navy Monument at Battery Selfridge (NPS Stop 7). Park.

Walk down to the Union Second Missouri Light Artillery Battery overlooking the museum site of the USS *Cairo*. From here, you have a good view of the Mississippi River. What you can see today is part of the Yazoo River Diversion Canal, but at the time of the siege it was the main channel of the Mississippi River.

STOP 11A, NAVAL OPERATIONS DURING THE SIEGE

The Union navy played a significant role in the siege of Vicksburg. What Grant's field army lacked in large guns necessary to support a siege was offset by the numerous heavy-caliber guns made available by Admiral Porter. He ordered heavy guns to be taken from his gunboats and hauled into positions from which they could pound the Confederate defenses. In addition, a battery of naval guns manned entirely by sailors was put into position at this site. The battery was under the command of Lt. Comdr. Thomas O. Selfridge Jr., an aggressive and distinguished officer who had been in command of the ironclad *Cairo* when it struck a mine and sank in the Yazoo River in December 1862 (see Stop 11B for more on the *Cairo*). The Union navy thus supported the siege from a land-based battery as well as from the gunboats under Admiral Porter's command on the Mississippi River. The continuous, heavy shelling by these guns played an important role in the defeat of the Confederate garrison.

See Part I, Chapter 14, "Narrative of Adm. David D. Porter, USN," for the naval report on this action.

Return to your car. Drive 0.3 mile to the USS *Cairo* Museum parking area.

STOP 11B, NAVAL OPERATIONS (CONTINUED): THE USS CAIRO

The USS *Cairo* was a steam-driven thirteen-gun ironclad typical of those the Union navy used on the major waterways. It was sunk by an electronically detonated mine in the Yazoo River on December 12, 1862, the first documented sinking of a vessel by an electrical mine (called torpedoes at the time). The museum here has the complete details on the sinking as well as a large number of artifacts showing how Union sailors lived during the Civil War. The *Cairo* was discovered on the bottom of the Yazoo River in 1956 and raised in 1964. This display offers a rare opportunity to see an actual iron-plated wood gunboat from this era.

Get back in your car. Drive 0.7 mile to Fort Hill (NPS Stop 9). Park in the lot and climb to the fort.

Fort Hill offers a tremendous view of the old Mississippi River channel, which is now part of the Yazoo River Diversion Canal. The new river channel can barely be seen to your west (left, as you face the river), nearly on the horizon. To appreciate the significance of this position, the reader must understand that all river traffic coming down the Mississippi River in 1862–63 had to pass under the guns of Fort Hill.

STOP 12, CONFEDERATE DEFENSES ON THE MISSISSIPPI RIVER

Fort Hill was the northern stronghold of the Confederate defenses around Vicksburg. Deemed too strong to attack by the Union on May 19 and 22, it was never assaulted by an infantry force. Confederate guns on the hill where you are now standing, together with another strong battery on the riverbank beneath the fort, dominated the Mississippi. Admiral Porter's running of the Vicksburg batteries (see Part I, Chapter 6) began as his ironclads passed this position. The Union gunboat USS *Cincinnati* tested the river battery on May 27, 1863, and was sunk by the combined Confederate fires. The boat was eventually raised after the capture of Vicksburg and returned to action with the Union navy.

Report of Col. Edward Higgins, CSA, Commanding River Batteries

The line of batteries extended along the river front, commencing at a point above Fort Hill, on the right of my line, to a redoubt which terminated the extreme right of the rear lines and met my left, a distance of 3 miles, and consisted of 8 10-inch Columbiads, 1 9-inch Dahlgren, 1 8-inch Columbiad, 1 7.44-inch Blakely gun, 1 7-inch Brooks, 1 6.4-inch Brooks, 3 smooth-bore 42-pounders, 2 smooth-bore 32 pounders, 8 banded and unbanded 32-pounder rifles, 1 18-pounder rifle, 1 20-pounder Parrott, 1 Whitworth, 1 10-inch mortar, 1 8-inch siege howitzer, making in all 31 pieces

View from Sherman's lines looking south at Fort Hill. (*Harper's Pictorial History of the Civil War*)

of heavy artillery, besides 13 pieces of light artillery, which were placed in position to prevent a landing of the enemy on the city front. These batteries were divided into three commands: . . . The upper batteries, from Fort Hill to the upper bayou, . . . the center batteries, or those immediately on the city front . . . [and] the lower batteries. . . .

On the evening of May 18, the investment commenced in rear of the city. At the same time five of the enemy's gunboats (four of which were iron-clads) came up from below, and took up a position in the river just out of range of our guns, while the river above and in front of the city was guarded by three gunboats, thus completing the investment.

On the evening of the 19th, the enemy's sharpshooters, having obtained possession of our abandoned line of outer works, opened a fire upon the upper four-gun water battery . . . thus rendering the battery temporarily untenable. Advantage was taken of the darkness of the night to construct traverses on the flank and in rear of the guns of this battery, and at daylight there was ample protection afforded to the men while at the guns. The enemy also commenced feeling our batteries, and opened a heavy fire from three of his iron-clads upon . . . the left of my line. Their fire was kept up for several hours, but without any serious damage.

At daylight on the . . . 20th, the enemy opened fire upon the city and batteries with seven mortars placed under the bank of the river on the Louisiana shore. Three iron-clads also shelled the lower batteries at long range.

On the 22d, at 9 A.M., four iron-clads and one wooden gunboat engaged the lower batteries, and after an engagement of one hour and a half were repulsed. Two of the iron-clads were seriously damaged. This engagement was creditable to the First Louisiana Artillery, who, with ten guns, mostly of small caliber, contested successfully against thirty-two heavy guns of the enemy. Our casualties were only 2 wounded during the fight; one 10-inch Columbiad and the 18-pounder rifled gun were temporarily disabled. The Blakely gun burst at the muzzle.

On the 23d, eleven of the light pieces on the river front were ordered to the rear, and were there fought by detachments from my command during the remainder of the siege.

From the 24th to the 26th, mortars kept up a steady fire upon the city and batteries. The 8-inch siege howitzer, one smooth-bore

Col. Edward *Higgins*, CSA, Commander, Confederate batteries protecting the river approaches to Vicksburg. (U.S. Army Military History Institute)

32 pounder, the 20-pounder Parrott, and the Whitworth gun were removed to the rear with their detachments.

Soon after daylight on . . . the 27th, the enemy's iron-clad gunboat *Cincinnati,* mounting fourteen guns, was observed approaching our upper batteries, while four iron-clads approached the lower batteries. An engagement took place, which resulted in the complete repulse of the enemy, and the sinking of the *Cincinnati* in front of our guns, after an action of thirty minutes. Great credit is due to Captains [J. P.] *Lynch* and [T. N.] *Johnston,* of the First Tennessee Heavy Artillery, for the handsome manner in which their guns were handled during the engagement.

The enemy's loss was severe, many of their men being killed in the port-holes by our sharpshooters. As the river fell, attempts were made by the enemy to recover the guns of the *Cincinnati* by working at night, to prevent which fire was opened on the sunken boat every night from one or two of my guns during the siege.

On the 28th, the 18-pounder rifled gun was sent to the rear lines. . . .

At daylight on the 31st, a tremendous fire was opened on the city from the enemy's guns in the rear, which did some damage to the works of the upper batteries. A battery of two small Parrott guns which opened upon my left at the same time was silenced by Captain *Capers'* 10-inch Columbiad.

June 1, a large fire broke out in the city, close upon the magazine of the Whig Office battery, which was at one time in great danger. The ammunition was taken out and placed in a more secure position. All the men of my command that could be spared from the guns were ordered out immediately to assist in arresting the progress of the conflagration.

From June 2 to 8, the enemy kept up an incessant fire from the mortar flats on the city and batteries, and each day the gunboats below shelled the woods and lower batteries. Two of the field pieces in my command were turned over to Maj. Gen. M. L. *Smith,* to be placed in the rear defense.

June 9 and 10, the fire from the mortars continued at irregular intervals. The enemy succeeded in placing sharpshooters in the woods on the Louisiana shore opposite the city, but they were driven off by a few well-directed shots from one of the light field pieces. . . .

On the morning of June 11, the enemy opened fire from a 10-inch gun placed in position at a point about a mile above the bend of the river, opposite the upper batteries, mortars and gun-boats still keeping up a brisk fire.

June 12, the 10-inch mortar was ordered to our works in the rear, and was placed in Major-General *Forney*'s line. . . .

June 13 to 15, a 30-pounder Parrott gun opened on the upper batteries from the same position as the 10-inch gun mentioned previously. Several of the mortars dropped down the river some 500 yards, and opened a heavy fire on the upper batteries. The two Parrott guns opened again on Captain *Capers,* but were silenced after five shots.

June 16, enemy opened fire on Captain *Lynch*'s battery (upper batteries) from a new work between Edwards' negro quarters and the river, doing considerable damage to the parapets, traverses, etc, but not injuring any of our men or guns.

June 17, 18, and 19, mortars still keeping up an irregular fire. The guns on the Louisiana shore fired very rapidly in the morning and evening. Our batteries replied slowly. The Parrott battery opened again on Captain *Capers,* but never fired after our guns opened. Since the surrender it has been ascertained that those two guns were totally disabled by Captain *Capers'* fire.

June 20, about 3 A.M., the enemy opened a heavy fire from both front and rear upon the city and batteries. Firing ceased at 7:30 A.M.

June 21, mortars ceased firing. The enemy mounted a 100-pounder Parrott gun on the Louisiana shore, under the bank of the river, at a point about 500 yards above the mortar-boats. It opened upon the city during the evening, doing a great deal of damage. Captain [R. C.] *Bond,* in the lower batteries, opened fire with his 10-inch Columbiad and 32-pounder rifled gun, when, after a few shots, the enemy's gun ceased firing.

June 22 to 27, firing from the guns on the Louisiana shore was kept up on the city and batteries with great vigor. Our guns replied slowly and with deliberation, but in consequence of the timber on the Louisiana shore affording ample means of masking batteries, it was very difficult to arrive at any satisfactory results.

On the 26th, the mortars resumed their fire upon the city, and on the same day numbers of the enemy's sharpshooters opened upon the city from the brushwood on the Louisiana shore.

June 28, firing still kept up. The 10-inch Brooks' gun in the upper batteries burst one of the bands and also at the breech. At 4 P.M. the 100-pounder Parrott gun and two mortars opened upon the lower batteries.

June 29 and 30, heavy firing all along the river front. The gunboats shelled the woods around Captain *Capers'* battery. The mortar was brought from the rear, and remounted in its old position in the redoubt on the extreme left of my line. It was very successfully used in driving off sharpshooters from that point. In addition to the other guns on the Louisiana shore, the enemy opened two small Parrott guns close to the bank in front of the city. Their fire was very slow and at irregular intervals.

July 1, the enemy opened fire on the mortar redoubt from his lines. Our works were somewhat damaged by it. The mortar replied, and almost immediately afterward the enemy's fire ceased.

July 2 and 3, heavy firing from all points. At 4 P.M. on the 3d, I opened fire all along my lines, and at 5 P.M. the last gun was fired by the river batteries in defense of Vicksburg.

July 4, the city capitulated.

During this long and tedious siege . . . the officers and men under my command discharged their duty faithfully and with alacrity. Owing to the weakness of our infantry force, they were called upon to perform other duties than those of fighting their guns. They formed a portion of the city guard, discharged the duties of firemen in case of fire, policed the river, etc., and the reliefs were almost nightly under arms as infantry in the trenches.[25]

Return to your car and drive 1.7 miles. You are driving along the line of Confederate fortifications facing the Union siege lines you have recently passed. You may park near the Stockade Redan (NPS Stop 10) to look at the action covered in Stop 8B if you have not done so previously. (Turn to the Stop 8B section for the readings that apply here.) Now drive 0.9 mile to Pemberton Avenue. Turn left and drive 0.1 mile. Turn left into the parking area for the old park museum and administration building.

Walk to the cannon marking the location between the Union and Confederate lines where Grant and Pemberton met on the afternoon of July 3, 1863, to discuss surrender terms.

STOP 13, THE CONFEDERATE SURRENDER

As the Union forces edged ever closer to the Confederate lines, Grant planned a grand assault for July 6. In the meantime, the Confederate forces under *Johnston* had moved toward Vicksburg to distract the Union army and allow *Pemberton* one last chance at breaking out on July 7. However, Grant's lines around the city were so impenetrable that word of *Johnston's* plans did not reach *Pemberton*. On July 2, *Pemberton* consulted with his division commanders to determine the feasibility of a breakout. His subordinates told him that the inactivity of being forced to remain in the siege lines, combined with the reduced rations and the overall stress of defending against siege operations, had sapped the strength from the Southern force. There would be no breakout.

Pemberton decided to try to negotiate favorable terms of surrender, hoping to have his troops paroled instead of becoming prisoners of war. He knew that Grant was concerned about capturing nearly 30,000 prisoners that he then would be responsible for guarding, feeding, and transporting to Northern prisoner-of-war camps. This knowledge came from intercepting signals between Grant and Admiral Porter. On the morning of July 3, *Pemberton* sent Brig. Gen. John *Bowen,* who had fought so well during this campaign—and formerly had been Grant's neighbor when they were both stationed in St. Louis in the prewar army—to open negotiations. Grant called for unconditional surrender. At approximately 3 P.M. Grant and *Pemberton* met near the position where you now stand. Early in the morning of July 4, the Confederate forces surrendered. The Vicksburg campaign was over.

Even before the surrender had occurred, Grant already had dispatched Sherman's corps to move against *Johnston*. The men, supplies, and boats that would have been required to care for Confederate prisoners were put into motion toward Tennessee and the Union armies there.

On July 4, one day after Lee's defeat at Gettysburg, Vicksburg surrendered. Approximately 30,000 Southern troops were paroled out of the city, some of whom again fought for the South, most of whom simply went home. More than 170 cannon and 60,000 rifles were captured. A surprising amount of artillery and rifle ammunition was captured. The Mississippi River was again open (the defenders of Port Hudson surrendered on July 9 upon hearing the news of Vicksburg's fall).

The Surrender

Grant to Halleck, July 4, 1863, 10:30 A.M.

The enemy surrendered this morning. The only terms allowed is their parole as prisoners of war. This I regarded as of great advantage to us at this juncture. It saves probably several days in the

Photo of the Confederate South Fort, taken in 1899. (U.S. Army Military History Institute)

captured town; leaves troops and transports ready for immediate service. General Sherman, with a large force, will face immediately on *Johnston* and drive him from the State. I will send troops to the relief of General Banks, and return the Ninth Corps to General Burnside.[26]

For detailed information on the surrender of Vicksburg, see Part I, Chapter 15, "The Surrender."

Return to your car. Turn right out of the parking area and drive 0.1 mile to Confederate Avenue. Turn left and drive back to the Visitor Center or out of the park.

This concludes the third phase of the campaign for Vicksburg. Those who desire to see the Confederate fort that anchored the southern end of the river defenses may follow these directions:

From the traffic light at the exit from the Visitor Center, turn left on Clay Street (U.S. 61); in 0.2 mile turn right onto I-20 West. Drive

to Exit 1A (3.7 miles). Follow State Welcome Center signs. Park in the Welcome Center lot.

Walk across the stairway over the road to Navy Circle, which was the most advanced Union position along the river. From Navy Circle, you can walk north through several commercial areas for approximately 250 yards. There you will find South Fort, the Confederate position overlooking the southern river approaches to Vicksburg.

OPTIONAL SITE: SOUTH FORT

Just as Fort Hill was the key to defending the northern approaches down the Mississippi, South Fort played the same role on the south side of Vicksburg. Confederate artillery here commanded the river from its dominating position. The batteries were part of the gauntlet that Porter's fleet ran on April 16, 1863. They traded fire with the Union fleet, and later Federal land batteries in the vicinity of Navy Circle, throughout the siege. There was no Union infantry assault against the position at South Fort, and it surrendered with the rest of the garrison on July 4, 1863.

NOTES

1. *O.R.*, XXIV, pt. 2, pp. 366–67.
2. *O.R.*, XXIV, pt. 2, pp. 385–91.
3. *O.R.*, XXIV, pt. 2, pp. 140–42.
4. *O.R.*, XXIV, pt. 2, pp. 343–45.
5. *O.R.*, XXIV, pt. 2, pp. 240–41.
6. *O.R.*, XXIV, pt. 2, p. 174.
7. *O.R.*, XXIV, pt. 1, pp. 153–56.
8. *O.R.*, XXIV, pt. 1, pp. 102–3.
9. William T. Sherman, *Memoirs of General William T. Sherman, by Himself*, 2 vols. (New York: Appleton, 1875), 1:354–56.
10. *O.R.*, XXIV, pt. 2, pp. 292–93.
11. *O.R.*, XXIV, pt. 2, pp. 367–69.
12. *O.R.*, XXIV, pt. 2, pp. 293–95.
13. *O.R.*, XXIV, pt. 2, pp. 257–60.
14. *O.R.*, XXIV, pt. 2, pp. 414–15.
15. *O.R.*, XXIV, pt. 2, pp. 374–76.
16. *O.R.*, XXIV, pt. 2, pp. 370–71.
17. *O.R.*, XXIV, pt. 2, p. 371.

18. *O.R.*, XXIV, pt. 2, pp. 371–72.

19. *O.R.*, XXIV, pt. 2, p. 373.

20. *O.R.*, XXIV, pt. 2, p. 374.

21. Sylvanus Cadwallader, *Three Years with Grant, as Recalled by War Correspondent Sylvanus Cadwallader,* ed. Benjamin P. Thomas (New York: Alfred A. Knopf, 1955), p. 100.

22. Ulysses S. Grant, *Personal Memoirs*, 2 vols. (New York: Charles L. Webster, 1885), 1:534–40.

23. Adam Badeau, *Military History of Ulysses S. Grant, from April 1861 to April 1865,* 3 vols. (New York: D. Appleton, 1868–81), 1:333–34, 338–40, 361, 370–71.

24. William T. Sherman, *Memoirs of General W.T. Sherman* (New York: Library of America, 1990), pp. 353–62 passim.

25. *O.R.*, XXIV, pt. 2, pp. 336–39.

26. *O.R.*, XXIV, pt. 1, p. 44.

APPENDIX
ORDER OF BATTLE, UNITED STATES ARMY AND CONFEDERATE STATES ARMY[1]

Organization of the Union forces operating against Vicksburg, May 18–July 4, 1863

THE ARMY OF THE TENNESSEE
Maj. Gen. Ulysses S. Grant

Escort
4th Illinois Cavalry, Company A, Capt. Embury D. Osband

Engineers
1st Battalion Engineer Regiment of the West, Maj. William Tweeddale

NINTH ARMY CORPS*
Maj. Gen. John G. Parke

FIRST DIVISION
Maj. Gen. Thomas Welsh

First Brigade	Third Brigade	Artillery
Col. Henry Bowman	Col. Daniel Leasure	Pennsylvania Light,
36th Massachusetts	2d Michigan	Battery D
17th Michigan	8th Michigan	
27th Michigan	20th Michigan	
45th Pennsylvania	79th New York	
	100th Pennsylvania	

SECOND DIVISION
Brig. Gen. Robert B. Potter

First Brigade	Second Brigade	Third Brigade
Col. Simon G. Griffin	Brig. Gen. Edward Ferrero	Col. Benjamin C. Christ
6th New Hampshire	35th Massachusetts	29th Massachusetts
9th New Hampshire	11th New Hampshire	46th New York
7th Rhode Island	51st New York	50th Pennsylvania
	51st Pennsylvania	

Artillery	Artillery Reserve
2d New York Light, Battery L	2d United States, Battery E

---

*Joined from the Department of the Ohio, June 14 to 17.

THIRTEENTH ARMY CORPS
Maj. Gen. John A. McClernand
Maj. Gen. Edward O. C. Ord

Escort
3d Illinois Cavalry, Company L, Capt. David R. Sparks

Pioneers
Kentucky Infantry (Independent Company), Capt. William F. Patterson

NINTH DIVISION
Brig. Gen. Peter J. Osterhaus

First Brigade	Second Brigade	Cavalry
Brig. Gen. Albert L. Lee	Col. Daniel W. Lindsey	2d Illinois
Col. James Keigwin	54th Indiana	3d Illinois
118th Illinois	22d Kentucky	6th Missouri
49th Indiana	16th Ohio	
69th Indiana	42d Ohio	
7th Kentucky	114th Ohio	

Artillery
Capt. Jacob T. Foster
Michigan Light, 7th Battery
Wisconsin Light, 1st Battery

TENTH DIVISION
Brig. Gen. Andrew J. Smith

Escort
4th Indiana Cavalry, Company C, Capt. Andrew P. Gallagher

First Brigade	Second Brigade	Artillery
Brig. Gen. Stephen G. Burbridge	Col. William J. Landram	Illinois Light, Chicago
16th Indiana	77th Illinois	Mercantile Battery
60th Indiana	97th Illinois	Ohio Light, 17th
67th Indiana	103d Illinois	Battery
83d Ohio	19th Kentucky	
96th Ohio	48th Ohio	
23d Wisconsin		

TWELFTH DIVISION
Brig. Gen. Alvin P. Hovey

Escort
1st Indiana Cavalry, Company C, Lt. James L. Carey

First Brigade	Second Brigade	Artillery
Brig. Gen. George F.	Col. James R. Slack	1st Missouri Light,
McGinnis	87th Illinois	Battery A
11th Indiana	47th Indiana	Ohio Light,
24th Indiana	24th Iowa	2d Battery
34th Indiana	28th Iowa	Ohio Light,
46th Indiana	56th Ohio	16th Battery
29th Wisconsin		

FOURTEENTH DIVISION
Brig. Gen. Eugene A. Carr

Escort
3d Illinois Cavalry, Company G

First Brigade	Second Brigade	Artillery
Brig. Gen. William P.	Brig. Gen. Michael K.	2d Illinois Light,
Benton	Lawler	Battery A
Col. Henry D. Washburn	21st Iowa	Indiana Light,
Col. David Shunk	22d Iowa	1st Battery
33d Illinois	23d Iowa	
99th Illinois	11th Wisconsin	
8th Indiana		
18th Indiana		
1st United States (siege guns)		

FIFTEENTH ARMY CORPS
Maj. Gen. William T. Sherman

FIRST DIVISION
Maj. Gen. Frederick Steele

First Brigade	Second Brigade	Third Brigade
Col. Francis H. Manter	Col. Charles R. Woods	Brig. Gen. John M. Thayer
Col. Bernard G. Farrar	25th Iowa	4th Iowa
13th Illinois	31st Iowa	9th Iowa
27th Missouri	3d Missouri	26th Iowa
29th Missouri	12th Missouri	30th Iowa
30th Missouri	17th Missouri	
31st Missouri	76th Ohio	
32d Missouri		

Artillery	Cavalry
Iowa Light, 1st Battery	Kane County (Illinois)
2d Missouri Light, Battery F	Independent Company
Ohio Light, 4th Battery	3d Illinois, Company D

SECOND DIVISION
Maj. Gen. Francis P. Blair Jr.

First Brigade	Second Brigade	Third Brigade
Col. Giles A. Smith	Col. Thomas Kilby Smith	Brig. Gen. Hugh Ewing
113th Illinois	Brig. Gen. Joseph	30th Ohio
116th Illinois	A. J. Lightburn	37th Ohio
6th Missouri	55th Illinois	47th Ohio
8th Missouri	127th Illinois	4th West Virginia
13th United States	83th Indiana	
1st Battalion	54th Ohio	
	57th Ohio	

Artillery
1st Illinois Light, Battery A
1st Illinois Light, Battery B
1st Illinois Light, Battery H
Ohio Light, 8th Battery

Cavalry
Thielemann's (Illinois) Battalion,
  Companies A and B
10th Missouri, Company C

THIRD DIVISION
Brig. Gen. James M. Tuttle

First Brigade	Second Brigade	Third Brigade
Brig. Gen. Ralph P.	Brig. Gen. Joseph A.	Brig. Gen. Charles L.
Buckland	Mower	Matthies
Col. William L. McMillen	47th Illinois	Col. Joseph J. Woods
114th Illinois	5th Minnesota	8th Iowa
93d Indiana	11th Missouri	12th Iowa
72d Ohio	8th Wisconsin	35th Iowa
95th Ohio		

Artillery
Capt. Nelson T. Spoor
  1st Illinois Light, Battery E
  Iowa Light, 2d Battery

Unattached Cavalry
4th Iowa

SIXTEENTH ARMY CORPS
(Detachment)
Maj. Gen. Cadwallader C. Washburn

FIRST DIVISION
Brig. Gen. William Sooy Smith

Escort
7th Illinois Cavalry, Company B

First Brigade	Second Brigade	Third Brigade
Col. John M. Loomis	Col. Stephen G. Hicks	Col. Joseph R. Cockerill
26th Illinois	40th Illinois	97th Indiana
90th Illinois	103d Illinois	99th Indiana
12th Indiana	15th Michigan	53d Ohio
100th Indiana	46th Ohio	70th Ohio

Fourth Brigade
Col. William W. Sanford
48th Illinois
6th Iowa

Artillery
Capt. William Cogswell
1st Illinois Light, Battery F
1st Illinois Light, Battery I
Illinois Light, Cogswell's Battery
Indiana Light, 6th Battery

FOURTH DIVISION
Brig. Gen. Jacob G. Lauman

First Brigade	Second Brigade	Third Brigade
Col. Isaac C. Pugh	Col. Cyrus Hall	Col. George E. Bryant
41st Illinois	14th Illinois	Col. Amory K. Johnson
53d Illinois	15th Illinois	28th Illinois
3d Iowa	46th Illinois	32d Illinois
33d Wisconsin	76th Illinois	12th Wisconsin
	53d Indiana	

Cavalry
15th Illinois, Companies F and I

Artillery
Capt. George C. Gumbart
2d Illinois Light, Battery E
2d Illinois Light, Battery K
Ohio Light, 5th Battery
Ohio Light, 7th Battery
Ohio Light, 15th Battery

PROVISIONAL DIVISION
Brig. Gen. Nathan Kimball

Engelmann's Brigade	Richmond's Brigade	Montgomery's Brigade
Col. Adolph Engelmann	Col. Jonathan Richmond	Col. Milton Montgomery
43d Illinois	18th Illinois	40th Iowa
61st Illinois	54th Illinois	3d Minnesota
106th Illinois	126th Illinois	25th Wisconsin
12th Michigan	22d Ohio	27th Wisconsin

SEVENTEENTH ARMY CORPS
Maj. Gen. James B. McPherson

Escort
4th Company Ohio Cavalry

THIRD DIVISION
Maj. Gen. John A. Logan

Escort
2d Illinois Cavalry, Company A

First Brigade	Second Brigade	Third Brigade
Brig. Gen. John E. Smith	Brig. Gen. Mortimer D.	Brig. Gen. John D.
Brig. Gen. Mortimer D.	Leggett	Stevenson
Leggett	Col. Manning F. Force	8th Illinois
20th Illinois	30th Illinois	17th Illinois
31st Illinois	20th Ohio	81st Illinois
45th Illinois	68th Ohio	7th Missouri
124th Illinois	78th Ohio	32d Ohio
23d Indiana		

Artillery
Col. Charles J. Stolbrand
1st Illinois Light, Battery D
2d Illinois Light, Battery G
2d Illinois Light, Battery L
Michigan Light, 8th Battery
Ohio Light, 3d Battery

SIXTH DIVISION
Brig. Gen. John McArthur

Escort
11th Illinois Cavalry, Company G

First Brigade	Second Brigade	Third Brigade
Brig. Gen. Hugh T. Reid	Brig. Gen. Thomas E. G.	Col. William Hall
1st Kansas	Ransom	Col. Alexander
16th Wisconsin	11th Illinois	Chambers
95th Illinois	72d Illinois	11th Iowa
	14th Wisconsin	13th Iowa
	17th Wisconsin	15th Iowa
		16th Iowa

Artillery
Maj. Thomas D. Maurice
2d Illinois Light, Battery F
Minnesota Light, 1st Battery
1st Missouri Light, Battery C
Ohio Light, 10th Battery

SEVENTH DIVISION
Brig. Gen. Isaac F. Quinby
Brig. Gen. John E. Smith

Escort
4th Missouri Cavalry, Company F

First Brigade
Col. John B. Sanborn
48th Indiana
59th Indiana
4th Minnesota
18th Wisconsin

Second Brigade
Col. Samuel A. Holmes
Col. Green B. Raum
56th Illinois
17th Iowa
10th Missouri
24th Missouri
80th Ohio

Third Brigade
Col. George B. Boomer
Col. Holden Putnam
Brig. Gen. Charles L.
Matthies
93d Illinois
5th Iowa
10th Iowa
26th Missouri

Artillery
Capt. Frank C. Sands
Capt. Henry Dillon
1st Missouri Light, Battery M
Ohio Light, 11th Battery
Wisconsin Light, 6th Battery
Wisconsin Light, 12th Battery

HERRON'S DIVISION
Maj. Gen. Francis J. Herron

First Brigade
Brig. Gen. William Vandever
37th Illinois
26th Indiana
20th Iowa
34th Iowa
38th Iowa
1st Missouri Light
Artillery, Battery E
1st Missouri Light
Artillery, Battery F

Second Brigade
Brig. Gen. William W. Orme
94th Illinois
19th Iowa
20th Wisconsin
1st Missouri Light
Artillery, Battery B

Unattached Cavalry
Col. Cyrus Busey
5th Illinois
3d Iowa
2d Wisconsin

DISTRICT NORTHEAST LOUISIANA
Brig. Gen. Elias S. Dennis

Detached Brigade
Col. George W. Neeley
63d Illinois
108th Illinois
120th Illinois
131st Illinois
10th Illinois Cavalry,
Companies A, D, G, and K

African Brigade
Col. Isaac F. Shepard

Post of Milliken's Bend,
Louisiana
Col. Hiram Scofield
8th Louisiana
9th Louisiana
11th Louisiana
13th Louisiana
1st Mississippi
3d Mississippi

Post of Goodrich's Landing, Louisiana
Col. William F. Wood
  1st Arkansas
  10th Louisiana

ORGANIZATION OF THE CONFEDERATE STATES ARMY OF VICKSBURG

Lt. Gen. John C. Pemberton, Commanding
As of July 4, 1863

STEVENSON'S DIVISION
Maj. Gen. C. L. Stevenson

First Brigade	Second Brigade	Third Brigade
Brig. Gen. S. M. Barton	Brig. Gen. Alfred	Brig. Gen. S. D. Lee
40th Georgia	Cumming	20th Alabama
41st Georgia	34th Georgia	23d Alabama
42d Georgia	36th Georgia	30th Alabama
43d Georgia	39th Georgia	31th Alabama
52d Georgia	56th Georgia	46th Alabama
Hudson's (Mississippi)	57th Georgia	Alabama Battery
Battery		
Pointe Coupee (Louisiana)		
Artillery, Company A		
Pointe Coupee (Louisiana)		
Artillery, Company C		

Fourth Brigade	Waul's Texas Legion	Attached
Col. A. W. Reynolds	Col. T. N. Waul	1st Tennessee Cavalry
3d Tennessee	1st Battalion (infantry)	Botetourt (Virginia)
(Provisional Army)	2d Battalion (infantry)	Artillery
39th Tennessee	Cavalry battalion	Signal Corps
43d Tennessee	Artillery company	
59th Tennessee		
3d Maryland Battery		

FORNEY'S DIVISION
Maj. Gen. John H. Forney

Hebert's Brigade
Brig. Gen. Louis Hébert

3d Louisiana	43d Mississippi
21st Louisiana	7th Mississippi
36th Mississippi	2d Alabama
37th Mississippi	Appeal (Arkansas) Battery
38th Mississippi	

MOORE'S BRIGADE
Brig. Gen. John C. Moore

37th Alabama	40th Mississippi
40th Alabama	2d Texas
42d Alabama	Alabama battery
1st Mississippi	Pointe Coupee (Louisiana)
35th Mississippi	Artillery, Battery B

SMITH'S DIVISION
Maj. Gen. M. L. Smith

Baldwin's Brigade	Shoup's Brigade	Vaughn's Brigade
Brig. Gen. W. E. Baldwin	Brig. Gen. Francis A. Shoup	Brig. Gen. J. C. Vaughn
17th Louisiana	26th Louisiana	60th Tennessee
31st Louisiana	27th Louisiana	61st Tennessee
4th Mississippi	28th [29th] Louisiana	62d Tennessee
46th Mississippi	McNally's (Arkansas)	
Tennessee Battery	Battery	

Mississippi State Troops
Brig. Gen. John V. Harris
5th Regiment
3d Battalion

Attached
14th Mississippi Light Artillery
Battalion
Mississippi Partisan Rangers
Signal Corps

BOWEN'S DIVISION
Maj. Gen. John S. Bowen

First (Missouri) Brigade	Second Brigade	RIVER BATTERIES
Col. Francis M. Cockrell	Col. T. P. Dockery	Col. Ed Higgins
1st Missouri	15th Arkansas	1st Louisiana Artillery
2d Missouri	19th Arkansas	8th Louisiana Heavy
3d Missouri	20th Arkansas	Artillery Battalion
5th Missouri	21st Arkansas	22d Louisiana
6th Missouri	1st Arkansas Cavalry	1st Tennessee Heavy
Guibor's (Missouri)	Battalion	Artillery
battery	12th Arkansas Battalion	Tennessee Battery
Landis's (Missouri)	(sharpshooters)	Tennessee Battery
battery	1st Missouri Cavalry	Tennessee Battery
Wade's (Missouri) battery	3d Missouri Cavalry	Vaiden (Mississippi)
	3d Missouri Battery	Battery
	Lowe's (Missouri) Battery	

MISCELLANEOUS
54th Alabama (detachment)
City Guards
Signal Corps

NOTES

1. *O.R.*, XXIV, pt. 2, pp. 148–58 and 326–28.

BIBLIOGRAPHY

Badeau, Adam. *Military History of Ulysses S. Grant, from April 1861 to April 1865.* 3 vols. New York: D. Appleton, 1868–81.

Bearss, Edwin C. *The Vicksburg Campaign.* 3 vols. Dayton, Ohio: Morningside, 1985–86.

Boatner, Mark Mayo, III. *The Civil War Dictionary.* New York: David M. McKay, 1959.

Cadwallader, Sylvanus. *Three Years with Grant, as Recalled by War Correspondent Sylvanus Cadwallader.* Edited by Benjamin P. Thomas. New York: Alfred A. Knopf, 1955.

Dyer, Frederick Henry A. *A Compendium of the War of the Rebellion.* 3 vols. 1908. Reprinted as 2 vols.; Wilmington, N.C.: Broadfoot Publishing, 1994.

Grant, Ulysses S. *Personal Memoirs.* 2 vols. New York: Charles L. Webster, 1885.

Guernsey, Alfred H., and Henry M. Alden. *Harper's Pictorial History of the Civil War.* Chicago: Star Publishing, 1894.

Halleck, H. Wagner. *Elements of Military Art and Science.* New York: D. Appleton, 1862.

Johnson, Robert U., and Clarence C. Buel, eds. *Battles and Leaders of the Civil War.* 4 vols. New York: Century, 1887–88.

Kennedy, Frances H., ed. *A Guide to the Campaign and Siege of Vicksburg.* Jackson, Miss.: Mississippi Department of Archives and History, 1994.

Korn, Jerry. *War on the Mississippi.* Alexandria, Va.: Time-Life Books, 1985.

Leslie, Frank, and Rossiter Johnson. *The American Soldier in the Civil War.* New York: Bryan, Taylor, 1895.

Leslie, Frank, John C. Ridpath, and Marcus J. Wright. *Battles and Commanders of the Civil War.* Washington, D.C.: Government Printing Office, 1891–1922.

Miller, Francis T., and Robert S. Lanier. *The Photographic History of the Civil War.* 10 vols. New York: The Review of Reviews, 1912.

Moat, Louis S., and Frank Leslie. *Frank Leslie's Illustrated Famous Leaders and Battle Scenes of the Civil War.* New York: Mrs. Frank Leslie, 1896.

Mullins, Michael A., and Terrence J. Winschel. *Vicksburg: A Self-Guiding Tour of the Battlefield.* Wilmington, N.C.: Broadfoot Publishing, 1990.

Nye, Wilbur S., ed. *Struggle for Vicksburg.* Harrisburg, Pa.: Historical Times, 1967. Reprint, Conshohocken, Pa.: Eastern Alcorn Press, 1982.

Pemberton, John C. *Pemberton: Defender of Vicksburg.* Chapel Hill: University of North Carolina Press, 1942.

Scott, Henry Lee. *Military Dictionary: Comprising Technical Definitions; Information on Raising and Keeping Troops; Actual Service, Including Makeshift and Improvised Matériel; and Law, Government, Regulations, and Administration Relating to Land Forces.* New York: D. Van Nostrand, 1861.

Sherman, William T. *Memoirs of General William T. Sherman, by Himself.* 2 vols. New York: Appleton, 1875.

U.S. Military Academy. *The West Point Atlas of American Wars.* 2 vols. New York: Frederick A. Praeger, 1959.

U.S. Navy Department. *Official Records of the Union and Confederate Navies in the War of the Rebellion.* 31 vols. Edited by Richard Bush et al. Washington, D.C.: Government Printing Office, 1894–1927.

U.S. War Department. *Atlas to Accompany the Official Records of the Union and Confederate Armies.* 5 vols. Washington, D.C.: Government Printing Office, 1891–95.

———. *War of the Rebellion: Official Records of the Union and Confederate Armies.* 128 vols. Edited by Robert N. Scott et al. Washington, D.C.: Government Printing Office, 1891–1901.

Vicksburg. Brochure prepared by the Vicksburg, Mississippi, Convention and Visitors Bureau, 1996.

Warner, Ezra J. *Generals in Blue: Lives of the Union Commanders.* 1964. Reprint; Baton Rouge: Lousiana State University Press, 1981.

———. *Generals in Gray: Lives of the Confederate Commanders.* 1959. Reprint; Baton Rouge: Lousiana State University Press, 1981.

Winschel, Terrence J. *Champion Hill: A Battlefield Guide.* Flowood, Miss.: Boyanton Brothers Printing, 1989.

———. *Chickasaw Bayou: A Battlefield Guide.* Flowood, Miss.: Boyanton Brothers Printing, 1987.

———. *Port Gibson: A Battlefield Guide.* Flowood, Miss.: Boyanton Brothers Printing, 1989.

INDEX

Gregg, John, 57, 58, 206, 208, 214, 221, 223, 280, 281, 382, 383; defense of Jackson, 218–20; report of fighting at Raymond, 211–13
Gregg's Brigade, 58, 64, 156
Grenada, Mississippi, 32
Grierson, Benjamin, 124, 128, 130, 150, 152, 153, 370; map of Grierson's raid, 134; photograph, 131; report on cavalry operations, 132–42
Griffin, Simon G., 461
Griffith, Joseph E., 301, 404
Griffith's Battery (Carr's Division), at Port Gibson, 166
Guertner, Gary L., xi
Guibor's Missouri Battery (Cockrell's Brigade), at Port Gibson, 173

Hall, Cyrus, 465
Hall, William, 466
Halleck, Henry W., 4, 26, 29, 42, 114, 115, 130, 305, 307, 308, 310, 349, 366, 381, 413, 444, 457; photograph, 197; suggests Grant and Banks unite forces after Port Gibson, 198
Hall's Ferry road, 295
Hamilton, C. S., 29
Hand-grenades, 394, 395, 402, 427; lithograph showing use of at Vicksburg, 395
Hankinson's Ferry, 175, 190
Hardee's Tactics, 6
Hard Times, 156, 157, 162, 370, 378
Harris' Brigade, 282
Harrison, Isaac, 171
Hatch, Edward, 132
Haynes' Bluff, 6, 44, 81, 99, 337
Hébert, Louis, 282, 393, 434, 468; condition of his soldiers, 442; reports, 436–42
Hébert's Brigade (Forney's Division) (Army of Vicksburg), 282; order of battle of, 468
Henderson, Samuel, 152
Herron, Francis J., 309, 314, 325, 326, 467; approach to Confederate lines, 325
Herron's Division (Seventeenth Army Corps) (Army of the Tennessee), order of battle of, 467
Hicks, Stephen G., 465
Higgins, Edward, 283, 338, 450, 469; photograph, 453; River Batteries, 469
Higgins, Thomas, Private, U.S.V., 396
Hill's Plantation, 103, 105
Holly Springs, 26, 46, 128, 364; capture of by Van Dorn, 33
Holmes, Samuel A., 238, 467
Hoskin's Battery, 219

Hovey, Alvin P., 52, 165, 180, 182, 186, 230, 233, 235, 239, 241, 249, 314, 380, 385, 408, 414, 462; Champion Hill, 236–39; photograph, 231; report of fighting at Port Gibson, 182–86; report of fighting on May 22, 411
Hovey's approach to Confederate lines, 323–24, 412–13; lithograph of assault by Twenty-fourth Indiana, Champion Hill, 384
Hovey's Division, 165
Hudson Battery, 174, 187
Hurlbut, Stephen, 77, 127, 136, 195, 201, 369, 444; photograph, 129; plans for Grierson's raid, 130–32; success of Grierson's raid, 128–30
Hurst, D. W., 109

Indian mound(s), 57, 104, 374–75; fighting at, 58
Iron-clads, 19, 64, 68, 74n2

Jackson, Adams, 203
Jackson, Mississippi, 128, 144, 205, 264, 280; attacked by Union forces, 213–16; Confederate defense of, 218–20; map of battle, 214
Jackson, W., 288
Johnson, Amory K., 465
Johnston, Joseph, 4, 125, 145, 147, 150, 154, 157, 214, 215, 218, 222, 226, 258, 264, 280, 281, 282, 284, 299, 301, 306, 307, 309, 310, 314, 348, 351, 358, 382, 383, 391, 444; asks for additional forces from Lee, 36; assigned to command in the west, 34–36; defense of Mississippi, March–May 1863, 220–22; defense of Vicksburg, 341–44; directs Pemberton to concentrate his forces, 159, 202; orders evacuation of Port Hudson and promises to send forces to Vicksburg, 287–88; photograph, 35; reactions to Champion Hill and Big Black, 270; strategic situation, January 1863, 36–37
Johnston's Battery (Botetourt Virginia Artillery) (Tracey's Brigade), 175, 247, 254

Kelton, J. C., 34
Kimball, Nathan, 465
Kinsman, Colonel, 276
Klauss, M., 463
Klauss' (First Indiana Light) Battery, 166, 183

Lafayette, U.S.S., 120, 161
La Grange, Tennessee, 128, 130; base of operations, 2